John Edward Hasse

DA CAPO PRESS

BEYOND

The Life and Genius of Duke Ellington

CATEGORY

This Da Capo Press paperback edition of *Beyond Category* is a
republication of the edition first published in New York in 1993,
with textual emendations. It is reprinted by arrangement
with Simon & Schuster, Inc.

Copyright © 1993 by John Edward Hasse

10

Published by Da Capo Press, Inc.
A Member of the Perseus Books Group

All Rights Reserved

Manufactured in the United States of America

Library of Congress Cataloging in Publication Data

Hasse, John Edward, 1948–
  Beyond category : the life and genius of Duke Ellington / John
Edward Hasse.
      p.   cm.
  Originally published: New York: Simon & Schuster. 1993.
  Includes bibliographical references (p.   ) and index.
  ISBN 0-306-80614-2
  1. Ellington, Duke, 1899–1974.   2. Jazz musicians—United
States—Bibliography.   I. Title.
ML410.E44H37   1995
781.65'092—dc20
[B]   94-45928
                                                                 CIP
                                                                 MN

The author gratefully acknowledges permission to use material from the following copyrighted
works:
  From *Boy Meets Horn* by Rex Stewart, edited by Claire P. Gordon. Copyright © 1991 by the estate
of the late Rex Stewart and Claire P. Gordon. Reprinted by permission of the University of Michigan
Press.
  Excerpts from *Duke Ellington: An Intimate Memoir* by Mercer Ellington with Stanley Dance.
Copyright © 1978 by Mercer Ellington and Stanley Dance. Reprinted by permission of Houghton
Mifflin Co.
  From "The Ellington Effect" by Billy Strayhorn, from *Down Beat* magazine. Copyright © 1952
by Down Beat, Inc. Reprinted by permission of *Down Beat*.
  From "The Hot Bach" by Richard O. Boyer. Reprinted by permission: © 1944, 1972 The New
Yorker Magazine, Inc.
  From *Of Minnie the Moocher and Me* by Cab Calloway and Bryant Rollins. Copyright © 1976 by
Cab Calloway and Bryant Rollins. Reprinted by permission of Cab Calloway.

(Continued on page 479)

$\mathcal{A}$CKNOWLEDGMENTS

This book would not have been possible without the kindnesses of many researchers, colleagues, and friends. For reading some or all of the manuscript and offering advice, I deeply thank my friends David Baker, Jared Carter, Scott DeVeaux, Krin Gabbard, Sandra Gregory, Rob Gross, Andrew Homzy, Theodore Hudson, Kip Lornell, Tom Piazza, Jessie Rodrique, S. Frederick Starr, Bruce Talbot, and especially Robert Toll. Their suggestions enabled me to avoid a number of pitfalls and make many improvements. For generosity with their information and research materials, thanks to George Avakian, Gordon Ewing, Morris Hodara, Brooks Kerr, Steven Lasker, Susan Markle, Dan Morgenstern, and Klaus Stratemann.

For their generous help with photographs, thanks to Frank Driggs, Duncan Schiedt, and *Down Beat*'s Frank Alkyer and Dave Helland. Other photographic assistance came from Ray Avery, Julia Jones, Dennis Kan, Josephine Mangiaracina of Sony Music, Trina Sobotka, and Mark Tucker. For the pleasure, over the years, of stimulating conversations about Ellington, I wish to thank David Berger, Anthony Brown, Stanley Crouch, Stanley and Helen Dance, Andrew Homzy, James T. Maher, Wynton Marsalis, Albert Murray, Gunther Schuller, Bruce Talbot, Jack Towers, Mark Tucker, Patricia Willard, and the late Martin Williams. Thanks to Mercer Ellington, Ruth Ellington Boatwright, and Clark Terry for their friendship.

To the staffs of the Schomburg Center for Research in Black Culture, Boston University's Mugar Library Special Collections, Ken Crilly of the Yale University Music Library, and Vivian Perlis and Janice Fournier of Yale's Oral History, American Music, and especially the Institute for Jazz Studies at Rutgers University, my thanks for help in accessing collections.

The decision to devote my evenings and weekends to writing this book was made easier by the support of my colleagues at the Smithsonian's National Museum of American History: Roger Kennedy, former director; Spencer Crew, acting director; Lonnie Bunch, Assistant Director for Curatorial Affairs; former chair, Tom D. Crouch, and chair Anne Golovin of the Department of Social and Cultural History; and James Weaver, supervisor, Division of Musical History, all gave the project their encouragement.

Other Smithsonian colleagues made available materials from its massive Ellington collections or proffered other kinds of assistance: Ildiko DeAngelis, Kelly Fennell, Nancy Fischer, John Fleckner, Marquette Folley, Marilyn Graskowiak, Alison Huff, Reuben Jackson, Karen Linn, Kip Lornell, Deborah Macanic, Elizabeth McCullough, Mary Ellen McCaffrey, Dane Penland, Rhoda Ratner, Deborra Richardson, James Roan, Jessie Rodrique, Gary Sturm, Betty Teller, Fitzroy Thomas, Jane Woodall, and Bill Yardley.

I was grateful to draw on a voluminous Ellington bibliography, as well as summaries of some interviews, on which, over the years, a series of interns and volunteers have worked: Cindy Agustin, Kristen Brown, Lyn Causey, Anne Conant, Leisl Dees, Scott Faulkner, Sherman Fine, Mildred Hall, Alice Heywood, Holland Hopson, Jolanta Juszkiewisz, Brendan Keegan, Maureen Keegan, Karen Lund, Noel Manalo, Hope Michael, Monica Moore, Vivian Morris, Kareem Murphy, Jennifer Perry, Lee Puricelli, Dwan Reece, Rebecca Sokolowsky, Hillery Stubbs, Herbert Toler, Marie Vachon, Ann Wagner, and Sylvia Wall.

I would like to express my gratitude for his aid to my literary representative, Gabriele Pantucci, and for his many editorial contributions, my editor, Bob Bender, as well as his associate editor, Johanna Li, and production editor Gypsy da Silva and copy editor Bruce Macomber. Finally, a special thanks to Ellen and John Buchanan for their backing, and to my wife, Nancy Rallis, my daughter Leanne, and entire family for their loving support and understanding.

March 1993   J.E.H.

To the memory of my parents
and of Ruth Philips Fenton

and to the inspiration of Duke Ellington
and his musicians

Contents

OREWORD

He didn't sleep at night
He liked to eat large meals—steak, vegetables, and grapefruit
He drank Coca-Cola with sugar in it
He hated the color green, especially wallpaper
Duke Ellington liked to eat ice cream
He was constantly clean—sartorially speaking
He was the greatest flirt—ever
He respected his elders
He thought that the 13th was a lucky day and Friday the 13th was
    an especially lucky day
He loved the differences in people and revered originality above all
    else
He liked kangaroos
Duke Ellington remembered people's birthdays
He was patriotic
He worshiped his mother
He was a very good dancer
He liked blue, royal blue, especially curtains
He had good manners and loved New Orleans
Duke Ellington was always calm, even though he was the leader of
    an orchestra of 16 musicians—all characters—ready, willing,
    and inclined to express themselves
Duke Ellington touched more people than confetti
He captured the sound of trains, planes, baby(s), lions and ele-
    phants
He liked simple songs with complicated developments and pretty
    endings

He didn't change with the style; he developed

He invented a new system of harmony based on the blues—whole musical forms that have yet to be imitated

He invented new logics of part writing and orchestration for each composition

In other words, he was slave to no systems

Duke Ellington combined the sensuality of the blues with the naïveté of society music to create blue mood pieces

He understood that music is neither new nor old

He believed that there were two kinds of music: the good kind and the other kind

He was the world's most prolific composer of blues, blueses of all shapes and sizes

Duke Ellington wrote music based on Shakespeare's themes

Wrote music to accompany the paintings of Degas

Wrote thousands of inventive arrangements for instrumentalists and vocalists of various levels of sophistication

Wrote music in all 12 known keys and some keys that are still unknown

Wrote music about romantic life under Paris skies

Wrote music about little bugs and other Night Creatures

Wrote music about countries all over the world from Nippon to Togo

Wrote music to accompany movies, television shows, ballets, Broadway shows, and the exercise of horizontal options

Wrote music to be played in gymnasiums, street parades, and charades

Wrote sacred music

Wrote music about the human experience; if it was experienced, he stylized it

In other words, Duke Ellington had a lot on his mind.

—WYNTON MARSALIS

$\mathcal{P}$REFACE

By the time Duke Ellington reached his diamond jubilee—his last birthday—he had heard himself called America's greatest composer and had been honored throughout the world. The French government had given him its highest award, the Legion of Honor. The government of the United States had bestowed on him its high civilian honor, the Presidential Medal of Freedom. Four nations had issued postage stamps to celebrate his achievements. In his fifty-year career, he had played perhaps 20,000 performances in Europe, Latin America, the Middle East, and Asia as well as in the United States; his music had reached tens of millions of people in person and via the mass media; he had made thousands of recordings; and most important of all, he had written several thousand compositions, the best of which are likely to resound through the ages. By any standard, Duke Ellington was a giant of twentieth-century music.

There has been an enormous amount written about Ellington and his work. Many of the writers have emphasized his recordings, which are unquestionably the most public part of his work and legacy but which represent only a portion of his varied musical career. His phonograph records provide only a partial picture of what and how he performed before audiences at dances, theaters, and concerts. Many of the pieces that he played he did not record, or recorded only years later with different players and thus with a rather different sound. And there was more to Ellington and his career than recordings—personnel, engagements, management style, audiences, economics, race, repertoire, his creative process, and much more. But the emphasis on his recordings and scattered interviews was understandable, because those were the principal sources available. But that changed in 1988.

Although Ellington himself showed little interest in preserving records of his past, a massive body of material has been saved through the foresight and diligence of his son, Mercer, who kept stashing things away until he had filled a room in a Manhattan warehouse. The existence of this body of material was largely unknown to the public, even to Ellington biographers of the 1980s. But in 1985, the author, then a new curator at the Smithsonian Institution, initiated conversations with Mercer Ellington and the Ellington estate about providing a permanent home for the archive. In 1986, due especially to the efforts of U.S. Representative Louis Stokes and other members of the Congressional Black Caucus, the Smithsonian received an appropriation from Congress toward the purchase of the materials. This funding, along with a decision by Mercer Ellington to donate a substantial portion of the collection, resulted in the March 1988 move of the archive to Washington, where a staff of four began the enormous task of cataloging it.

The acquisition sent a wave of excitement through the worldwide community of people who cared about Duke Ellington's music. No wonder! The 600-cubic-foot treasure trove contains 200,000 pages of documents and other materials. About half of this is music scores, lead sheets, parts for players, textual sketches, scenarios, and scripts for stage works—virtually all of it unpublished. In addition to twenty-four leather notebooks of his compositions that were transcribed and presented to him on his sixtieth birthday, there are seventy-eight publicity scrapbooks, containing thousands of domestic and international newspaper and magazine clippings dating from 1930 to 1973. The approximately five hundred objects include more than three hundred trophies, medals, plaques, and other awards, a complete set of the band's custom-made music stands, his gold-covered Bible and gold crucifix, and clothing he wore on stage. About two thousand photographs, boxes of business records, concert programs, posters, Ellington's personally designed Christmas cards, and some five hundred recordings round out the collection.

In 1991, the Smithsonian acquired and added to the archive a smaller but substantial collection of music manuscripts and other unpublished materials from Ellington's sister, Ruth Ellington Boatwright, including more than a thousand pieces of music, and long-time Ellington cornetist Rex Stewart's scrapbooks, photographs, and writings. The preservation of this previously unavailable national treasure of Ellington materials should make possible a new era of Ellington scholarship. And in 1993, to disseminate the Ellington collection and legacy widely, the Smithsonian opened a new exhibition, *Beyond Category: The Musical Genius of Duke Ellington*, to tour the United States for several years, part of a ten-year program called "America's Jazz Heritage: A Partnership of the Lila Wallace-Reader's Digest Fund and the Smithsonian Institution."

Drawing on the Smithsonian's Ellington collections as well as a range of other sources, this book seeks to introduce the general reader to the overall development of Duke Ellington's career and to foster an appreciation of his most important accomplishments. Although his personality, private life, and relationships with family and friends are discussed occasionally in the book, the focus is on the development and evolution of Ellington the musician. This is primarily a career biography, not a personal biography. The book includes new information and imagery that may be of interest to specialists, but it assumes no prior knowledge of music, jazz, or Ellington. Throughout the book, there are mini-essays on the "Essential Ellington" that highlight and briefly discuss some of his notable recordings from each period and also direct the reader to available sources of these recordings. Listening to these will significantly enrich the reader's appreciation of Ellington's work since words alone simply cannot do justice to his music.

As the critic Martin Williams once observed, Ellington, who had a fifty-year career of innovation and creativity, stands as the largest, most challenging single topic facing American-music critics, musicologists, and historians. Fortunately, Ellington himself may have left us some of the keys to beginning to come to grips with and understand his life's work. "I have two careers," he once said, "and they must not be confused, though they almost always are. I am a bandleader and I am a composer." In 1961, he reflected, "My biggest kick in music—playing or writing—is when I have a problem. Without a problem to solve, how much interest do you take in anything?"

Combining these observations, this book examines the development and evolution of Duke Ellington's "two careers" as he dealt with a series of problems throughout his life. His two careers were so often confused because they were not two truly separate careers in the sense that he spent part of his time as a bandleader and part as a composer. The two were inseparable from the time the fourteen-year-old Ellington improvised his first tune on the job while playing piano at a soda fountain. They remained intertwined and mutually interdependent throughout his career. He probably would not have been the bandleader he was if he had not also been a composer; he certainly would not have been the composer he was if he had not also been a bandleader; and he undoubtedly would not have been the bandleader and composer he was if he had not also relished, even artistically sought out, problems.

Each chapter discusses how Ellington responded to the major problems he faced in that period of his life: growing up in Washington, D.C., and choosing a career; finding mentors to guide him; learning his craft as a pianist and starting to compose; testing himself in the big time in New York and learning what it took to succeed; developing his own sound and realizing that his destiny— as a musician and as a composer—was more as a bandleader than as a soloist; developing an orchestra with a unique sound and distinctive soloists and tailoring his compositions to that group; learning to manage a temperamental group of artist-musicians; becoming a prominent figure through high-profile nightclubs, records, and radio; facing the challenges of economic depression and continual touring; coping with major changes in music, musical tastes, and technology; composing with a partner and reaching new musical heights; struggling to maintain a big band in tough times; securing control of his business affairs; seeking new challenges as a composer of concert and sacred music; and dealing with the losses of key people. Running throughout his entire life were the problems that all African-Americans and all jazz musicians faced in Eurocentric America as well as the "problems" Ellington created for himself with his insatiable need to break old rules, write new ones, break new ground, and to create and innovate.

In later years, Ellington used the phrase "beyond category" as a term of the highest possible praise for artists such as Ella Fitzgerald. Because of the unmatched sound of his orchestra, the extraordinary range of his music, the dedication of leading a band for over fifty years, and the astonishing artistic heights to which his music soared, no one deserved his phrase "beyond category" more than he did. And in its other, literal, sense, "beyond category" aptly describes Ellington's life and work: each was one of a kind. If this book induces more people to appreciate Duke Ellington, to want to learn more about him, or to listen to his music, the author will feel richly rewarded.

ONE

·

Enjoying a
capital childhood

·

1 8 9 9 — 1 9 1 3

Duke Ellington came into the world as Edward Kennedy Ellington on April 29, 1899, in Washington, D.C. He would spend the first twenty-four years of his life— nearly one third—in the nation's capital. During those years, his character and personality would take shape, largely as a result of his relationship with his parents, and he would choose the career he would devote his life to. His parents and his experiences with community, church, and music would shape his character and ultimately his music.

His mother, Daisy Kennedy Ellington, was a beautiful, soft-spoken woman. Born in 1879 in Washington, D.C., she came from a middle-class family and had completed high school, a remarkable achievement at that time. Her father had been a District of Columbia policeman, a coveted job for a black man in those days. Daisy raised young Edward with love, praise, and encouragement and always treated him as someone very special, telling him, "Edward, you are blessed. You don't have anything to worry about. Edward, you are blessed." Young Edward would maintain this confident feeling of being favored for the rest of his life. Daisy regarded him as her jewel, and when he came down with pneumonia, she refused

Daisy Ellington was a devoted and loving mother to young Edward.

to leave his bedside. "I was pampered and pampered," Ellington recalled, "and spoiled rotten by all the women in the family."

In his memoirs, Ellington mentions only one sibling—Ruth Dorothea, who was born when he was sixteen. Edward's birth certificate, however, specifies that he was the *second* child of Daisy and James Ellington; the first must have died in childbirth or infancy. If Daisy had already lost one child, this could help explain her coddling, protectiveness, special treatment, and preoccupation with Edward. She may also have reacted to the worsening situation for black Americans during Edward's early years by investing in him intense emotion, love, and hope. Daisy undoubtedly hoped that her son would be able to rise above the troubles and make a better life for himself.

Edward Ellington devoutly loved his mother, who projected a refined manner and became a rather prim and serious parent. He later wrote, "Because . . . no one else but my sister Ruth had a mother as great and as beautiful as mine, it is difficult to put into understandable words an accurate description of my mother, Daisy." As Ruth recalled in 1989, "He said that when he was a little boy and sitting on his mother's lap, he looked into her face and he knew that she was the most beautiful mother in the world. And he felt that way about her until the day she died." Throughout her life, he would seek and relish her approval.

Edward's father, James Edward Ellington, had been born in Lincolnton, North Carolina, in 1879, the same year as Daisy. Like so many other southern blacks, before and after, he had migrated north hoping for a better life, settling in Washington, D.C. James —his friends called him J. E. and his relatives called him Uncle Ed —had not completed eighth grade. The senior Ellington held a series of occupations from the late 1890s until about 1920. He worked first as a driver, then as a butler for the family of Middleton F. Cuthbert, a prominent white physician with whom he enjoyed a close relationship. Sometimes Ellington got work as a caterer and a few times served as a butler for catered events at the White House.

James often brought home fine steaks and terrapin and acted as if he were a rich man, or so it seemed to young Edward, who later wrote, "He raised his family as though he were a millionaire. The best had to be carefully examined to make sure it was good enough for my mother." Edward's sister, Ruth, sixteen years his junior, recalls that her "father kept the house as he had at Cuthbert's— cut glass and silver, with lace curtains in the living room." This was a refined, cultivated household, which suited Daisy as well as James.

Between 1898 and 1921, James and his family lived in fourteen different locations, all in Northwest Washington. According to Rex Stewart, who later played cornet with the Duke Ellington orchestra, people who lived in Northwest "were the lighter complexioned people with better-type jobs, such as schoolteachers, postmen, clerks or in government service. . . . The southwest area . . . [had] the working class, the coal men, the fishmongers, the gamblers, pimps and sporting females." Most of the Ellington family homes were situated in the near northside area now known as Shaw. In Ellington's day, the neighborhood comprised pleasant middle-class houses; his family occupied a middle economic position within the black population.

J. E. taught his son the importance of good manners, such as knowing how to select the proper knife, spoon, and fork. As Edward adored and even worshiped his mother, he admired his father. The son regarded J. E. as a great ballroom dancer, convivialist, wine connoisseur, and wit, who knew exactly what to say to please a woman. "Gee, you make that hat look pretty," was a classic J. E. line, one which Ellington would use as a song title in 1968. As Edward grew to maturity, he picked up and carried on this kind of florid flattery. Like the father, the son would earn a reputation for his way with women. Even before he acquired the nickname "Duke," young Ellington was a natural aristocrat—in bearing, manners, taste, dress, and self-confidence. Cultivating airs and graces, and foreshadowing his future relationships with women, he even had his female cousins bow down to him as a sign of respect.

Ellington's father and mother possessed divergent temperaments. Daisy was, in the words of Barry Ulanov, "a woman of rigorous moral principle, stiff-lipped, and in direct contradiction of her beautiful face and figure, prim of mien and manner." J. E., by contrast, was easygoing and fun-loving; nothing troubled him much. Daisy had more education and came from a higher social stratum than he. Moreover, they attended different churches: she the Nineteenth Street Baptist, at which many old-line families worshiped, while he preferred the John Wesley African Methodist Episcopal Zion. Yet they seem to have had a warm, close relationship with one another and with their son.

Both parents came from large families and, while they had only two children of their own, their house buzzed with aunts, uncles, and cousins. By one count, Edward had twenty-eight cousins. Growing up, Ellington always found plenty of playmates.

Both Daisy and J. E. also played the piano—his father played operatic arias by ear and his mother played parlor songs and rags by note. One of Edward's earliest memories was that of his mother playing *The Rosary* so beautifully that "I bust out crying." As a small boy, then, Edward learned that music could evoke strong feelings and spiritual uplift.

At age four, Edward Ellington was already demonstrating the sartorial and personal style that would later earn him the nickname "Duke."

Washington's Nineteenth Street Baptist Church, Daisy Ellington's church, which young Edward attended every week.

Washington's Pennsylvania Avenue, with the U.S. Capitol in the background, in the early 1900s. When Ellington was born, Washington had the largest black population of any American city, concentrated in neighborhoods where black people developed their own churches, clubs, and cultural organizations.

When he was seven or eight, attending Garnet Elementary School, his mother signed him up for his first formal training in music. Edward studied for a time with a teacher who was evidently named Mrs. Marietta Clinkscales. No evidence survives, however, that the lessons had much effect. At that age, he showed far more interest in playing outdoors and watching baseball. Playing baseball on Sixteenth Street, he would sometimes notice President Theodore Roosevelt ride by on horseback, stop, and watch the boys; as he left, he'd wave to them and they'd wave to him. "Washington was in the American League and every day I had to see the game," Ellington remembered. So he got a job hawking peanuts, popcorn, and candy at the ballpark; at first he faced stage fright, he later said, but soon overcame it.

Edward liked "putting on a show," and at a very young age revealed a theatrical flair by telling jokes, dancing, and playing the Jew's harp. By the age of twelve, he was slipping surreptitiously into the Gayety Theater to watch the burlesque shows. "The shows were very good," he said, "and I made a lot of observations, on show business techniques, on the great craftsmanship involved, and on the rather gorgeous girls." Throughout his life, in fact, Ellington constantly looked for lessons in his experiences.

No doubt without his mother's knowledge, at age fourteen Ellington began sneaking into Frank Holliday's poolroom, situated only seven blocks from Ellington's home. Located next to the well-known Howard Theater, Holliday's unusual pool parlor demonstrated, as Ellington put it, "how all levels could and should mix." Waiters, porters, students, piano players, and doctors—they all came to Holliday's place. Here, Ellington learned to appreciate the value in mixing with a wide range of people. Railroad porters told of having just been in New York, Detroit, and Chicago, and whetted Ellington's appetite for travel.

Edward's sister, Ruth Ellington Boatwright, noted that she and her brother were raised in a house "full of love, where people [did] not talk about hostile incidents . . . I guess that was their way of protecting us." There was much from which to protect a youngster like Edward. While his family evidently did not speak of racially motivated lynchings and other outrages, at some point in his youth, Ellington must have learned of their existence.

The Gayety Burlesque Theater, where, beginning in his tenth year, Ellington sneaked in to watch the shows (seen here in the 1930s).

Ellington, in fact, was born into one of the most difficult periods African-Americans have experienced. Indeed, the historian Rayford W. Logan considers the period from 1897 to 1901 to have represented black Americans' absolute lowest point. African-Americans faced two basic facts of life during Ellington's boyhood: socially and politically, things were getting worse—most of all in the South but also in the North, and increasing numbers of them would make the fateful decision to leave the South and move north.

When Ellington was an infant, racist ideology considered "scientific" at the time was on the rise in both Europe and the United States. In 1896, the U.S. Supreme Court, in the case *Plessy* v. *Ferguson*, legalized racial segregation in public facilities. Throughout the American South, legislatures in state after state then passed laws establishing "separate but equal" facilities for persons of color. In addition to being separate, facilities for blacks were almost always inferior and usually markedly so.

With racism the official policy of federal and state governments, a small but vociferous and ugly minority of white Americans physically attacked black men and women in a series of bloody race riots in the first two decades of the twentieth century. In May of 1910, in response to the growing injustices, a biracial group of intellectuals and activists met in New York to form a pioneering civil rights organization, the National Association for the Advancement of Colored People. At this point, Ellington had just turned eleven; when he was much older, the NAACP would bestow upon him its highest honor.

The downward spiral of justice and opportunity for African-Americans that gripped the nation also affected Ellington's hometown. In Washington, equal treatment under the law had largely disappeared by the time of his birth. And professional opportunities for black people were few. In 1900, to serve its 87,000 black citizens, Washington had only 400 black teachers, 90 ministers, 50 physicians, 30 lawyers, and 10 dentists. For every teaching opening in the school system, there were ten applicants. Teaching loads were higher in segregated black schools, salaries lower. Between 1900 and 1909, civil service offered fewer opportunities for blacks than it had in the 1880s and 1890s. Jobs in other fields, especially domestic service, also declined. Trade unions discriminated against black working people. Control of many institutions—schools, businesses, hospitals, government—lay in the hands of whites. Residential segregation increased during Ellington's first twenty years, and in 1915, attempts were made to segregate even the streetcars in Washington. In 1913, Booker T. Washington, the foremost African-American leader of the day, wrote, "I have recently spent several days in Washington, and I have never seen the colored people so discouraged and bitter as they were at that time." And though the Lincoln Memorial, completed in 1921, proclaimed equality of humankind, across town, the capital's leading newspaper, the *Washington Post*, rarely mentioned blacks except to report their involvement in crimes.

Through all these problems, the support of family, the richness of their culture, the comfort of folk traditions, a belief in God, a strength of spirit, and a gift for laughter kept many black Americans going. And yet, declining possibilities for economic parity and social justice for blacks meant that it took a very strong person, who could draw fully on his or her community and own strength, to firmly withstand the unending battering of self-respect. Ellington was such a strong individual.

During Ellington's youth, Washington, D.C., was considered "the undisputed center of American Negro civilization," due to its population, socioeconomic structure, and educational and cultural opportunities. The city was a leader in the education of African-Americans, home to Howard University, established in 1867, the most distinguished black university in the United States. And the poet Paul Laurence Dunbar wrote in 1900 of Washington as having "a higher standard of culture among people of color than obtains in any other city." In 1900, Washington had the largest black population of any American city, and it was a higher proportion—31 percent—of the city's population as a whole. (Blacks represented between a quarter and a third of the city's population from 1870 to 1950.) Racial segregation forced blacks to live separately from whites, as they did most other places in the rural and urban South. In these neighborhoods, black people developed their own communities, churches, and cultural organizations.

Ellington's Washington: Monumental, Ironical —and Inspirational?

In many ways Washington was a southern city. In neighboring states situated below the Mason-Dixon line, slavery had been legal, and Washington had been a center for the domestic slave trade and also an important stopping point on the Underground Railroad. From the Washington Monument one could see Virginia, a half mile to the south across the Potomac River, part of the old Confederacy. Visible a half mile to the west was the home of General Robert E. Lee.

The Washington Monument, completed in 1884, towered majestically over the city of Ellington's youth, visible from nearly all quarters. In 1901, when Ellington was two, the city resurrected the original city plan developed by Pierre L'Enfant. Twentieth-century Washington implemented a grid pattern crossed by streets radiating diagonally outward from the Capitol and the White House. The design also included public squares and circles reserved for monuments and an extensive park system.

The city assumed an aura of dignity as railroad tracks were cleared from the National Mall and a host of new government buildings was erected. The city returned to neoclassical architecture. Landscaping increased in importance as the federal government built Rock Creek Park, landscaped the Tidal Basin, and, beginning in 1911, planted cherry trees. Recalling a visit in the 1910s, Langston Hughes felt that "Washington is one of the most beautiful cities in the world. For that I remember it with pleasure."

The new buildings symbolized the expanding visions and hopes of Washington's white populace. To some in the black community, these grand buildings may have heightened the pain of their declining fortunes. Even at the dedication of the Lincoln Memorial in 1922, blacks were forced to sit in a roped-off area across a dirt road. The irony of shrinking black vistas

(continued)

beside expanding white horizons could not have been lost on someone as discerning as Duke Ellington.

Characteristically optimistic, however, Ellington evidently chose not to dwell on the negative but to take what he could from his environment. Did the visual beauty of Washington influence him? Did the grand vistas stimulate in him not only a sense of order and proportion but also his own ambition?

The Washington Monument loomed over Ellington's Washington.

Within this population, people drew strong class distinctions. The black populace was structured like a pyramid. A small aristocracy, comprising about sixty or seventy families, made up the top. They were mostly descendants of Washington's antebellum free blacks. The poet Langston Hughes was harshly critical of Washington's "Negro society." "Never before, anywhere," he wrote, "had I seen persons of influence—men with some money, women with some beauty, teachers with some education—quite so audibly sure of their own importance and their high places in the community. So many pompous gentlemen never before did I meet."

Immediately beneath the top of the pyramid was a middle class of government workers, professionals, and businessmen. The Ellington family, with its refined, middle-class life-style and moderate income, fit in this group. The largest and poorest sector—most of the pyramid—comprised recent migrants from the South, many of whom lived lives of destitution and deprivation.

Most people of color were aware of differences in hue among themselves. Thus Washington's black community recognized caste as well as class lines. There were three castes corresponding to the three classes. More often than not, the most successful people had the lightest skin. "I don't know how many castes of Negroes there were in the city at that time," wrote Ellington, "but I do know that if you decided to mix carelessly with another you would be told that one just did not do that sort of thing." Rex Stewart described "the indisputable differentiation between negro people of various hues. There was very little mixing in the homes, in the churches or in the dance halls." Sonny Greer, Ellington's drummer beginning in 1919 or 1920, told interviewer and jazz drummer Stanley Crouch:

> Washington, D.C.—all them pretty girls from all over the country used to go to Howard University. Man, a guy like me and you, we're dirt, we're nothing. We're nothing. If you wasn't a doctor or some of that crap . . . you ain't got a chance. We'd be too dark for them.

Having enjoyed rubbing elbows at Frank Holliday's poolroom with all levels of the black community, Ellington must have grown impatient with discrimination based on skin color, income, and occupation.

As part of his education, Ellington was taught pride in his race and responsibility to represent it well. His eighth-grade English teacher, Mrs. Boston, emphasized, according to Ellington, that "everywhere you go, if you were sitting in a theater next to a white lady or something like that, or you were on stage representing your race, no matter where you go or what you do, you are representing your race and your responsibility is to command respect for the race. They taught that. I've always had that."

"What one did with one's mind had a lot to do with one's station," declared Theodore Hudson, a retired professor of English from Howard University, who grew up in a middle-class Washington family. "It was an era when you put your best foot forward, when you didn't go to movies, play cards, or listen to light music on Sundays. In polite black society in Washington, you didn't offend people. You couldn't say 'lie,' you had to say 'wasn't telling the truth.' "

In Washington, many middle- and upper-class blacks expected their children to become achievers—for example, doctors or teachers. Jazz pianist Billy Taylor, who attended Dunbar High School, attested that career expectations and Washington role models yielded positive results. Ellington's sister, Ruth, perceived that making a mark in the world "was a norm for that Washington black American middle class group" that Ellington grew up in. Edward himself later declared: "The driving power was a matter of wanting to be—and to be heard—at the same level as the best." The writer Albert Murray, who knew Ellington, observed that he always stressed that he "was born and raised among people to whom quality mattered and who required your personal best no less as a general principle than as a natural reaction to the folklore of white supremacy. In neither case would they accept excuses for failure. You either had what it took or you didn't."

Besides making him feel privileged, well fed, confident, special, and very loved, Ellington's parents also instilled a pride in the person he was and the achiever he might become. They taught him and Ruth that they could do anything, encouraged them, and instilled in them a positive attitude toward life. With all this as a foundation, Ellington built a strong sense of self-confidence. With a reservoir of love, self-assurance, and racial pride, Edward Ellington, about to become a teenager, began to explore what his life's calling might be.

TWO

·

$\mathcal{S}$TARTING A

CAREER

·

1913 – 23

Moving from boyhood to young manhood, Ellington showed talent in several of the arts and would have to choose what he would make his career. His decision would not only chart his career path but also reveal a great deal about how he would solve problems.

As he proceeded through grade school and entered junior high school in 1911, Ellington's piano lessons had faded into memory and he was now showing a flair for art. In 1913, as he prepared to enter high school, Edward might have gone to M Street High School (the predecessor to Dunbar High, which opened in 1916), an academically oriented school founded in 1870 as the nation's first public high school for blacks. Instead, he entered the neighboring Armstrong Manual Training School to study commercial art. According to Mercer, Ellington's son, Armstrong was "a kind of rough high school. If you went there you were practically regarded as incorrigible."

And yet, music still tugged at Ellington, too. The musical world Edward Kennedy Ellington was born into was very different from that of today. During his youth, people mostly heard music performed live—at home, in church, or in a wide range of places that employed musicians. Sound recordings, then in their infancy, were made acoustically; without benefit of electrical microphones, they suffered from extremely poor fidelity. Radio, talking motion pictures, and television lay in the future. The word *jazz* was unknown. Blues music was virtually unheard of outside the black community, and within it, shunned by most of the middle class. Even by 1920, very few black performers were recorded. Like the rest of the society, the record business had barred many doors to blacks.

When Ellington was a youngster, piano sales were booming and in 1909, when he was ten, the sale of pianos hit an all-time high in the United States. The upright piano stood as the symbol of middle-class respectability, in both black and white homes. "Back in those days . . . all *big* families had to have a piano," Mercer Ellington would say of his father's youth, "and it was a matter of culture to have someone to play it, or someone studying and taking lessons once a week. Before radio, you had to have it to help entertain guests on Sunday."

The piano seduced many of Ellington's contemporaries with its multiple attractions. A rank amateur could make sounds. A piano was the compleat instrument, like a one-man orchestra. Great contrasts were a snap: you could play higher and lower, louder and softer, on a piano than on virtually any other instrument. Today, most people do not realize how mellifluous the pianos of Ellington's youth sounded. Later, cheap-sounding little spinet pianos flooded the nation. But the heavy wooden pianos of Ellington's youth resonated richly through the wooden floors and walls of homes and dance halls. Whether you were playing or listening, the sound of the piano was full, palpable, and pleasurable.

Ruth Ellington recalled the family's pianos. "We had two pianos —one in the living room and one in the dining room. My mother's brother, James Kennedy, lived with us. He brought his piano, and my parents had a piano. My brother used to practice on them both. He was always playing the piano. . . . It was marvelous to watch him play."

Like many people his age, Ellington was drawn to ragtime. The new ragtime music had first appeared on the scene just a couple of years before Ellington. Black musicians developed it, one could argue, partially in response to the uncomfortable stereotypes that lingered from nineteenth-century blackface minstrelsy. Ragtime relied on the respectable piano, sparked competitions and contests among players, and, at its best, offered musicians rhythmic challenges and required technical virtuosity. Many youngsters turned to popular songs and ragtime, though typically their parents disapproved because, as Rex Stewart recalled, in those days "ragtime had an unspeakable connotation." Among both black and white young people, however, ragtime thrived, drawing in young people with its terrific repertoire—*Maple Leaf Rag, Cannon Ball Rag, Twelfth Street Rag,* and hundreds of other snazzy rags. The latest, smartest thing in popular music, it was "their" music, flourishing despite adult objections, much as rock'n'roll would generations later. This was young Ellington's music. In a real sense, Ellington, ragtime, and the new century were born and grew up together.

In the late nineteenth and early twentieth centuries, many white and black pianists partook of a large common literature, part of a shared American culture. Syncopated popular music—ragtime—was played by black and white pianists, whether amateurs playing in their parlors or professionals performing at dances, saloons, or restaurants. A shared musical culture facilitated constant interchange between black and white musical traditions.

Ellington was beginning to go out and listen to sharp ragtime pianists in Washington and, occasionally, elsewhere. During the summers, J. E. sent Daisy and Edward on vacations to Philadelphia, or to Atlantic City, New Jersey, then as now a popular vacation resort. One summer, evidently in 1913, they vacationed instead in Asbury Park, another oceanside resort in New Jersey. There he heard of a hot young pianist named Harvey Brooks. At the end of the summer, on the way home, Ellington made a detour to Philadelphia to meet Brooks, who showed Ellington some pianistic tricks and shortcuts. "I cannot tell you what that music did to me," Ellington said. "He was swinging, and he had a tremendous left hand, and when I got home I had a real yearning to play. I hadn't been able to get off the ground before, but after hearing him I said to myself, 'Man, you're just going to *have* to do it.' "

To do it, he had to learn to play by listening, watching, and imitating others. He had to learn his craft and it did not come easy at first. But he developed his talent by doing, by trial and error, as he would through much of his life. "I played piano by ear then," he recalled in 1933, "but I didn't have much of a repertoire. In fact, I didn't have one at all. I used to go to rent parties and hear popular pianists really play the piano, but they would hit so many keys that I couldn't begin to play the tunes they played."

Despite the daunting difficulty of the music, he kept on listening. "Oh, I was a great listener!" wrote Ellington. Washington bred many fine pianists—the unschooled ones such as Ralph Green, Shrimp Bronner, Lester Dishman, Clarence Bowser, Sticky Mack, Blind Johnny, and the Man with a Thousand Fingers, and the ones who read music, like Claude Hopkins, Roscoe Lee, Gertie Wells, Doc Perry, Louis Brown, and Louis Thomas. Because he couldn't read music very well, Ellington listened carefully to other pianists and tried to reproduce their ragtime, popular songs, and dance numbers.

"Those ragtime pianists sounded *so* good to me!" declared Ellington. "And they looked so good! Particularly when they flashed their left hands." The piano was ideally suited to provide the music for the growing frenzy for social dancing. And on the piano you could develop your own musical, physical, and visual style. That suited Ellington, a growing individualist, just fine. He was already choosing his career even if not fully aware of it yet.

Even at this early stage, he began to compose music, though he started more by necessity than by design. During the summer of 1913, he took a job as a soda jerk in the Poodle Dog Cafe on Georgia Avenue.

We had a piano player in the Poodle Dog who was one of the best when he was sober, but that wasn't often. When he got to where he couldn't play any better than I could, the boss would throw him out, take my place behind the soda fountain, and have me play piano. The only way I could learn how to play a tune was to compose it myself and work it up, and the first one was *Soda Fountain Rag,*

which was also known as the *Poodle Dog Rag.* Ellington later recalled the tune's birth this way:

I began by tinkering around with some old tunes I knew. Then, just to try something different, I set to putting some music to the rhythm that I used in jerking ice-cream sodas at the Poodle Dog. I fooled around with the tune more and more until at last, lo and behold, I had completed my first piece of finished music. It was an extremely fast tune, requiring very tricky finger work, and I called it *The Poodle Dog Rag*.

This first, almost unconscious, composition involved the processes he would later refine—listening to others, composing by playing, reworking memorable elements, and refining the piece in later performances. Composing and performing grew out of each other— even for fourteen-year-old Ellington.

Ellington attracted some attention with *Soda Fountain Rag*. (He never, however, wrote it down, and in the early 1930s claimed he couldn't remember how it went; his band members teased him by frequently requesting it.) Soon Ellington composed another piece, which he called *What You Gonna Do When the Bed Breaks Down?*, a slow-dancing number he later termed "a pretty good 'hug-and-rubbin' crawl." The piece was never published or formally recorded, but its bawdy lyrics have been preserved:

> Tried it on the sofa, tried it on the chair,
> Tried it on the table, didn't get nowhere,
> What you gonna do when the bed breaks down?
> You've got to work out on the floor.
>
> If you can't be good be careful.
> And if you can't be careful, name it after me.

Ellington's teenage audiences, with their raging hormones, loved the song.

In 1913, just before entering high school, Edward picked up his now world-famous sobriquet. According to Ellington, his pal Edgar McEntree—"an elegant cat, a swinger of his day"—looked at Ellington's polite manners, fashionable clothes, and aristocratic bearing and nicknamed him "Duke."

After Ellington entered high school, McEntree pushed him into playing a number for the seniors' dance. He made a hit. From then on, Duke Ellington was in demand as a pianist at dances and parties. He quickly noticed that "when you were playing piano there was always a pretty girl standing down at the bass-clef end of the piano. I ain't been no athlete since." Music, he realized, could lead to a rich social life as well as to a career.

The more he played the more numbers he needed. But he knew very few. So again, out of necessity, he learned a lesson he would build on all his life. Taking *Soda Fountain Rag*—less a completed composition than a structure for improvisation—he changed the beat and tempo, and played it as a one-step, two-step, fox-trot, tango, and even as a waltz. His unsuspecting listeners thought he had a real repertoire. Later, *Soda Fountain Rag* would show up as part of Ellington's *Oklahoma Stomp* (1929) and *Swing Session* (1937). Another piece he created about 1914, called *Bitches' Ball*, would reappear in 1943 as part of *Black, Brown, and Beige*. These recyclings, as musicologist Mark Tucker has observed, typified one of Ellington's most fundamental principles of composition: reusing older material in new contexts. Not just examples of thriftiness, Ellington's reworkings can also be seen as part of black artists' tradition of "signifying," as Henry Louis Gates, Jr., describes it: commenting on previous versions but adding ironic, subtle twists, creating "repetition with a signal difference."

In the early 1900s, it was becoming acceptable for "nice" people to dance in public—at restaurants and ballrooms. Then, from 1912 to 1916, a zeal for social dance raged across the United States. New steps, coming out of black communities, surged into middle- and upper-class white strata. These ragtime and "animal" steps included the turkey trot, grizzly bear, bunny hop, kangaroo hop, slow drag, and ballin' the jack. These percussive steps, which allowed for individualism and improvisation, were part of the great, long-term Afro-Americanization of European dance sensibilities in America. Beginning in 1912, Irene and Vernon Castle helped legitimize some of the new black dance steps, popularized the one-step and tango, and introduced the fox-trot.

To accommodate the mushrooming number of dancers, cabarets and nightclubs—previously disreputable places for women to patronize—sprang up in many American cities. Nocturnal dancing became a regular public form of entertainment in American cities for young people and also married men and women. Couples treated one another with more casualness, and women experienced new social and physical freedom. Publishers now demanded that all popular songs be danceable. As ballroom dancing increased, demand for dance bands rose, too. These changes were to have a lasting effect on Ellington's musical world.

By around 1920 or 1921, and probably earlier, Washington was rife with dance halls for the outspread African-American population. As Rex Stewart recalled,

> I don't think there were many towns with more dance halls than Washington, excluding only maybe that fabled New Orleans scene. Starting with the then spanking new Lincoln Colonnades, there was Murray's Casino, True Reformer's Hall, Eye Street Hall, Stack O'Lee's in Foggy Bottom, Odd Fellows Hall in Georgetown, the Woodman's Hall in Anacostia, Eagle's Hall in the Northeast section, the Masonic Hall in midtown, and Convention Hall, plus at least ten or so smaller halls.

Soon, Ellington would find himself part of this beguiling scene.

By the time he was in his early teens, Ellington was learning to be clever. Sometimes he would steal his father's Chandler automobile at night, drive around, then refill the gasoline to the exact level it had started at, and let the engine cool. People thought Duke Ellington owned the Chandler and was prosperous.

Though becoming artful, Ellington was only a middling student in high school. His grades were average to poor, except in mechanical and freehand drawing, in which they were generally very good. The one semester he took music—spring 1914—he nearly failed the course, receiving a D. His academic studies held less interest than art courses and, especially, extracurricular music. He liked to cut classes to play piano in the gymnasium, and to skip school to hang out with other pianists. His most important lessons would come from outside the classroom.

There were many male role models, national and local, for Ellington to admire. "There were a lot of great piano players in Washington," he recalled. "Some of them were conservatory men and some of them played by ear, but one was always interested in what the other was doing. . . . I absorbed the emotional values and . . . the technical values. It was a very good climate for me to come up in musically." At the age of fifteen, at a party, he heard Lester Dishman playing and took another "lesson." "He was terrific—really good. The piano jumped. The air shook. With his left hand he really yum-yummed, while with his right he played intricately woven melodic things. But fast!" Besides the local pianists, Ellington was impressed, he said, "by men like James P. Johnson and Luckey Roberts when they came visiting from New York."

His tutors were working musicians. "Every time I reached a point where I needed direction," Ellington reflected, "I ran into a friendly advisor who told me what and which way to go to get what or where I wanted to get or go or do." One of those advisors or mentors was Oliver "Doc" Perry, a popular Washington band-leader, who took Ellington in hand and taught him to read music. Ellington said, "He was my piano parent and nothing was too good

Doc Perry, Ellington's "piano parent."

The Washington pianist Louis Brown, one of Ellington's influences.

for me to try." Perry and fellow pianist Louis Brown deeply influenced Ellington with their poise, manners, discipline, musical skill, and broad-mindedness. "Brown had unbelievable technique," Ellington recollected. "He played chromatic thirds faster than most of the greats of that time could play chromatic singles."

Soon Perry invited Ellington to fill in for him at Wednesday-afternoon dances. Another of his early playing jobs was accompanying an itinerant performer known as "Joe" who was both fortune-teller and magician. Ellington began filling in at clubs and cafes in black Washington.

Yet he was still exploring career options. In 1916, he entered a poster contest sponsored by the civil rights organization the National Association for the Advancement of Colored People (NAACP). And he won. The prize was a scholarship to study art at the prestigious Pratt Institute of Applied Arts in Brooklyn. Now, he had to decide. A career in art or music? He turned down the scholarship to stay in Washington and pursue music. He claimed he was making too much money at his music, but that was probably only part of the reason, maybe a minor part. Besides having been raised by parents who made music, Ellington enjoyed the social aspects of music making, and music appealed to him at a very deep level. "Music is everything," he would write in his memoirs. "Music is the oldest entity. . . . The scope of music is immense and infinite. . . . Without music I may feel blind, atrophied, incomplete, *inexistent*." He still faced, however, the enormous problem of how to learn his craft for his new career.

In about February 1917, three months shy of graduation, Ellington left Armstrong School. His departure from high school marked the beginning of his career as a professional musician. He was by then a fairly good pianist, but he was also a practical young man. To make a living, he worked by day painting signs and posters, soon becoming a partner with Ewell Conaway in a sign-painting business, and by night performing music. After quitting high school, he got his first music jobs playing in the ensembles of Washington bandleaders Louis Thomas, Russell Wooding, and others. Ellington still had much to learn about what it took to be a member of a band. One day Perry bawled him out for showing up at a British embassy gig wearing a bright shepherd's plaid suit instead of formal wear. And Wooding fired him from his large dance orchestra because Ellington chose to embellish the music instead of playing it as written.

Besides learning what it meant to be part of a band, Ellington was also learning new music. Though the death of Scott Joplin, "the King of Ragtime Writers," in April 1917, symbolized the close of the ragtime era, many musicians, including Ellington, already had moved beyond the kind of composed ragtime Joplin published to its looser, more modern offspring then spelled variously "jas," "jass," "jaz," and "jazz."

The new jazz owed a great deal to ragtime. The conventional

view that ragtime was a notated music and jazz an improvised one is grossly distorted. From the time it first was published, in 1896, ragtime encompassed two performing traditions—an as-written approach maintained mostly by amateurs, and an improvisatory approach practiced by professionals. (Many of the professional piano "professors" or "ticklers" were black.) The latter tradition comprised an early form of jazz in everything but name. When the transition from ragtime to jazz occurred is impossible to pinpoint. It is like trying to specify precisely when twilight becomes night.

The earliest documented use of the term *jazz* appeared in San Francisco in 1913. During the middle and late 1910s—in New Orleans, San Francisco, New York, Chicago, Washington, and elsewhere—black musicians, and their white counterparts, were experimenting with the new style. They were trying out looser rhythms, fooling around with given melodies, embellishing and syncopating them, creating their own tunes, and otherwise elasticizing the original pieces. They were going from 2/4 to a more swinging 4/4 beat, bending notes, creating their own "breaks." The first jazz recordings were made in 1917 by the Original Dixieland Jazz Band, a white group. When their recordings and their appearances in New York caused a sensation, the new style came to be in demand. The next year, black and white Washington would begin discovering jazz.

Five days after Joplin died, the United States declared war on Imperial Germany and somewhat reluctantly entered World War I on the side of England, France, and their allies. During the war, Ellington got a job as a messenger at the Navy Department, then at the State Department. The war mobilization created for Washington, as the nation's capital, an upsurge in government visitors, a buildup in the armed services, and a flurry of social activities, many requiring music. It brought work for Washington musicians, and Ellington and his colleagues kept busy entertaining at all sorts of functions.

In 1917 or perhaps early 1918, Ellington took the next step on the road to becoming a full professional: he formed his own group and named it The Duke's Serenaders. At first, the Serenaders comprised two to four players: Ellington on piano, along with drums, banjo or guitar, and saxophone. "I played my first date at the True

True Reformer's Hall, where Ellington played his first dance engagements.

Reformer's Hall, on the worst piano in the world," Ellington remembered. "I played from 8 P.M. to 1 A.M. and for 75 cents. Man, I snatched that money and ran like a thief. My mother was so proud of me." Here was his beloved mother giving her approval to his choice of bandleading as a career.

During Ellington's musically formative years, from the age of eleven through seventeen, he lived with his family a scant two and a half blocks from True Reformer's Hall, a large, well-equipped public facility in the heart of black Washington, at Seventh and T streets, Northwest. (Musicians—including Claude Hopkins, Doc Perry, Elmer Snowden, and Ellington—used to hang out on the street corner outside.) Room 10 became a gathering place for aspiring teenage musicians and their fans. Ellington's group became popular there and, Rex Stewart remembered, Ellington was crowned "king" of Room 10. "I can still see young Ellington playing the piano," recalled Stewart decades later, "and fixing that famous hypnotic smile on the nearest pretty girl."

Ellington sometimes performed with a neighborhood friend, Otto —or "Toby," as he liked to be called—Hardwick, five years his junior, who played bass and saxophone, and trumpeter Arthur Whetsol, six years younger than Ellington. They formed the nucleus of what eventually became the Duke Ellington orchestra. Whetsol stood for neatness, dependability, and sobriety. Many Washington musicians, in fact, especially those Ellington admired, demonstrated dignity. Ellington said that Washington had a "disciplinary climate." Barry Ulanov wrote of "a Washington pattern" among musicians. "It involved a certain bearing, a respect for education, for the broad principles of the art of music; a desire for order, for design in their professional lives."

What repertoire did Duke's Serenaders play? No one is entirely sure. But almost certainly they performed some instrumental rags such as Scott Joplin's *Maple Leaf Rag*, ragtime songs like Irving Berlin's *Alexander's Ragtime Band*, W. C. Handy's *St. Louis Blues* and other blues songs, such popular song hits as *Pretty Baby* and *Indiana*, and instrumental dance tunes—including waltzes, two-steps, fox-trots, and tangos. The Serenaders may also have played a few originals by Ellington and, possibly, other members of the band. One thing is clear: Ellington had become the leader of a jazzy, working dance band.

By March of 1918, Ellington had taken three additional steps toward independence and professionalism. First, he moved out of his parents' home and into a place of his own. Second, he got a telephone—at that time, still a luxury. He acquired a telephone two and a half years before his parents did. (He would become a great user of the telephone, and typically would avoid written communication—except for his musical compositions—in favor of the phone.) And third, he bought a listing for himself as "musician" in the classified section of the telephone directory. Through this listing, or perhaps his father's society contacts, Ellington secured his first jobs playing outside the black community at venues such as the Women's Democratic Club.

Sometime in about 1918, Louis Thomas sent Ellington to play a solo piano job at the Ashland, Virginia, Country Club. Thomas took 90 percent of the fee as commission. Stunned by the possibilities, Ellington decided to serve as his own booking agent. In January 1919, he took out a display advertisement in the telephone directory's classified pages. As Hardwick remembered, "All of a sudden

. . . we began to get a lot of 'dicty' [high-toned] jobs. . . . Duke would direct us to drive to an embassy or private mansion." Other times, they would drive into Virginia to play for society balls after fox hunts and horse shows, usually with a four-piece band. Like his father, Ellington was now working for "society," except not as a provider of food and personal service but as a supplier of dance music. Playing for this stratum of society must have enhanced Ellington's professionalism and his desire to evolve a stage presence.

Duke Ellington was also becoming a canny businessman. A friend named "Black" Bowie came up with schemes for the band to play in nearby cities such as Baltimore. "From then on," asserted son Mercer,

> Duke Ellington began to realize the significance of the interplay between management and artist and the necessity for it. . . . He had begun to learn the art of hustling in back halls and dark alleys, how to play at top level in places that were prepared for "sport." His mastery of this developed as a parallel until he was no longer a hustler but a businessman.

When people telephoned, he would speak quickly so as to sound rushed. Soon, he secured so much work that by October 1919 he was listing himself as "manager" of The Duke's Serenaders. He

By 1919, Ellington was performing regularly, in part the result of an advertisement for his band, The Duke's Serenaders, in the Washington, D.C., telephone directory of October 1919.

Ellington's wife,
Edna Thompson Ellington,
in the 1930s.

The versatile Henry Grant,
Ellington's neighbor and
music teacher.

sent out other bands under his name, as many as five bands on a busy night. Yet he was practical enough to keep his sign-painting business and tie it into his music business. "When customers came for posters to advertise a dance, I would ask them what they were doing about their music. When they wanted to hire a band, I would ask them who's painting their signs."

Where did Ellington get his business sense? Perhaps from hustling in Washington poolrooms, perhaps in part from his father, who in addition to his regular job as butler for Dr. Cuthbert had peddled his services as an independent caterer. Whatever the source, Ellington was and would remain an independent businessman desirous of controlling his own affairs.

By 1919 he was doing well enough to buy a car and a house. As a shareholder in the American Dream, he wanted the house for the family he was establishing. On July 2, 1918, Ellington had married a neighborhood sweetheart, Edna Thompson. That fall he registered for the draft, but was never called up. On March 11, 1919, Duke and Edna had a baby, whom they named Mercer Kennedy Ellington. Mercer has said he doesn't think his parents would have gotten married had they not wanted to legitimize their son. "There was too much pulling them apart. My mother's folks were from a higher station of black society than my father's. They were school-teachers and principals, and they considered all musicians, including Duke Ellington, low-life. Ironically, though, Ellington's parents thought my mother wasn't good enough for *him*. You know how parents are, and his were even more so." A second child, born to the Ellingtons the following year, didn't survive. Mercer would be their only child.

Even as he was becoming a successful family man, Ellington also realized he needed more musical "schooling" to keep growing. "I was beginning to catch on around Washington," Ellington wrote, "and I finally built up so much of a reputation that I had to study music seriously to protect it." He found an ideal teacher: Henry Grant, who lived in Ellington's neighborhood. Ellington went to Grant's twice a week for lessons. Grant taught him harmony, and probably improved Ellington's music-reading abilities, too. Grant's musical activities covered a lot of ground: he taught music at Dunbar High School, conducted church choirs, gave solo piano recitals, played in a classical music trio, conducted a group of folk singers, in 1919 helped found the National Association of Negro Musicians, and edited its magazine, *The Negro Musician*. For someone so well trained in European "classical" music, Grant was unusual: he didn't condescend to or scorn popular music.

Under Grant, "the whole thing suddenly became very clear to me, just like that. I went on studying, of course, but I could also hear people whistling, and I got all the Negro music that way. You can't learn that in any school. And there were things I wanted to do that were not in books, and I had to ask a lot of questions."

The summer of 1919 saw the worst interracial strife the United States has ever experienced. Whites attacked blacks in race riots in more than two dozen cities and killed scores of black people. There were lynchings, too, of seventy-six blacks—the highest number ever after 1909. The bloody racial violence moved the writer-activist James Weldon Johnson to call it the "Red Summer." In Washington's stifling July, armed white soldiers and sailors attacked unarmed black civilians, injuring dozens. Ellington's reaction to the brutality in his city went unrecorded, but the pain of it, along with the other events in his life and in the land, may not only have thrust him into adulthood but also given him a new worldliness.

His people victimized by racial prejudice, Ellington chose now to deal with the larger world by outsmarting it, by playing the trickster, the sly fox, garbed in the sheep's clothing of charm. He would dazzle them with his manners, polish, style, and entertainment, all the time pursuing his own goals. And he would walk with pride, head held high, everywhere he went.

Due to his experiences as a young man, Ellington developed an aversion to restrictive categories, one he increasingly voiced throughout his life. His sister, Ruth, has said one of his mottoes was "No boxes." As Ellington disliked the way that black Washington maintained strata based on income and pigmentation, he could only have chafed at the greater restrictions the white community placed on him, his family, and friends—restraints based solely on his racial category. And the way many of his teachers, performers, audiences, and venues would mix one kind of music with another probably led him to feel that the musical categories the larger society imposed had little meaning. Later, other experiences would intensify his aversion to categories, for example, the way people would limit their praise with the word "Negro": "Ellington is a fine Negro composer." The designations "jazz musician" and "jazz composer" served to restrict his music, and in later years he would speak out against such labels.

Ellington already had developed a magnetic presence, as testified by William Greer, a singing drummer born about 1895 in Long Branch, New Jersey, one of a number of out-of-town musicians attracted to Washington's thriving musical scene. An irrepressible hipster, bon vivant, and born showman known as "Sensational Sonny" or just Sonny, he met Ellington in 1919. "From the moment I was introduced to Duke, I loved him," Greer said years later. "It was just something about him. He didn't know it, but he had it then. I've never seen another man like him. When he walks into a strange room, the whole place lights up. That's how he likes people, and how he impresses them."

Just as his father had developed his own florid style, Duke Ellington was creating his own personal, conversational, sartorial, and musical style, and his own public image. "In those days," Rex Stewart related, "the fashion in D.C. was to have a tailor-made suit with some feature that no one else was wearing. One memorable evening Ellington astonished everybody by strolling up to the corner attired in a shimmy back herringbone suit (this was shirred and pleated in the back). To all of the style-conscious musicians, Duke was considered the epitome of elegance from then on."

Ellington's need to stand out and be treated royally can be traced back to his mother calling him "blessed"—and his naturally aristocratic tendencies. According to Mercer Ellington, his father "had Black Bowie . . . go ahead to the club or dance hall where he was appearing and announce: 'Duke Ellington is going to be here this evening.' When he arrived, Jerry Rhea [another Washington friend] would be with him to fling open the door and tell the people, 'Get out of the way, 'cause here comes Duke.' "

In 1920, Greer landed the drummer's chair in the Howard Theatre pit band. The Howard, which had opened in 1911 as Washington's first large theater for blacks, engaged the services of a growing number of musicians. At the Howard, Ellington's band and several others played for preperformance supper shows, from 5:00 to 6:30 P.M. These shows featured as many as five local bands, who competed for the applause of the audience to determine the most popular. Later, after becoming famous, between the 1930s and the 1960s, Ellington's orchestra would frequently play the Howard as the featured attraction. It was at the Howard, in 1920, that Ellington made another important connection: he met Juan Tizol, a Puerto Rican–born valve trombonist whom Ellington would recruit in 1929 for his orchestra.

The Howard Theatre, Washington's foremost black theater, where Ellington performed often.

Ellington at Louis Thomas's Cabaret, Ninth and R streets, in Washington, ca. 1920.
From left: Sonny Greer, Bertha Ricks, Ellington, Mrs. Conaway, Sterling Conaway.

By the early 1920s, Ellington's band was playing many kinds of engagements for both blacks and whites. These experiences with different types of audiences would prove valuable in his career. In Washington's hot, humid summers, he played for outdoor dances at New Fairmount Park and the Anderson Open Air Gardens. Some of the indoor dances featured costumed dancers, elaborate decorations, and exotic themes, and the jazz bands spiced up their music with novel effects, which probably helped prepare him for his engagement, some years later, at the Cotton Club.

As Ellington and his band quickly learned, the life of a dance-band musician had its rewards but also its risks. Rex Stewart recalled Southwest Washington in about 1920. "This was a wild area. There'd be all kinds of interruptions during rehearsals, like a brawl or some woman screaming 'He's going to kill me.' Once the police shot it out with bootleggers, right across the street from [bandleader] Ollie's house! It was the closest thing to New Orleans's Storyville at that time. . . . There was a dance somewhere every night," Stewart remembered. "Of course, you had to know what the social climate might be before venturing into a hall where you were not known, as the natives were mighty clannish in those days. Sometimes you might have to leave a dance without your overcoat, your hat or even your head! Ambulances were rarely seen in a colored neighborhood in those days, and the victim generally bled to death."

If there was trouble, the musicians themselves were not necessarily safe. Stewart, eight years Ellington's junior, recalled peeking into the Odd Fellows Hall in Georgetown, probably in 1921, where Ellington and a quartet were playing for a Saturday-night dance. The foursome

> sounded great to us kids because they played the popular tunes of the day, such as *It's Right Here for You, and If You Don't Get It, It's No Fault of Mine; Walking the Dog; He May Be Your Man, But He Comes to See Me Sometime.* We gaped over the fence, drinking in the bright lights, the pretty girls, the festive atmosphere, and the good music. . . . These dances always started sedately, but as the night wore on and the liquor flowed faster, the tougher element went into action, and the customary fight erupted. This time it was a real brawl, and the Georgetown toughs ran the band out of the hall. . . . The band [was] hotfooting it down Twenty-ninth Street [with Duke in the lead].

So far as is known, Ellington was never seriously injured at any of his engagements.

If he was to move up from this rowdy scene, Ellington would have to stand out from his competitors. He knew that in this period the better ragtime or jazz pianists strove to develop their own style of stage manners and of playing. Typically they also composed a signature piece, a "theme song" with which they would become identified. One of the best such pianists was New York's James P. Johnson and his showpiece was *Carolina Shout*, first issued on piano roll in 1918, and a brilliant, virtuosic piece of eastern-style ragtime. *Carolina Shout* became a test piece among professional pianists, especially those in the East.

One day in about 1920, Ellington's friend Percy "Brushes" Johnson, a drummer, invited him over to his home on T Street. He told Ellington, "You've got to listen to this." He put James P. Johnson's (no relation) piano roll of *Carolina Shout* onto the player piano. "This was, of course," Ellington recalled, "an entirely new avenue of adventure for me, and I went back every day and listened." Always keen to learn any way he could, Ellington had his friend slow down the tempo of the roll, so he could watch each key go up and down and begin learning the piece. After a lot of practice, he could play it perfectly. Brushes Johnson took Ellington around town to show off him and the piece.

Then, probably on November 25, 1921, James P. Johnson himself came to town to perform at a large jazz revue at the Convention Center. After Johnson, as expected, played *Carolina Shout*, Ellington's friends egged him to get up on the bandstand and "cut" the master. Ellington, "scared stiff," played the difficult piece for the older man, and when he finished, the master applauded along with

James P. Johnson, known as "the Father of Stride Piano," and an influence on Ellington.

Ellington's friends. Johnson was a magnanimous musician who liked to encourage younger players.

Again realizing here was a true master from whom he could learn a lot, Ellington hovered over the piano, watching Johnson play the rest of the evening. "I took him out that night for a tour of the Southwest [entertainment] district, and I stayed up till ten A.M. listening to him." Later Ellington wrote, "What I absorbed on that occasion might, I think, have constituted a whole semester in a conservatory." Ellington was a student in what could be called a "conservatory without walls." He mostly taught himself by imitating piano rolls, listening to recordings, watching and listening to pianists more skilled than he, and, occasionally, taking informal piano lessons. His son, Mercer, observed, "Throughout his whole life he had a disdain for formalized training."

In trying to best James P. Johnson, Ellington was participating, albeit in a limited way, in an established tradition. In a "cutting contest," two or more pianists competed to establish a clear winner. They performed difficult pieces, brought out their pianistic tricks, showed off their own styles, and strove to put their own stamp of individuality upon what they played. These spirited, muscular competitions were akin to boxing matches, contests to determine a champion of the place or time. A different arena, a different type of expression, but the same principle.

Jazz bands also competed in the same type of event, called a "band contest" or a "battle of the bands." "The jazz band battle was not only fun, it was also an education," declared Rex Stewart, "a proving ground and a moment of truth for many a musician." As well as playing in piano contests, Ellington himself played in the occasional band battle in Washington. Stewart remembered one at the then-new Lincoln Colonnade, about 1922. The main battle was between Doc Perry, the favorite of Northwest Washington, and Sam Taylor, Southwest's "homeboy." Ellington led a third, pickup, group. "I can see the scene as if it were yesterday," wrote Stewart. "It looked like the entire police force was on hand to keep order, whiskey was flowing like water and guys were betting on who had the best band. Artie Whetsol, John Adams from Annapolis, and I suppose every musician within 40 miles was there."

Whether he won or lost the contests, Ellington learned from them about music, show business, and competition. "Whenever we had a contest to play we used to go all out for psychology," Ellington revealed. "We'd tell the fellows in the other band they were going to get cut that night. They'd be so rattled they'd even get to calling out the wrong numbers."

His ears always open to new sounds, Ellington sought out opportunities to hear musicians who visited Washington, mostly from New York City. Besides James P. Johnson, Ellington also heard pianists Eubie Blake and Luckey Roberts, blues singer Mamie Smith, and bandleader LeRoy Smith, whose group impressed Ellington greatly. "It was well dressed and well rehearsed, and all the musicians doubled on different instruments. This created an effect of . . . magic that caused an explosion in my desire to explore the further reaches of music's possibilities."

Duke Ellington was doing well in Washington. He could have remained there and probably led a comfortable life as a dance-band leader and booking agent. But, somehow, that was not enough. He had the drive to excel, to rise to the top, and the top at the time was New York. The imaginations of Ellington and his buddies were fired with stories of New York City's great talents in blues, jazz, vaudeville, popular songwriting, and other entertainments.

In Ellington's Washington circle, Greer had the New York connections. He had grown up in New Jersey and done some playing in New York. Greer gave Ellington's crowd glowing accounts of the scene in New York, whetting their appetites for a taste of the action. "So I come in there and started that jive talk . . . ," Greer recalled, "telling them cats about New York, painting a glorious picture about New York, and right away them cats they was on me like white on rice."

In February 1923, the vaudeville bandleader Wilbur Sweatman wired Greer from New York that he needed a new drummer. Greer accepted the gig on the condition that Sweatman also hire Otto Hardwick and Ellington. Sweatman agreed. Ellington hesitated. He was securely entrenched in the band business in Washington. But in the end he accepted, tempted by the lure of Manhattan and the challenges awaiting him there. "Harlem, in our minds, did indeed

Sonny Greer, the singing drummer from Long Branch, New Jersey, teamed with Ellington in the early 1920s.

have the world's most glamorous atmosphere." He realized, "We had to go there."

So Ellington made a fateful decision in 1923. He decided to leave the warmth of his family, the security of his many established customers and clients, and the whole familiar world of his native Washington. Leaving so much behind, he must have felt some apprehension. But like countless other young people, he felt he needed to test himself against the world-class challenges of New York, to go for more opportunity, for the "big time," in fact, "the biggest-time" entertainment arena of all.

Ellington had by now established his personality. He was tied strongly to his mother, secure, self-confident, optimistic, prideful, aristocratic in demeanor, charming, well mannered, easy with people from all walks of life, religious, ambitious, clever, didactically oriented, street smart, shrewd in business, restive with categories, averse to writing while inclined toward oral communication, a styl-

Duke Ellington in the early 1920s.

ish dresser, and a growing individualist. His decision to leave for New York proved that he was also a risk taker.

Diverting from, but not abandoning, visual art, he had settled on music as a career. He had completed his musical apprenticeship in the nation's capital and become an avid listener and absorber of other black pianists and black music generally, a decent pianist, a budding bandleader and composer, and a pleasing entertainer.

In New York he would face terra incognita, the rough-and-tumble world of nightclubs in the gangster-ridden Prohibition era. He would be a black man trying to make it in a highly competitive, white-dominated realm, relying on musical talents that were still relatively undeveloped. Yet, he headed north to New York City, north to Harlem to test himself and to face the problem of what it took to survive and to succeed in the big time.

THREE

SEEKING
SPECIAL SOUNDS

1923 – 27

If Washington provided Ellington his basic musical education, Manhattan would be his graduate school and more than he reckoned on, it would be a school of hard knocks. Here he would encounter intense competition, learn new music, experiment as a soloist and band member, and realize that his fortune lay with leading a band with a distinctive sound of its own that set it off from all others.

When Ellington stepped off the train in New York in March 1923, just before his twenty-fourth birthday, it was evidently his first time there. When he reached Harlem, he was excited and awed. "The world's most glamorous atmosphere," he is said to have remarked. "Why, it is just like the Arabian nights." Harlem contained the largest concentration of black people in the nation and probably in the world. As bandleader Cab Calloway commented, "I had never seen so many Negroes in one place before in my life." Long-time Harlemites, new arrivals from the South, immigrants from the West Indies—they all were Harlem.

For a young musician, the competition in Harlem could not have been more intense since talented African-American musicians were part of the rush to the new black Mecca. Between 1910 and 1920, New York City had surpassed Washington, D.C., as the

American city with the largest black population. Similarly, Harlem had eclipsed Washington as the capital of black America. Unlike Washington, Atlanta, and Nashville, New York City had no well-known black university. It nonetheless became the center of black intellectual, political, and cultural life and a magnet for aspiring young black men and women. As a result of events in the 1920s, James Weldon Johnson could write in 1930 of Harlem: "It is a Mecca for the sightseer, the pleasure-seeker, the curious, the adventurous, the enterprising, the ambitious, and the talented of the entire Negro world; for the lure of it has reached down to every isle of the Carib Sea and penetrated even into Africa."

Crowds throng Lenox Avenue in Harlem, where Ellington moved in 1923.

Without doubt, Harlem was a magnet and cultural capital, the home of the "Harlem Renaissance." First, there was the sheer size of its black population. In 1920, it had 73,000 black residents, and by 1930, 165,000 blacks in an area about twenty-five blocks long and six blocks wide. Second, it was increasingly the center of political activity. Harlem was home to two important civil rights groups. Founded in 1910, the National Association for the Advancement of Colored People (NAACP), was headed by the Harvard-trained intellectual-activist W. E. B. DuBois. The National Urban League was founded in 1911 to help new arrivals from the rural South. And beginning in 1916, the charismatic Marcus Garvey made Harlem the base for his romantic, doomed brand of black nationalism. Third, black writers were drawn to New York to participate in its growing literary scene, and perhaps for greater potential access to publishers. Fourth, entertainers, actors, and musicians were drawn there for opportunities to play before the nation's largest black *and* white populations, and because New York was serving as the headquarters for national mass media networks: publishing, booking agencies, recording, and radio.

The Harlem Renaissance, also known in its day as the "Negro Renaissance" or the "New Negro movement," was an attitude or psychology centering on racial pride and a burst of creative activity in the 1920s. Most books on the Harlem Renaissance have defined it as essentially a literary movement. Certainly Harlem was home to a phenomenal gathering of writers. Its luminaries included the poets Jean Toomer, Frank Horne, Arna Bontemps, Langston Hughes, and Countee Cullen; novelists Zora Neale Hurston, Walter White, Jessie Fauset, Rudolph Fischer, Claude McKay, and Wallace Thurman; playwrights such as Rose McClendon; and the versatile writer James Weldon Johnson.

Indeed, it was perceived as mostly a literary movement by people like bandleader Cab Calloway, who said, "Those of us in the music and entertainment business were vaguely aware that something exciting was happening, but we weren't directly involved . . . the two worlds, literature and entertainment, rarely crossed. We were working hard on our thing and they were working hard on theirs." Probably also at work here were African-American class and cultural distinctions. Literature and painting appealed more to the elite, while jazz, blues, and pop were in the realm of the masses of black folk. And some intellectuals tended to regard African-American folk practices as raw material that needed to be "refined" before it could count as art. Thus jazz artists were regarded with some suspicion because they accepted folk blues too uncritically.

Black music and dance were also flowering during this period, and, regardless of how the movement has been defined, Duke Ellington must be seen as a key figure of the cultural awakening of Harlem. He would achieve as much as any literary figure of the Renaissance, and would keep on achieving after most of the writers had faded or died. That Ellington is given little role in the standard histories of the Renaissance has more to do with literary historians' understandable focus on literature of the period and cultural historians' lack of knowledge about him and unpreparedness in assessing music than anything else.

In the black community, music reached more people than did literature. Music was more accessible because you did not have to be educated or even literate to listen to it. You could experience music in all sorts of informal gatherings, including rent parties and fish fries. Through the spreading medium of radio, you could listen to music for free, and by the mid 1920s, listeners around New York City might sometimes tune in to Duke Ellington, Fletcher Henderson, or other musicians. Records cost only about one third of books. Music was, then, more democratic. Music had a visceral, physical appeal: you could tap your toe, pop your fingers, dance to it. And, finally, music was more participatory: you could sing along or swing your lady around the dance floor.

Ever since composer Will Marion Cook and poet Paul Laurence Dunbar wrote *Clorindy, the Origin of the Cakewalk* in 1898, there had been all-black revues and musicals on Broadway. But in 1921, when the musical comedy *Shuffle Along*, with songs by Eubie Blake and Noble Sissle, and featuring an all-black cast, had become an unexpected smash hit, Broadway began a vogue for black revues that helped spark a market for black entertainment and art. The vogue for African-Americans that went hand-in-hand with the Harlem Renaissance opened doors for Ellington. Arriving in Manhattan in the early years of the Renaissance, he was in the right place at

Ellington inscribed this publicity photo "To the dearest mother in the world."

the right time—to find reaffirmation in the African-American cultural tradition, to be discovered by an ambitious impresario, to be accepted by a growing public, black and white.

Shuffle Along, in the words of writer Arna Bontemps, was "an announcement, an overture to an era of hope" for African-Americans. It was *Shuffle Along*'s dances that above all caught the public's fancy. Opening in October 1923, the revue *Runnin' Wild* popularized the knee-bending exhibition dance, the Charleston, which became a huge national fad for about three years, in the process generating tremendous controversy because of its movements, which seemed wild to most white Americans. The irresistible Charleston broke American dance away from European norms for good, popularizing an African-American sensibility in dance.

The African-American dances that created a sensation among theater audiences spurred a growing interest in public dancing. In 1923, New York City had 786 dance halls, 238 of them in Manhattan. Nearly 88 percent of the Manhattan halls were open to the general public, and that year collected a total of 6 million paid admissions.

Despite these statistics, when Ellington got to New York, he found, as in Washington, that blues, jazz, and dancing were suspect among many people, black and white. Public dancing faced great opposition early in the decade. "Dancing," wrote the *Ladies' Home Journal* in 1921, was "moral ruin," carried out to "cheap, common, tawdry music." Moralists drew a close link between dancing, loose language, immodest dress, sex, and jazz—not to mention nightlife, alcohol, and crime.

Nightclubs stood as "emblems of 1920s values—consumption, sexual expression, youth culture, and social informality," historian Lewis Erenberg has observed. Prohibition "governed night life by placing it outside the domain of acceptable middle-class mores. . . . Nightclubs helped form the mystique of the big city. They provided settings for the fantasies money might buy."

One of the things money could buy was live jazz music. And traditionalists despised it. "Does Jazz Put the Sin in Syncopation?" asked a 1921 article in the *Ladies' Home Journal*. "Does Jazz Cause Crime?" asked the *Musical Observer* in 1924. Both periodicals answered their rhetorical questions with emphatic affirmatives. White religious periodicals denounced jazz dances as "impure," "polluting," and "debasing." The music played in nightclubs and speakeasies—and their illegal booze, late-night hours, and aura of loose sexual mores—flew in the face of the respectability many were striving for. Thus, Ellington and his colleagues were working in a realm of which many people disapproved. He would later describe jazz as "the music that somebody likes to look down on."

Jazz also faced an uphill struggle for acceptance among middle-class black families during the early and mid 1920s. Recalls the African-American clarinetist and saxophonist Garvin Bushell:

> Most of the Negro population in New York then [around 1920] had either been born there or had been in the city so long they were fully acclimated. They wanted to forget the traditions of the South and were trying to emulate the whites. You couldn't deliver a package to a Negro's front door. You had to go down to the cellar door. And Negroes dressed up to go to work, then changed into work clothes when they got there. You usually weren't allowed to play blues and boogie woogie in the average Negro middle-class home. That music supposedly suggested a low element. And the big bands with the violins, flutes, and piccolos didn't play it either. You could only hear the blues and real jazz in the gutbucket cabarets where the lower class went.

The low status of jazz, and the notion that jazz music is a frill, would haunt Ellington for the rest of his life. Despite his substantial later accomplishments, people like Ellington would even be dismissed as "the glitter of more substantial and more solid progress" by the writers of *The Negro in New York*, a book that grew out of the Federal Writers Project in the late 1930s.

The 1920s saw a great clash between modernism and traditionalism on many fronts—modern versus premodern art, alcohol versus Prohibition, evolution versus Biblical literalism, new sexual mores versus conservative ones, urban versus rural values, youthful abandon versus parental stuffiness. Jazz was caught up in the swirling controversies. "Americans shared a common perception that jazz had transforming qualities that could last beyond the time of a song and the space of a cabaret act," Kathy Ogren has noted. "For many Americans, to argue about jazz was to argue about the nature of change itself." People on both sides of the controversy saw jazz as signaling the end of one era and the beginning of another, more modern, period.

When Ellington arrived in Manhattan, he found a pulsating entertainment scene. Besides a growing interest in blacks by the musical theater, an emerging jazz scene, and booming dance business, the blues were gaining currency—at least among the segment of the public open to change. As a type of song, the blues had arisen when Ellington was a child, when it was a new, hip kind of music. Originally a southern folk expression, the blues remained largely unknown to white Americans until they were written down, regularized, popularized, and commercialized by the black bandleader and composer W. C. Handy. Beginning in 1912 with his *Memphis Blues*, the blues became a popular kind of song and instrumental in sheet-music form, and on piano roll. In August 1920, black singer Mamie Smith made the first blues record, *Crazy Blues*, and it opened the way for a flood of "race records" made expressly for black consumers, though there were some whites who bought them, too.

In the early 1920s, jazz maintained a strong element of novelty— for example, through humorous instrumental sounds or antics on the bandstand. "When I began my work," Ellington related later, "jazz was a stunt, something different. Not everybody cared for jazz and those who did felt that it wasn't the real thing unless they were given a shock sensation of loudness or unpredictability along with the music." The vaudeville entertainer Wilbur Sweatman was a very large man best known for such a gimmick—his ability to play three clarinets simultaneously. Sweatman's band, including Ellington and his comrades from Washington, Sonny Greer and Otto Hardwick, opened at the Lafayette Theatre in Harlem on March 5, 1923, for a week's run as part of an "all-star vaudeville show." The band sat on stage, possibly the first time Ellington had done so, at least in a vaudeville show.

After playing a few more gigs with Sweatman, the trio from Washington faced a decision. Should they stick with Sweatman as he toured to other cities? Or should they remain in New York, striking out on their own?

They chose the latter path, which proved bumpy. There was no immediate work for them, and breaking into the hotly competitive music scene in New York was difficult. By day, they went around Harlem, hustling games of pool. When they got two dollars, they'd go buy a meal. By night, they went from club to club, trying to rustle up work. Out of cash, they slept at the homes of various aunts.

Yet despite the economic woes, Ellington's smart style of dress, good grooming, manners, and charm helped him gain entrée into the inner circle of top Harlem pianists, including Willie "The Lion" Smith. He appreciated Ellington right from the start, finding him a "good-looking, well-mannered fellow; one of those guys you see him, you like him right away; warm, good-natured. I took a liking to him and he took a liking to me." The gruff, cigar-chomping Smith even shared his money with Ellington's struggling trio of friends.

Ellington tagged along with Smith at speakeasies, cabarets, and other engagements. After the gig ended in the wee hours, they would haunt other nightspots, looking for musical action. If they couldn't find it, they would go to someone's apartment, and drink and play music till morning, even noon. Again, Ellington was learning both by observing and by doing. He was also trying his hand at being a solo entertainer.

Another kind of affair to which Ellington tagged along with Smith was house-rent parties, a characteristically Harlem institution that flourished in the 1920s because most Harlem residents could not

Harlem's Lafayette Theatre and Connie's Inn, with the Tree of Hope.

afford the nightclubs. An outgrowth of church fund-raising affairs and "parlor socials," house-rent parties became very popular as exorbitant rents caused financial hardship at the same time as Prohibition created a quest for drink. For an admission price ranging between twenty-five cents and a dollar, you could enter a private apartment, with soft, low lights—red or blue—and enjoy good times. The only furniture was an upright piano, where a pianist played hot rhythms. Drinks typically cost twenty-five cents. The host paid the rent from the receipts.

Willie "The Lion" Smith has left a vivid description of these affairs:

> They would crowd a hundred or more people into a seven-room railroad flat and the walls would bulge—some of the parties spread to the halls and all over the building. . . . The rent party was the place to go to pick up on all the latest jokes, jive, and uptown news. . . . The parties were recommended to newly arrived single gals as the place to go to get acquainted. . . . The best time of all at these parties came early in the morning. . . . During these early hours close to dawn the dancers would grab each other tightly and do the monkey hunch or bo-hog. Their shuffling feet would give everything a weird rhythmic atmosphere. The lights would be dimmed down and the people would call out to the piano player, "Play it, oh, play it" or "Break it down" or "Get in the gully and give us the ever-lovin' stomp." Those were happy days.

"In New York the gigs were few and far between, but we could always count on Saturday," recalled Ellington. "We could get all the food we wanted and take some home, and a dollar besides. . . . We played the house rent parties every Saturday night. That was home sweet home."

Usually all the music at rent-parties came from a piano. Besides Ellington, the pianists who entertained at rent parties included Claude Hopkins, Cliff Jackson, Stephen "Beetle" Henderson, Abba Labba (Richard McLean), Raymond "Lippy" Boyette. Later in the decade, the "Big Three"—the most sought after—at rent parties would be James P. Johnson, Willie "The Lion" Smith, and their young protégé, Thomas "Fats" Waller.

Sometimes the pianists would compete against one another in

"carving" or "cutting" contests, taking their turns at the piano. "We would embroider the melodies with our own original ideas and try to develop patterns that had more originality than those played before us," said Willie "The Lion" Smith. "It was pure improvisation. . . . You had to have your own individual style and be able to play in all the keys." Clearly, to succeed in Harlem required both virtuosity as a musician and originality as a stylist.

This bravura keyboard style, in which Ellington was apprenticing, came to have its own name—Harlem "stride" piano. Growing out of ragtime, the style called for rapid tempos, virtuosic devices borrowed from classical music, and use of the piano's full register. Named "stride" for the large strides or leaps in the left hand, the style developed tremendous rhythmic propulsion. It is the most comprehensive of all jazz piano styles (played on the most self-contained of all jazz instruments) as it provides its own bass, rhythmic and harmonic accompaniment, and melody.

Finally, "we were getting more bored with our situation than desperate," Ellington would recall, but things were, in fact, getting thin. When he found fifteen dollars lying in the street, he and his friends bought themselves a good meal and three train tickets, and headed back to Washington. " 'Course," he would say later, "all we need to have done was to send home and they would have sent us some money anyway, but we preferred to do it this way so we could make an entrance. You know, 'Just back from New York for a little holiday,' something like that."

It must have been a great letdown to leave such a Mecca, and to leave far less than a success, far less than the best that he had aspired to since he was a boy. But Ellington was at least wiser for the experience. In a short time, he had observed the smart show business acumen of Wilbur Sweatman, heard some very good (as well as mediocre) music, begun learning tricks from the top Harlem pianists, won the patronage of Willie "The Lion" Smith and the friendship of other musicians, and, perhaps above all, developed a sense of what it would take to make it in New York City.

"We got to Washington on a Sunday morning," Ellington recalled in 1944. "I still remember the smell of hot biscuits when we walked in. There was butter and honey. My mother broiled six mackerel. There was lots of coffee. Uncle Ed [his father] got out the old decanter and we lay there drinking corn in the sunshine." (Ellington was, in fact, a somewhat heavy drinker, and would be for years to come.) He went back to his life in Washington, playing music, making signs, and seeing wife Edna and son Mercer, who had remained behind.

Soon, however, another invitation came his way. In about June of 1923, Elmer Snowden, Otto Hardwick, Sonny Greer, and Arthur Whetsol took a train back to New York. They sent for Ellington, promising him work. Leaving his family again, Ellington, confident of employment, traveled in ducal fashion, buying a first-class train ticket and ordering an expensive meal. When he arrived, he found the job had vanished and his friends were broke.

They hit the streets again, scuffling for work. "It was summertime, it was hot as hell," recalled Ellington in 1956. "We used to have to ride that subway in the morning and go downtown and audition and all that sort of thing." Their auditions, however, yielded no bookings.

In late June, led by Snowden, the band took a gig at Atlantic City's Music Box. A real break came when the singer Ada "Bricktop" Smith landed them a job at Harlem's prestigious Exclusive Club. Run by Barron Wilkins, the club catered to wealthy whites and tolerated light-skinned blacks. "A hundred-dollar bill will not go very far," reported an observer, "and it is not intended to do much service in this luxuriously fitted-out cabaret. But what charm! What exoticism!" The band, Ellington recalled, played soft, "conversation" music. "We used to get about thirty dollars apiece in tips every night," Ellington said, "in addition to the salary . . . which was real great."

He was beginning to feel settled and to feel he was learning the ropes. After getting established at the Exclusive Club, Ellington sent for Edna. They rented a room, while Mercer stayed behind under the care of Ellington's parents.

In 1923, New York saw an increasing demand for black floor shows. Stars like Florence Mills spurred the trend, as did, ironically, Prohibition. Nightclubs heightened the polish of their entertainment for the more sober and discerning patrons. In the summer of 1923, Connie's Inn opened next to the Lafayette Theatre. Connie's was a swank "black and tan" cabaret, open to blacks and whites, and its opening was a notable event. Ellington took on the daytime job of rehearsal pianist, learning how a revue is put together. This lesson would prove invaluable to him in the coming years.

By this time, Ellington had learned that anyone could submit a song to a Broadway publisher, and in the summer of 1923, he teamed up with Jo Trent, a young black lyricist and record producer. They made the rounds of publishers, auditioning their new songs, but typically met rejection.

The ambitious Ellington pursued other entries into the entertainment world. In July 1923, as part of Snowden's five-piece Novelty Orchestra, he made his first recording. Though it was never issued, it marked the beginning of a crucial aspect of his musical legacy—that of recording artist, though here as a band member, not a band leader. In August 1923, Ellington and a band under his nominal leadership evidently made a radio broadcast on station WDT, accompanying a blues singer. There were probably very few listeners, however, as commercial radio broadcasting, yet in its infancy, was still largely an electrical tinkerer's hobby. It would be another four years or so until radio would come out of the attic and go into the living room, becoming family entertainment. But again Ellington was trying his hand at every phase of show business he could.

Ellington's spring stint in New York had been difficult but instructive. In the summer of 1923, he opened for himself new vistas of opportunity—performing at some of the top night spots in Harlem, making his first record and radio broadcasts, observing how revues are put together, and writing songs for Broadway publishers. The Washington pianist had made an encouraging start in New York.

Now came an important move. Elmer Snowden and his Black Sox Orchestra landed a six-month contract at the Hollywood Club and opened in September 1923. It was at this club, wrote Ellington,

The Broadway entertainment district with marquee of the Roseland Ballroom at Fifty-first and Broadway. The Hollywood Club was two blocks south at Forty-ninth and Broadway.

"that our music acquired new colors and characteristics." The colors would come especially from several highly individual instrumental voices that would soon join the band. The orchestra—whose initial lineup included Ellington, Whetsol, Greer, Hardwick, and Snowden as leader—would play at the Hollywood Club for four years. Ellington performed there for forty of the next forty-eight months, comprising the longest more or less continuous engagement of his career. Here, as part of a band that worked together night after night, he would grow considerably as a musician.

Despite its glamorous-sounding name, the Hollywood Club was a small, dingy, basement dive with a low ceiling and plumbing pipes protruding over the bandstand. Willie "The Lion" Smith described the joint:

The bandstand was up under the sidewalk in a corner. The bandsmen had to walk up three stone steps to get on the stand. Their dressing rooms were like "the Black Hole of Calcutta." . . . The stand there . . . only held six men and Duke had to play piano and direct from the dance floor. If you worked up on the deck long enough, you wound up with hunched shoulders for good because the stand was about five-and-a-half feet from the glass grill up in the sidewalk.

Greer called the bandstand "one of them back-in-the-hole things." The club could hold only 130 people, but it had an excellent location. Situated near Forty-ninth and Broadway in the heart of the entertainment district near Times Square, the club was a great place to attract notice.

Soon the band, now seven strong, proudly changed its name to The Washingtonians. They came, after all, from the nation's capital, the city that had only recently been eclipsed by New York as the "undisputed capital of black America." "We paid quite a lot of attention to our appearance," recalled Ellington, "and if any one of us came in dressed improperly Whetsol would flick his cigarette ash in a certain way, or pull down the lower lid of his right eye with his forefinger and stare at the offending party. Whetsol was our first unofficial disciplinarian."

In short order the band landed a regular radio broadcast, every Wednesday at 3:45 P.M. on station WHN. And soon it drew the attention of the press. In November, Abel Green wrote in the *Clipper*, "This colored band is plenty torrid and includes a trumpet player who . . . exacts the eeriest sort of modulations and 'singing' notes heard."

This trumpeter was James "Bubber" Miley, who replaced Arthur Whetsol in the fall when he returned to Washington to finish at Armstrong High School. Born in Aiken, South Carolina, but raised in New York, Miley had been deeply influenced by the New Orleans jazz cornetist Joe "King" Oliver's authority, melodic gifts, and use of mutes. Miley dramatically altered the sound of The Washingtonians and became the centerpiece of the orchestra. "Our band changed character when Bubber came in," said Ellington. "He used to growl all night long, playing gutbucket on his horn. That was when we decided to forget all about the sweet music." The

Trumpeter Bubber Miley
became the centerpiece
of the Ellington orchestra.

growl, as Mercer Ellington once explained, is made up of "three basic elements . . . the sound of the horn, a guttural gargling in the throat, and the actual note that is hummed. The mouth has to be shaped to make the different vowel sounds, and above the singing from the throat, manipulation of the plunger adds the *wa-wa* accents that give the horn a language."

Before Miley's arrival, The Washingtonians had been something of a polite dance band. Miley took them irrevocably into the realm of jazz, echoing back to New Orleans and earlier. Arthur Whetsol had had a sweet sound that evoked polite society; his "tonal character," Ellington said, was "fragile and genteel." Miley, in contrast, brought a gruff, raspy sound that evoked the low-down sound of blues shouters. In its tone and percussive attack, it was more traditionally African-American. Miley's use of wah-wah mutes imbued the trumpet with shades of the human voice—which echoed

In early 1924, The Washingtonians were a sextet comprising Sonny Greer, Charlie Irvis, Bubber Miley (seated), Elmer Snowden, Otto Hardwick, and Ellington.

back to the African practice of blending speech and song. Miley used the unusual tones not as mere novelties, but to serve the melody, and used melody to produce and sustain a mood. More than anyone else except Ellington himself, Miley helped define an Ellington sound. Miley also played mellophone, and because most of the players in The Washingtonians could double on a second instrument, the band achieved a variety of tonal colors.

Ellington continued to try his hand at songwriting with Jo Trent, and in October a song of theirs, *Blind Man's Buff,* was copyrighted, though never published. Late in December 1923, the prominent popular-music publisher Fred Fisher hired Ellington to work in his professional department.

Meanwhile, Ellington continued to expand his circle of contacts and mentors. He had a knack for making friends of older, more established musical figures. The African-American songwriter Maceo Pinkard, later known for *Sweet Georgia Brown*, helped The Washingtonians secure a second recording date with Victor in October 1923. Victor, however, never issued their two numbers.

The African-American composer and conductor Will Marion Cook, thirty years Ellington's senior, befriended him. Having studied at Oberlin, in Berlin, and in New York at the National Conservatory, a forerunner of Juilliard, Cook was perhaps the best musically educated person who influenced Ellington. "I got most of my instruction riding around Central Park in a taxi," Ellington would say in 1944. "He and I would get in a taxi and ride around Central Park and he'd give me lectures in music. . . . He was a brief but a strong influence. . . . Some of the things he used to tell me I never got a chance to use until years later." Cook, who after failing to make a career as a concert violinist, went into writing musical comedy, in his later years became bitter and perhaps guilty about having not pursued High Art. He may very well have planted seeds in Ellington's mind that would eventually lead him to write long concert works. In any event, Cook made an enduring impression on the young musician when he advised him, "First you find the logical way, and when you find it, avoid it, and let your inner self break through and guide you. Don't try to be anybody else but yourself." This advice became Ellington's private musical credo. In time, Ellington and his men would achieve a supreme expression of the tenet of individuality, held in high esteem by many African-Americans.

Around the first of the new year, 1924, trombonist Charlie Irvis, a blues specialist, joined the orchestra. With Irvis and Miley, the band took on a more robust sound. By February, Elmer Snowden, the leader of the group, left. The band evidently rebelled because they found out he was taking more than his fair share of the money. Ellington now found himself in the role of bandleader, a capacity he had assumed in previous ensembles back in Washington and would maintain for the next fifty years.

By March 1924, The Washingtonians were also playing at the Cinderella Ballroom, off Times Square at Broadway and West Forty-eighth Street, before their show at the Hollywood Club began. The idea was to expose the band to dancers at a different venue to increase business at the Hollywood. In April 1924, they played for several weeks in Salem, Boston, and Lynn, Massachusetts—the first of many trips the orchestra would take to New England.

In November 1924, Ellington made seven records, with various combinations of his musicians. On three of them, for the first time he received credit as composer, a milestone in his career. One of them was *Choo Choo*, a train-effects piece. In Bubber Miley's "hot" trumpet playing, one can already hear the distinctive growls and muted effects that would become a hallmark of the Ellington sound.

Sometime early in 1925, the Hollywood suffered a fire and closed down for repair. As Sonny Greer recalled, when "business would get slack . . . the boss Leo Bernstein come up and say, 'You all take your horns home, we're going to have an accident down there tonight.' " During this hiatus, in February 1925, The Washingtonians took a series of dance engagements in Haverhill, Massachusetts. In March 1925, the Hollywood Club reopened, with a new name, the Club Kentucky, or as most people called it, the Kentucky Club. By the middle of that year, The Washingtonians had added a tuba to their lineup, in the person of Henry "Bass" Edwards.

At the Kentucky Club, The Washingtonians worked extremely hard, playing music for dancing from 9 or 10 P.M. until midnight. They also accompanied comedy sketches and comely female singers and dancers at midnight and 2 A.M. Then after sending the band home, Ellington, wheeling around a small upright piano, and drummer Sonny Greer would "work the floor" for tips. "I was making good money and I had my hustle," Greer recalled, "me and the piano player [Ellington] going around the tables." The tips could indeed be large. It was the era of the big-spending businessmen, celebrities, and mobsters. "The Kentucky Club was something and the money flying," said Greer. "Money is flying. Partner, the money is flying." This intensive learning of how to please an audience would benefit Ellington the rest of his career. At this time, and until the 1940s, Ellington was proudly and unapologetically an entertainer serving primarily the nightclub world. Only later would he create art with a self-conscious quality. Now he was making

utilitarian music, *Gebrauchsmusik,* and developing it quite splen-
didly.

Greer remembered that "we . . . stayed open till 7:00 in the
morning. . . . Our club was a little small place and after 3:00 in the

Ellington (right) poses with his father, J. E. Ellington, and banjoist/guitarist Fred Guy.

morning you couldn't get a seat. They'd stand around and it got so popular, we were packed and jammed. . . . The floor was so crowded you couldn't dance."

Sometime around this period, the great soprano saxophonist Sidney Bechet, originally from New Orleans, played with the Ellington orchestra. "Bechet and Bubber used to have what we called cutting contests," Ellington recalled. "One would go out and play ten choruses, then the other would do the same. And while one was on the other would be back getting a little taste to get himself together and finding a few new ideas. It was really something."

New Orleans, in some ways the mother city of American music, had already affected The Washingtonians through Miley, who had absorbed King Oliver's sounds. Now Bechet increased this influence through his propulsive swing. Despite Bechet's superior musicianship, however, Ellington had to ask him to leave because of his lack of punctuality and discipline. The passionate, rhapsodic Bechet, however, had a lasting effect on the Ellington sound—especially through his influencing young Johnny Hodges and Barney Bigard, who would soon join the Ellington orchestra.

The Washingtonians attracted musical celebrities such as Paul Whiteman and celebrities-to-be like Tommy Dorsey. Evidently the hot playing of Miley and Irvis, and Greer's flashy drumming and singing drew them. "Paul Whiteman would bring all his friends and band down there," remembered Greer. "But it was so small, a lot of times the guys would want to sit in and play with the band, but they had to sit on the floor."

Also, the orchestra was one of the best-rehearsed small bands in the country. Most other bands played from published standard or "stock" arrangements, which left the orchestras sounding somewhat alike. Or the bands played loose, more or less on-the-spot arrangements. By contrast, The Washingtonians avoided "stock" orchestrations and instead worked out their own arrangements in advance, with a lot of give-and-take among Ellington and his individual players. To some extent, the arrangements were collectively arrived at. They were generally worked out orally and aurally: the band would talk them through, play them, listen, and make adjustments. This "communal spirit" would mark much of the work of the Ellington orchestra in coming years. "The Washingtonians," observes Mark Tucker, "aimed for a balance between improvisation and composition, between the individual and the group."

Ellington's career as a composer was also progressing if more fitfully. One day in March or April 1925, Jo Trent hurried up to Ellington on Broadway. "He had a big proposition and there was urgency in his voice," wrote Ellington. " 'Tonight we've got to write a show,' he said. '*Tonight.*' " They wrote at least four songs —*Jim Dandy, Jig Walk, With You,* and *Love Is Just a Wish for You* —around which an all-black revue was built. Though *Chocolate Kiddies* never played Broadway, and Ellington saw it only in rehearsal, it did tour in Europe for two years, playing Hamburg, Berlin, Copenhagen, Stockholm, and ending in Leningrad and Moscow. He said it made publisher Jack Robbins a "rich man," and that he got $500 for his efforts—that's about $4,000 in 1993 terms.

For the band, the gig at the Club Kentucky was not continuous. Besides the fires that periodically closed the joint, the owners may have brought in other bands. In any event, The Washingtonians played a number of engagements around Manhattan—for example, Ciro's, a West Fifty-sixth Street cabaret and restaurant, in the spring of 1926, and the Plantation Club in June 1926. As well, they

The sheet music for *Jig Walk,* one of Ellington's early published works, from the revue *Chocolate Kiddies.*

occasionally took out-of-town dance jobs, such as at Nuttings-on-the-Charles (River) in the Boston suburb of Waltham, Massachusetts. While Ellington's group was playing regularly, progressing musically, and doing fairly well, it was still a second-string band. The white bandleaders Paul Whiteman and Vincent Lopez and the black Fletcher Henderson—these were the leaders of top dance orchestras, playing the best establishments, recording prolifically, and gaining considerable publicity.

In June of 1926 Duke Ellington and His Washingtonians, as the band was now known, made a record that summarizes Ellington's many musical influences and points to future directions. *Li'l Farina*, as Mark Tucker has observed, indicates that Ellington was inspired by "Louis Armstrong, Don Redman, Fletcher Henderson, Paul Whiteman, black musical theater, popular song, New Orleans," and the "jungle" brass style of Bubber Miley. Although Ellington's first ten records, made through June 1926, are plagued with rhythmic and other weaknesses, they still reveal, as Tucker asserts, "a moderately accomplished dance band with one outstanding voice (Miley), three talented soloists (Hardwick, Irvis, Ellington), a good rhythm section, and a leader-arranger who was gaining in confidence and ability."

Late in June, Ellington made a significant change in personnel. He replaced trombonist Charlie Irvis with Joe "Tricky Sam" Nanton. Born in New York of West Indian parents, Nanton was by now something of a veteran of New York after-hours clubs. He would become known to his colleagues in the Ellington orchestra as a source of strength in a crisis, a follower of the black nationalist Marcus Garvey, an intelligent reader on many subjects, yet fun-loving and fond of practical jokes.

Nanton brought a new trombone sound to the Ellington orchestra, expanding the Miley influence with his own growl sounds and plunger-mute technique. Like Miley, Nanton would *personalize* his instrument to remarkable heights of individuality. "Tricky possessed the gift of communication that is the essence of any music," wrote Rex Stewart, later a band mate. "What a variety of sounds he evoked from his instrument! From the wail of a new-born baby to the raucous hoot of an owl, from the bloodcurdling scream of an enraged tiger to the eerie cooing of a mourning dove, Tricky had them all in his bag of tricks, and he utilized them with thoughtful discretion and good taste." Nanton and Miley became Ellington's most valuable players of this period. The two "got great pleasure from playing something together in harmony that came off well," recalled baritone saxophonist Harry Carney, who would later join the Ellington orchestra. "They were always blowing for each other and getting ideas together for what they were going to play."

A major part of Ellington's nascent genius as a composer was his ability to seek out and highlight the individual gifts of his players. After Miley joined the band, Ellington generally picked players who would add a special sound to the orchestra. He opted not to hire stars—they were too expensive, too set in their ambitions and ways —rather Ellington chose to find "raw material" and explore its strengths while avoiding its weaknesses. Through this process, some of his players would *become* stars.

"All these people were valuable to me," wrote Ellington, "because each one's effective range or scope was limited. . . . You take the limitations on how many notes you can make effectively, and you have a little problem with your writing. In other words, you have to write to fit the limitations. But any time you have a problem you have an opportunity. It was all a matter of the kind of sound you wanted to make with the available equipment. If you had just seven good tones, those were the tones that had to be used, no matter how many tones were within the compass of the instrument." Barney Bigard, who would join Ellington in 1928, agreed: "He knew your limits up and down and he would build the things around a given soloist's voice." "You can't write music right unless you know how the man that'll play it plays poker," Ellington would say later. "You've got to write with certain men in mind," Ellington revealed. "You write just for their abilities and natural tendencies and give them places where they do their best—certain entrances and exits and background stuff." His careers as bandleader and composer were one and both were moving toward a unique Ellington sound.

Ellington's musicians were, as his later record producer Irving Townsend observed, "like all who were close to Duke, extensions of himself. . . . Each, in an odd way, personified a part of the total Ellington personality." Or perhaps it was that his family, friends, and players completed him. Thus, for instance, Ellington balanced his essential musical urbanity, learned in his native Washington, with the earthy styles of Miley and Nanton. Part of the secret of Ellington's gifts at creating enduring art would be making one of these and other opposites: for example, major and minor tonality, speech and song, the extant (composition) and the spontaneous (improvisation), the familiar and the fresh, and the expected and the unexpected.

Ellington's fate as a composer would always be inextricably linked to that of his orchestra, for he wrote solely for *his* orchestra. The orchestra, *his* orchestra was his instrument. And he was building an orchestra that, like the best of his compositions, would comprise a whole greater than the sum of its parts. And what "parts" his players represented! From 1923 on, the beginning year of what became his orchestra, he would find gifted and distinctive musicians.

In the summer of 1926, the Kentucky Club was padlocked, probably due to violations of liquor laws. As the summer doldrums hit Manhattan in July and August, Ellington and his men headed north to cooler New England. There they toured for at least four weeks. The Washingtonians opened on July 12, 1926, at Nuttings-on-the-Charles and then played other spots in Massachusetts, Maine, and Rhode Island. The tour proved successful, partly due to Charles Shribman, who spotted their talent and promoted them vigorously. He often put Ellington's group and a white band on the same bill, encouraging both ensembles to play their best. The orchestra's month-long tour included dance engagements at ballrooms small and large: Nuttings-on-the-Charles and Mosley's-on-the-Charles in the Boston suburb of Dedham could each accommodate at least a thousand people.

The 1920s were seeing the establishment of public dance halls as never before. If by streamlining steps and stressing elegance and refinement, Irene and Vernon Castle had made public dancing respectable in the 1910s, the new jazz music, along with new dance halls and ballrooms, helped make it a national pastime in the 1920s, especially among young people. The 1920s and 1930s were, as

Russell Nye has observed, the time when "public dancing in America reached its highest point of popularity and profit, and the dancehall became one of the nation's most influential social institutions."

The kind of dance hall that drew the largest attendance was the dance palace: "Huge, brilliantly lighted, elaborately decorated with gilt, drapes, columns, mirrors, and ornate chandeliers, often with two bands, these became synonymous with glamor and romance." The most celebrated dance palaces were the Roseland and Savoy in New York City; the Trianon and Aragon in Chicago; the Graystone in Detroit; the Indiana Roof Garden in Indianapolis; and the Avalon Casino on Santa Catalina Island, California. A step down in space and fanciness were Minneapolis's Marigold, Kansas City's Pla Mor, and Louisville's Madrid ballrooms. Several nightclubs with big ballrooms opened in the 1920s and became famous: Glen Island Casino in New Rochelle, New York; Castle Farm in Cincinnati; and Shadowland in San Antonio. Except for New York's Roseland Ballroom, established in 1919, all of these establishments opened their doors during the 1920s. In coming years Ellington would play nearly all of these ballrooms.

The Washingtonians returned to New York refreshed and more experienced. They began their third year at the Kentucky Club, with an eight-month contract. The club reopened with a new show on September 25, 1926. Ellington was now expanding the group, and evidently used eight players at the club. For recording, however, he sometimes added a ninth or even a tenth musician. With each additional player, Ellington could exploit an increased range of volume, tonal colors, and arranging possibilities.

Meanwhile, Ellington must have kept one ear open to the competition. Sam Wooding had established one of Harlem's first big bands. But in 1923, Fletcher Henderson established a nine-piece dance orchestra that quickly ascended to preeminence. Part of Henderson's success resulted from having hired Louis Armstrong to play jazz. Another important element was Don Redman, Henderson's principal arranger, who was developing the fundamental for-

Fletcher Henderson. His orchestra initially offered Ellington a musical role model.

mat of big-band arrangements: sections of reeds and brass pitted against each other, sometimes in call-and-response patterns, and sometimes with one section playing supporting motifs or riffs behind the other. In 1924, Henderson had begun playing at the Roseland Ballroom (a couple of blocks from the Kentucky Club), from which, during the next decade, he catapulted to national fame. In March 1926, he played at the grand opening of Harlem's opulent Savoy Ballroom, which held 3,500 people and would become celebrated for its hot music, torrid dancing, and special events. By 1926, Henderson's was unquestionably the band to beat—as, for example, the heady *Henderson Stomp*, recorded in November 1926, demonstrates. His players read music with agility—something Ellington's musicians could not do nearly as well. Ellington admired Henderson, later recalling, "When I first formed a big band in New York, his was the one I wanted mine to sound like."

With a nicely developing sound and ensemble, what Ellington needed most was exposure. He soon got it. It was probably in the fall of 1926 that Ellington began a relationship with Irving Mills— short, clever, feisty, and fast-moving—which was to prove highly beneficial to both. Indeed, of all the people Ellington met in the 1920s, Mills and Bubber Miley would become the most significant to the establishment of his sound and career. Born in New York

The canny music publisher and impresario Irving Mills, who began a crucial association with Ellington about 1926.

City in 1894, Mills, who was Jewish, became a song plugger in 1913 and in 1919 founded a publishing firm with his brother Jack. The brothers Mills made a career of finding and publishing unknown but gifted composers and songwriters—Hoagy Carmichael, Dorothy Fields, Jimmy McHugh, Harold Arlen, Mitchell Parish, and others. In a 1984 interview with the author, Mills described himself as cocky, determined, and successful. "We were very aggressive and colorful," he recalled, "and up-to-the-minute with ideas and new things to do." Projecting enormous confidence, he talked his way into many deals in the hectic music business.

The brash, shrewd Mills was scouting talent for his music publishing company and recording ventures when he heard Ellington one night at the Club Kentucky. He offered The Washingtonians a chance to record on Vocalion, a subsidiary of the big Brunswick record company. They jumped at the opportunity to get their music for the first time on a major record label. "This was," said Ellington, with an evident mixture of gratitude, irony, and his characteristic public generosity, "really the beginning of a long and wonderful association."

In the first few decades of the twentieth century, ethnicity was a major theme, stated and unstated, in American society, culture, and entertainment. This preoccupation was reflected in American songs, entertainment, humor, and folklore. At that time, Jews and blacks were on the outskirts of American society. Yet they both used music and entertainment to circumvent certain barriers and find a more visible place in the mainstream of American culture. Blacks such as Bert Williams, Eubie Blake, Florence Mills, and Duke Ellington seized opportunities to take center stage. While a number of Jews—Al Jolson, Fanny Brice, Eddie Cantor, Sophie Tucker—also took center stage, others—Harry and Albert Von Tilzer, Irving Berlin, George Gershwin, Billy Rose—wrote songs for that stage. Some—Leo Feist, Ted Snyder, the Witmarks, Shapiro and Bernstein—published their songs. And still others—like Irving Mills, Florenz Ziegfeld, Joe Glaser, the Shuberts—found the talent for that stage. One of the richest sources for the talent and the songs was African-Americans who saw new opportunities opening through these new ethnic entrepreneurs. The two groups, blacks and Jews, formed a symbiotic relationship.

Probably formalized by 1928, an agreement between Mills and Ellington would call for each to own 45 percent of a corporation, with the remaining 10 percent going to Mills's lawyer. In exchange for giving up 55 percent, Ellington was given an interest in some Mills properties, according to Barry Ulanov, who did not specify them. This large a share gave Mills a huge stake in Ellington's success, and the impresario worked tirelessly to advance the maestro to recognition and reward. In addition, this arrangement would give Ellington more control over the musicians in the band, because it would give him the power of having a deal with Mills. If others in the band didn't like the arrangement, they would have little recourse but to quit. It was more clearly Ellington's band, not the cooperative Washingtonians of a few years earlier.

Mills may have recognized that Ellington's orchestra stood out from the crowd when it played his own compositions. Mills may also have spotted Ellington's emerging gifts in composition, which would grow to become his towering contribution to music. But Mills certainly knew that he could make more money if Ellington composed pieces and Mills published them. So the publisher insisted that Ellington record mostly his own pieces. This, in turn, helped Ellington financially and artistically, since it gave him royalties and increasing experience as a composer. This particular confluence of art and commerce, artist and entrepreneur, black and white, would come to greatly enrich twentieth-century culture. And too, it increased the intimate interrelationship and mutual interdependency of Ellington's two careers.

Ellington's initial Mills-arranged recording session evidently took place on November 29, 1926, under the name "Duke Ellington and His Kentucky Club Orchestra." For the first time Ellington got to record four of his own compositions, notably *Birmingham Breakdown* and the moody *East St. Louis Toodle-Oo*. These were the first Ellington compositions copyrighted and published by Mills, registered for copyright on February 10, 1927. After that, Ellington allowed Mills to publish nearly all his work for years to come.

Ellington later recalled that "practically everything we wrote back then was supposed to be a picture of something, or represent a character." Referring to *East St. Louis Toodle-Oo*, he wrote later in a British magazine, "Those old Negroes who work in the fields for year upon year, and are tired at the end of their day's labour, may be seen walking home at night with a broken, limping step locally known as the 'Toddle-O,' with the accent on the last syllable. I was able to get a new rhythm from this, and what better title could I find than the original?" (On his record, "Toddle-O" was rendered "Toodle-Oo," a spelling which stuck.) The piece ranks as Ellington's first significant recording, one that critics consider an early masterpiece.

The association with Mills brought Ellington quick results. Besides Brunswick, other major record companies—Victor and Columbia—began recording him. The distribution of his recordings and his resultant recognition increased sharply. His publicity in

Ellington inscribed this 1925 photograph "To Pop—Edd 'The greatest father in the world' From Son Edward."

An advertisement for *East St. Louis Toodle-Oo* (1926), Ellington's first significant recording.

Orchestra World, Metronome, and other periodicals picked up. And his compositions were copyrighted and published by Mills Music, probably the leading house for jazz and blues. Other publishers even came calling on him.

During 1927, Ellington made thirty-one recordings, nearly twice as many as he had made previously. Besides *East St. Louis Toodle-Oo,* he created two other seminal masterworks—the unique *Black and Tan Fantasy* and the celebrated *Creole Love Call.* Thus, 1927 represented a breakthrough year for Ellington as a composer and conductor. Later that year, as we will see in the next chapter, Ellington would secure another break with far-reaching implications.

As Ellington was breaking new ground for himself as a composer and bandleader, he was differentiating his from run-of-the-mill compositions through their emotional and pictorial content. "Our aim as a dance orchestra," Ellington would write a few years later, "is not so much to reproduce 'hot' or 'jazz' music as to describe emotions, moods, and activities which have a wide range, leading from the very gay to the sombre." Increasingly, Ellington would broaden the emotional range of his compositions. "Every one of my song titles is taken," Ellington continued, "principally from the life of Harlem. . . . [I look] to the everyday life and customs of the Negro to supply my inspiration." While Ellington's sources of inspiration would expand in later years, throughout his life America remained one of his main themes—especially Harlem and African-American life.

Perhaps spurred by Mills, Ellington quickly grasped the potential of phonograph records for his music. While most musicians considered recordings as mere promotion for their live performances, Ellington realized that they were a new performance medium. As pianist-composer Jelly Roll Morton had already been doing, Ellington devoted great care to tailoring his compositions and arrangements to fit the exacting demands of the ten-inch record. Each work had to be as close to three minutes in duration as possible. To make a piece good for dancing at a performance, or listening once through, was one thing. But to make it listenable over and over again, via record, provided the composer a bigger challenge. Ellington worked to meet that challenge by writing interesting introductions, interludes, and codas, and, moreover, by crafting the shape of his pieces.

If Ellington strove to achieve recordings of high musical quality, he also aimed at a high sonic quality. Drawing on his strengths as a listener, he worked to ensure optimal balance of the instruments in relation to one another and, crucially, to the microphone that was just then being introduced to record making. (Previously everyone made recordings by playing into a large acoustic horn that resembled a gigantic ear trumpet. Ellington's first electrically made recordings were in June 1926, and the improvement in technology produced a quantum leap in fidelity.) Like conductor Leopold Stokowski, Ellington seized on the electrical recording process —especially the microphone—and mastered its potential for his music. As jazz historian Dan Morgenstern has written:

> Take any 1920s record by Fletcher Henderson and compare it with a contemporary Ellington disc, and you will hear that Henderson didn't care about studio balances or (except on very rare occasions) tailor his recorded performances to best fit the time limit imposed by the 78 rpm format. Paul Whiteman was well ahead of Henderson in this respect, but even he lagged behind Ellington. . . . But what other band . . . comes across with such presence and impact? Where else do we hear the string bass in such a forward position in the sonic spectrum? Where else are the piano and drummer's kit so well balanced with the horns, and the particular sounds of those horns . . . so strong and true?

When the Club Kentucky contract expired in April 1927, Ellington prepared for another summer tour of New England arranged by Charles Shribman. By this time he had added three new players to the band. Harry Carney, just seventeen, played clarinet and alto sax. Ellington called him "a very well-behaved, well-organized young man, [who] was immediately nicknamed 'Youth' by Sonny Greer." Carney increasingly would turn to his preferred instrument, the low-pitched baritone sax, which became the musical anchor for the Ellington orchestra. "His massive tone," recalled Mercer Ellington, "not only gave the saxophone section a depth and roundness no other had, but it gave the whole ensemble a rich, sonorous foundation that proved inimitable." Ellington would often assign Carney the seventh tone, rather than the expected root note, of a chord, and these unusual low notes contributed to the uniqueness of the Ellington sound. In time Carney would become the leading player of the baritone saxophone and make it recognized as an instrument capable of sustaining solos. The quiet, handsome Carney would stay with the orchestra until Ellington died, the longest tenure of any Ellington musician.

Another new band member, Rudy Jackson, a Chicago-bred clarinetist, had previously played with the great King Oliver of New Orleans and brought a flavor of that city's jazz tradition. Another Crescent City native, the bassist Wellman Braud, brought more New Orleans influence and his big tone to the Ellington sound. Ellington's eight-year-old son, Mercer, along for the tour, vividly recalls Braud's slap-bass style of playing: "pulling the single strings up on one beat and slapping them against the board on the next."

The advance publicity on the tour carried notices such as this: "Duke Ellington and His Washingtonians, Columbia and Brunswick Record Orchestra, Featuring Bub Miley, America's Hottest Trumpet Player." With increased experience, greater confidence, and enhanced personnel, the orchestra was better equipped than the previous summer to win fans. And this they did, in droves. The *New York Tribune* reported that they were "taking the territory by storm," becoming "New England's favorite dance-orchestra."

By now, Ellington was establishing life goals and lifelong work habits. He was aiming at the top, and working hard to get there. Unless he had an afternoon gig, he rehearsed his band during the afternoon, performed at night, and then stayed up into the wee hours to compose, with the instrumentalists' sounds fresh in his ears.

After the tour finished on Labor Day, Ellington and his band returned to New York again reinvigorated with increased experience and confidence. The regenerative powers of touring—or at least of certain tours—would become a recurrent theme in Ellington's career.

Back in Manhattan, the orchestra did not return to the Club Kentucky. Possibly Irving Mills had other plans for them. Instead, they performed for three weeks at Club Ciro's. They then landed engagements in three revues combining song, dance, and comedy. The first, in mid-October, was held at Harlem's Lafayette Theater, about two blocks from Ellington's apartment. The revue was called *Jazzmania*. The *New York Age* raved about Ellington's ensemble: "Both in the orchestra pit and on the stage their performance was superb. With the possible exception of Fletcher Henderson's band, Duke Ellington seems to head the greatest existing aggregation of colored musicians." The cast included the singer Adelaide Hall. Perhaps inspired by working with her, during the engagement, Ellington wrote and recorded *Creole Love Call* to feature her. While Ellington had never been anywhere near Creole country, the title fit the exotic sensibilities of the music. In this number, Ellington added an entirely new sound to his orchestral colors by having Hall sing an extraordinary wordless vocal.

The second revue, in October, was *Messin' Around*, at the Plantation Club. Third, in November, was *Dance Mania*, back at the Lafayette. This time, Adelaide Hall was a singular sensation: she sang, danced, and played ukulele.

No one knew it at the time, but a stroke of luck, or at least a twist of fate, was about to mark the end of one period in Ellington's career and the beginning of another that would transform his music and reputation.

Duke Ellington's first four and a half years in New York had been very good for him. After a disappointing beginning, he had greatly improved his skills as a bandleader and composer-orchestrator. He built and maintained an orchestra; began signing a cadre of gifted musicians, each with a special sound; began to internalize their strengths and weaknesses and to develop his own vision as a composer, and the orchestra's unique identity, based on the musicians at hand; began to master the aesthetic integration of opposites; and established a crucial association with Irving Mills, a master publicist and promoter.

What Duke Ellington now needed were more challenging opportunities to compose and orchestrate, and a platform from which to launch his music nationally.

Essential Ellington,
1923–27

Ellington began making records in 1923, and by December 1927, he had made more than sixty recordings. During these early years, the sound of growling brass became an Ellington trademark. Most of the early recordings show more promise than accomplishment and many are dominated by trumpeter Bubber Miley. But three stand out as seminal and significant.

From November 1926, *East St. Louis Toodle-Oo* rates as Ellington's earliest important recording. While rudimentary, it is a genuine composition with connected sections, not just a series of strung-together improvisations or an on-the-spot "head" arrangement. Bubber Miley probably wrote most of the piece with Ellington. The recording reveals Miley as a brilliant creator of melody and an equally artistic innovator of the "growl-and-plunger" technique. Miley took a cornet straight mute and a trumpet plunger mute, which the New Orleans pioneer trumpeter King Oliver had exploited separately, and combined them, producing new tone-color effects. Miley became the most important developer of muted effects on trumpet.

A chorus of dark reeds frames and provides a countermelody to Miley's minor melody. The melody of this main section echoes a low-down, minor blues, and sounds moody, even ominous. Trombonist Tricky Sam Nanton solos on the bridge, or B section, using his own growl-and-plunger technique. Upon first hearing this piece when he was sixteen, Sy Oliver, who would become one of the swing era's greatest arrangers, felt it "actually changed my life . . . it sounds almost too simplistic, but it's true."

The Ellington orchestra made four early recordings of *East St. Louis Toodle-Oo*—on Vocalion, Brunswick, Columbia, and Victor. They have been reissued, respectively, on *The Brunswick Era* (MCA), *The Chronological Duke Ellington, 1924–1927* (Classics), *The OKeh Ellington* (Columbia), and *Beyond Category* (Smithsonian/BMG). In some ways the

(continued)

first version remains the best. Until 1941, the piece served as the orchestra's signature tune, but after that they seldom performed it.

Black and Tan Fantasy, composed by Ellington and Miley, dates from October 1927. Largely written by Miley, the piece is essentially a variation on the blues, beginning in minor and modulating to major. In his majestically constructed solo, Miley demonstrates his gifts as Ellington's best soloist of this period. Who else would open with a four-measure-long high note and then break loose into a bluesy and dirty—yet measured and beautiful — creation? Miley's solo ranks as one of the greatest plunger-mute trumpet solos ever recorded. Ellington plays some fetching "stride" piano, including a bit of trick or offbeat left hand, and Nanton takes a good solo, replete with a little horse whinny. The ending borrows from Chopin's *Funeral March*. This version of the piece has been reissued on *Beyond Category* and *Early Ellington*, among others. The piece remained in Ellington's repertoire throughout his career.

Also from October 1927, *Creole Love Call* achieved fame for the hauntingly beautiful, wordless vocal of Adelaide Hall. She turns the human voice into a new and expressive orchestral instrument. Hall colors her voice with multiple shadings, including vocal growls. She recorded briefly with Ellington, then spent her subsequent career singing mostly in cabaret and musical theater.

Evidently Bubber Miley created most of *Creole Love Call* with some help from Ellington and clarinetist Rudy Jackson. Parts are borrowed and transformed from a 1923 recording by King Oliver of *Camp Meeting Blues*. Ellington retains the flavor of New Orleans, especially through the trio of clarinets playing the main theme and through the luminously singing solos of Miley and Jackson. The recording has been reissued on *Beyond Category* and *Early Ellington*.

Creole Love Call found a permanent place in the Ellington repertoire, but only one other Ellington singer—Kay Davis in the 1940s—could convincingly sing its wordless melody. Before and after Davis's tenure, the orchestra played it as an instrumental.

FOUR

*C*OMPOSING AT

THE COTTON CLUB

•

1 9 2 7 — 3 1

ight Life is cut out of a very luxurious, royal-blue bolt of velvet," Ellington once said. As the 1920s progressed, Harlem was becoming more of a magnet, pulling in many whites to explore its rich and seemingly exotic nightlife. In the fall of 1927, Harlem's prominent nightspot the Cotton Club had a vacancy. Andy Preer, the leader of the house band, the Missourians, had died in May. Bandleader King Oliver reportedly turned down the job because the money was too low, and Sam Wooding refused it because he wanted to perform in the Broadway area. The club was overdue to start its autumn show, and, with no new house band in late November, its management grew worried.

There are conflicting versions of what happened next. By banjoist Fred Guy's account, while performing in *Dance Mania*, Ellington was approached by the management of the Cotton Club. Songwriter Jimmy McHugh, who was writing a new revue for the club, liked Ellington's music and convinced the general manager, Herman Stark, and Dan Healy, the show producer, to hear Ellington. They liked what they heard and went to a tavern adjoining the Lafayette Theater. There, they persuaded Ellington to sign a contract to perform with his orchestra in the forthcoming Cotton Club revue.

The entrance to Harlem's Cotton Club (1930), with its log-cabin exterior meant to evoke the South.

By Ellington's account, the club held auditions. He and his orchestra arrived late, after six other groups had shown their stuff. By chance, the club's overseer, Harry Block, was late, too. Not having heard the other groups, he hired Ellington's. "That's a classic example," Ellington remarked, "of being at the right place at the right time with the right thing before the right people." If this is what indeed happened, then it may represent the luckiest thing that ever befell Ellington. (His other great break of the 1920s—meeting Mills—seems in retrospect to have been more a matter of fate than luck: the two men, both very ambitious and both seeing possibilities in African-American jazz, with places of employment a mere two and a half blocks apart, were perhaps fated to connect.)

Yet, in the meantime, the band had a commitment to play in a road version of *Dance Mania* on the Keith-Albee theater circuit. Their first stop was in Philadelphia at the Gibson Standard Theater. Before they could finish their two-week run, the Cotton Club

Ellington with Sonny Greer and his array of percussion instruments, which impressed
many other drummers, ca. 1940.

called them back to New York. What about their obligation in
Philadelphia? The Cotton Club's gangster owners sent an associate
named Yankee Schwarz to see the theater manager in Philadelphia. "Be big or you'll be dead," he advised. The manager decided
to be big.

While the Cotton Club employed blacks as entertainers and waiters, it admitted only whites as customers, a policy that was not
unusual at the time. However Ellington felt about it, he must have
decided that the advantages of working there outweighed the dis-
advantages. He was always a practical man who maintained his
personal dignity and realized when to play the sly fox. After all, the
Cotton Club promised a prestigious venue with steady work, good
money, new kinds of experiences from which to learn, lots of op-

portunities for exposure to the press and other influential people, not to mention pretty young women who danced and sang in the show. How could he not accept this offer? His problem was to make sure he and his band took full advantage of the opportunity in the spotlight.

The Cotton Club:
"The Aristocrat of Harlem"

The owners were gangsters. The help and entertainment were black. The customers were white.

Located on the second floor, over the Douglas Theater, at the northeast corner of 142nd Street near Lenox Avenue, the Cotton Club opened in the fall of 1923. The English-born gangster Owney Madden, who was paroled in 1923, soon took it over. He made his bootleg liquor—"Madden's No. 1"—at a plant on West 26th Street. He hired Harry Block as overseer and Herman Stark as general manager.

The club was forced to close in 1925 due to its violation of Prohibition laws. But it soon reopened—another of the estimated 32,000 to 100,000 illegal drinking establishments in New York City. The Cotton Club had a log-cabin exterior and interior and featured jungle decor, a proscenium stage, and a dance floor. Beginning in 1926, the irrepressible Dan Healy— a singer, dancer, and comic—staged and produced the shows. Jimmy McHugh wrote the songs, usually with Dorothy Fields, through 1929. Lady Mountbatten dubbed the club "the aristocrat of Harlem."

"There were brutes at the door," observed Carl Van Vechten, "to enforce the Cotton Club's policy which was opposed to [racially] mixed parties." Occasionally, however, a star performer such as Bill "Bojangles" Robinson or Ethel Waters could get a table for friends.

During Ellington's tenure, the club typically opened at 10 P.M. and closed

(continued)

at 3 A.M. There were two different shows nightly, one at 12:00 (or 12:15) A.M. and another at 2:00 A.M. Showtimes were designed specifically to attract a high-spending after-theater crowd. "Join the crowds after theater," read one advertisement from 1929. "All Broadway comes to Harlem."

This was no ordinary nightclub. Printed programs announced the musical songs and sketches and identified the vocal and dance soloists. In time, the programs grew more high toned in their language. One from 1931 noted, "Entr'acte: Dance to the strains of the incomparable Duke Ellington and His Recording Artists."

The club could accommodate between 500 and 700 customers, seated at tables on two tiers by the dance floor and booths at the perimeter. Cab Calloway, who first performed there in 1930, vividly recalls the club:

> It was a huge room. The bandstand was a replica of a southern mansion, with large white columns and a backdrop painted with weeping willows and slave quarters. The band played on the veranda of the mansion, and in front of the veranda, down a few steps, was the dance floor, which was also used for the shows. The waiters were dressed in red tuxedos, like butlers in a southern mansion, and . . . there were huge cut-crystal chandeliers.

"The floor shows at the Cotton Club," recalled Marshall Stearns, "were an incredible mishmash of talent and nonsense which might well fascinate both sociologists and psychiatrists." The shows combined hot music, snappy dancing, vaudeville, and even burlesque. The job of chorus girl was highly coveted. A chorus girl had to be no older than twenty-one, at least five feet eleven, light-skinned ("high yaller"), dance and carry a tune, and be glamorous. "Them girls stopped the show", recalled drummer Sonny Greer.

> Oh, just the girls, the chorus. Stopped them cold. . . . Sixteen of them, they were handpicked, like you pick a beauty contest. . . . The prettiest colored girls in the world. . . . You better believe they could dance! . . . Because they made plenty of money, couldn't nobody hit on them, because they had their pocketbook full of money. . . . My wife was one of the Cotton Club girls. [At first] she couldn't see me with a telescope.

(continued)

The costumes were sensational, as Calloway testifies:

> The sets and costumes were stunning and elaborate, like operatic settings almost. The chorus girls changed costumes for every number, and the soloists, dancers, and singers were always dressed to the hilt—the women in long flowing gowns, if that was appropriate, or in the briefest of brief dance costumes. Talk about the String—these chicks wore less than that. Low cut and very, very risqué.

The cast could be large: the spring 1929 review had thirty in the company, plus Ellington's orchestra. The fall 1930 show had an even larger cast, and the club advertised "50—most beautiful Creoles—50."

On one level, the Cotton Club provided a hell of a good show. A well-produced, fast-paced string of acts, unusual music, original songs, sexy dancers, a racy song or two, a professional announcer, in a place to be seen in, with exotic decor, that served illegal (and expensive) booze in Prohibition America. But on a deeper level, the Cotton Club served as a safe haven, however highly stylized and restricted, for whites to encounter aspects of black *culture*. In a decade when the Ku Klux Klan was nationally resurgent, and opportunities for whites to encounter blacks were circumscribed in many ways, the Cotton Club provided a view of black Americans as handsome, accomplished, gifted, and yes, elegant. That view was highly stylized and limited: the African-Americans at the Cotton Club— Ellington included—all wore invisible theatrical masks.

Ellington and his men, who had been rehearsing for the new show while playing in Philadelphia, hurried back to New York on December 3. On Sunday, December 4, they opened at the Cotton Club. Because his engagement there would prove pivotal to his continued artistic and commercial growth, Ellington's opening is now regarded as one of the most celebrated premieres in American music. Yet at the time, opinion was divided. Ned Williams, later Ellington's publicist, heard the orchestra that first month. "I can't say I was too much impressed with the Ellington crew on that visit," he said.

There are several reasons that Ellington's orchestra may have gotten off to a slow, if not bumpy, start. First, there were several temporary musicians in the band, including a violinist. At the Cotton Club, many of the pieces they played were chosen by the singers and other acts they accompanied. Yet, the band was used to playing Ellington's music, which various members sometimes had a hand in creating. At this Cotton Club revue, however, they had to play other people's music. In addition, the band could not sight-read music very well. And it had precious little time to rehearse the new Cotton Club show.

Ellington's orchestra was ten strong, comprising trumpeters Bubber Miley and Louis Metcalf; trombonist Tricky Sam Nanton; reedmen Otto Hardwick, Rudy Jackson, and Harry Carney; guitarist/banjoist Fred Guy; drummer Sonny Greer; bassist Wellman Braud; and the maestro himself at the piano. At that time, the orchestra neither had nor needed a regular vocalist, since the Cotton Club revue featured its own singers.

Ellington's first Cotton Club revue was a long, demanding show —fifteen numbers for singing or dancing, plus encores. Jimmy McHugh wrote the music, and the young Dorothy Fields supplied the lyrics. Ellington's orchestra accompanied the singing by Aida Ward and Edith Wilson, sinuous dancing by Earl "Snake Hips" Tucker, and other acts. They played for both the midnight and 2:00 A.M. shows, and in between provided dance music for the patrons.

One of those who liked the show was Abel Green, the editor of the show-business magazine *Variety*. He wrote of the Cotton Club's revue:

> It is the foremost black and tan cafe, featuring a whale of a colored revue that matches any of the preceding editions, all of which have been noteworthy for their artistry and talent. . . . [The show] compels attention and any over-length is only the result of audience demand. The big attraction are the gals, 10 of 'em, the majority of whom in white company could pass for Caucasians. . . . In Duke Ellington's dance band, Harlem has reclaimed its own after Times Square accepted them for several seasons at the Club Kentucky.

Ellington's jazzique is just too bad . . . for a "hot" show and something different from the general nocturnal fare, get a load of the Cotton Club.

Green praised the costumes, Fields's lyrics, and the clever floor direction of Danny Healy. The dancing was a sensational part of the show: "The . . . high yaller gals look swell and uncork the meanest kind of cooching ever exhibited to a conglomerate mixed [gender] audience. . . . Mae Alix [is] jazzy, hot, and a fool for the splits."

The music included Fields and McHugh's *Harlem River Quiver*, *Doin' the Frog*, and *Red Hot Band*, and probably *Blue Bubbles*, composed by Ellington and Bubber Miley. Undoubtedly during his first Cotton Club revue Ellington wrote *Jubilee Stomp* and, probably with Miley, the sublime *Black Beauty*.

The dynamic drummer Sonny Greer became something of a percussionist, and provided a visual focus for the band. As he related later:

When we got into the Cotton Club, presentation became very important. I was a designer for the Leedy Manufacturing Company of Elkhart, Indiana, and the president of the company had a fabulous set of drums made for me, with timpani, chimes, vibraphone, everything. Musicians used to come to the Cotton Club just to see it. The value of it was three thousand dollars, a lot of money at that time, but it became an obsession with the racketeers [who owned nightclubs], and they would pressure bands to have drums like mine, and would often advance money for them.

Working as part of a slickly produced show, night after night, Ellington and his men soon learned how to pace their programs. Although it did not perform on stage, the orchestra served as an important part of the entertainment. The engagement undoubtedly served to stimulate the theatrical flair Ellington had shown as a boy.

There was a more profound connection between Ellington's music and the theater. "I am a man of the theater," Ellington declared years later. As Charles Fox has observed, "His music has a theatrical dimension, soloists being deployed rather like characters in a play, their comings and goings planned and orchestrated." Playing on the phrase "dramatis personae" in his memoirs, Ellington discussed his musicians under the heading "Dramatis Felidae" (the "cats" in the play). During the Cotton Club period, Miley and Nanton provided bursts of dramatic solos that Ellington wrote his compositions to highlight.

The specific talents of not only Miley and Nanton but of all the members of his orchestra, then and later, helped determine what Ellington would compose. Like the playwright fortunate enough to have a repertory company of actors for which to write, Ellington was able to compose specifically for the various instrumental voices in his band. He would work hard to keep his principal players together for years (and decades), assuring himself of leading and writing for a group with great continuity, which Ellington managed to sustain for fifty years.

The mobsters who ran the Cotton Club reportedly did not like Ellington's music at first. "Too weird," they are said to have responded. But soon they relaxed: business evidently picked up as Ellington won over not only the old Cotton Club customers but musicians and critics. They were impressed with his orchestra's unique sound, especially its so-called jungle music, which had antecedents in American popular music. For several decades it had shown a fascination with far-off or exotic peoples: there were vogues for oriental fox-trots, Hawaiian songs, and songs about American Indians and Africans, among others. Under the veil of exotica, a songwriter or performer could do all sorts of raucous, bold, unconventional things. The Cotton Club was decorated with southern and African motifs, and the whole experience was intended to give its patrons a respite, however brief, from the cares of the present time. The audience would be transported to some far-off, exotic place for an hour of fast entertainment, energetic dancing, skimpy costumes, and unusual music.

The chief exponents of the jungle-music style were Miley and Nanton. As a composer-orchestrator, Ellington succeeded in transforming their growls from novelties into real art—a sign of his growing originality and skill. The jungle could also be suggested by Barney Bigard's sometimes mysterious-sounding clarinet, and by

Feathered dancers, like the kind who performed at the Cotton Club,
with the Duke Ellington orchestra, in a still from the 1929 motion-picture short *Black and Tan.*

certain somewhat exotic chord progressions Ellington wrote, such
as, for example, the opening of *The Mooche.* Ellington also suggested a jungle connection with the titles of some of his pieces—
Hottentot, Harlem River Quiver, Jungle Blues, Jungle Jamboree,
and *Jungle Nights in Harlem.* After leaving the Cotton Club, as
Mark Tucker has observed, Ellington "moved away from the stylized primitivism" of these pieces, and found ways to work "its
surface manner deeper into the substance of his music."

At this early stage, it was Bubber Miley and Tricky Sam Nanton
who exerted the greatest influence on Ellington. Miley, in particular, helped compose some of the orchestra's most characteristic
and illustrious recordings of this period.

The Cotton Club engagement was affording Ellington an opportunity to experiment and find his own way as a composer and arranger, stimulating him to pursue two formal problems inherent in jazz
arranging. Ellington was taking up what André Hodeir and Gunther
Schuller have called "the formal problem of jazz arrangement—
how best to integrate solo improvisation." This was really two problems.

First, how do you integrate the soloist with the group without overwhelming either one? In other words, how do you achieve a balance? In many of his early recordings, before Ellington learned to achieve a balance, Bubber Miley seems to dominate. To prevent a soloist from dominating the proceedings, Ellington learned to assign several soloists to take their turns, at the right moments; this was common practice among jazz arrangers. Beyond that, however, to achieve a balance, Ellington, in the words of Hodeir and Schuller, "learned to exploit expertly the contrast produced by the soloist's entry, so as to project him into the music's movement and entrust him with its development. This partly explains why even Ellington's finest soloists seemed lusterless after leaving his orchestra." He also learned to compose striking musical accompaniments for his soloists, so that the audience would find musical interest in both solo and orchestral background, thus enriching the listening experience.

The second problem was, How do you allow for spontaneity within a controlled structure without giving way to musical chaos? Put another way, how do you maintain musical order while offering the excitement and spontaneity of an inspired creation of the moment? To achieve a balance between composition and improvisation, Ellington sought to create works that had carefully laid-out spaces for a soloist to improvise. The space could be as brief as two or four measures, though six and eight bars were more common. Ellington planned these spaces in such a way that they provided a high degree of contrast, maintained musical interest and forward momentum of the pieces, and made for a musically satisfying whole. There would be a few pieces in the Ellington repertoire that seemed to be loose jams—the *C-Jam Blues* of 1942, for example. But even this piece would be deceptive—Ellington had a master plan, a hidden script and structure, behind all the blowing. Another of the ways Ellington achieved a balance between the preordained (the composition) and the spontaneous (improvisation) was by employing, beginning in the 1930s, what could be considered a musical sleight of hand: writing solos that, when played by his musicians, *sounded* improvised. *Old Man Blues* of 1930 is a good early example of Ellington's gift for balancing soloist and group, as well as balancing improvisation with composition.

Most orchestral composers—whether classical or jazz—wrote for sections of players—trumpets, trombones, etc.; Ellington often composed for individual players. Thus, increasingly he was limited only by the number of permutations that his musicians could produce.

The importance of the Cotton Club engagement to Ellington's development as a composer cannot be overemphasized. It represented, as Gunther Schuller has written, a kind of "prolonged workshop period." Ellington had to compose, not just arrange, works; he tried his hand at different kinds of music to accompany diverse acts; every six months there was a new show to write for; because he played six or seven nights a week, he could learn intimately the abilities of his players and could fine-tune his creations. The other leading black band of the day, Fletcher Henderson's, played mostly dances, and so Henderson did not have the opportunity to write the varied music that Ellington had.

"You know what?" Ellington once asked big-band expert George T. Simon. "My biggest ambition was to sound like Fletcher. He had such a wonderful band. But his was basically an ensemble group, and in our band the solos—you know all the various stars we have had—always dominated everything." Ellington was being modest: what would increasingly set his music apart from the others were his growing gifts as a composer and orchestrator.

As Ellington settled in at the Cotton Club, American entertainment was changing. New technology had added voices, sound effects, and music to the formerly silent movies. One by one, the great vaudeville houses were adding the new sound films to their offerings. *Variety* dubbed them "vaudfilm" houses. By February 1928, there were only a few holdout theaters offering vaudeville shows alone. Alert to new opportunities, Ellington must have wondered if and when he would get an opportunity to break into pictures.

In late December 1927, within a few weeks after beginning at the Cotton Club, Ellington began to refine his sound with new

At the Cotton Club, patrons sat close to the show stage.

"voices." He decided to replace clarinetist Rudy Jackson with Barney Bigard. Born Albany Bigard in 1906 in New Orleans, he was a light-skinned product of the proud, French-speaking, mixed-race people known as "Creoles of color." After settling in New York in 1927, he was hired by Ellington, who wanted someone who could read difficult parts easily, soar above the brass without screeching, and inject agile obbligatos as a counterweight to the saxes and brass. Bigard had a beautiful sound, with a clear, warm tone; phrased elegantly; played precisely in tune; and could sweep nimbly from one end of the register to the other. As Bigard recalls, he was summoned to Ellington's apartment near the Lafayette Theater: " 'I want you to join my band,' he says. 'I don't know how long we're going to stay here, but we are trying to build up a good band. If we can do it, and the boss likes us, then we can stay at this Cotton Club a long time. We'll have a good job there.' " Bigard accepted the offer and proved to be one of Ellington's most distinctive players.

"We were doing real good through those first months and things just kept getting better," remembered Bigard. "We worked seven nights a week at the Cotton Club and very seldom had an off night."

In May 1928, Ellington brought in another unique voice, Johnny Hodges, a young alto saxophonist from Boston. Hodges, who would be nicknamed "Jeep" and "Rabbit," would spend nearly his entire career with Ellington and develop into arguably his greatest soloist. With steady assurance and technical brilliance, Hodges pioneered a style that took full advantage of the saxophone's potential. He would offer passion, a rich tone, lyric phrasing, florid runs, and glorious glissandos. Hodges would grow to become a supreme melodist, with an inexhaustible fund of splendid melodic figures. He became known as unflappable, untalkative, shy and solitary, and shrewd and stubborn. Both Bigard and Hodges brought elements of New Orleans jazz: Bigard as a Creole of color from the Crescent City and Hodges as a disciple of the extraordinary New Orleans reedman Sidney Bechet.

By June 1928, trumpeter Louis Metcalf would leave the orchestra, to be replaced as lead trumpeter by Ellington's old buddy from Washington, the decorous, sweet-toned Artie Whetsol. "A great organization man," Ellington recalled, "he would speak up in a minute on the subject of propriety, clean appearance, and reliability. If and when any member of our band made an error in grammar, he was quick to correct him. He was aware of all the Negro individuals who were contributing to the cause by *commanding respect.*" Someone nicknamed him "Flickering Phil," because while talking Whetsol would constantly flick ashes from his cigarette.

Within a short time, the fame of Ellington and his top soloist Bubber Miley was spreading via radio broadcasts from the Cotton Club. Commercial radio broadcasting had only begun in the United States in 1920. The early stations sent out a mixture of news, drama, and musical entertainment, virtually all of it live. Since 1923, radio stations had been hooking up with each other to create networks, and by February 1928, the National Broadcasting Corporation (NBC) network boasted fifty-six stations, from Boston to San Francisco, including two in New York City (WEAF and WJZ). Sales of radio receivers were skyrocketing. From 1927 to 1929, they grew by 250 percent. Radio transformed American life, creating instantaneous common experiences throughout the vast nation, linking city with farm, east with west, north with south, and reducing the public's need to create its own entertainment at home.

The Cotton Club was outfitted with a microphone connected to radio stations, and this gave Duke Ellington and His Cotton Club Orchestra, as it was now called, an opportunity to be heard far and wide. Most such opportunities were restricted to white bands, which may have given Ellington's distinctive sound even more impact on audiences. "One of the hottest bands on the air," reported *Variety*, "is Duke Ellington's from the Cotton Club Monday midnights. One torrid trumpet brays and blares in low-down style that defies passiveness on hearing it."

Sometimes the orchestra made dinner-hour broadcasts. Sonny Greer recalled, with his typical swagger, "From the Cotton Club, we used to broadcast . . . from 6:00 to 7:00. The world was waiting for that. Everybody was waiting for that from New York to California and coast to coast, was waiting for that. Of course, you know, that's suppertime. All the people didn't anybody get anything to eat until we come off. Cats working all day, starved to death until we get off." Under the headline ELLINGTON SUBDUED, Abel Green of *Variety* reviewed one session: "Duke Ellington and his heated jazzpators from the Cotton Club in Harlem are not as 'dirty' as they are of midnights, such as Monday when broadcasting during the dinner sessions. They lean more to the 'sweet' type of syncopation but can't refrain from slipping in a real wicked ditty off and on." Knowing that different people listened at suppertime than at midnight, Ellington was learning to master his audience—or rather, audiences.

The Ellington orchestra itself became a draw. "The band was becoming much more of a drawing card than the location it played in," according to Bigard. "At first you could have put anyone in at the Cotton Club and the crowd would have gone along there, but now the band was gaining fans so fast that if we had moved to another place I think the people would have come along with us." Among the clientele were mobsters, but Ellington had the good sense to be very discreet about whom and what he saw. "People would ask me if I knew so-and-so," he said. " 'Hell, no,' I'd answer. 'I don't know him.' . . . But I knew all of them because a lot of them used to hang out at the Kentucky Club, and by the time I got to the Cotton Club things were really happening!"

Meanwhile, Fletcher Henderson's orchestra, until now Ellington's main competition, went into a period of relative decline in 1928, just as Ellington's stature was shooting skyward. Another band was coming on strong. "Charlie Johnson's Paradise Band in its time was regarded by many as highly as Duke Ellington's," writes Schuller. "In a sense the band, located at Small's Paradise, a Harlem nightclub, was Duke's closest competitor, for he also provided show music and jungle tableaux for white patrons from downtown. Through Johnson's band passed a host of fine musicians"—including Jabbo Smith, Benny Carter, Sidney de Paris. While in many ways on a par with Ellington's and Henderson's, Johnson's suffered from poor promotion: he recorded only fourteen pieces, and after the beginning of the depression in 1929, he never recorded again. Both Henderson and Johnson sorely needed a canny agent-promoter-publicist-manager like Irving Mills. If they had been able to link up with such a person, their careers might have turned out to be more successful.

Over at Harlem's prominent Savoy Ballroom, lesser but popular bands held forth, normally two at a time, alternating sets between two bandstands. Savoy standbys in the late 1920s included the bands of Fess Williams, Chick Webb, Cecil Scott, Luis Russell, and the Alabamians, fronted by Cab Calloway. In 1928, an exciting new dance step, the lindy hop, burst forth—probably from the Savoy, where it would be developed in the 1930s to exceptional heights, literally and figuratively. It featured "breakaways" for improvisation, athletic aerial movements or "air" steps, and the "geechie walk," which has been described as "a strutting step performed with a shimmy." Twirling dancers, swirling skirts, exuberant smiles, youthful energy, the night charged with excitement —that was the lindy hop.

Harlem nightlife was full of possibilities—some licit, some illicit. In some of the entertainment district there were drugs and prostitution, fed in part by the throngs of whites who came to Harlem for exotica. Complaining of the show-business newspaper *Variety*'s role in promoting Harlem nightlife, the black-run, conservative *Amsterdam News* railed: "That idea of taking a residential community and making it the raging hell it is after dark is something that should arrest the attention of even ministers of the gospel." "That part was degrading and humiliating to both Negroes and whites," Ellington would recall in later years. "But there was another part of it that was wonderful. That was the part out of which came so much of the only true American art—jazz music."

Excluded from most Broadway dance halls and cabarets and from places such as the Cotton Club, and looking for something closer to home, blacks opened their own establishments. By 1929, there were "eleven class white-trade night clubs" and more than five hundred "colored cabarets of lower rank," according to the *Amsterdam News*. Harlem had about "300 girl dancers continuously working in the joints" and 150 young male dancers, "fifteen major bands and more than 100 others in action every night." At the top remained the Cotton Club.

On Sunday, April 1, 1928, Ellington and his orchestra opened in their second Cotton Club revue, called *Cotton Club Show Boat*. The club advertised, "It is a glittering pageant of thrills and a triumph of scintillating beauty." On October 1, 1928, toward the end of the second revue, Ellington recorded three masterworks: the piano solo *Swampy River*, the quintessential jungle-music piece *The Mooche*, and *Hot and Bothered*. The latter was a reworking of the old New Orleans standard *Tiger Rag*. It was one of at least seven such transformations Ellington would make of the old piece, demonstrating his jazzman's gift for turning something old and familiar into something new and fresh.

Then, on October 7, 1928, *Hot Chocolate*, Ellington's third Cotton Club revue, opened. The club advertised:

a real production—a cast of 50 people—beautifully costumed
clever stars—beautiful girls
all ingredients that make for joy
stirring music—fine acting and the drollest comedy.

The *New York Evening Post* called it "a snappy and colorful revue," singling out the dancing Berry Brothers, the singer Leitha Hill for her double-entendre song *Handy Man*, and others, but failed to mention Ellington. "The Cotton Club has always present[ed] a fine revue, but its latest attempt outshines all former endeavors. Slightly augmented, it would be an instant success at one of the downtown [white] theatres. It is colorful and vigorous and goes through with speed and snap."

Also in October 1928, Ellington brought another talented musician into the fold: the diminutive New York native Freddie Jenkins to play, left-handedly, third trumpet. His extroverted stage presence brought him the nickname "Posey," as in posing for audiences. Jenkins's jaunty style would contribute to a number of Ellington's recordings in the late 1920s and early 1930s—among them *Tiger Rag, High Life,* and *In the Shade of the Old Apple Tree.* Jenkins's arrival enlarged Ellington's brass section to four—three trumpets and a trombone. Now he could write for eleven different instruments (including piano), expanding his compositional possibilities.

When he had joined Ellington's orchestra, one of the things that first struck Barney Bigard was the "weird chords that would come in behind us. I wasn't used to that kind of chording at all . . . [Ellington would] break all the principles of arranging too. He'd give a guy different notes to what he should have had for his instrument."

Ellington wanted not only to make new rules but to set new records. Like other jazz musicians, his recordings, and thus his compositions, were restricted by the record industry to issue on 78-rpm records that were ten inches in diameter. These discs played only about three minutes. There were twelve-inch records, which lasted another minute or two—a significant difference. The record executives, however, reserved these more desirable discs largely for classical music.

On January 8, 1929, Ellington's became only the second jazz ensemble to record a two-sided piece (the first had been the obscure Troy Floyd, in 1928). Part 1 of *Tiger Rag* was issued on one side of the disc, and Part 2 on the other, yielding a total duration of nearly six minutes. While Ellington had not composed the piece, he and his men put their own distinctive stamp on it. He must have been anticipating the day when he could not only record but *compose* a six-minute work.

By the time Bigard joined the band, Ellington was already a master psychologist. He needed to keep in line ten creative artists —young, male, and some of them temperamental or rambunctious. "Duke was a real good leader from the start," said Bigard. "I never knew him to fire anyone. But I'll tell you, he was a slickster. He would make life so miserable on that job that you would just quit."

Bubber Miley and especially Otto Hardwick had fallen into very bad habits: they would get drunk and not show up for several days. Their erratic behavior caused them to miss recording sessions and also evenings at the Cotton Club when people with good connections in the music business showed up. "Finally," Bigard recalled, Ellington "got so disgusted with them that he got rid of both of them by making life so unpleasant that they quit." Hardwick was the first to go—by about May 1928. (He would return to Ellington's band four years later.)

In late January or early February 1929, shortly after participating in the *Tiger Rag* recording, Bubber Miley also left Ellington. "The reason why [Ellington] fired Bubber Miley," asserted Miley's replacement, trumpeter "Cootie" Williams, "was every time some big shot come up to listen to the band, there wasn't no Bubber Miley and he had the whole band built around Bubber Miley." His departure could have struck a great blow as he was Ellington's best-known and leading soloist. Miley, along with Nanton, also gave the Ellington orchestra the reputation, rightly or wrongly, of being one of the "dirtiest" jazz groups. The "dirty" or earthy sound they got through growls and mutes excited many listeners.

Ellington moved quickly to replace Miley and hired seventeen-year-old Charles "Cootie" Williams to take over Miley's "growl" chair in the trumpet section. A native of Mobile, Alabama, Williams proved to be one of Ellington's most serious, sober, and reliable players. Nanton taught Williams the growl-and-plunger technique, much as Miley had taught it to Nanton some thirty months earlier. The technique was thus passed through succeeding generations of Ellington brass players. As Martin Williams has ob-

By 1929, the Ellington orchestra had grown to twelve players.
Standing, from left: Tricky Sam Nanton, Harry White (trombones); Sonny Greer (percussion);
Ellington (piano and leader); Fred Guy (banjo and guitar); Wellman Braud (bass).
Seated, from left: Freddie Jenkins, Cootie Williams, Artie Whetsol (trumpets); Harry Carney,
Johnny Hodges, and Barney Bigard (saxophones and clarinets).

served, it was Williams "who brought the [Louis] Armstrong style and spirit into the Ellington orchestra. He also brought a sound brass technique and the ability not only to take over the plunger trumpet role that Miley had created but to expand it, in flexibility, in varieties of sonority, and in emotional range." Cootie Williams would spend twenty-three years with Ellington, in two different stints.

More attention was focused on jazz soloists and trumpet players after Louis Armstrong and His Hot Five recorded a piece called *West End Blues* in June 1928. Armstrong electrified listeners with his sensational opening cadenza and brilliant chorus. More than any single recording, *West End Blues*, Martin Williams has argued, helped transform jazz from a group into a soloist's art. Armstrong took his place as the leading soloist in jazz, and influenced countless musicians, including from then on, directly or indirectly, every trumpeter who would join the Ellington orchestra.

Ellington's fourth Cotton Club revue opened on Sunday, March 31, 1929. *Spring Birds*, with a cast of thirty and the Ellington orchestra, again offered songs specially written by Fields and McHugh and with direction by Dan Healy. *Variety* found the show "disappointing," especially in comparison to the nearby club Connie's Inn, but praised Ellington's orchestra and its "wicked trumpet player" who "heightened the effect to riotous returns." The reviewer speculated that part of the problem with the show itself was that whites created it, while over at the competition, "native Afro-Americans [Leonard Harper, et al.] were primarily concerned in the Connie's floor show." This review indicates another talent of Ellington's: like Louis Armstrong, he could rise above poor material.

By 1929, Irving Mills's press campaign was in high gear. As he described it, he strove to present to "the public a great musician who was making a lasting contribution to American music." Mills wanted to spotlight Ellington not as a popular bandleader but as a conductor and composer—in short, as an artist. This sophisticated image was one Ellington had largely cultivated back in Washington, before coming to New York. All indications are that Ellington was not only aware of and pleased with his growing celebrity, he was in fact continuing to invent his own public image. In Mills he had found a perfect ally and partner.

In 1929, Mills secured another break for Ellington—in motion pictures. It seems inevitable that jazz and the movies would get together. Both grew up in the early twentieth century. Both were considered strictly entertainment at the time, and both suffered ill repute in their early days. Both are collaborative, dynamic art forms. In October 1927, Al Jolson's voice had come magically out of the screen in *The Jazz Singer*, the first successful full-length "talking picture." The craze for "talkies" spread rapidly, and by

1929, the United States had 1,300 movie theaters equipped to show the new sound films.

That summer, at the invitation of the motion-picture studio RKO, Ellington and his orchestra went out to Astoria Studios on Long Island to make their first film. This must have fulfilled a goal for the ambitious maestro. The nineteen-minute short subject, *Black and Tan,* was built around the orchestra, playing such unique Ellington pieces as *Black and Tan Fantasy* and *Black Beauty.* David Meeker has called the film "a rare example of a film which uses jazz both organically and dramatically, with stunning effect." In fact, it was only the second such film to use jazz as the basis for narrative and music. There was a slight plot involving a romance between "Duke," a jazz bandleader, and "Freddie," a dancer played by the lovely Fredi Washington. The film was directed by Dudley Murphy, who in 1929 also made a now-famous short with Bessie Smith called *St. Louis Blues.* Ironically, Ellington's first motion picture of many would be almost his only opportunity to have an acting role—in later movies he was normally seen only as a musician.

Both of these films featured only African-Americans on screen. The motion-picture executives knew that white audiences, at least in the South, did not want to see mixing of the races on the screen, so frequently the producers observed segregation by using all-black casts. Alternatively, they could plan the films so that scenes with black musicians could easily be edited out, which was a major reason ongoing roles for blacks were so rare in general-release films.

Still, Black American entertainers continued to make new opportunities for themselves. On June 20, *Hot Chocolates* opened, an all-black Broadway revue with songs such as the durable *Ain't Misbehavin'* written by Fats Waller and Andy Razaf. It ran for six months. Louis Armstrong was called from the orchestra to play an onstage solo.

At this time, Ellington secured another break, akin to his motion-picture debut. Through the recommendation of Will Vodery, a respected black arranger who served for years as musical director for Florenz Ziegfeld, Ellington landed a spot for himself and the band

In this scene from *Black and Tan,* Ellington and Artie Whetsol rehearse a musical passage as dancer Fredi Washington looks on.

Opposite: A poster for Ellington's first movie, *Black and Tan*, 1929, which featured the orchestra performing five pieces.

A dramatically lit still photo from the film short *Black and Tan* clearly reveals a facial scar said to have been inflicted on Ellington by his wife during a marital fight.

in Ziegfeld's *Show Girl*. The impresario wanted to pack the musical with calculated showstoppers from vaudeville and cabaret to ensure a longer run. So he lined up Ruby Keeler, Jimmy Durante, Eddie Foy, Jr., and Duke Ellington and his orchestra. George Gershwin wrote the music, which included the ballet *An American in Paris*. Ira Gershwin and Gus Kahn supplied the lyrics. On several nights, Al Jolson sang *Liza* from the audience to his new wife, Ruby Keeler, on stage. Opening on July 2 at the Ziegfeld Theater, *Show Girl* ran for 111 performances.

Ellington's role was to play, from the stage, some of the band's recent successes. According to the *Variety* reviewer, "Duke Ellington's colored jazz band of 10 pieces did much better on the stage [than the pit orchestra]. They worked with the three boys in the cabaret scene, also playing on the top layer of the minstrel platform, as 45 girls in minstrel costume sat beneath them." Mercer Ellington remembers, "The guys were sitting on steps in red uniforms, playing almost as though they were in a jam session. Their big number was 'Liza,' and they used to play it at the Cotton Club, too."

Ziegfeld himself wrote in the *Telegram:*

> It was probably foolish of me, after spending so much money on a large orchestra, to include a complete band in addition, but the Cotton Club Orchestra, under the direction of Duke Ellington, that plays in the cabaret scene is the finest exponent of syncopated music in existence. Irving Berlin went mad about them, and some of the best exponents of modern music who have heard them during rehearsal almost jumped out of their seats with excitement over their extraordinary harmonies and exciting rhythms.

While playing nightly (except Sunday) in *Show Girl*, Ellington and his orchestra were still playing shows each night at the Cotton Club—midnight and 2 A.M.—and making occasional recordings. This demanding routine continued through October 5, when *Show Girl* closed, the victim of heaviness and slow pacing. Ellington must have been sorry to see the show end; he felt the engagement was "valuable in terms of both experience and prestige."

It was also rewarding financially. According to Mercer Ellington, "For their spot in this show they were paid $1,500 a week, but there was enormous prestige to appearing in a Ziegfeld show, and after they finished that engagement they could get almost $1,500 a night, a phenomenal amount of money then." A few weeks after *Show Girl* closed, Ziegfeld would lose all his money—a million dollars—in the stock-market crash.

Perhaps during the run of *Show Girl*, Ellington received what he later termed "valuable lectures in orchestration" from Will Vodery. This instruction, along with some help from Will Marion Cook, was atypical, for evidently Ellington was mostly self-taught as an arranger, initially simply transferring notes from the piano to the various members of his band. Also during *Show Girl*, in August or September, Ellington hired a second trombonist, Juan Tizol. No doubt Ellington wanted to keep up with Fletcher Henderson, who had been employing two trombones since January 1927. Ellington had met the trombonist in Washington in 1920, when Tizol played in the Howard Theater pit band. Tizol, a Puerto Rican, was lighter skinned than everyone else in the early Ellington orchestra with the possible exception of the Creole Barney Bigard. Tizol was known for his punctuality and moderation yet, surprisingly, also for his practical jokes. Tizol complemented Nanton. In contrast to the latter's slide trombone playing a "hot" style, replete with growl-and-plunger techniques, Tizol played valve trombone, which provides for greater melodic mobility. Also, he was more of a reading, "legit" player than a typical jazzman. Now, for the first time, Ellington had twelve players, giving him his fullest and richest sound yet, and, in combination with his other players, expanding his possibilities for creating tonal colors and harmonies.

Ellington's fifth Cotton Club revue opened on Sunday, September 29, 1929. Employing the racial stereotyping of the time, the producers called the show *Blackberries*. During this run, Ellington evidently composed *Oklahoma Stomp* and *Lazy Duke*, which if not part of the *Blackberries* revue, certainly were part of his dancing-music entr'acte.

Less than a month after the opening of Ellington's new revue, Wall Street suffered a disastrous day on Thursday, October 24, 1929. The following Monday saw another big drop, and Tuesday,

A rare advertising handbill for the Cotton Club's
1929 production *Blackberries*.

October 29, witnessed record-breaking losses of nine billion dollars. An economic slide began that would continue largely unabated
until hitting rock bottom in 1933. The downturn would make life
especially difficult for many African-Americans, and all others in
the lower economic rungs of society. It would later affect Ellington,
too.

"Had jazz not been so stanch, it would surely have received the
coup de grace in 1929," wrote *Fortune* magazine in 1933. Writing
of affluent white society, it continued, "That year skirts as well as
stocks descended; there was a perceptible revival of gracious manners. The national thirst yearned for something less positive than
gin, the tail coat replaced the dinner jacket, and ladies who had
sworn never to submit to corsets again were shaping themselves to
meet the new order of things." With his suaveness and elegance,

Ellington may have benefited as the national mood and fashions changed.

Despite the economic situation, aided by Irving Mills, Ellington was securing wide exposure on records. In 1929 and 1930 Ellington was recording for all the big record companies. To maintain an appearance of loyalty to each record company, his records had to be released under various pseudonyms. On the Banner/Perfect family of labels, Ellington's orchestra became the "Whoopee Makers." On Brunswick, they were "The Jungle Band." OKeh called them the "Harlem Footwarmers," while Diva and Clarion dubbed them "Ten Black Berries," after the Cotton Club review of 1930.

On March 2, 1930, Ellington opened in his sixth revue, *Blackberries of 1930*. Jimmy McHugh and Dorothy Fields had left the Cotton Club. Irving Mills and Duke Ellington offered their services as songwriters, and management accepted. However, none of the duo's songs—evidently including *Bumpty Bump, Doin' the Crazy Walk,* and *Swanee River Rhapsody*—would gain currency outside the revue. The dances were staged by Clarence Robinson, a black producer who had worked extensively in Harlem. The cast included eight "principals"—singers Celeste Cole, Leitha Hill, Cora La Redd, and the dance teams of Henri Wessels and Mildred Dixon, and the Berry Brothers—and twenty-four chorus girls.

The opening drew a raft of Broadway and other celebrities, including dance director Busby Berkeley, bandleaders Ben Pollack and Guy Lombardo, and many others. " 'The Black Berries of 1930' premiere at the Cotton Club packed in the orchid-ermined crowd when social registerites and stage celebrities milled up-town to flash Harlem's hot spot," wrote *Morning Telegraph* nightlife watcher Lee "Harlemania" Posner, revealing the degree to which whites in search of an "in" spot with robust and somewhat racy entertainment dominated the audience.

Soon another break came Ellington's way. Irving Mills succeeded in persuading Broadway producer Charles Dillingham to book the Ellington orchestra to perform with the famous French singing star

Maurice Chevalier. They opened at New York's Fulton Street Theatre on Sunday, March 30, 1930, for a two-week run. Recalled Ellington, "This was about the only time I ever used a baton!"

Ellington's orchestra played the first half of the evening, fifty minutes, in part with dancers from his Cotton Club show, Ananias Berry and Henri Wessels. The *Daily News* wrote that "Chevalier is aided by Duke Ellington's colored bandmen and an amazing young dancer who calls himself Ananias Berry. The program opens with an Ellington concert in which strange, tricky things that only Duke's men know are done to brasses and tunes. What a band!" The orchestra played, among other numbers, *St. Louis Blues*, *Dear Old Southland*, *Liza*, *Mississippi Dry*, and the Ellington compositions *The Mooche*, *Black Beauty*, *Swampy River*, *Awful Sad*, and *East St. Louis Toodle-Oo*. During the second half of the program, Ellington's orchestra accompanied Chevalier.

The first half of the Chevalier show probably represented Ellington's first concert engagement. Normally, he accompanied a stage show or played for dancing. Having an audience watch and listen to the musicians for an hour must have been slightly intimidating, yet at the same time flattering. It also must have whetted his ambitions to be taken seriously as a composer and musician. The Chevalier show represented one of the earliest concerts by any jazz band. But it would be years before Ellington would be able to play many concerts in his native country.

At the Cotton Club, there was a master of ceremonies to keep things moving. Not so at the Fulton Street Theatre. Ellington had to talk on stage. "I didn't know the first thing about how to M.C.," he confessed, "and the thought of it had me half scared to death. Then, there we were on the stage and I opened my mouth and nothing came out." It was only gradually that he developed his smooth speaking manner before an audience.

It was a busy spring. While continuing to play at the Cotton Club, appear regularly on radio, and make records, Ellington was booked to play a revue at Harlem's Lafayette Theater. Clarence Robinson, the choreographer from the Cotton Club, produced *Pepper Pot Revue* for one week. This show, and a dance played at Harlem's Savoy Ballroom, afforded black Harlemites a rare opportunity to hear Ellington in person.

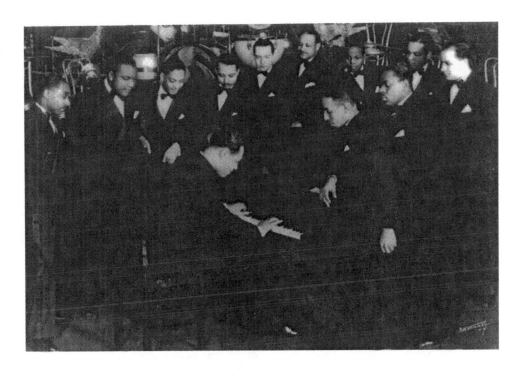

The Ellington orchestra at New York's Fulton Street Theatre, with Sonny Greer's percussion instruments in the background.

Then in May, evidently through Irving Mills's initiative, Ellington and his men got still another break. The Ellingtonians played the Palace Theater, the nation's foremost vaudeville house, for two weeks. *Variety* found the band "not fully prepared for vaude," citing its inability to play slow material well: "When not torrid it's not good." The reviewer, however, loved the solo work in general and especially the brass section's trick plunger work: "What they can do with a bell of a trumpet or trombone makes anybody's feet move."

The success and publicity Ellington was enjoying encouraged Mills to seize opportunities beyond New York. In June, the orchestra left the Cotton Club temporarily for a tour of theater and dance engagements that took them to Baltimore; Boston; Buzzards Bay on Cape Cod, Massachusetts; Pittsburgh; Detroit (where they played the famous Graystone Ballroom); and Chicago (where they

In this frozen film frame from *Check and Double Check*, Ellington's brass players manipulate derby mutes over the bells of their horns, "vocalizing" their instruments' sounds. The "wah-wah" was a vital color in the Ellington orchestral palette. Seated, foreground, from left: Freddie Jenkins, Cootie Williams, Artie Whetsol. Standing, background, from left: Tricky Sam Nanton and the Puerto Rican Juan Tizol, whom the movie's producers forced to wear blackface makeup.

appeared at that city's Savoy Ballroom). By this time, the national debate over dancing that had raged ten years earlier was largely over, and dance halls and public dancing were a firmly established entertainment, especially among young people. While the band was on tour, the Cotton Club replaced it with The Missourians, a band fronted by Cab Calloway.

Then Irving Mills succeeded in booking the Ellington orchestra as part of a Hollywood feature-length film, Ellington's first. *Check and Double Check* was an RKO feature starring Amos 'n' Andy, played by wildly popular white radio comedians wearing blackface makeup and speaking in exaggerated black dialect. "Couple of

ofays put on blackface and win popularity for Negroes, give Negroes jobs. What irony!" commented Otto Hardwick. Amos 'n'
Andy play bumbling taxicab drivers in this dreadful movie. Due to
the movie studios' strictures, bandmembers Juan Tizol, a Puerto
Rican, and Barney Bigard, a Creole, were forced to put on black
makeup so they would appear to be Negro. Racial mixing, even on
a bandstand, was opposed by some whites, especially in the South.
History does not record what Tizol, Bigard—or Ellington—thought
of this affront.

Ellington's orchestra did, however, get a good spot in the film,
introducing portions of *East St. Louis Toodle-Oo*, *Three Little
Words*, *The Mystery Song*, and a full version of the driving *Old Man
Blues*, which provides a wonderful glimpse of the mute work of the
brass and trombones, and gives a feel of the musical vitality of the
Ellingtonians at that time. For *Check and Double Check*, the band
got $5,000 a week plus expenses.

It was with *Ring Dem Bells* that Irving Mills began taking credit
as lyricist on some Ellington pieces—eventually totaling sixty numbers. No one knows if he wrote these lyrics by himself, or had a
staff lyricist do it under contract, or if, in some cases, Ellington
contributed part of the text. Later, Mercer Ellington would say
flatly that Mills did not write any of the lyrics but took 75 percent
of the royalties—the entire publisher's share and half the author's
share. At the same time Mills was evidently being unfair to people
like Ellington, he was also helping them and doing good by breaking
"down so many darned barriers for Negro musicians," according
to Cab Calloway, whom Mills also managed, "you couldn't count
them." For Mills there was evidently no contradiction in both
chiseling royalties and pressing for employment, publicity, and dignity for his artists. It was all part of business.

If Ellington's professional successes were boosting his fame and
finances, his marriage was deteriorating. The previous year or so,
Ellington and Edna had sent for their son Mercer to join them. But
reportedly both Ellington and Edna were having extramarital affairs, and when an argument between the two escalated into a fight,
Edna slashed Ellington's cheek with a razor or knife. The scar is
clearly visible in some photographs. The couple separated, but
never divorced—nor reconciled, either. It was probably in 1929

Ellington was enormously attractive to women, as symbolized by this staged publicity photo shot on the Hollywood lot of RKO Pictures.

Mildred Dixon
lived with Ellington
beginning in 1929.

that Ellington found a new paramour—Mildred Dixon, a dancer who was Henri Wessels's partner at the Cotton Club. "I came home from school one day," Mercer recalled, "and there was a strange woman living with my father and taking care of me and Ruth. My mother, it turned out, had moved. . . . They had separated without telling us. Nobody in my family liked to be the bearer of bad news."

Then, around May of 1930, Ellington took a large three-bedroom apartment at 381 Edgecombe Avenue, on Sugar Hill, described as "a citadel of stately apartment buildings and liveried doormen on a rock, [that] soared above the Polo Grounds and the rest of Harlem like a city of the Incas." Sugar Hill and Striver's Row, along 138th and 139th streets, were Harlem's most prestigious addresses. "On Sugar Hill . . . Harlem's would-be 'sassiety' goes to town," Adam Clayton Powell, Jr., would write in 1935, rather sarcastically. Powell would take note of the "paneled walls, parquet floors, electric refrigeration, colored tile baths, luxurious lobbies, elevators and doormen resplendent in uniforms." Into this spacious and gracious place, Ellington moved his mother, father, sister, son—and Mildred. She and Duke Ellington would live together as man and wife until the late 1930s.

It was after moving into the Edgecombe place that young Mercer Ellington became aware of how his father worked. Sometimes, in the wee hours of the night, he would hear soft sounds coming from the piano. His father "would be out there writing, playing the piano softly so as not to wake everyone up, but I could hear the notes and chords he was hitting." Duke Ellington was becoming a perpetual composer, often at night, just about the only time he could compose in solitude.

When Ellington returned to the his old venue on September 14, 1930, the Cotton Club heralded him with an announcement, "Hail the Conquering Hero." Two weeks later, on Sunday, September 28, 1930, Ellington opened in his seventh Cotton Club revue, *Brown Sugar: Sweet but Unrefined*. For this revue, there was a new songwriting team, Harold Arlen and Ted Koehler. Ellington would work with them again in a few years. "Those shows by Arlen and Koehler," remembered Cab Calloway, "were a combination of vaudeville, burlesque, and great music and dancing."

"Dorothy Fields wasn't really funky enough to write the kind of songs that would carry a Negro revue of that type," he recalled.

The real down-to-earth Cotton Club shows, with the double-entendre nasty songs and the hurly-burly and bump-and-grind mixed with high-class swinging jazz, were produced by Harold Arlen and Ted Koehler beginning in 1930.

It's no accident that the name Cotton Club has come to be synonymous with the greatest Negro entertainment of the twenties and thirties. A lot of people worked hard as hell to pull those shows together. . . . That was the Cotton Club spirit. Work, work, work. Rehearse, rehearse, rehearse. Get it down fine. Tops and professional in every sense of the word. The club was alive with music and dancing at night, but it was also alive all day long. If the chorus line wasn't rehearsing, then the band was. If the band wasn't rehearsing, then one of the acts was. We knew we were performing before some of the most critical audiences in the world. We knew we had a standard of performance to match every night. We knew we couldn't miss a lick. And we rarely did.

The club advertised "Your visit to New York is incomplete until you've been to the Cotton Club." By now, the club had become a draw for well-heeled white tourists.

Calloway also recalled Ellington's self-confidence was already strong at this time: "I had always considered myself a pretty suave guy. But Duke was more than suave. He had something special and he carried it with him all the time. He was a handsome, almost shy-looking man, with his hair brushed straight back and a thin mustache. He wore loose-fitting comfortable clothes, and he was almost always smiling. But mostly it was that air of self-assurance that got to me." Whether Ellington's composure was entirely natural, or partly a mask of theatrical suaveness, he wore it on stage and off.

Several weeks later, on October 16, Ellington was booked into the famous Roseland, "America's foremost ballroom," located at Broadway and Fifty-first Street, for its "Monster fall opening. Internationally famous stage and screen favorite making his first ballroom appearance on Broadway with his universally acclaimed sensational rythm [sic] orchestra." Roseland presented the revue "exactly as presented at the Famous Cotton Club."

By 1930, millions of people were unemployed. Harlem was already suffering under the yokes of racism, high rents, low wages—which caused poverty, crowded and unsanitary living conditions. One historian asserts that the "most profound change that Harlem experienced in the 1920s was its emergence as a slum. Largely within the space of a single decade Harlem was transformed from a potentially ideal community to a neighborhood with manifold social and economic problems called 'deplorable,' 'unspeakable,' 'incredible.' "

In Harlem, and in fact everywhere, musicians were hard hit. The advent of talking and singing motion pictures had caused most theaters to abandon their orchestras, typically replacing them with a single organist. Tens of thousands of musicians were thrown out of work as the general belt tightening left most people with less to spend on entertainment. Increasingly, radio became the "poor man's phonograph" and brought Ellington even more recognition.

By 1930, the radio wire from the Cotton Club was broadcasting Ellington far beyond Lenox Avenue. During the first several years of the orchestra's engagement at the Cotton Club, the young CBS radio network had sent Ellington's music across America. By late in 1929, CBS rated Ellington's as the only black orchestra among its most commercially valuable bands, and second only to Will Osborne's among bands playing for private parties, balls, and other private engagements.

By May 1930, Ellington could be heard five or six nights a week from the Cotton Club over New York's radio station WABC, at either 11:00 P.M., 11:30 P.M., or midnight—the time varied. In September, Ellington landed a regular national program on the largest and most prestigious network, NBC radio, via the pioneering New York station WEAF, each Saturday night from 11:15 until midnight. During this time, Ellington continued to broadcast on other stations. In a one-week period in early October 1930, for example, he was heard in four broadcasts from the Cotton Club transmitted over three New York City radio stations. Significantly, Ellington was broadcast on both NBC's Red Network (through its anchor station WEAF), which aired popular entertainment, and, through flagship station WJZ, its Blue Network, which featured more refined, sophisticated fare.

Radio's effect was not just one way. One night in October 1930,

Ellington and six players from his band of eleven played a piece they called *Dreamy Blues* on the band's radio broadcast. "The first tune I ever wrote specially for microphone transmission," Ellington called it. "The next day," he remembered, "wads of mail came in raving about the new tune, so Irving Mills put a lyric on it." Retitled *Mood Indigo,* the work became one of Ellington's evergreens, one of his all-time masterpieces. This peerless work still sounds compelling some sixty years after it was created.

The original trio that accomplished the
never-before-heard sound on *Mood Indigo:*
Tricky Sam Nanton, Artie Whetsol, and Barney Bigard
at a microphone, ca. 1935.

Ellington's Musical Sources: A Treasury of Traditions

Ellington was heir to a veritable treasury of musical traditions which he drew on throughout his career in his compositions and orchestrations. Contemporary American composers such as Walter Piston, Howard Hanson, and Roger Sessions drew primarily on the European forms of rondo, sonata, theme-and-variation, and others. Ellington, in contrast, drew on vernacular American and African-American forms, techniques, and sensibilities. In fact, as he put it to an interviewer in 1964, "My strongest influences, my inspirations, were all Negro."

First there was an African-American musical sensibility which stresses, among other things, individuality, improvisation, and participatory interrelationships within the band and between performers and audience. Important, too, is what Robert Ferris Thompson described in African art and dance as "high-affect combinations"—bringing into balance "high and low, gentle and sudden,...hot-against-cool, male-within-female, angles and curves, 'loud' colors against 'dark,'...simplicity beside elaboration." Ellington managed to balance his own debonair tendencies with his earthy qualities and those of his players, Bubber Miley and Tricky Sam Nanton; to balance the soloist with the group, improvisation with composition; and, in many of his compositions, to achieve the equilibrium of various kinds of musical opposites. *The Mooche*, for instance, is a brilliant integration of musical opposites into a satisfying and aesthetic whole.

As in jazz generally, Ellington's melodies included the famous bent or "blue" notes, short repeating motifs or riffs, and other African-American traditions; his rhythms included syncopation, swing, and off-beat phrasing; there was an emphasis on percussive or staccato timbres in many pieces; and his orchestrations sometimes featured call-and-response between soloist and band, between sections of instruments, or even between instru-

(continued)

The latter work's lovely section called *Come Sunday* would reappear twenty years later as part of *My People* and twenty-two years later as part of his *Concert of Sacred Music.*

The players in his band were a fundamental source of inspiration and ideas. Sometimes he'd like a certain lick or phrase one of them was playing and would develop it into a full-blown piece. Other times, the procedure might be mutually collaborative. As many as two hundred pieces bear Ellington's name along with that of Billy Strayhorn, Johnny Hodges, Barney Bigard, Rex Stewart, Mercer Ellington, or others. Still other pieces may have originated in rehearsals but remain credited only to Ellington.

As a composer Duke Ellington drew on all these sources. All of them, and his own ceaseless creativity, provided a treasury from which he gained musical ideas throughout his life.

That fall, more engagements in uptown Harlem theaters and downtown vaudeville houses followed, including a two-week stint at Broadway's Paramount Theater—the first time a black orchestra had played there. Between the Cotton Club, other gigs, and recording and radio work, Ellington found the time to work on a new, ambitious composition. He wanted to stretch his wings as a composer beyond the miniature, three-minute pieces whose length was proscribed by the 78-rpm disc. So he pursued the problem of larger form, specifically a six-minute piece. He called the work *Creole Rhapsody.* The Ellingtonians recorded it January 20, 1931, and Brunswick issued it on opposite sides of a record. It ran nearly six and a half minutes. While the form seems somewhat strung together, it does represent a bold move forward, anticipating Ellington's longer works of the late 1930s and beyond. *Creole Rhapsody* has several other innovations, especially its unusual phrase lengths and trombone duet.

Ellington must have been looking ahead to other challenges he could pursue. His popularity and fame had spread far beyond New York, and the ever enterprising Mills was ready to exploit it. Late in January came word that Ellington would leave the Cotton Club on February 2, 1931, to go on a national tour. It would be several years before the Ellington orchestra would perform at the Cotton Club again. Thus closed a short but crucial era for Duke Ellington.

In a matter of thirty-eight months, the span of his Cotton Club engagement, Ellington—his experience, talents, orchestra, repertoire, and reputation—had grown remarkably. He had also become a public figure. Through occasional live performances and, especially, records and radio, Ellington had developed a great following in the black community. Through his Cotton Club shows, special performances downtown, film appearances, and, again, records and radio, he was building a national following among music lovers and especially among aficionados of the still-young jazz music. Ellington had taken a position equal to Louis Armstrong as the leading figure in jazz. Armstrong was the greatest soloist, Ellington the greatest bandleader and composer. Ellington was poised to take his music personally to the rest of the country, and to seek more opportunities for musical growth. He would now face the problem of almost continual touring.

An advertisement, aimed at after-theater audiences, for the Cotton Club's 1929 production *Spring Birds*.

An early caricature of Ellington by Al Hirshfeld.

Essential Ellington,
....

1927–31
....

During its Cotton Club years, the Ellington orchestra made about two hundred recordings. The orchestra grew from ten to twelve players, offering Ellington more challenges and opportunities for composing. Ellington's now-famous jungle-music style, created to entertain the Cotton Club audiences, originated during this period. And Ellington's constant experiments in finding his own way bore delectable fruit. Here are eight of the most significant recordings.

After opening at the Cotton Club, Ellington's band took on new polish. Barney Bigard joined early in 1928, and *Jubilee Stomp* was one of the first pieces the band recorded—four times in the space of two months. The best version—recorded on March 26, 1928—features strong solos by Bigard, Tricky Sam Nanton, and especially Bubber Miley. The band is tight rhythmically and builds considerable momentum in this driving, fast dance number. Ellington takes a hot, albeit rushed, piano solo in the Harlem stride style. The piece has been reissued on *Great Original Performances*, Vol. 1 (ABC), and *Jubilee Stomp* (Bluebird).

The mooche was a slow, shuffling dance, similar to the grind, that African-Americans from the South brought to New York. In October 1928, Ellington and his orchestra made several recordings of their unforgettable *The Mooche*. It boasts one of the most eerie and haunting melodies of its time, arranged for wailing clarinets. The best early version of *The Mooche* has been reissued on *Great Original Performances*, Vol. 1, *Reminiscing in Tempo* (Columbia), and *The OKeh Ellington* (Columbia), with a good alternate version on *The Brunswick Era,* Vol. 1 (MCA).

On the version recorded originally for OKeh, high keening clarinets state the theme, as Bubber Miley answers. The New Orleans clarinetist Barney

(continued)

Bigard then plays a low-register call-and-response with guest guitarist Lonnie Johnson, also from New Orleans. Guest singer Baby Cox growls some scat in a duet with Johnson. Miley returns for a muted solo, with a young Johnny Hodges behind him. In the climax, Miley wails his trumpet like a singer with a choir. Like *East St. Louis Toodle-Oo*, *The Mooche* represents a prime example of Ellington's jungle-music style intended to evoke exotic images for the Cotton Club audiences. *The Mooche* brilliantly balances contrasts in high and low registers, major and minor keys, soloist and ensemble, and call-and-answer between players. There is nothing like *The Mooche*.

Ellington dedicated *Black Beauty* to the memory of Florence Mills, the attractive and gifted singer-dancer who died at a tragically young thirty-two, and whose Harlem funeral was thronged by 150,000 people. Evidently another collaboration between Bubber Miley and Ellington, *Black Beauty* ranks as one of the orchestra's most resplendent compositions.

A recording from March 1928 by the Ellington orchestra is available on *Beyond Category*, *Early Ellington* (Bluebird), and *Great Original Performances*, Vol. 1. His arrangement is not very creative—he simply transferred notes from the piano to his players. But he was learning quickly, and soon he would succeed at more imaginative scoring. Here, Bigard takes an affecting solo, and Wellman Braud, another New Orleans native, plays a well-miked slap-bass part. In his piano solo, Ellington demonstrates his musical debt to the Harlem pianist Willie "The Lion" Smith.

The following October, Ellington made a fine solo-piano version, which is available on *The OKeh Ellington* and *The Chronological Duke Ellington, 1928* (Classics). The way he "voices" his left-hand chords is an indication of his growing gift for unusual ways of expressing harmonies. In 1929, when Ellington made his first motion picture, *Black and Tan*, he chose to include *Black Beauty*, to which the Five Hot Shots—a quintet of tuxedo-clad dancers from the Cotton Club—tapped synchronously on a mirrored floor.

(continued)

In August 1930, Ellington and his men were in Hollywood to make their first feature film, *Check and Double Check*. Having replaced the masterly Bubber Miley in the "growl" trumpet chair, Cootie Williams was finding himself with large shoes to fill. He acquitted himself, however, in *Ring Dem Bells* with two brilliant trumpet choruses. A version available on *Early Ellington* has a strong solo by Williams, but the version issued on *The Chronological Duke Ellington, 1930*, Vol. 2 (Classics) is even more memorable. In both recordings, Johnny Hodges engages Williams in a marvelous call-and-response duel of saxophone playing vs. scat singing.

In *Old Man Blues*, from the same film, Ellington achieved, as Gunther Schuller has observed, a remarkable balance between composition and improvisation. Moreover, the piece created an equilibrium among various soloists, and between the soloists and the band. Baritone saxophonist Harry Carney and trombonist Tricky Sam Nanton play especially strong solos. This exciting recording is available on *Beyond Category*. Notable in the film version are young Johnny Hodges on soprano saxophone, the brass section wah-wahing with hands and mutes, and the showy body language of trumpeter Freddy Jenkins, who can't sit still to the music. He's a delight to watch.

In October 1930, Ellington and his men recorded *Dreamy Blues*, written by clarinetist Barney Bigard and Ellington. Soon retitled *Mood Indigo*, it ranks as one of the most original and memorable miniatures of the twentieth century. Ellington turned on their heads the usual roles of trombone, trumpet, and clarinet, assigning the trombone the *high* notes and the clarinet the *low*. As Gunther Schuller has asserted, the resulting tonal colors probably had never been heard before in all of music history. This brilliant, unique piece, with its unusual harmonies, can be heard in three versions from the fall of 1930, on *The Jungle Band* (MCA), *The OKeh Ellington*, and *Beyond Category*. The first two, recorded in October, are spare and elegantly simple. For the next version, recorded in December, Ellington

(continued)

adds an orchestral accompaniment that showcases the poignant solo of trumpeter Arthur Whetsol and the gentle, flowing sound of clarinetist Bigard.

Credited to Ellington, saxophonist Harry Carney, and Irving Mills, *Rockin' in Rhythm* was first recorded in January 1931, as the orchestra's Cotton Club engagement was coming to a close. One of Ellington's most characteristic pieces, *Rockin' In Rhythm,* the maestro once said, is "as close as an arrangement gets to sounding spontaneous." With its loosely swinging and instinctive feel, it points the way to similar pieces by swing bands of the 1930s.

Rockin' in Rhythm is a showcase for the section work of the saxophones and clarinet and for Cootie Williams's trumpet. The piece builds contrast by going from major to minor (the passage played by Barney Bigard on clarinet) and back again to major.

This rhythmic dance number stayed in the band's repertoire until the end, ever changing along the way. The first version remains the most relaxed and in some ways the best: it has been reissued on *Reminiscing in Tempo, The OKeh Ellington,* and *Swing, 1930 to 1938* (ABC). A second version is on *Early Ellington* and *Beyond Category. The Chronological Duke Ellington, 1930–1931* (Classics) has three different early versions.

Not recorded until June of 1931, the composition *Echoes of the Jungle* probably dates from 1930. Cootie Williams wrote it, probably as a production number for the Cotton Club, where the "mink set" gathered to watch scantily clad women dancing to "exotic" music supposedly evocative of Africa. Despite its ironic title, this piece is sophisticated. Williams plays two superb choruses—the first one with open horn, the second dramatic chorus with a mute. Barney Bigard injects an element of mysteriousness. Alto saxophonist Johnny Hodges contributes his lyrical sound, and Tricky Sam Nanton does a "yah-yah" talking trombone. This marvelous piece, sounding as fresh today as when made, can be heard on *Early Ellington.*

FIVE

•

TAKING THE

ROAD

•

1 9 3 1 – 3 5

For the next four years, despite the nation's economic difficulties and their impact on the entertainment industry, Ellington traveled, enlarged his audience, expanded his band, experimented musically, and received greater recognition.

Leaving the Cotton Club early in 1931, Ellington embarked on a series of tours. Why he left the Cotton Club is not clear. It is possible that Ellington's popularity at the Cotton Club had begun to decline, but it seems more likely that Mills, exploiting Ellington's growing fame, found that he and Ellington could make more money by touring the country.

Ellington took with him a Cotton Club busboy named Richard B. Jones. "Jonesy" became the "band boy," responsible for handling the trunks, helping Sonny Greer set up his elaborate drum set and keep it polished, handing out musical arrangements, and acting as something of a bodyguard for Ellington.

Impresario Mills gave out typewritten itineraries, and each member of the orchestra knew "what bus, train or boat to catch. They'd all be there too. . . . Duke had the easiest band to handle in those years that he ever had," asserted Bigard. "I mean the bunch he had much later, that was another world he had to be in."

The first stop was Boston. After a week at the Metropolitan Theater, the band headed to Chicago, where Ellington played for a month at the Oriental, Regal, Uptown, and Paradise theaters. From there, the orchestra went to Detroit, Omaha, Minneapolis, Des Moines, Denver, Kansas City, St. Louis, Indianapolis, Chicago, Toronto, Philadelphia, Toledo, Cleveland, back to Chicago, Cincinnati, Pittsburgh, Philadelphia, and Washington, D.C. By then it would be early October.

With this tour the orchestra established a pattern of travel that would persist until the end of Ellington's life. Though there were some one-night stands in 1931, the engagements typically lasted a week or more. By comparison with the three-plus years at the Cotton Club, the travels that began in February of 1931 must have seemed hectic to the musicians. Later, when Ellington was performing mostly one-nighters and constantly had to pick up and go to the next city, the pace of 1931 must have seemed leisurely by comparison.

Until this time, the Duke Ellington orchestra had consisted entirely of instrumentalists. If singing was needed, before 1931, it was handled by drummer Sonny Greer or, on an occasional and reluctant basis, by trumpeter Cootie Williams. At the Cotton Club, where the orchestra accompanied a number of singers, the Ellingtonians had not needed their own. And relatively few of the other bands regularly featured singers.

But now, for stage shows on the road, Ellington decided to add a vocalist. In Chicago he tested a singer named Ivie Anderson for two weeks, and then hired her. Anderson, twenty-five, had been sent over from the Grand Terrace by fellow bandleader Earl Hines. Trim and vivacious, Anderson sang with sensitivity, relaxed rhythm, a smoky tone, excellent pitch and diction, and considerable respect for lyrics. She also developed strong rapport with audiences, and she and drummer Sonny Greer created musical interplay on stage. Though on stage she appeared almost angelic, dressed characteristically in white, off stage she was quite another person, in the words of future band mate Rex Stewart, "bossing the poker game, cussing out Ellington, playing practical jokes or

Ivie Anderson inscribed
this photo to Ruth Ellington.

In 1931, Ellington performed at Chicago's Oriental Theater five times,
breaking the theater's records as well as his own.

giving some girl advice about love and life." Remaining with the orchestra for eleven years, Anderson became Ellington's most versatile singer.

Ellington opened at the enormous Oriental Theater, situated on Chicago's equivalent of Broadway, on Friday, February 13, 1931, with Ivie Anderson. The show was a sensation, and Ellington, who had a number of superstitions, from then on considered Friday the 13th a *lucky* day for him. "His is a band that really entertains," wrote the *Chicago American*. "The program he presents is swift moving. It takes about thirty-five or forty minutes, yet seems far shorter. . . . The wah wah cornetist, trombonist and other soloists were so eloquent, indeed, during the performance we attended that the audience would not stop applauding some of their numbers for many minutes." In the first show, Ivie Anderson was "forced to take four bows and a speech to get off the stage." The Oriental's bill featured Ellington and a now-forgotten movie, *Truth about You*. Due largely to Ellington, the 3,200-seat theater grossed $49,900 in one week, nearly beating the previous record.

After Chicago, they went on a barnstorming tour of one-night performances. For a fourteen-week tour, the Publix theater chain paid them $3,500 per week plus traveling expenses. In Detroit, they broke all records. In Peoria, a fifth performance had to be scheduled to accommodate a thousand extra people. The local newspaper called their appearance "the biggest sensation ever to hit the city in a theatrical way." Many people, the paper noted, were from out of town and "had come long distances." After the Publix tour, the National Broadcasting Company's (NBC) artist bureau booked the Ellington orchestra for a ten-week tour of the central United States, beginning on June 2. Wherever a hookup was possible, NBC Radio broadcast the performances.

The reviewer of the *Cleveland Plain Dealer* singled out the orchestra's distinctive tonal colors. The critic found that the tunes "rush at you with a kind of frenzied madness, spiced with tricky rhythms and garnished with strange, half eerie tonal backgrounds. They ripple and swell through the house . . . [with] their flashing, artful way of almost completely submerging the melody to give you effects and colors no other orchestra seems to have been able to do."

Back in Chicago, the fans had not gotten enough of Ellington, so he was booked into the Oriental Theater four times in 1931. He broke the theater's previous monetary records as well as his own, and played to an estimated cumulative total of 400,000 people. He packed 1,100 people into the Lincoln Tavern, an exclusive dancing and dining spot three miles west of Evanston, Illinois. Ellington was seen by the *Chicago Defender* as paving the way for black musicians to perform not just in black neighborhoods but throughout the city in venues that previously hired only white performers. Wanting to share his success with loved ones, Ellington brought his mother, father, sister, and son out to be with him.

But in Chicago all was not roses. A long-standing enmity between Irving Mills and musicians' union boss James Petrillo resulted in the union's hauling Ellington before a tribunal and slapping him with a $2,000 fine—a little less than half the band's weekly salary—for accepting $4.92 less per man per week than the union scale. The disputed amount totaled about $60. During one of his frequent visits to Chicago in the early 1930s, some gangsters threatened Ellington with extortion or kidnapping, depending on the report. Ellington got some help from Owney Madden, the owner of the Cotton Club, who called the Chicago gangster Al Capone. "When the kidnapping party arrived at the club," recalled Barney Bigard, "three of Al's men stepped out from behind pillars with drawn guns. 'Where you fellows going?' 'To see our friend.' 'What friend?' 'The Duke.' 'Since when has he been a friend of yours? Get the hell out of here!' That was the end of the threats."

And Ellington was caught up in what was evidently a romantic hoax that must have embarrassed as well as flattered him. A well-refined man, convincingly posing as Ellington, telephoned prominent married women to ask for a "quiet date." As the handsome Ellington told the story, for five nights running, he returned to his hotel to find messages from the wives of noted physicians, undertakers, and others asking him to please call as soon as he could. Some husbands found out and word leaked to the press. To put the matter to rest, Ellington informed the newspapers of the situation, saying, "Being a married man, you can imagine just how embarrassing it was." Despite their best efforts, the infuriated husbands never caught the imposter.

The Duke Ellington orchestra at the Oriental Theater, Chicago, 1931. Standing, from left: Freddie Jenkins, Cootie Williams, Artie Whetsol, Juan Tizol, Tricky Sam Nanton, Sonny Greer, and Duke Ellington. Seated: Wellman Braud, Harry Carney, Johnny Hodges, Barney Bigard, and Fred Guy.

Not only was Ellington blessed with good looks but he dressed carefully and elegantly. One journalist described him this way: "Handsome in his square shouldered double breasted blue suit, with maroon tie and pencil striped soft shirt, glistening black hair slicked back, a wisp of a mustache, diamond ring and gold cuff links as his only bits of flash, he appeared much more the conformist than a 'violator' of any sort [of musical rules]."

But in his music, Ellington, ever the innovator, was continuing to ignore the normal rules. "We violate more laws of music than anyone else," Ellington said after a rehearsal, "and then just go right along violating." He told another reviewer, "My own music, if you wish a succinct definition, is 'screwy.' We have not followed the fetishes of symphonic musicians and have not hesitated to break the rules and even make new rules. We know that we have offended a great many people in the process, particularly 'legitimate' musicians, but I think we have also made a few friends."

What rules was Ellington breaking? Classical music's rules on harmonic progressions, counterpoint, blending of different instruments, proper instrumental tone—a whole range of codified practices and conventions to which Ellington paid no heed. He continued to follow the advice of Will Marion Cook to find his own way—for example, in the daring harmonies in *Blue Tune*, the unusual phrase lengths in *Creole Rhapsody*, and the enigmatic muted brass sound that opens *The Mystery Song*. Musicians scratched their heads on how Ellington created the latter effect. The secret? Partly it was his clever staggering of the players at farther and farther remove from the microphone. He missed no opportunity to expand upon his orchestra's distinctiveness.

Radio continued to serve as a tool to reach more people, but for an African-American, no matter how popular on tour, radio remained a sporadic vehicle at best. August of 1931 found the orchestra broadcasting over Chicago radio station WGN twenty-eight times a week. During this period, Ellington was broadcasting on local stations, but not nationally for some months. Evidently a dispute with NBC kept him off the air. But this absence from the airwaves underscored the fact that Ellington's orchestra was one of the few nationally famous groups that could not find a regular sponsor. Evidently no national company wanted to link its name to black performers in the 1930s. "I do not think," said a writer for the *Bridgeport Herald*, "I am telling any stories out of school when I submit that the reason such great names as Ellington and Calloway haven't profited commercially in radio is because national sponsors steer clear of arousing southern race prejudices. Too bad."

Though never blatant, Ellington, in his own quiet way, did address racial issues. While in Washington, he played a benefit concert for the "Scottsboro boys," nine black youths who were convicted without benefit of adequate counsel, by an all-white jury, of raping two white women and were sentenced to death. Ellington also called at the White House to meet President Hoover. The musician must have been very proud of the fact that this marked the first time a black entertainer would be received by the president. Yet despite the fact that the meeting was publicized in the newspapers, it never took place, according to the Hoover presidential papers. Evidently it was stopped because the man who set it up, Charles Lucien Skinner, had a police record. Perhaps too proud for himself and his race to admit to being rebuffed, or perhaps wanting to make a statement, Ellington posed for photographers on the White House grounds, without anyone from the presidential staff. The African-American press accused Hoover of being afraid to be photographed with black visitors.

In Philadelphia, Ellington encountered more trouble. Thugs smashed the windows in his automobile and stole a few valuables. One report said that the hoods, who escaped in a car with New York license plates, had wanted to kidnap the musician. Another report said the vandalism was intended to protest Ellington's playing in a neighborhood—presumably a white one.

Racial discrimination was a frequent indignity Ellington had to face. For instance, in St. Louis, he and his band went to the Melbourne Hotel to make a broadcast at the studios of WIL Radio, on the sixteenth floor. The white elevator operator refused to take them up or down. Ellington and his esteemed company had no choice but to ride up in the freight elevator. The next night, however, he played a concert for charity at the Hotel Coronado, where, as a newspaper noted, "he was accorded all of the respect due to an American citizen." Two years later, he'd be back in St. Louis, playing the exclusive Club Avalon—reportedly the first African-American to break the color barrier there—and was "received with overwhelming success."

By this time, Ellington's growing celebrity reportedly brought him as many as two hundred fan letters a day. He put his father to work answering them. Among the reasons for Ellington's celebrity was the relentless Mills publicity machine. It moved into a higher gear when, in September 1931, Mills hired Ned Williams as a public relations person and assigned him to spend half of his time promoting Ellington (the other half on Calloway). Williams's first assignment was to produce an advertising manual for Ellington—probably a first for a "dance band." During his seven years with Mills, Williams would become, in the words of Mercer Ellington, a general "trouble-shooter, office and personnel manager, booker, and road manager!"

Duke Ellington was becoming a household name, though not everyone who had heard of him could correctly identify him. According to the *Los Angeles Examiner*, "Two applicants for a guide position at the [1933 Chicago] World's Fair answered in a questionnaire that Duke Ellington was an English nobleman and that he defeated Napoleon at the Battle of Waterloo."

Ellington was gaining fans not only in the United States but in Europe as well—especially in England and France, where his few available records made quite an impression. The noted English composer Constant Lambert observed that "Duke Ellington is notable in that he is not only a first-class jazz-composer, but a fine orchestrator and executant as well. His works are conceived directly for his medium, and it is he who gives them their final stamp. He gives the same distinction to his *genre* that Strauss gave to the Waltz or Sousa to the March."

Ellington was becoming a culture hero among many black Americans. The black newspaper *Pittsburgh Courier*, which had something of a national readership, began a contest among readers to vote for the most popular orchestra. Ellington won the contest in 1931, with 50,000 mailed-in ballots—far more than the runners-up: McKinney's Cotton Pickers (42,000 votes) and Cab Calloway (32,500). At an award ceremony, the newspaper presented Ellington with a large loving cup. Always wanting to share his successes with his mother, Ellington brought her, his sister, and son to Pittsburgh. Not only was Ellington influential musically, but also sartorially. In an article on fashion among African-Americans, the *New York American* would assert, "The supremest dandies are the jazz exponents, Duke Ellington and Cab Calloway, who set the style pace."

During this time, Ellington grossed $5,000 to $5,500 weekly. By December 1931, he was commanding as much as $6,000 per week (that's $55,000 in 1993 dollars). Beginning in the fall of 1931, he and Mills began to secure an optional 50 percent of the house gross. Even this deal, however, still put him behind the popular white bands such as Paul Whiteman ($7,500), Ted Lewis ($7,500), Ben Bernie, and Guy Lombardo, or other white attractions such as Eddie Cantor ($8,800) and the blackface comedians Amos 'n' Andy ($7,500). Yet considering that jazz—of which Ellington was the practitioner of the highest standard—was then ardently embraced by only a small minority of the public (the mass popularity of jazz was yet to come), his fee was, if not fair, then at least impressive.

Meanwhile, Ellington's fame had spread through his recording of *Mood Indigo*. Victor Records had named it "the popular and concert record-of-the-month for February 1931." While continuing to make occasional records of the three-minute variety, Ellington still chafed under this arbitrary time limitation. A recently discovered homemade recording, taken from a radio broadcast in late 1931 or early 1932, preserves a rendition by Ellington of *When It's Sleepy*

When this picture of Ruth Ellington was taken in 1932, she was sixteen and her brother, Duke, was thirty-three.

The sheet music for *It Don't Mean a Thing*, 1932, whose title presaged the swing era.

Time Down South that lasts five and a half minutes. This reveals that in performance, Ellington ignored the arbitrary three-minute limit. It raises the question of how accurate his recordings are in documenting what Ellington actually played before audiences.

Not everyone wanted to hear longer Ellington pieces. One observer, Constant Lambert, noted that all of Ellington's pieces, except *Creole Rhapsody*, "only occupy one side of a 10 in. record and are all the better for this limitation. A jazz record should be as terse as possible, and it would be a pity if Ellington started to produce rambling, pseudo-highbrow fantasies such as Gershwin's more ambitious essays. The two best Ellington records obtainable in England are *Hot and Bothered* . . . and *Mood Indigo* . . . and neither of them attempts any change of mood."

But Ellington was determined to spread his wings and Victor gave him the opportunity. In early 1932, Victor recorded Ellington's orchestra in two experimental long-playing, 33⅓-rpm recordings. On February 3, 1932, Ellington gathered his men in RCA Victor Studio No. 1, on Twenty-fourth Street in New York City. Unusually, *two* microphones were set before the band. The orchestra recorded a medley of *Mood Indigo*, *Hot and Bothered*, and *Creole Love Call*. On February 9, they recorded a second medley: *East St. Louis Toodle-Oo*, *Lots o' Fingers*, and *Black and Tan Fantasy*. Both recordings were made in an early, experimental form of stereo. Unfortunately, Ellington strung together a medley of mostly well known numbers, instead of recording a longer, unified work which would have taken better advantage of the opportunity to stretch out. Meanwhile, however, Ellington made another normal-length recording in February that became one of his most emblematic: *It Don't Mean a Thing (If It Ain't Got That Swing)*.

In addition to featuring Ellington compositions such as *Mood Indigo*, the orchestra also performed "standards" such as *St. Louis Blues*, *Tiger Rag*, and *Memories of You*, and popular pieces of the day, such as *Stardust*, *Rockin' Chair*, and *Three Little Words*. These standard pieces, which were widely available in published "stock" arrangements, became the staple of most dance bands. Thus, most dance bands across the country played the same arrangement of *Stormy Weather*. Even with standards, Ellington, however, set his orchestra apart from the crowd by avoiding stock arrangements. "We do not use any printed orchestrations," he wrote in 1931. "These are much too stereotyped. For a band to keep in the top flight to-day it must be original. I therefore make all my own arrangements."

In April 1931, the enterprising Mills had begun issuing dance-orchestra arrangements of Ellington's pieces, including *Mood Indigo*, *The Mooche*, *Black and Tan Fantasy*, for seventy-five cents apiece. Orchestra leaders could then feature Ellington's works in something like their original style. The arrangements, however, were not entirely faithful to Ellington's records, and without his brilliant soloists, these other leaders could only approximate the Ellington sound.

As 1931 drew to a close Ellington must have felt that he had much to celebrate. Though he and his band made fewer records that year than in any year since 1926, in many ways it had been a very good year. The added luster brought by Ivie Anderson, the huge crowds, the strong response, the favorable press notices, the awards and honors, the breaking down of barriers, the growing salary—these must have pleased him enormously.

Ellington would maintain this momentum throughout 1932, and, in fact, for years: touring constantly—playing a theater typically for one week, and sometimes a dance; benefiting from Mills's relentless promotion; wowing audiences and making new converts in cities that he had never visited; on special occasions, bringing out his family to share in his success; earning good money; enduring occasional scrapes; encountering uncounted racial slights and barriers and increasingly breaking through them.

The year 1932 found him playing for the first time in Warner's Earle Theater in Washington; the Paramount Theatre in Brooklyn; and then going across country in a 3,000-mile beeline to San Francisco, in a special railroad car. There the Ellington troupe impressed the critics. Several commented on Ellington's poise and restraint as a conductor. "That a personality headed the organization was apparent from the start. The leader is a poised though ingratiating type, not given to antics. His eternal smile aided in an early intimacy with his audience." One reviewer noted the "thud-thud from an audience that can't make its feet behave." In Los Angeles, Ellington's orchestra was welcomed at the railway station by hundreds of people, including Les Hite's band, who formed a long parade of cars to welcome him down the avenue. Signs along the street said WELCOME DUKE, and he was the guest at a gala reception. Ellington earned this headline in the *Los Angeles Times:* MUSIC SCORCHES HEARERS.

Los Angeles boasted the most popular nightclub west of Chicago —Sebastian's Cotton Club (unrelated, except in name, to Harlem's

Cotton Club). At the enormous Sebastian's, Irving Mills, traveling as usual with Ellington, heard a trombonist execute an impressive piece, almost a concerto for trombone, called *Trees*—a musical setting of the familiar Joyce Kilmer poem. Mills asked the musician —Lawrence Brown was his name—if he would join the Duke Ellington orchestra. Brown said he was willing to go see Ellington. "I don't know you and I've never heard anything about you," Brown said Ellington told him, "but Mr. Mills says to get you. So come on in the band." Brown agreed, reckoning he'd be back in Los Angeles within a year. He stayed with the Ellingtonians for nineteen years.

Brown would transform trombone playing with his seemingly effortless technical skills, legato phrasing, mellifluous tone, eloquent and well-organized melodic ideas, romantic way with ballads, and

Ellington's unmatched trombone section—much later dubbed "God's trombones": Tricky Sam Nanton, Juan Tizol, and Lawrence Brown.

inimitable overall style. The son of a minister, he earned the nick-names "Deacon" and "Rev" (short for "Reverend") for his strict morals and serious demeanor. He was grumpy and aloof from the other players' ongoing rumpus on the road.

Brown was a sublime trombonist and enhanced the orchestra's sound. By comparison, at this time, Fletcher Henderson's orchestra used only one or two trombonists. The addition of Brown provided Ellington nine melody voices—three saxophones/clarinets, three trumpets, and three trombones. The size gave him a full and rich brass sound, and presented many possible ways of voicing his melodies and harmonies. To highlight his new trio of trombones, Ellington wrote *Slippery Horn* (first recorded on May 18, 1932), and it influenced other musicians, especially Don Redman and Jimmy Mundy. Soon, following Ellington's lead, big bands made three trombones the standard.

"Negro bands like plenty of brass," said Ellington in 1932, "and it is as the result of this influence that many white bands which formerly utilized a single trombone and two trumpets are now using two trombones and three trumpets or cornets. I have these five [*sic*] instruments in my band, with three saxophone players, all of whom double on the clarinet; a banjo, a bass, drums and piano. With the aid of mutes we are able to play just as 'sweet' as bands with violins or other instrumentation."

Despite believing Friday the 13th a lucky day for him, Ellington wouldn't let Brown play at first because he was the thirteenth band-member. So perhaps both to avoid bad luck and to enhance his sound, in April or May, Ellington enlarged his band again, bringing in a fourth saxophonist, Otto Hardwick, who returned to the band after an absence of four years. Ellington now had fourteen players and a singer, providing him as a composer-orchestrator still more possibilities in textures, tonal colors, dynamics, and moods.

If there had been any doubt, it was now clear this was *Ellington's* orchestra. Hardwick noticed a change in the governance of the orchestra. "It wasn't *our* thing any longer," he said. "It had become Ellington's alone. This was inevitable, I guess. Ten years ago it was 'We do it this way,' and 'We wrote that.' Now the we was royal." This change may just have reflected the need for a strong hand and clear line of command to run a growing organization of disparate individualists, but it probably also represented Ellington's growing confidence and sense of authority as a musician, composer, and bandleader.

Ellington's players now came from Boston, New York, Washington, Alabama, New Orleans, California—even the West Indies. Part of the contribution that each made to the orchestra was his or her regional musical accent.

How did Ellington keep his men sounding fresh? He related his secret to a reporter from the *Cleveland Press* in June 1932.

> Sometimes, I have pretended to the men that they've got lazy, but they know I didn't mean it. Not an instrumentalist in my band is lazy. But they get shiftless. Playing the same numbers four or five times a day gets to be routine. And they mustn't get "routine" in Duke Ellington's orchestra.
>
> Know the cure? Every once in a while, you'll notice that I drop out of vaudeville for a week or a few weeks and play dance engagements. That wakes up the boys and they get back into form. When they see people moving around the floor, they've got to put snap and ginger into their work.
>
> Why, it works like magic. We come back into the theater after these dance engagements and the boys put all of their vim and vigor into their work. Perhaps [they] imagine they see the members of the audience circling around the floor. Anyway, there's a big difference in their work; and perhaps there's a difference in my work.
>
> Probably you have noticed that when we play, we play! There's no half-way about it. And when the audiences hear us, they know there's music in the air—no mistake. Somehow, I always feel that we're not playing for them; we're playing with them and entertaining them. We like to know that they feel they're taking part in it with us, that they'd like to sing or dance.

Some of the best-known orchestras of the 1930s were led by musicians who conducted in front of the band—Paul Whiteman, Cab Calloway, and Jimmie Lunceford. Ellington mostly led from the piano. With his hands on the keyboard, how could he direct the band? His secret was visual cues. He would raise or lower his eyebrows to indicate he was pleased, or not, with the performance;

he'd purse his lips into a "shh" motion to indicate playing more softly; and he'd tilt his head up for a faster tempo and lower it for a slower tempo. Though audiences might not realize it, Ellington was in full control of the orchestra—and the music, which may have appeared spontaneous but was always worked out in advance.

For most of its early history, the Ellington orchestra avoided using written orchestrations in public. As Ellington told an interviewer, when they played at, say, the Paramount Theater, they were on for about twenty minutes and played four numbers.

> In the old days, you know, when you played on the stage, you just never brought music on the stage, you just didn't . . . because that wasn't very theatrical, to see . . . all 15 guys up there blowin' into some music. You just didn't do that . . . And so I found out that guys memorize things that they heard much more quickly and much more easily than they did if they read it. And what I would do is hold a rehearsal at night, after the theater, and give them notes to play— to say, "You play this." [Plays phrase at the piano.] . . . And the next guy I'd give him [plays another phrase]. Well, so, you know, and [plays another phrase]—I mean, just give out the parts like that, and he would remember it . . . and it would be indelibly stamped in their mind. The next day they would come and play it. No music. And that was it. . . . And then it . . . just got to be too damn much music.

A number of commentators noted the absence of written music when Ellington played in public. This statement also reveals how Ellington worked individually with his players, literally *teaching* each of them their parts personally.

Other than a lack of written music and of an obvious conductor, what was a performance of the Duke Ellington orchestra like during this period? A careful review of eyewitness reports allows a reconstruction of a typical dance at a large midwestern ballroom. Even before showtime, the front of the ballroom, the area near the bandstand, would be crowded with fellow bandleaders and jazz buffs craning their heads to take in every nuance of the unique Ellington sounds. The band of fourteen men would be dressed in simple white suits. With little theatrics Ellington would announce the numbers; for some numbers, drummer Sonny Greer would share the announcing duties. Tonight, there would be as an added attraction a little show featuring the dancer Earl "Snake Hips" Tucker and a quartet of tap dancers. Wellman Braud would slap "his first triumphant bass-fiddle note in *Ring Dem Bells*," stony-faced Johnny Hodges would take a ravishing solo, and the five-foot, 107-pound trumpeter Freddie Jenkins would astonish the audience with his blowing power and showmanship. Jenkins and Greer would tickle the audience with some comedy bits. On *Mood Indigo*, three players carrying the melody—trumpeter Artie Whetsol, clarinetist Barney Bigard, and trombonist Tricky Sam Nanton—would step to the front of the stage, while the rest of the band played ever so softly behind them. The orchestra would perform a mix of old and new Ellington originals including *Black and Tan Fantasy* and *Sophisticated Lady*, and pop and jazz standards such as *Bugle Call Rag, My Blue Heaven, I Got Rhythm, Lazy Bones*, and the old *Tiger Rag*. "Send me, man!" Greer would shout as he launched a percussion volley. Later on he would sing *Dinah*. Mostly the band would play at a low to medium volume; on some numbers it would let loose with blasts of brass. Ivie Anderson, ever dressed in white, would skip out on stage, looking, as one reviewer wrote, like "a million dollars," and singing without a microphone "as well as any man," would wow the crowd with *It Don't Mean a Thing, Stormy Weather*, and *Minnie the Moocher*, which would draw two encores. She and Greer would create a visual, verbal, and musical interplay, to the great delight of the crowd. The audience would respond enthusiastically to the overall event, or as one reviewer would put it the next day, "the young folks danced and perspired and danced and perspired again and applauded the music to the echo." Afterward, admirers would crowd around to meet Ellington, and musicians to ask a question or seek encouragement.

While he played occasional dances, during this period Ellington mostly performed stage shows—that is, his sets alternated with movies. His increasing polish and effectiveness on stage, undoubtedly assisted by the canny Irving Mills, would by mid-1932 establish him, in the words of one entertainment columnist, "as one of the outstanding stage attractions in the country." This degree of success was surprising, given the fact that jazz was "a type of music not noted for its box-office appeal," as *Fortune* magazine put it. In the view of *Fortune*, while part of his popularity on stage resulted from his "feature singers such as Ivie Anderson and dancers like the gelatinous 'Snake Hips' Tucker . . . there can be little doubt that Ellington's success is mainly due to his music itself."

The fact of his success on the stage has escaped many writers on Ellington, because they have focused single-mindedly on his recordings. Those recordings, in fact, only partially represent the Ellington that his audiences at dances and stage shows knew. For one thing, his stage shows included other acts—dancers like Fredi Washington, Bessie Dudley, Earl "Snake Hips" Tucker, the tap-dancing Four Blazers, the novelty dancers Jerry and Terry—or an additional singer, like Bobby Caston, described by one reviewer as a future "Ethel Waters." In fact, Ellington often traveled with his own revue; the version he offered in early 1934 was called *Harlem Speaks*.

The recordings give a partial view in other ways: recorded versions of pieces were often shortened to fit into three minutes; many songs that were a mainstay of Ellington performances during the 1930s never made it to record—the *Scat Song, How'm I Doing*— or made it to record decades later when the band sounded quite different—*Trees, Minnie the Moocher, When It's Sleepy Time Down South*. The comedy, interplay with other musicians, and visually arresting playing of his percussion battery that made Sonny Greer a standout are lacking from recordings. There is no way to recapture the dynamics of a live Ellington performance; the closest one can come now is by watching his band perform in movies, particularly those few showing the band performing before an audience. (One of the most realistic glimpses of Ellington and his audience would come in 1942, in the motion picture *Cabin in the Sky*.)

In early November 1932, Ellington received an invitation from Percy Grainger, the noted composer and chairman of the Music Department at New York University. Ellington and his orchestra played for a class in music appreciation, and Grainger casually compared his genius for melodic invention to that of Delius and Bach. This is how the persistent misconception arose that Ellington was influenced by Delius. In fact, Ellington had never listened to

In November 1932, the noted composer Percy Grainger (center) invited Ellington (seated) to address his class at New York University. Irving Mills looks on at left.

Delius. After Grainger made his comparison, Ellington quipped, "I'll have to find out about this Delius." It is not likely he did, because his own music kept him so occupied that he did not usually listen even to his own recordings.

Grainger and Constant Lambert were among a growing number of classical musicians who recognized Ellington's genius. Since 1927, the Harvard-trained writer R. D. Darrell had been writing positive pieces on Ellington in the *Phonograph Monthly Review*.

Now, in 1932, he wrote a knowing and glowing piece on Ellington called "Black Beauty" for the American record review *Disques*. He found Ellington's mind

> resourcefully inventive, yet primarily occupied not with the projection of effects or syncopated rhythms, but the concern of great music —tapping the inner world of feeling and experience. . . .
>
> . . . gifted with a seemingly inexhaustible well of melodic invention, [Ellington is the] possessor of a keenly developed craftsmanship in composition and orchestration. . . . A man who knows exactly what he is doing: exercising his intelligence, stretching to new limits his musicianship, while he remains securely rooted in the fertile artistic soil of his race. A man who . . . out of a group of some ten [*sic*] men has built his own orchestra [into] a superb and personal instrument.
>
> The most striking characteristic of all his works, and the one which stamps them ineradicably as his own, is the individuality and unity of style that weld composition, orchestration, and performance into one inseparable whole.
>
> In the exploitation of tonal coloring . . . Ellington has proceeded further than any composer—popular or serious—of today. His command of color contrast and blend approaches at times an art of polytimbres.
>
> Ellington's finest tunes spring into rhapsodic being as simply, as naturally as those of Mozart or Schubert. Characteristic of even the lesser tunes is their astounding fluidity and resilience of line. . . . Over the straining, strongly pulling bass and the fundamental beat, the true melody, or more often two or more melodies dip, curvet, swoop, and spiral in the untrammelled, ecstatic freedom of soaring gulls.
>
> To me the most daring experiments of the modernists rarely approach the imaginative originality, mated to pure musicianship, of a dozen arresting moments in Ellington's works.

The discerning Darrell observed that many of Ellington's commercial pieces—he recorded many pop tunes of the day—fell into the trap of popularity or the orthodoxy of dance music or lost their footing for the "delusion of grandeur." But he presciently predicted that Ellington would "give us again more than a few moments of the purest, the most sensitive and ineluctable revelation of feeling in music today." Finally, noting that Ellington's "atmosphere is sustained only over small canvasses," the critic argued that "intensity and not size is the true measure of musical worth."

On January 8, 1933, the New York School of Music presented its award for best composition of the year to Ellington, for *Creole Rhapsody*. The piece was chosen "because it portrayed the Negro life as no other piece had." Mayor O'Brien presented the award. As further indication of the respect Ellington was receiving as a composer, on January 25, Paul Whiteman featured the piece in a concert at Carnegie Hall.

While Mills's publicity machine had for several years striven to portray Ellington as a talented composer, the praise of people like Grainger, Lambert, and Darrell was of a far different and higher order. The canonization of Duke Ellington had begun in earnest, and it would continue throughout his life and after.

In the words of *Fortune* magazine in 1933, Ellington was "an idol of the jazz cult, which has developed a critical canon as precise and exacting as that applied to porcelains or plain song. The jazz cult is apathetic to nine-tenths of modern dance music." The jazz cult, however, comprised only a very small number of people—not enough to sustain a traveling orchestra during the depression's depths. So now—and throughout his career—Ellington would strive for a balance between what the public wanted to hear and what *he* wanted to play, between the familiar and the new, between the accessible and the challenging, and between dance/stage entertainment and fine art. This balancing act was intertwined with the ongoing problem of having two careers—bandleader and composer. But he continually found ways to advance both careers, even in America's worst depression.

The Great Depression hit rock bottom in 1933. A fourth of the labor force was out of work. Since 1929, the gross national product had fallen by nearly 50 percent. The economic disaster and pain were unprecedented in scope and duration. By the end of 1931, the entire entertainment industry had already been suffering mightily from the nation's economic woes. "Show business, as the current year closes out, is in the most chaotic condition it has ever known," reported *Variety* magazine. By 1932, every aspect had been suffering—records, music publishing, theaters, vaudeville, movies, everything. At one point, more than eight hundred movie theaters with stages were closed.

The record industry's fortunes had nose-dived from a sale of 75 million records in 1929 to only 6 million in 1933—a twentieth-century low and a decline of 92 percent. The average number of copies a hit record sold plummeted also, meaning recording artists and songwriters earned far less money. Many musicians were dropped from the rosters of the record companies.

Ellington was one of the five most successful bandleaders on the Victor label, yet Victor cut back his recording activity drastically. In 1931, he made only twenty different records, thirty-three in 1932, and twenty-eight in 1933.

In this weak record market, Ellington made very little money from his recordings. In fact, sales of records would not bounce back to their predepression levels until 1945, and by then, changing tastes in music would deny Ellington large record sales. Fortunately for Ellington, Mills proved adept at booking him stage shows and dances throughout the country. During this time, personal appearances were Ellington's bread and butter.

In depression America, besides being the poor man's phonograph, radio became enormously popular among the middle class too. In 1930, radio had penetrated to one third of U.S. homes. Rapidly falling costs of radios—in 1933, you could get a table model for $12.95 or twenty-five cents down and fifty cents a week —helped the figure to jump to two thirds of households in 1935. By 1934, more than 650 American radio stations were on the air.

Since 1932 or so, the press had been proclaiming that the radio had surpassed the phonograph in popularity and influence. While Ellington was touring, his radio broadcasting was sporadic, though in large cities such as Los Angeles and San Francisco, he usually managed to make some broadcasts. It was only when he returned to New York in March 1933, that he could again broadcast regularly. That month, Mills hired Martin North to handle Ellington's commercial radio business. And North earned his money that month. He landed the Ellingtonians nightly broadcasts at 1:30 on WMCA and NBC, midnight programs on Tuesdays and Fridays on WJZ and NBC, Thursdays at midnight on WEAF. By April 1933, forty-five radio stations were broadcasting Ellington around the country, reportedly a record for a dance program beginning at midnight.

In 1933, while the record industry bled, Ellington devoted his energies to personal appearances. There would be four triumphs—a return to the Cotton Club, a trip to Europe, a tour deep into the South, and a series of stellar recordings.

When Mills succeeded in booking Cab Calloway for a tour of southern states, Ellington substituted for Calloway at the Cotton Club. On opening night, Thursday, March 9, celebrities such as George Raft, Bert Lahr, Frances Williams, Ray Bolger, and Eddie Duchin turned out. One night, during a radio broadcast, Paul Whiteman, sitting at a ringside table, mischievously sucked on a lemon and, according to press reports, "put three trumpets, three trombones, and four clarinets out of commission." But then Ellington saved the day by quickly having his men look elsewhere.

The Ellington orchestra accompanies Ethel Waters and chorus line at the Cotton Club in 1933.

After a month of filling in for Calloway, Ellington opened the twenty-second Cotton Club revue, *Cotton Club Parade*, on Sunday, April 16, at midnight, with "an all star cast of 50 artists" and a "chorus of 18 girls." There were eighteen scenes, plus the Ellington orchestra's overture, finale, and numbers in between. Ted Koehler and Harold Arlen composed the songs. The highlight was Ethel Waters singing *Stormy Weather*, which became not only *the* popular song of the season but, in the words of *Variety*, "the biggest song hit of the last 10 years." The opening night drew Eddie Cantor, Sophie Tucker, Jimmy Durante, Vincent Lopez, Johnny Weismuller, Ethel Merman, Ray Bolger, Carl Van Vechten, Eddie Duchin, Fatty Arbuckle, Milton Berle, and many other celebrities. The show did not seem to do much for Ellington's music—it does not appear that he wrote any of the pieces in the production itself —but it added a bit more luster to his already luminous name in New York. In May, the Ellingtonians recorded an instrumental version of *Stormy Weather* coupled with his new composition, *Sophisticated Lady*, which went to the top of Brunswick Records' sales for May and June.

Ellington exercised a strong hold over many listeners. Some of them used the same kind of descriptions as earlier generations had when they encountered black ragtime music. "Barbaric," "weird," "intoxicating"—these are the adjectives that both generations

Ellington donned a top hat for this 1933 publicity photo made before his tour of England.

The Ellington orchestra created a sensation at the London Palladium
during their triumphant 1933 tour of Britain.

used to describe this exotic music. One reviewer wrote that the
Ellingtonians' music "inspires some to dance, holds others to the
bandshell front to listen and intrigues me to the extent of rapt
attention for almost five hours."

Mills, continuing to seek new opportunities for his artists—Ellington, Calloway, Mills' Blue Rhythm Band, the Mills Brothers—
traveled to Europe in November 1932. The result was a European
tour by the Ellington orchestra in the summer of 1933, sponsored
by the British bandleader Jack Hylton. The dancer Bessie Dudley,
best known for the shake, was part of the act, as were the tap
dancers Bailey and Derby. The Ellingtonians left New York on the
S.S. *Olympic* on June 2, arrived in Southampton on June 9, and
embarked upon a fifty-five-day tour of Great Britain, Holland, and
France.

With Hylton and Mills working on generating publicity, the Ellington tour was much ballyhooed weeks in advance. Louis Armstrong had played in England in 1932, to decidedly mixed response. Now, some were especially hungry to hear Ellington. "We are of the opinion," wrote the British magazine *Rhythm*, "that the time is ripe for the advent of another coloured band in this country, as our bands have been lately sinking into a stereotyped rut and it is time that a certain judicious kick in the pants was administered." Arriving at London's Waterloo Station, the Ellington party was greeted by thirty-seven photographers. The orchestra members found, however, that no decent hotel would rent them rooms because of their race. They split up and managed to find accommodations at assorted Bloomsbury hotels and rooming houses.

For two weeks they played last on a thirteen-act bill at the Palladium, considered by some the world's foremost vaudeville or variety theater. The stage featured twelve-foot banjoists decked with ducal crowns. The houses were sold out and the audiences exceptionally enthusiastic. *Rockin' in Rhythm*, a pianissimo version of *Tiger Rag* called *Whispering Tiger*, *Mood Indigo*, Ivie Anderson's feature *Stormy Weather*—all were sensations. "This was a night that scared the devil out of the whole band," Ellington wrote later, "the applause was so terrifying—it was applause beyond applause. On our first show there was 10 minutes of continuous applause. It was a tremendous thrill." *Billboard* reported, "On the first day of his appearance, the Palladium broke all box-office records, with over $3,800 being taken at the two performances."

After closing in London, the orchestra traveled to Liverpool, Bolton, Blackpool, Glasgow, Harrogate, and Birmingham—then more engagements in London. The Prince of Wales (later the Duke of Windsor) attended one of the concerts in Liverpool, where the Ellingtonians made thirteen curtain calls and played four encores. And there was a round of social activities, including hobnobbing with Prince George (who repeatedly asked Ellington to play his piano solo *Swampy River*), playing a piano duet with the Duke of Kent, and permitting the Prince of Wales to sit in at the drums.

Ellington broke precedents as well as records. Even before his arrival, his phonograph records reportedly outsold all others in Great Britain. Then, for a forty-five-minute broadcast, the BBC paid the most ever for an orchestra; Ellington's fees were the highest ever paid in Britain to American entertainers; he ran up the largest grosses and scored the "biggest personal and professional success ever achieved by an American attraction in Great Britain"; and he would pack the Trocadero Theatre with 4,000 seated fans and 1,000 standees, and many more would be turned away. Overall, a reported 100,000 people listened or danced to Ellington during his stay in England.

Besides the stage shows and a few dance engagements, Ellington was booked for three Sunday concerts—the first at the Palladium. The Palladium engagement delighted most of the audience, though not all the zealous fans and musicians. So musician Spike Hughes, who hated commercial compromises, organized—on behalf of *Melody Maker* magazine—a special concert at the Trocadero, the largest movie theater in Europe. Stanley Dance, there at both the Palladium and Trocadero, has said that no jazz musicians, before or since, had such an effect on an English audience. "The cream suits, orange ties, brown shoes, and tan skins," Mercer Ellington has said, "made for an attractive appearance." The audience loved Ellington, his musicians, their comport and dress, and above all, their music.

The musicians were presented in elaborate twenty-four page programs as serious artists, Ellington as an important composer, and his compositions as true works of art. Nothing like this had ever been done for Ellington in the United States. Even when he would finally be invited to perform concerts at Carnegie Hall in the 1940s, the program booklets were not nearly as elaborate.

Two controversies broke out over Ellington, one among the general British public, another among dance-band musicians and critics. The public and daily press were divided about the *merits* of Ellington's music. "With just one exception," wrote one reviewer, "every layman I have questioned concerning the Ellington broadcast disliked it." "Is this music?" asked one bewildered audience member at the Palladium. The music was too new, adventurous, or jazzy for much of the public. Their discomfort or dislike was echoed by some music critics and expressed in letters to the editor. The *Manchester Guardian* complained, "When all arguments are finished it is surely true to say that something that is thoroughly ugly from start to finish is fairly to be opposed. Even the 'music' would be more bearable if the words were not so stupid and if the ideas which exist vaguely behind it were not so pathetically crude." These reactions underscored the point that Ellington did have a very different, very advanced sound that many people were not quite ready for.

On the other hand, critics, musicians, and listeners predisposed to jazz tended to like Ellington's fresh sounds. Constant Lambert, writing in the *London Sunday Referee*, said, "I received the thrill of a lifetime to hear what is unquestionably the world's greatest brass section." The *London Era*'s S. R. Nelson raved:

> Ellington the Amazing. Ellington the Musician. Ellington the Showman. Ellington the Artist. How can I in such a limited space, describe the unbelievable spectacle I have just beheld at the Palladium on the occasion of the Duke's initial performance in London? . . . How to describe in so many words the most vital emotional experience vaudeville in England has ever known? . . . Where oh where are the renowned British qualities of aloofness, coldness, unemotionalism, self-restraint?
>
> I am not ashamed to say that I cried during the playing of "Mood Indigo." Here was a music far removed from the abracadabra of symphony. . . .
>
> For one brief, fleeting moment I looked around the auditorium. More than half of that usually phlegmatic sea of faces was bathed in an ecstatic adoration of that tall, distinguished, grey-suited figure at the piano and the triangle of musicians building up to the back of the stage.
>
> Ellington has yet stamped indelibly his personal touch on even the most banal of tunes. . . . Musically he is unique in the sense that, as a composer, he has his own orchestra to play his compositions. It is doubtful whether any other orchestra in the world could interpret Ellington's music in the manner of his band. . . . I say that in Duke Ellington we have one of the foremost musical figures of the time, a view which will be shared by all far-seeing musicians.

Another London critic wrote of hearing Ellington at the Palladium: "His music has a truly Shakespearean universality, and as he sounded the gamut, girls wept and young chaps sank to their knees." This brings into focus another problem Ellington faced with his two careers—the problem of pleasing knowledgeable fans yet generating enough popular appeal to fill large houses. Again, a careful, tricky balancing act was needed, one that simply could not please everybody.

The second controversy arose among jazz aficionados over Ellington's *selection* of works. Some wanted him to play his "purest," "least commercial" pieces, such as *Blue Tune* and *Creole Rhapsody.* "The Palladium concert greatly disappointed me in one particular respect," wrote critic Peter Rush. "Number after number was the music of Ellington of the stage. I wanted more of the music of Ellington of the records. Possibly he gave the audience what he judged it wanted and considered that enough of his art had already been given via the wax."

Ellington's orchestra triumphed in three concerts in Paris at the huge Salle Pleyel. "It was perhaps the most riotous scene of joy ever witnessed within the four walls of this building," raved the African-American writer J. A. Rogers in the *Amsterdam News.* Rogers asserted that "apart from the waltz and tango, the European orchestras cannot play good dance music—that is, the jazzy, peppy kind. They simply haven't got the feeling for it. The Duke Ellington concerts . . . have shown that the European public is . . . eager for properly played jazz." The orchestra also presented a special concert at the Casino du Deauville in the famous seaside resort.

In Paris, Ellington's band members were startled at how seriously their European fans treated their music—memorizing solos from records that the players themselves had forgotten. "This was respect and knowledge of a kind they seldom encountered at home," Mercer Ellington wrote later, "at least from white folks. The affection and admiration they received more than balanced whatever prejudice and surviving ignorance on racial matters that they met."

What was the significance of this tour? Ellington had proven himself in the capitals of cosmopolitan culture. During this tour, Ellington's music and—as Mercer Ellington has written—his "composure, wit, and innate dignity had 'commanded respect'—to use a phrase he always liked—in the two most sophisticated capitals of the world, London and Paris." Despite some negative reactions, he was now hailed by some as "probably the first composer of real character to come out of America."

Freddie Jenkins, Lawrence Brown, Cootie Williams, and Juan Tizol
during a BBC radio broadcast for which Ellington was paid a record sum.
Artie Whetsol's face is obscured by the microphone.

Abroad, Ellington's music challenged and stimulated musicians, critics, and the public. "Ellington's visit has been of great advantage to us in many ways," wrote *The Melody Maker*. He "has shown us that we must look elsewhere than in this country for a band which can keep an immaculate tempo. Until hearing Ellington in the flesh, I never realised how ragged and chancy our bands are." *The Metronome* agreed that "the greatest impression made by the orchestra was upon the musicians in England, both professional and amateur." Wrote critic Peter Rush:

With such a high standard of playing talent coupled with organised team work and led by a master artist it is easy to understand why the band has such an astounding record of success to its credit, and why it is able to challenge musical thought in this country to the extent of making tongues wag and heads think hard. . . . Duke Ellington has shaken up the ideas of English musicians and caused them to put on their thinking caps.

Some years after his 1933 tour, the English music press credited Ellington with raising performance standards among British musicians.

Finally, the tour had several effects on Ellington, one fundamentally commercial, the other more substantive. The orchestra's smashing success was seized on by Mills and his staff in their subsequent publicizing of Ellington—now they called him "internationally famous"—and no doubt increased Ellington's commercial viability and public stature.

Like his men, Ellington returned from Europe more seasoned and somewhat changed. "The main thing I got in Europe was *spirit,*" he said. "That kind of thing gives you courage to go on. If they think I'm *that* important, then maybe I have kinda said something, maybe our music does mean something." "We were absolutely amazed by how well informed people were in Britain about us and our records," Ellington wrote. But it wasn't just the adulation he received (R. D. Darrell and others had heaped critical praise on him in his homeland), it was the way his music and performances were treated. In the United States, Ellington was booked to play dances, stage shows, and theatrical performances—almost never concerts. But this European tour was different—primarily stage shows and concerts. The experience stimulated his ambitions in his career as a serious composer. In 1935, he would tell interviewer Frank Marshall Davis, " 'A musician should have both Europe and America.' These United States are better for dance stuff," Davis wrote, "but for concerts he'll take the other side of the Atlantic. It seems Europeans, because of a different cultural background, have a general understanding and appreciation of art not found on these shores." Put simply, the bandleader in Ellington liked America, while the composer in him preferred Europe.

. . .

After returning to the United States, the band toured New England. Then it embarked on a twelve-week southern tour. Ellington had resisted such a trip, according to biographer Barry Ulanov. " 'I won't go south,' Duke had said, many times. 'I don't care what they offer me.' " He didn't want to be in places where black people had been—and still were—treated so shamefully.

Cab Calloway's experience may have reinforced his reluctance. In 1931, Mills had persuaded Calloway to make, in his words, "the first tour of a big Negro band through the deep South." "The trip was trouble from the beginning. . . . Benny Payne, our pianist . . . used to tell me . . . 'They've got us coming in and leaving from the backs of theaters, dressing in toilets, and eating while we sit on potato sacks in the kitchen. You know damned well they don't treat white bands like this.' " When most of Calloway's band was delayed by a bus breakdown, the white audience in Virginia Beach, Virginia, grew angry and "somebody shouted, 'Let's take this nigger out and lynch him.' All of this was going on while I was trying to sing."

"It was tough traveling through the South in those days," agreed Pops Foster, bassist in the Luis Russell and Louis Armstrong bands. "It was very rough finding a place to sleep in the South. You couldn't get into the hotels for whites, and the colored didn't have any hotels. You rented places in private homes, boarding houses, and whorehouses. The food was awful."

But Ellington was in an upbeat mood after Europe, and Mills promised him good money if he went south. Mills's publicity people made sure the newspapers on the band's itinerary were well supplied with advance publicity, and this tactic seems to have generated considerable interest along the route. The southern tour began in Dallas on September 30. Using new scenic equipment built for them in New York City, they played five shows per day. They took Dallas by storm and the Majestic Theater grossed $22,000 in one week, breaking its previous record. The *Dallas News* reviewer was enthralled, calling Ellington "something of an African Stravinsky" and asserting that five Ellington compositions—*Ring Dem Bells,*

Sophisticated Lady, It Don't Mean a Thing, Black and Tan Fantasy, and *Mood Indigo*—"erased the color line" between jazz and classical music.

> They are veritable symphonic studies which pluck nerve-strings never before in the reach of a composer. They bear titles in the jazz idiom, have tunes that catch immediately, but they are harmonized in substantial and permanent vein. This is not butterfly jazz with three months' life. It can and probably will be performed whenever you can find musicians to play it. Whether such musicians exist outside the dark ranks of the Ellington band is doubtful.
> The Ellington program has two distinct phases, one a first-class Cotton Club floor show and the other a revelation in modern harmony. The latter, which is one of the most remarkable things ever to smite the ear, may prove bewildering to the light-minded.

When Ellington made his first tour of the Deep South in 1933, large crowds turned out, as at the Majestic Theatre in Dallas.

As this review indicates, Ellington shrewdly used his popular appeal to advance his musical interests: after the floor show, he offered a musically advanced program. Here is another example of Ellington balancing the roles of, on one hand, bandleader and entertainer with, on the other hand, composer. Ellington openly embraced the ambiguity of his public roles—as utilitarian dance-band leader, entertainer, and, at least in Europe, concert artist. From Dallas, the orchestra traveled across Texas and Oklahoma; to New Orleans, Birmingham, Atlanta; and through Tennessee. Segregation ruled at Ellington's performances. At Dallas's Ice Palace, one dance was held for whites and a few days later another was held for African-Americans, at which white "spectators" were allowed to sit in a reserved area. There was a special midnight show at the Majestic on October 4, with a 200-voice black choir whose program included several Negro spirituals; the balcony was reserved for blacks. "Duke was a big name," Bigard recalled, "even in the South, but they always had to have four cops stationed at each corner of the place so that the local people wouldn't get any ideas." There was tension, but evidently no major incidents. One policeman would say to Ellington, however, during one of his travels in the early 1940s, "If you'd been a white man, Duke, you'd been a great musician."

Bob Udkoff, who began an association with Duke Ellington in 1934 and traveled with the band beginning in 1936 as an advance man to find accommodations, recalled that

Duke had the ability to rise above the petty discrimination. He says, "I'm not going to allow that to set me aside and distract me. That's their problem, that's not my problem." However, there were occasions, I'd see where it could get to him. But by and large, he maintained an attitude—attitude was such an important thing to him. He'd lift his head and just rise above it. Wouldn't hear it, wouldn't see it. It was there—he was aware of it. He knew how far he could go. But he never apparently would allow it to bother him. He felt he was as good as anyone. He had a creed, and he'd say, "You've got to love yourself before you can love anyone else." And he loved himself, and he loved those around him.

Ellington himself would tell an interviewer in 1944, "You have to try not to think about [discrimination] or you'll knock yourself out." His attitude must have grown out of his parents' avoiding discussing unpleasant incidents.

When Ellington got to Oklahoma City in October, among the audience was a young man named Ralph Ellison. "I was but a young boy in the crowd that stood entranced around the bandstand at Slaughter's Hall," recalled the great novelist and essayist.

> And then Ellington and the great orchestra came to town; came with their uniforms, their sophistication, their skills; their golden horns, their flights of controlled and disciplined fantasy; came with their art, their special sound; came with Ivy [sic] Anderson and Ethel Waters singing and dazzling the eye with their high-brown beauty and with the richness and bright feminine flair of their costumes, their promising manners. They were news from the great wide world, an example and a goal. . . .
>
> . . . a few years later, when I was a student in the music department at Tuskegee [Institute in Alabama], I shook his hand, talked briefly with him of my studies and of my dreams. He was kind and generous even though harassed (there had been some trouble in travel and the band had arrived hours late, with the instruments misplaced and the musicians evil as only tired, black, Northern-based musicians could be in the absurdly segregated South of the 1930s), and those of us who talked with him were renewed in our determination to make our names in music.

No one knows how many young people were influenced or encouraged by Duke Ellington, but judging from other reports and newspaper accounts of musicians thronging him after performances, the figure is probably high.

Electrified by European esteem and favorably surprised by his southern reception, Ellington enjoyed an upsurge of creativity in his career as a composer. Within about a year of returning to the United States from Europe, a series of acclaimed pieces—from the latter part of 1933, *Jive Stomp, Rude Interlude, Dallas Doings,* and *Daybreak Express,* and from 1934, *Delta Serenade, Stompy Jones,*

Solitude, Blue Feeling, and *The Saddest Tale*—would come from Ellington's fertile mind. Yet he also had to deal with the practical problems of the bandleader.

By early 1934, there was a change in Ellington's travel arrangements. Now, the Ellington orchestra had its own private railroad cars: two sleepers and a baggage car for their musical instruments, and sound and lighting equipment. Sometimes they had a dining car, and sometimes they cooked on a hotplate stove on the train. Sleeping and eating on the train eliminated the difficulty of finding accommodations in the segregated South, to which they returned in August 1934 for a second tour.

The writer Nat Hentoff said that

> once in a while Ellington would talk about Jim Crow, and the abiding delight he'd had in traveling through the South from 1934 to 1936 with two Pullman cars and a seventy-foot baggage car. "We commanded respect. We parked those cars in each railroad station and we lived in them. We had our own water, food, electricity, and sanitary facilities."
>
> Duke smiled. "The natives would come by and they would say, 'What on earth is that?' And we would say, 'That's the way the President travels.' That was in the thirties." Duke looked at me. "You do the very best you can with what you've got."

In Atlanta, in the heart of the old Confederacy, Ellington continued to raze racial barriers. In August 1934, the *Atlanta Constitution* reported:

> Approximately 7,500 persons shoved, pushed and perspired Tuesday night at the city auditorium to hear Duke Ellington's 15-piece orchestra. . . . More than 2,000 were turned away from the box office. . . . The white people who crowded the gallery were loud in their applause of the orchestra and the dancers. The dance and concert were a decided hit, both from the white patrons' standpoint and the colored dancers'.

This trip also took them to New Orleans. They came in triumphantly, as thousands met them at the railway station. The hometown boys, Bigard and Braud, were especially welcomed, and college bands serenaded them into the depot.

According to records at the Franklin D. Roosevelt Library, in February 1934, while Ellington was performing at Washington's Howard Theater, he offered to perform for Mrs. Roosevelt. Ellington was politely rebuffed with the explanation that Mrs. Roosevelt

Traveling from city to city in their own private railroad car, the Ellingtonians often passed the time by playing cards. Here, Barney Bigard and Johnny Hodges match their skills.

After one of Ellington's tours, the noted Harlem nightclub Smalls' Paradise welcomed him back to New York with a party on July 1, 1934. By the mid 1930s, Ellington's was the most popular black orchestra in the United States.

was away and the president was busy and not planning any entertainment that week. The newly discovered evidence of Ellington's
attempted contacts with Hoover and the Roosevelts increases the
estimation of Ellington's ambition—for himself, his band, his
music, and his race. Not overtly political, Ellington sought these
and later contacts with the president because they would confer a
legitimation by the highest civil authority in the land and thus
would advance his aims. And besides, Ellington, having naturally
aristocratic tendencies, a royal nickname, and introductions to
princes in England, probably figured the American president is the
closest thing the United States has to a king. Why shouldn't an
American duke meet the American king?

In a publicity photo for the 1934 movie *Murder at the Vanities*, Ellington
and his orchestra pose at a railroad station. From left: dancer Earl "Snake Hips"
Tucker, Juan Tizol, Artie Whetsol, Ivie Anderson, Tricky Sam Nanton, Harry Carney,
Wellman Braud, Otto Hardwick, Ellington, Fred Guy, Freddie Jenkins, Barney Bigard,
Johnny Hodges, Lawrence Brown, and Sonny Greer.

But for other reasons, the English—royalty and commoner alike —were now out of reach. In September 1934, Ellington was set to return to England for two weeks at the Plaza Cinema in London and four weeks' tour of Paramount theaters in the provinces. But the British Ministry of Labour refused to grant a permit for the Ellingtonians to play in British motion picture theaters, fearing competition with native bands. This made the tour economically infeasible, and the trip was canceled. It would be twenty-six years until the Ellington orchestra would return to England.

Ellington was securing increasing opportunities for exposure through motion pictures. In 1933, he had made two short subjects —a Paramount newsreel and *A Bundle of Blues*—in New York. Now, between February and May of 1934, he stayed in Los Angeles, doing club and theater work, making recordings and radio broadcasts, and appearing in two Paramount feature films—*Murder at the Vanities* and *Belle of the Nineties*—and recording music for the sound track of a third—*Many Happy Returns*. In *Murder at the Vanities,* a furious classical conductor mows down the entire Ellington orchestra with a machine gun because they have dared to jazz up Liszt's *Hungarian Rhapsody*. Accompanying Mae West singing four numbers in *Belle of the Nineties*, the Ellington orchestra, as Klaus Stratemann has observed, received Hollywood exposure then unprecedented for a jazz band, black or white. The orchestra's role, however, was still somewhat incidental to the film as a whole.

Mills had negotiated a third Paramount film for Ellington, this time an entire short subject to himself. In December 1934, the orchestra went to Astoria Studios on Long Island to record the soundtrack, and returned in March 1935 to do the actual filming. *Symphony in Black: A Rhapsody of Negro Life* contained four sections: *The Laborers*, showing the hard physical labor of loading huge cotton bales onto a boat and tending a blast furnace; *A Triangle*, which in three parts depicts the hurt of a woman (played by the soon-to-be-discovered young Billie Holiday) who is rejected by her man for another woman; the haunting *A Hymn of Sorrow*, show-

ing a minister and congregation mourning the death of a baby; and
Harlem Rhythm, celebrating nightlife with the sinuous swiveling of
Snake Hips Tucker. Ellington adapted three previous pieces of his,
in abbreviated form, and created anew the rest of the work, his
longest score to date.

The composer revealed in an interview in *New Theatre* his disappointment that the producers had changed the order of the sections and had abbreviated his grand design. Referring to the *Hymn
of Sorrow*, he said he had "put into the dirge all the misery, sorrow,
and undertones of the conditions that went with the baby's death,"
and felt it was "the high spot and should have come last."

After making the soundtrack, Ellington never again performed
the score. Nonetheless, this nine-minute film stands as a milestone
in Ellington's musical and film career. The music is affecting—
revealing Ellington's growing mastery of moods—and is a pre-
cursor to later ambitious works that depict the life of African-
Americans, notably *Black, Brown and Beige.* Though he and the
band previously had starred in another remarkable short subject,
the eighteen-minute-long *Black and Tan*, its music had comprised
separate pieces. But *Symphony in Black* allowed him to compose a
more integrated suite of nine minutes' length. The latter film also
represented something of a milestone in moviemaking: it marked
the first time a motion picture attempted to integrate music with
screenplay completely and do so with absolutely no dialogue.

For six years, the Duke Ellington orchestra had enjoyed one of its
periods of greatest stability: except for a brief absence or two,
no one had left the orchestra since Bubber Miley in 1929. Since
Miley's departure, four new "chairs" had been added—three for
instrumentalists and one for the singer—but these additions were
musically positive steps for Ellington. Now, in a six-month period,
there would be several changes in the band's personnel.

During the first week of December 1934, the dynamic trumpeter
Freddie Jenkins left. He had come down with tuberculosis and was
admitted to Harlem Hospital. Jenkins's departure was a loss to
Ellington on recordings, but—considering Posey's showmanship
and tremendous popularity—an even greater loss to Ellington on

Ellington's dapper dress, handsome looks, winning smile, and personal charm all contributed to his motion picture screen presence.

the stage. Ellington, however, moved quickly to secure a replacement, and during Christmas week 1934 tapped cornetist Rex Stewart for the job. Stewart, who had been raised in a musical family in Washington, D.C., had from 1926 to 1933 performed off and on in Fletcher Henderson's orchestra. Known as a sensitive, intelligent, and urbane person, Steward made music with great power, humor, wit, versatility, individuality, even unconventionality, especially as he developed a "talking" cornet style. Stewart proved to be an even more remarkable soloist than Jenkins.

In November 1934, just before losing Jenkins, Ellington brought in a second bass player, Billy Taylor (no relation to the pianist and broadcaster of the same name), from New York. For a jazz orchestra to employ two bassists was unprecedented. Was this a ploy designed to make Braud uncomfortable and get him to resign? At forty-four, he was the oldest player in the band by four years, and it is possible that Ellington was growing restive with his slap-bass technique, which by then may have sounded dated. Or was the addition of Taylor an experiment designed to create a rhythmically richer underpinning for the orchestra? It was probably the former, but it led to the latter.

Once a second bassist was added, Mills tried to force Braud to take a 50 percent cut in pay, but when other members of the band threatened to quit, Mills backed down. But Braud was disheartened, and by March 1935 he had left the orchestra. At the end of May, Ellington brought on another bassist, Hayes Alvis, who had been playing with (Irving) Mills' Blue Rhythm Band. By now, Ellington must have seen musical possibilities in having two bassists.

But before he could reckon with musical changes, Ellington had to deal with a great personal loss. In 1934, his mother had been diagnosed with cancer. She was sent to a sanitarium in Detroit, where the family gathered around her, and on May 27, 1935, she succumbed. At her funeral, Ellington honored her with 3,000 flowers valued at over $2,000. The ingot iron casket cost $3,500, weighed 1,000 pounds, and required twelve men to carry it. "His world had been built around his mother," wrote Mercer Ellington, "and the days after her death were the saddest and most morbid of his life . . . he just sat around the house and wept for days."

"When my mother died," Ellington revealed, "the bottom dropped out. I had no ambition. Before that I'd compete with anybody." He drank heavily for a while. In his memoirs, he wrote, "After my mother passed, there was really nothing, and my sparkling parade was probably at an end." It was a loss from which he never fully recovered.

Slowly, over the summer, he pulled himself out of the gloom and began composing a piece in memory of his mother. *Reminiscing in Tempo* was the grandest piece he had yet written—occupying *four* record sides—and can be seen as an effort by Ellington to break out of the commercial realm, just as he fought to break musical barriers and limitations. "I have always been a firm believer in musical experimentation," said Ellington. "To stand still musically is equivalent to losing ground." In noting that *Reminiscing in Tempo* comprised two more sides than *Creole Rhapsody*, Ellington said that "Irving Mills had twice as much trouble with the record companies, who threatened to throw us out of the catalog!" The Ellington orchestra recorded it on September 12, 1935. That same month, while Ellington was waiting for the record to be issued, Paramount Pictures released *Symphony in Black*.

Symphony in Black and *Reminiscing in Tempo* announced to the world that Duke Ellington, the composer, was diverging in even more pronounced ways from big-band jazz of the time—moving beyond the expected, beyond the category of jazz. These works proved again that with brilliant compositions and orchestrations a jazz orchestra could express a wide variety of emotions. Breaking through more restrictions that industry and society placed upon all musicians—black and white—who worked in jazz, these works hinted that Ellington had even more interesting ideas in store for the future.

Having maintained remarkable stability among his players while increasing the orchestra's size and expressivity, Ellington had increased his—and the orchestra's—polish behind both the microphone and the proscenium, had enjoyed a string of highly successful personal appearances at home and abroad, had been given recognition as an artist and composer, and had continued his musical experimentation and growth. He was taking the musical magic he and his musicians had created in 1920s Harlem, refining it, extending its reach, and raising its levels of achievement. The ascent of Duke Ellington would continue, as would his assault on the problems he faced.

Essential Ellington, 1931–35

From the time he left the Cotton Club, through the recording of *Reminiscing in Tempo* in 1935, Ellington was expanding the orchestra (bringing back saxophonist Otto Hardwick and adding trombonist Lawrence Brown, singer Ivie Anderson, and a second bassist) and continuing to experiment with harmonies, voicings, colors, and other musical elements, and with musical forms longer than three minutes. Of the hundred or so recordings Ellington made during this period, here are nine of the most significant.

Ellington initially recorded *Creole Rhapsody* in January 1931. It was his first "extended" composition—encompassing both sides of a ten-inch 78-rpm record (over six minutes in total length). Ellington said he wrote it, at Irving Mills's prodding, in one night, and this first version (available on *The Jungle Band*, MCA) sounds underrehearsed. That June, Ellington recorded a revised version (available on *Beyond Category*, Smithsonian/BMG) on both sides of a twelve-inch 78-rpm disc (running over eight minutes). This second performance is much better, offering—besides changing moods—numerous contrasts in tempos (indicating this was definitely a piece for listening, not dancing). In both versions, Ellington experimented not only with the long form but also with asymmetrical phrase lengths and a trombone duet. A bit grandiose and not entirely integrated formally, the work perhaps does not withstand the decades as well as others discussed here. Yet in *Creole Rhapsody*, we hear Ellington the composer taking the dominant role vis-à-vis his soloists (there's little improvisation),

(continued)

and the piece marks an important step for his composing, pointing the way to his later long works.

It Don't Mean a Thing (If It Ain't Got That Swing) represents Ellington as a prophet. Having written and arranged it in August 1931, during intermissions at Chicago's Lincoln Tavern, he then recorded it in February 1932—and three years later, the word *swing* was on everyone's lips as "the swing era" was launched. The piece, wrote Ellington, became "famous as the expression of a sentiment which prevailed among jazz musicians at that time." The title had been a credo of Bubber Miley's.

Making her debut on record, Ivie Anderson demonstrates her already considerable skills in her relaxed vocal. This piece is a showcase for call and response: as baritone saxophonist Harry Carney weaves a counterpoint to Anderson's vocal, she calls out "It don't mean a thing if it ain't got that swing," and the brass answers "do-wah, do-wah, do-wah, do-wah, do-wah, do-wah, do-wah, do-wah." The recording also becomes a vehicle for Johnny Hodges's passionate, highly ornamented alto saxophone. This trademark piece can be heard on *Swing, 1930 to 1938* (ABC).

Sophisticated Lady is famous as both an instrumental and a vocal. Beginning with his first recording in 1932, Ellington preferred to perform it as an instrumental. This harmonically rich ballad, with a highly contrasting and ingenious bridge, became a vehicle for Lawrence Brown's sentimental trombone and Otto Hardwick's florid alto saxophone. The piece's authorship is disputed—Ellington, Hardwick, and Brown have all been credited. Ellington said he wrote it as a composite tribute to three high school teachers. "They taught all winter and toured Europe in the summer. To me, that was sophistication."

In 1933, lyrics by Mitchell Parish were added. "Sentimentally didactic" is how Philip Furia described them; Ellington himself called them "not entirely fitted to my original conception." Despite the lyrics' weaknesses and the

(continued)

song's difficult-to-sing bridge, other performers have made *Sophisticated Lady* a pop standard. Ellington's well-known recording from May 1933 can be heard on *Reminiscing in Tempo* (Legacy).

Trains have long held a mythic position in American life. In African-American life, they have symbolized the flight to freedom (the underground railroad) and a means of getting to a better place, whether the North or, in the gospel train, to heaven. Ellington loved traveling on trains —it stimulated his creative juices—and he used to listen to the railroad sounds on his tours of the South that began in 1933. "Duke would lie there resting," Barney Bigard said, "and listening to the trains. Those southern engineers could pull a whistle like nobody's business."

Daybreak Express represents one of the most awesome performances in the Ellington oeuvre, and arguably the greatest train-inspired piece in music. At the beginning of the piece, the train is at rest, then it gradually accelerates, picks up steam, and barrels down the track at a breathtaking pace. After three choruses, it slows down, pulls into a station, and stops with a dissonant wheeze. *Daybreak Express* not only celebrates singing rails and wailing whistles but also suggests the romance of highballin' expresses, villages whizzing by in the dark, and blues echoing in the night. Ellington built this work on the harmonies of *Tiger Rag*, but used them to make something fresh and exciting. Virtuosic as both performance and composition, *Daybreak Express,* as Gunther Schuller has observed, proved that jazz could match or surpass "anything that was being done in classical program music." The work is included on *Early Ellington* and *Beyond Category.*

Perhaps inspired by his recent trip through the South, Ellington in 1934 composed the lyrical *Delta Serenade.* Artie Whetsol's poignant trumpet states the seven-note main theme, and it is echoed by Barney Bigard's liquid clarinet and Lawrence Brown's silken trombone. By combining tight instrumental voicings and brass muting here, Ellington created sonorities

(continued)

brand new to music. The piece sounds more modern than its actual date of composition would seem to indicate, and presages Ellington's compositions of the early 1940s. Taken together with other 1930s pieces of Ellington's, *Delta Serenade* shows clearly that Ellington's music could express a far greater emotional range than could the swing music that was about to become a national craze. The piece has been reissued on *Early Ellington* and *Beyond Category*.

Symphony in Black (1934) is a musical affirmation of Ellington's roots and an affecting and memorable work. Not actually a symphony, the piece is rather a nine-minute suite of four contrasting movements that depict some of the aspects of African-American life: labor, romance, sorrow, and nightlife. He shrewdly incorporated three of his previous pieces: *Ducky Wucky, Saddest Tale,* and *Merry-Go-Round.*

Its original score was lost, but it was reconstructed and recorded in 1981 by the Smithsonian Jazz Repertory Ensemble under Gunther Schuller on the LP *Symphony in Black* (Smithsonian Recordings). The original sound track has been issued on LP by Privateer, Biograph, and Sandy Hook. Portions are available on *Reminiscing in Tempo* (Columbia).

From April 1935, *In a Sentimental Mood* offers one of Ellington's most yearning, haunting melodies. No wonder it became, with lyrics added by Manny Kurtz and Irving Mills, a popular-song standard. As with *Sophisticated Lady,* however, Ellington preferred to showcase it as an instrumental. His recording spotlights a series of soloists—Otto Hardwick on soprano saxophone, baritone-saxophonist Harry Carney, trombonist Lawrence Brown, and the new cornetist, Rex Stewart—with inventive, contrasting, and highly orchestrated underpinnings. As Gunther Schuller has observed, the uncompromising sophistication of this recording probably accounts for its lack of commercial success: ironically, Benny Goodman's and Ozzie Nelson's simpler versions became the popular ones. The composer's own *In a*

(continued)

Sentimental Mood is available on *Drop Me Off at Harlem* (The Compact Selection).

Ellington wrote *Reminiscing in Tempo* in the summer of 1935 to reflect on his beloved mother's death. He said that the manuscript was stained with his tears. The piece was a breakthrough for him—at thirteen minutes, his longest composition to date and one that integrated the various themes into a whole. Comprising both sides of two records, *Reminiscing* stands as perhaps Ellington's most complex work prior to the 1940s. He advances the experiments of *Creole Rhapsody* with asymmetrical phrase lengths (here, seven-, ten- and fourteen-measure phrases), and again leaves little space for improvisation, preferring instead to offer composed solos. The piece is striking with its lovely melodies, harmonic invention, and mood of melancholy reminiscing. The work is featured on *Reminiscing in Tempo* (Columbia).

Truckin' (1935) is a pop tune (not from Ellington's pen) that describes a popular dance step. Recorded just weeks before *Reminiscing in Tempo*, it is also something of a milestone. The band sounds much better than on recordings made three years earlier. As in the aforementioned piece, bassist Wellman Braud has been replaced by *two* bass players. Ben Webster—who in 1940 would become Ellington's first real tenor saxophone player—joins him here for this single recording session and plays a confident, bold solo that points ahead to the catalytic *Cotton Tail* of 1940. *Truckin'* is available on *Swing, 1930 to 1938*.

SIX

•

$\mathcal{S}$WINGING TO

A DIFFERENT

DRUMMER

•

1935-39

esides the loss of his mother, Ellington would have to
deal with a number of serious problems in the mid to
late 1930s—new competitors, changes in musical
tastes, and slumps in both his careers. As usual, new
problems inspired Ellington to new achievements. But
they did not come overnight. Again, he would turn in-
ward, reassess his music, and reemphasize what he did best.

The fall of 1935 was not the happiest of times for Duke Ellington.
There was still the fresh, deep pain of his mother's death, and the
uncertainty of his old friend and band member Artie Whetsol's
health. He also faced adversity in his profession. Reaction to *Reminiscing in Tempo* was mixed. Once an Ellington champion, John
Hammond now savaged his work in *Down Beat*, calling the piece
"arty" and "pretentious." The following year, he would charge that
"once this was the greatest band in the country but the bogey of
Showmanship and Art have crippled it." Only a few recognized the
integration of the solos in *Reminiscing*, the subtleties of the piece
as a tone-poem, and what it revealed about Ellington as a com-

poser. In August 1935, publicist Ned Williams left the employ of Mills Artists (he would return later), and Ellington's publicity suffered. He played many one-night dances.

Altogether, in the first year after his mother's death, Ellington made only sixteen recordings. After *Reminiscing in Tempo*, Ellington made no more records in 1935. His first session for Brunswick Records, in January 1936, was a failure: of the four pieces recorded, none was released. The latter part of 1935 was generally undistinguished, and his popularity dipped until mid 1936.

Meanwhile, late in 1935, something was in the air.

Ever since the repeal of Prohibition, nightlife in New York, as elsewhere, had been on the rebound. The United States was continuing its long, slow ascent from the depths of the Great Depression, and as it did so, there was more disposable income that could be spent on entertainment. Nightclubs became a reputable part of the urban scene and a new nightclub area had sprouted along Fifty-second Street, soon to earn the nickname "swing street." It was the home especially to soloists (Art Tatum), small groups (Fats Waller), and singers (Maxine Sullivan). And across the nation, the 1930s saw dance halls, now widely accepted as a valid social institution, enjoying their golden decade.

There was a sense that jazz and dance music were growing phenomena, where there was money to be made. In Chicago, *Down Beat* had commenced publication in July 1934 to cover the scene. The longtime musicians' magazine *Metronome* had begun publishing dance band reviews by George T. Simon in April 1935. The growing band-booking business was dominated by the Music Corporation of America (MCA), sending groups out for one-night stands at ballrooms, dance halls, and college parties.

On August 21, 1935, after a disappointing and dispiriting tour of mid-continent dance halls, a band led by the twenty-six-year-old white clarinetist Benny Goodman had opened at the capacious Palomar Ballroom in Los Angeles. At first, the audience did not respond, but then when the men went into their hard-swinging numbers such as Fletcher Henderson's *King Porter Stomp* (Goodman had hired Henderson to arrange for him after Henderson's

Benny Goodman's ascension as "King of Swing" began in the latter part of 1935. In 1938, he would record Ellington's *I Let a Song Go Out of My Heart*.

band broke up late in 1934), the crowd reacted with wild enthusiasm. Here was a group of people who had been following Goodman's music via radio. In the East, the band had come on too late at night for many listeners. But the time difference—it was three hours earlier on the West Coast—ensured Goodman a much larger audience there. Swing as a phenomenon of mass popularity began, with the arrangements of the African-American Fletcher Henderson providing the framework.

Tapping into a pent-up demand for genuinely rhythmic music, Goodman helped ignite a national craze for swing. Swing became a way of life for countless young people who sought out radio broadcasts from remote locations, followed their favorite bands, auditioned the latest records, argued the merits of soloists and leaders, trekked off to famed dance halls, queued up to see bands perform on theater stages, and generally reveled in the music.

As swing became the rage, hundreds of bands were formed to satisfy young Americans' craving for the music. By 1939, there would be an estimated two hundred professional "name" bands, employing some three thousand musicians, playing swing across the United States. Ellington could not have looked at all this new competition with welcoming feelings. His was one of the top bands in the country, probably more popular than any other black band, and topped only by a handful of white bands, including Glen Gray's and Hal Kemp's. As more and more bands competed for the public's attention, Ellington potentially had a lot to lose: public taste is fickle and Ellington surely knew it. For this and more profound reasons, as we shall see, Ellington would have an uneasy relationship with the phenomenon of swing.

Ellington was slighted in the early years of swing. His band was too old, Barry Ulanov has suggested—or, perhaps more precisely, too familiar. And also too challenging for some tastes: the Dartmouth College stringer for *Variety* reported in early 1936 that students there felt that "Ellington's weird chords have grown stale." Only new bands—like the separate bands of Tommy Dorsey and Jimmy Dorsey, formed in mid 1935—qualified as swing bands. For about eighteen months, Ellington seemed out of the limelight.

In Harlem, the orchestras of Benny Carter, Teddy Hill, Don Redman, and Charlie Johnson entertained regularly, and Chick Webb and Jimmie Lunceford crowded Ellington for the public's affection. In Chicago, Earl Hines's broadcasts from the Grand Terrace ballroom reached across the country, and Cab Calloway's group continued to tour under the auspices of Irving Mills. But the music business was increasingly dominated by white swing bands —Benny Goodman, the Dorseys—and white dance bands such as those led by Isham Jones, Ozzie Nelson, and Paul Whiteman.

Variety reported that college students preferred the white bands. "The general preference of white masses for jazz by white musicians," observed Stanley Dance, "was never altogether the result of racial prejudice. Translations, and indeed dilutions, were understandably more to their taste." It was perhaps easier for some whites to identify with white musicians as musical heroes or role models.

By 1936, publicists in Chicago had dubbed Goodman "The King of Swing." There is great irony in the fact that Fletcher Henderson, Jimmie Lunceford, Bennie Moten, and other African-American bands had been playing jazz dance music with rhythmic swing for years. Moreover, Ellington had been offering the most creative big-band music for some years before, and, through his 1932 song *It Don't Mean a Thing (If It Ain't Got That Swing)*, had probably spread the term *swing* into the everyday language. He had even been discussing swing publicly since at least May 1933, when he had told a Cleveland newspaper that his "and a few other orchestras have exploited a [jazz] style characterized by 'swing' which is Harlem for rhythm." His reaction to the Goodman press agentry was not recorded.

What was swing? Swing music, one could say, was launched by two musicians: Fletcher Henderson and Louis Armstrong.

As noted in chapter 3, Fletcher Henderson's orchestra established the fundamental big-band format and the style of arrangements that others emulated. To fill the cavernous dance halls and theaters with sound, and to create additional musical interest, the bands kept growing in size. The larger bands required more skilled orchestrations, and the arranger became increasingly crucial. The job of the arranger was to create contrast and interest with the piece by, among other devices, offering timbral and ensemble effects through the various sections of the band, highlighting the band's soloists, and in short differentiating his version from any others that competing bands might offer. Fletcher Henderson employed arrangers Don Redman, Benny Carter, his brother Horace Henderson, as well as himself; Chick Webb had Edgar Sampson; Benny Goodman used Fletcher Henderson (after the latter's band folded late in 1934) and Edgar Sampson; Jimmie Lunceford had Sy Oliver; Count Basie played many "head" arrangements, and occasionally written-out arrangements by Jimmy Mundy, Herschel Evans, Buster Smith, and Andy Gibson. It was the era when the arranger became in some ways paramount, and the arrangements were written, in part, to feature the many brilliant soloists active then.

Above all else, what separated swing from previous jazz was rhythm. Louis Armstrong's rhythmic innovations loosened up the beat of jazz, provided a greater variety of rhythms, and made its momentum more flowing. Between 1930 and 1935, the rhythm of jazz was transformed through the influence of Armstrong, from whom musicians learned to elasticize the beat. In its most original and most fundamental sense, "to swing" means to play with that perceptible forward momentum, the propulsive rhythmic quality that is found in much African-rooted music. It is a looseness, almost an elasticity of the pulse. Ellington would tell an interviewer in 1939 that "swing is not a kind of music. It is that part of rhythm that causes a bouncing, buoyant, terpsichorean urge."

The change in rhythm was furthered when the plodding tuba was replaced as keeper of a two-to-the-bar beat by the fleeter string bass, which enabled an even, flowing feel of four to the bar. Also, the banjo was abandoned in favor of the guitar, and drummers shifted the fundamental pulse from the drum itself to the high-hat cymbal. These changes made the music feel less staccato and jerky, more long lined, forward moving, and, well, swinging.

Other bands began to follow the trend that Paul Whiteman and Ellington had helped set: hiring featured vocalists. In the 1930s, Goodman offered Helen Ward, Basie had Jimmy Rushing, Chick

In the 1930s, one of the most popular dance steps was the lindy hop, which whites called the jitterbug.

Webb featured Ella Fitzgerald, Earl Hines engaged Billy Eckstine, Harry James employed Frank Sinatra, and Artie Shaw presented Helen Forrest and Billie Holiday. At its essence, however, swing was instrumental music. "In the middle and late thirties," wrote Barry Ulanov, "swing lost its standing as a verb and was elevated to the stature of a noun and a category. Jazz was dead, long live swing."

Public dancing was by now a part of courtship rituals. For many young people, swing music and dancing were important emotional outlets; while for others, they offered escape from the economic difficulties of the lingering depression. Swinging your partner into mutual happiness and momentary forgetfulness, you could stomp your blues away. While the music's time surged forward, paradoxically, real-world time seemed to stop. Ears flooded with irresistible melodies and intoxicating rhythms, skin flushed with excitement, perspiration, and perhaps desire, and pulses pounding, the dancers lindy-hopped, big-appled, susy-qued, shagged, and shim-shammed the nights, and their cares, away. If ballrooms had won public acceptance in the 1920s, and offered a diversion from the depression of the early 1930s, now in the late 1930s, they achieved an all-time popularity.

Depending on the venue, listeners and dancers created an explosion in the popularity of jukeboxes, on which Ellington's music, and swing, could increasingly be heard. The number of jukeboxes in the United States jumped from 25,000 in 1933 to 300,000 in 1939, by then consuming 13 million discs a year. Spurred on by the recovering economy, the phonograph, the jukebox boom, the new low-priced (thirty-five-cent) discs issued by upstart Decca and others, and the craze for swing music, the record industry climbed to recovery. From a low of 6 million discs sold in 1933, sales surged to 33 million in 1938, and 127 million in 1941.

Especially in the swing era, the competition between bands took on the aspects of rivalry between great athletic teams. Bands attracted ardent followers, orchestras engaged in sometimes epic band battles, black newspapers and jazz magazines ran readers' polls to select the top groups.

One reason that swing drew so many passionate adherents was the depth of its meaning. Martin Williams has put it this way:

For I think that in evolving this musical art of the Swing Era, the American black man did what he so often does in his best music. He denied nothing, not the pain, not the anger, not the frustration—and not the joy and not the pride. For the music faces all the realities of being, including the reality that affirms for him that no matter what his circumstances do to him and how he is treated, he is a man. I will not succumb, the music says. I will stay in touch with my essential humanity. And I will survive as a man. This essential affirmation that the black American found through his music in the 1930s held a deep meaning for many. And for many of us, I think, it affirmed the human spirit.

And it affirmed the joy of sound, movement, and dance at a time when the country was still struggling to come out of the Great Depression.

What about Ellington and swing? In some obvious ways he was part of swing: he shared with the swing bands a similar instrumentation, employed a singer, played pop songs and original instrumentals, and performed rhythmic music typically for dancing.

But overall, Ellington operated in an artistic sphere different from swing's. One aspect that set Ellington apart was his drummer. In swing bands generally the drummer kept the time and drove the band—for instance, the great Jo Jones in the Count Basie band, Chick Webb in his own orchestra. Sonny Greer took a different course; he was less a driver of the band than a master colorist, with his subtle brush and tasteful stick work and novel use of percussive effects. Ellington never wrote out drum parts: Greer relied on visual cues, trial and error, his ear, intuition, and taste. A creative player of cymbals, he eschewed the flashy drum solos of a Gene Krupa or a Buddy Rich and never overpowered singers or the band. John Hammond called him "the most intricate of all *percussionists*." In addition to a different role for the drummer, no other band of the period had two bass players to increase harmonic and rhythmic interest.

Unlike most other bandleaders, Ellington was not interested primarily in establishing a good beat for dancing. He wanted to explore his musical imagination as a composer: melodies, harmonies, tonal colors, moods, emotions—these were his focal points. In contrast to Goodman, Basie, Lunceford, Webb, the Dorseys, and Bob Crosby, Ellington was not merely a gifted instrumentalist and band-

From 1934 to 1938, Ellington employed two bassists to provide a stronger and richer rhythmic and harmonic foundation. Shown in this 1936 photo from Chicago's Congress Hotel are Ellington's "rhythm section": (clockwise from top) Fred Guy, Billy Taylor, Sonny Greer, and Hayes Alvis.

Cornetist Rex Stewart joined
the orchestra in 1934 and became
known for his unusual, vocallike
inflections on his instrument,
achieved in part by depressing the
valves halfway down.

leader. He was the supreme composer and orchestrator for the medium of the jazz orchestra. His music expressed a far greater range of emotions than did the other bands, employed more sensitive dynamics and more of a sense of theater than most, featured the most distinctive players and most varied sounds and colors, experimented and innovated much more than anyone else, was less prone to fads, and presented far more original (and more challenging) pieces, particularly on records, than the other bands, whose staple tended to be pop tunes of the day. Ellington's ongoing problem was to find a workable balance between art and popularity.

Even the best of the other big bands suffer a certain sameness if their recordings are listened to one after the other; but Ellington's recordings, taken together, offer variety, contrast, and even surprise. The Duke Ellington orchestra predated the swing craze by a decade, helped in fact to foster it, popularized its catch phrase, and provided its highest benchmarks of originality.

Rex Stewart put it this way: After some months with Ellington, he found that "slowly the picture started to emerge. Not only did I perceive vast new vistas in music, but, to my amazement, an entire new spectrum of emotional experiences unfolded. . . . I'd been with other big and important groups [like Fletcher Henderson's], but never before or since has there been the camaraderie, the glamor, the excitement of creativity, and a time when so many new doors of experience were opened to us. We played music such as had never been heard before." In recognition, the influential French jazz critic Hugues Panassié devoted an entire chapter of his pioneering book *Hot Jazz*, first published in English in 1936, to Ellington.

Ellington benefited from the increased interest in swing, yet, despite his unmatched genius, saw many other bands, especially white ones, zoom past him in popularity and recompense. No wonder he once said, "Jazz is music; swing is business."

Ellington grew restive with both labels, "jazz" and "swing." By the late 1930s, he was preferring to call his art "Negro music." Rex Stewart later observed, "By his refusing to be placed in any particular category, he could stand above his contemporaries and feel free to give whatever he chose to give of his fertile imagination, not on a competitive basis but more in the manner of a god descending from Olympian heights. And why not? He had removed himself. Let the world catch up." Ellington's music exceeded the conventions, accomplishments, and boundaries of swing; gradually and increasingly, in fact, no single musical category could contain Ellington.

But in the short run, swing may have meant something of a drop in popularity and income. In some ways, the dip gave Ellington the composer even freer rein to experiment.

In 1936, Ellington had no real hits and made relatively few records. He introduced, however, two new musical ideas, each in its way designed to highlight his musicians' individual contributions. The first concept, which he brought out in January 1936 (a sign that he was coming out of the slump after his mother's death), was to write showpieces for some of his top players. Two of Ellington's most exciting recordings of the decade were made on this principle: *Echoes of Harlem* and *Clarinet Lament*. Feature numbers for Cootie Williams and Barney Bigard, respectively, these pieces were quite a departure: the typical work at that time featured perhaps half a dozen soloists. While these pieces were not constructed in the classical European concerto form, they had the same purpose —to show off a specific instrument and the talents of the person playing it. These "concertos" proved successful and later Ellington wrote more showcases for Williams and Bigard, as well as Johnny Hodges (*Jeep's Blues*, 1938), Lawrence Brown (*Yearning for Love*, 1936), and Rex Stewart. The latter took the spotlight in *Trumpet in Spades* (1936) and the slower *Boy Meets Horn* (1938), which became famous for the bent-note effects Stewart achieved by playing with his cornet valves half depressed.

Meanwhile, Ellington was developing his second major new idea of the period 1935–39: to pioneer the jazz equivalent of chamber music—making a series of recordings of sextets, octets, and nonets drawn from his fifteen-player orchestra. He had made his first two such records, as the Duke Ellington Sextet, on March 5, 1935. Then, perhaps inspired by Ellington's example, Benny Goodman had recorded his trio (himself, his band's drummer Gene Krupa, and one non-band member, the African-American pianist Teddy Wilson) in July 1935, and Tommy Dorsey his Dixieland-style Clambake Seven (the players drawn from his big band) in December of that year.

In the meantime, fate brought Ellington together with a young woman who would play a pivotal role in his small-group ventures. While Ellington was touring the central and eastern parts of the nation, playing one-night dances and weeklong theatrical engagements, Goodman was enjoying a highly successful seven-month engagement at the Urban Room of Chicago's Congress Hotel. During this period, Helen Oakley, a former Toronto debutante and now a writer on jazz (later she would marry the jazz critic Stanley Dance), was promoting Goodman, helping to organize Sunday-afternoon jazz concerts at the Urban Room, and writing about Ellington, among others, for the fledgling *Down Beat* and other jazz magazines.

Following Goodman, the Ellington orchestra played the Urban Room from May 8 through June 5, 1936, during which time it was heard two or three times a night on local radio, and twice weekly on the NBC network. These broadcasts broke something of a drought for radio fans of Ellington. For the last two years, Ellington was rarely heard on national radio, which the *Afro-American* newspaper implied had unfairly held him back at a time when many white bands were heard throughout the nation.

"Here is a very bright young thing," Ellington declared to Irving Mills about Oakley. "Latch onto her." He did, and she worked for him on and off for six years, becoming his jazz specialist and a member of the Ellington circle. About then, Mills was acquiring Brunswick's old recording studio and establishing his own record labels: Master would be the full-priced label (seventy-five cents), and Variety the budget line (thirty-five cents), targeted especially at black audiences and the jukebox market. Mills insisted that the Ellington orchestra record on Master, but he also needed "product" for the cheaper line. Oakley pestered Mills into agreeing to record small groups from within the Ellington band on the cheaper Variety label, and into allowing her to produce the recordings.

In December 1936, Ellington began a series of small-group record dates, under the nominal leadership of Cootie Williams, Rex Stewart, Barney Bigard, or Johnny Hodges—the man who was by now Ellington's leading soloist and biggest star, and whose name most often appeared on these records. Ellington, however, played on all the dates, probably selected the players and the tunes, and took the lead in collectively working out arrangements during the recording sessions. Making these band-within-a-band recordings may have appealed to Ellington for three reasons: for the opportunity to make some extra money; for a way to keep his star soloists happy; and for the musical variety and interest, perhaps even challenge. He was master of the jazz-orchestra idiom; why not explore a different medium?

Within two years of starting the series for Variety, the Ellingtonians would cut more than 60 records. By the time of the last session in the series, on September 29, 1941, they would make a total of nearly 140 recordings. Overall, these recordings were commercially successful; some, such as Hodges's *Jeep's Blues* from 1938, became jukebox hits.

While the Ellington small bands ranged between six and nine instrumentalists, typically they had seven. These records superbly balanced improvised solos with scored parts and—despite similar personnel on each date—presented the individual session leaders to very good advantage. While many of the early records are marred by inappropriate vocalists foisted on the band by Mills, some of these recordings live on as among the most enduring small-band jazz of the swing era.

Ellington in 1937.

By the end of 1936, Ellington's band was not winning any band polls (Goodman, Glen Gray, Jimmy Dorsey, and Jimmie Lunceford came in ahead of him for "Best Swing Band" in *Metronome*'s 1936 poll) but Ellington demonstrated in a couple of loose, swinging, jam-sessionlike pieces—*In a Jam* and *Uptown Downbeat*—that his band could swing with the best of them.

Mills and Ellington, both shrewd businessmen in their ways, knew how to keep the musicians in the Ellington orchestra happy. Mills saw to it that Ellington and the band continued to be treated well on their travels, and at year's end, Mills and Ellington rolled out the largesse for the players. Rex Stewart recalled one year receiving a $100 bill and a handsome personalized wallet. And in December 1936, in what must have been a rare honor for an African-American musician at the time, Ellington was presented the keys to the city by Mayor Shaw of Los Angeles.

During the following year, 1937, Ellington experienced some modest gains as well as several more losses. Swing in general and Benny Goodman in particular were given a well-publicized boost on March 3, when Goodman opened at the Paramount Theater in New York. The Paramount's admission of only thirty-five cents made Goodman, who had been playing mostly rather expensive hotel rooms, accessible to New York youngsters, and they responded enthusiastically. By 10 A.M., some 4,400 fans were standing in line to buy tickets. The band caused a sensation—there was a near riot —and it was held over three weeks. There was a bigger market for swing than most had realized.

Beginning early in 1937, the Columbia Broadcasting System— CBS Radio—offered a new series called *Saturday Night Swing Session*, and Ellington performed on three different occasions. In a widely reprinted article, the classical music composer and critic Deems Taylor credited Ellington and Guy Lombardo as "being the first orchestra leaders to determine the scientific possibilities of the microphone in radio broadcasting."

On March 17, 1937, Ellington returned to the Cotton Club, now relocated downtown at 200 West Forty-eighth Street, at Broadway, about a block south of the Kentucky Club. The original Cotton Club in Harlem had closed on February 16, 1936, the victim of a fall-off in business following the riot by black residents of Harlem in March 1935. This time the show, *The Cotton Club Parade, Second Edition*, had a huge cast including Ethel Waters, singer George Dewey Washington, shake dancer Bessie Dudley, and others. Waters and Ellington got top billing, followed by the tap-dancing Nicholas Brothers and Washington. Dudley shook to *Rockin' in Rhythm*, the exotic dancer Kaloah wriggled to *Black and Tan Fantasy*, but overall there was relatively little of Ellington in the show—except for his dance music at intermission and a medley of his hits, which became an obligatory part of his shows from then on. He was heard on twice-weekly broadcasts via WOR and the Mutual radio network. Ellington performed at the club through June 15. He had been out of the limelight for some time, and the Cotton Club show —received with raves by the critics—brought him back in a big way.

Ellington was always very image conscious—during stage show engagements he insisted the band change wardrobe several times a day and he expected exacting scrim and lighting for his shows— and this Cotton Club revue was visually memorable, as Rex Stewart recalled:

The Ellington orchestra at a recording session, ca. 1937. Seated, from left: Sonny Greer, Rex Stewart, Artie Whetsol, Fred Guy, Cootie Williams, Harry Carney, Tricky Sam Nanton, Otto Hardwick, Lawrence Brown, Juan Tizol, Johnny Hodges, Barney Bigard. Standing, from left: Billy Taylor, Duke Ellington.

The governor, as Duke was called by the guys in the band, had out-done himself in outfitting the band for this one. When we appeared on stage the audience gasped and applauded. We wore white mess jackets, boiled tuxedo shirts with wing collars, white bow-ties above crimson trousers and crimson shoes. . . . And of course the Duke personified elegance and contrast in his sombre midnight tails.

Ellington composed another extended work in September 1937 that occupied both sides of a 78-rpm record. The companion pieces *Crescendo in Blue* and *Diminuendo in Blue* are ambitious, difficult to perform, and like *Reminiscing in Tempo*, allow little room for improvisation. "Like all of our compositions," Ellington wrote in the *Chicago Defender*, " 'Blues Crescendo' and 'Blues Dimin-uendo' concern themselves with capturing and revealing the emo-tional spirit of the race. That is why so many white musicians find them difficult to understand and in several cases, meaningless." Along with the exotic *Caravan*, cocomposed with Juan Tizol, and the dulcet *Azure*, these were Ellington's most exceptional orchestra recordings of 1937. *Caravan* demonstrates Tizol's greatest contri-bution to the Ellington orchestra—his very personal tone, which Ellington exploited especially to create a Latin, Middle Eastern, or other exotic mood. *Caravan* became something of a hit and in rec-ognition of its popularity earned a quarterly award from the Amer-ican Society of Composers, Authors, and Publishers (ASCAP), to which Ellington gained membership in 1935.

But that fall Ellington experienced another personal loss. By the summer of 1937, the drinking problem that J. E. Ellington had developed years earlier had gotten out of hand and he headed for the Catskill Mountains for a cure, but it failed. He entered Colum-bia Presbyterian Hospital in New York for pleurisy and died on October 28. He was buried at Harmony Cemetery in Washington next to his wife. (Later the cemetery was closed and the caskets transferred to Woodlawn Cemetery in the Bronx.)

This was a very difficult time for Ellington, according to his son, Mercer: Duke had been having problems paying his parents' med-ical bills and owed people sums of money (he borrowed money from some and also took advances on his song royalties to keep the band going). On occasion the band would offer its own dance; these were a gamble—sometimes they paid off, sometimes they didn't. Renting the three railroad cars for touring transportation was expensive, too, especially when the band played in one town for a week, and the cars just sat on a siding.

While at the Cotton Club in 1937, Ellington had befriended a physician named Arthur C. Logan, whose friendship became close, constant, and enduring and helped fill some of the aching void left by the death of Ellington's parents. The older, able Logan became, in the words of his widow, "Edward's closest friend and his physician for thirty-seven years. They had a unique, incredible, unexplainable friendship." In later years Logan—who would also serve as physician to Martin Luther King, Jr.—would usually come to Ellington's side, even on international tours, if called.

After both parents were gone, Ellington took an even stronger interest in his younger sister, Ruth, acting as provider and, in effect, father. He was stern and very protective of her, and the only way she was allowed to go to Paris, in the summer of 1938, to continue her language studies at the Sorbonne, was with a chaperone sent by her brother.

Meanwhile, Artie Whetsol's health was getting worse, and in February of 1938, he left the band because a brain tumor had advanced to the point where he was having mental problems. Ellington had now lost his three earliest trumpeters—Bubber Miley, Freddie Jenkins, and Arthur Whetsol—because of physical impairments. The loss of Whetsol was especially keen as Ellington had been associated with him longer than with anyone else in the orchestra, dating back to the late 1910s in Washington. His sensitive playing would be dearly missed by many.

When Whetsol retired, according to Mercer, Ellington also retired a number of Whetsol's feature pieces. But Ellington had no choice but to maintain one of Whetsol's top numbers—*Mood Indigo*—even though, according to the younger Ellington, playing the high D note and sustaining it "haunted trumpet players for many years . . . to the extent that they never wanted to play the lead part." To replace Whetsol, Ellington chose Wallace Jones, who is little known today partly because Ellington, blessed with Cootie Williams and Rex Stewart, did not give Jones much solo space.

Ellington also faced new African-American competition. In 1936, at John Hammond's behest, Count Basie had brought his band from Kansas City to New York. By 1938, it would become champion of the hotly competitive Harlem ballrooms, edging out the orchestras of Ellington, Chick Webb, and Jimmie Lunceford. Basie's rocking Kansas City rhythm, his terrific soloists, extraordinary rhythm section, and emphasis on freewheeling "head" (unwritten) arrangements where a player could blow for several choruses were keys to his success. But above all, his beat was irresistible to dancers.

In 1938, swing took on new legitimacy as staid Carnegie Hall hosted one of a few jazz concerts in its history to then. The January 16, 1938, event featured Goodman's orchestra, with Count Basie's also on the bill. Whether it was for the publicity or to keep several of his stars happy, Ellington allowed Cootie Williams, Harry Carney, and Johnny Hodges to perform as part of the Goodman quartet's jam session.

Ellington reportedly had been invited to participate, but declined. It was Goodman's concert, and Ellington probably did not want to get second billing; or he may not have wanted to be categorized as swing, or lumped together with groups that operated on an aesthetic level different from his.

Yet head-to-head contests with other swing bands gave Ellington's players a boost. Later that night, Ellington attended a battle at the Savoy Ballroom between the bands of Basie and Webb. Ellington was willing to participate in band battles. While swinging the rhythm was not the Ellingtonians' raison d'être or even their forte, they could swing when they really wanted to—especially in the heat of a band battle. As Mercer Ellington wrote of his father, "His was a band that did not always play well together, but when its reputation was at stake the guys knew they had what it took to wipe out the competition. That was what would happen when it got involved in a battle of music. It was one of the few to overcome the valiant Chick Webb's band at the Savoy, and it triumphed over

Ellington jams in 1938 with the hunchbacked drummer Chick Webb and clarinetist Artie Shaw.
Stanley Dance, who would later become an aide-de-camp to Ellington,
is the tall man in the center of the back row.

Jimmie Lunceford's in its heyday." When Ellington's forces met
Webb's on March 7, 1937, the crowd of 3,100 they drew reportedly
set a record for the Savoy. On December 26, 1938, Ellington and
Lunceford met in a heated "battle of swing." Playing largely for
white college students in Philadelphia, the two pulled out all their
best polish, arrangements, and crowd-pleasers. By the *Chicago
Defender*'s account, Ellington emerged victorious—evidently by
playing a wider variety of music—jungle, sweet, and swing. But
the Lunceford men were generous in their praise, saying, "Those
guys are the Babe Ruths, Charlie Gehringers, Ty Cobbs, and Joe
DiMaggios of 'swing.' "

Since at least 1933, there had been announcements in the press
that Ellington would play Carnegie Hall, and now reports stated

he'd play there in the spring. But this announcement, too, would prove premature.

Ellington was, however, playing more concerts in his homeland than ever before. He had been performing the occasional American concert since 1930 and was thus one of the pioneers in jazz concerts. Before jazz concerts themselves, radio simulated what Albert Murray has called "a concert hall without walls . . . listeners huddled around radios all over the nation." Then, during the period 1935 to 1945, the face-to-face jazz concert was becoming established as part of American culture.

On May 29, 1938, the Ellington orchestra participated in a "Carnival of Swing"—really a big-band festival—on Randall's Island, organized by the WNEW personality Martin Block. Around 25,000 people went to hear the twenty-some orchestras. Primed by other bands, the crowd was wildly enthusiastic over Ellington's; even the reviewer from the stuffy *New York Times* caught the infectious spirit. One of the pieces that Ellington performed was his new *Diminuendo and Crescendo in Blue*. Scheduled to play two numbers, he was compelled by the crowd to play five numbers and three encores.

By mid 1938, swing was a big business. Some of the smaller booking agencies were eyeing the Music Corporation of America with fear, Mills was boosting his attention to the band business, and the earnings of certain black bands—especially Ellington's, Calloway's, and Armstrong's—were arousing the interest of some of the biggest agencies.

Ellington's tenth show at the Cotton Club began on Thursday March 10, 1938, in a revue called *Cotton Club Parade, Fourth Edition*. Ellington now received top billing: for the first time since *Blackberries of 1930*, he had written the score. He may well have been seeking a song hit, but ironically, the one that came out of the engagement—*I Let a Song Go Out of My Heart*—was dropped from the show itself, at Mills's urging. So Ellington played it during his regular radio broadcasts from the club, heard on WABC and the CBS network, and by one accounting it became one of his best-selling records ever. One of the sensations in the *Cotton Club Pa-*

rade was the "band feature," *Braggin' in Brass*, a virtuosic piece with a trio of interlocking, rapid-fire trombone notes that is still astonishing. The show was well received by critics, but it would be Ellington's final appearance at the Cotton Club, which would close for good in June 1940.

If 1937 had been a thin year for memorable recordings, 1938 picked up considerably. Besides *Braggin' in Brass*, that year the Ellingtonians produced two reworkings of his 1927 classic *Black and Tan Fantasy*, not to mention the popular-song hit *Prelude to a Kiss*, the timely *Battle of Swing*, and the "mood" piece *Blue Light*. *I Let a Song Go Out of My Heart* topped the list of popular songs for August, as compiled by ASCAP, and the *Chicago Defender* reported that month that recordings of it "have already reached the million mark." The small-group recording of *Jeep's Blues*, made in 1938, was creating audience excitement; at a performance at Kansas City's Roseland Ballroom, according to the *Chicago Defender*, *Jeep's Blues* "about brought the ceiling from the house." The band was recording more frequently now and produced more memorable records. The departure of Hayes Alvis, one of two bassists in the band, about early June did not seem to hold Ellington or the band back, and Ellington did not replace him. From then on, there would normally be just one bass player.

In the late 1930s, the jam session became popular among swing musicians. Ellington had strong reservations, however, about the way most musicians improvised, writing in 1937 that

> free improvisation, or "jamming," is a frankenstein that may destroy its parent, jazz.
>
> Jamming, which is the fundamental of modern swing, is an innocuous, even useful thing—when it is properly scored and played to heighten the rhythmic effect. Under such conditions jamming might even be the means of making modern jazz an enduring thing.
>
> But, unfortunately, jamming is treated like a new toy. The majority of jazz musicians have not learned to harness it, to put it in its place. Instead, they jam recklessly, indiscriminately. And it is this indiscriminate jamming that is the great banality of modern jazz.

Here is a composer writing. Not only does he seem to be calling for more discipline and forethought in improvising but perhaps even for scoring—that is, writing down the improvisations. This may seem contradictory, but in fact it was an important part of his method as a composer.

Ellington created many compositions based on a riff or phrase Johnny Hodges or one of his other players might toss off. As Stanley Dance has written, "Many a popular song grew out of a phrase improvised during a jazz solo, and few soloists were as prodigal of such phrases as Hodges. 'He has a million of 'em,' Ellington admiringly remarked as Hodges casually furnished the riffs for an impromptu studio blues." Moreover, some of Ellington's pieces, by his own declaration, were created communally, at least until the late 1930s. In 1937, he wrote that some of his numbers

> were composed almost by unanimous inspiration while the orchestra was gathered together for a practice session. New ideas are merged at each meeting, and each man contributes to the offerings of the other. . . . The name "Duke Ellington" is synonymous with "The Duke Ellington Orchestra."

Ellington's use of his players' melodic ideas became a bone of contention for some of his men—especially Hodges. "Every time Duke would take a few notes that were Johnny's," Helen Dance recalled, "Johnny would clear his throat and give him one of his looks out of the side of his eye, and Duke knew that Johnny figured this was a hundred dollars." At a December 1938 record date that produced a piece called *Hodge Podge* (credited to Ellington and Hodges), wrote Gary Giddins, "Hodges addressed to his leader an admonition that would become one of the taciturn saxophonist's trademarks. 'Come out of the kitchen,' he said, his phrase for 'Stop stealing my stuff.' " Rex Stewart, on the other hand, asserted that "we all brought bits and pieces of songs to the boss, maybe 16 bars, maybe only four, and then Duke added, changed or embellished, so really the finished product bore his stamp."

A comparison of music Ellington wrote for his players with the original recordings reveals that in some cases Ellington composed the solos for his players, solos that *sounded* improvised. He knew his musicians' styles so intimately that he could write a solo passage for, say, Bigard that sounded not only idiomatic to the great clarinetist but also fresh and spontaneous. Because the band used written music as little as possible, the audiences probably thought many of these prescribed passages were made up on the spot.

This revelation may surprise some longtime Ellington listeners, and it may seem, at first blush, to diminish the brilliance of some of the solos. A great solo, however, is a great solo, whether written out or created extemporaneously, whether played largely the same way time after time or played once and never heard again. This discovery does, on the other hand, suggest a higher valuation of Ellington's composing genius than some in recent years—for example, the biographer James Lincoln Collier—have been willing to concede him.

As a composer, Ellington seems to have done his best work when he was inspired by a mood or an image. He once said, "The memory of things gone is important to a jazz musician. Things like old folks singing in the moonlight in the back yard on a hot night or something someone said long ago." Mercer Ellington said, "He always wrote what he felt. I don't think he ever wrote in contrast to his mood. The only time he was off guard was in his music. The happy tunes were written during happy days and the sad things were written when he was feeling sad."

Ellington had long been a cultural hero to many African-Americans. In December 1937, he was named to the newly formed Negro Actors Guild, an essentially honorary post. In February 1939, the NAACP featured for its annual ball in New York City the Duke Ellington orchestra, which drew a record crowd of 12,000 people.

Besides the originality, quality, and emotional expressiveness of his music, Ellington gave African-Americans other reasons to look up to him: the way he maintained his integrity despite many pressures to do otherwise, his seeming financial success, and his poise, elegance, and dignity. When he was seventeen, in 1939, the photographer and writer Gordon Parks eagerly sought Ellington's autograph upon first meeting him.

Ellington had always been my hero. Unlike . . . black Hollywood stereotypes he never grinned, he smiled; he never shuffled, he strode. It was always, "Good evening, ladies and gentleman"; never "How y'all doing?" At his performances we young blacks sat high in our seats, wanting the whites to see us; to know that this handsome, elegant, sharply dressed man playing that beautiful, sophisticated music, was one of us.

And many African-Americans may have been proud of the way he continued to break through racial barriers—a result of his music, charm, and theatrical flair, and Irving Mills's efforts on his behalf. In November 1936, for instance, Ellington played a week at the Chez Maurice, reportedly the first black band to play an extended engagement at a downtown Dallas nightclub; his became the first black band to play, according to the *Chicago Defender*, "in a large Austin hotel for the elite of the state," and it was the first black orchestra to perform on the campus of the University of Texas at Austin.

In early February 1937, Ellington played for the President's Birthday Ball at the exclusive Hotel Oakland, about which the *Chicago Defender* proudly reported: "Over 8,000 of the elite of white society from the bay cities packed into the elaborate ballroom and many thousands more listened to the music broadcast from the band shell." In December 1937, the Ellingtonians played the Orpheum Theatre in Memphis, again, according to the *Defender*, "the first time a Race attraction ever played to a white audience of this kind here."

As a composer he was also reaching broader audiences through radio. Not only were his compositions being successfully recorded by his band and others but they were also being played as theme songs on more radio programs than those of any other composer. ASCAP found that "Ellington's melodies are heard as themes on 37 radio shows: 'Mood Indigo' on 16; 'Sophisticated Lady' on 12, and 'In a Sentimental Mood' on 9."

Yet, ironically, at the same time that white society was soaking in his music, leading magazines were hailing him, and the entertainment world was eagerly embracing his work, he could not eat in most American restaurants or secure a room in most hotels.

Once asked his reaction, he responded, "I took the energy it takes to pout and wrote some blues."

In the latter part of 1938, as Ellington came in sight of his fortieth birthday, he began to make a series of changes in his personal life, business affairs, and orchestra. During his Cotton Club engagement early in 1938, he had met an employee named Beatrice Ellis, whom everyone called Evie. Mercer Ellington described her as "a beautiful woman among a lot of beautiful women. . . . Evie was not a chorus girl, but one of those who walked and stood around and posed in beautiful gowns." She lived on St. Nicholas Place, and soon Ellington moved in with her and never went back to 381 Edgecombe Avenue. As when he left Edna for Mildred Dixon, he again left behind all his clothes. Soon there was a fire in Evie's

Evie Ellis, with whom Ellington fell in love in 1939, models a gown for a Cotton Club show.

apartment building, and by early 1939, they moved into an apartment at 935 St. Nicholas Avenue, where they would live until 1953.

When Ellington went off with Evie, Mercer and Ruth were still living with Mildred Dixon at 381 Edgecombe. They knew he would not return, so they moved out, to 409 Edgecombe, leaving the furniture with Mildred. By this time, Mercer was in high school and Ruth was at Columbia University Teachers College.

If Ellington's personal relationships were not always constant, by 1938 he had learned the value of good relations with the press. According to Mercer, he had learned in the Washington poolrooms how to manipulate people, and, from Mills, how to "handle situations of every kind." Ellington knew how to get into the press and how to stay out of it: he fed some reporters stories; he took out expensive ads in the trade press so they would not run bad publicity and fear losing a client. Some people were even paid off to remain quiet. Through these means, word of Ellington's abandoning his wife for extramarital relationships first with Mildred Dixon and then with Evie Ellis remained out of the press for decades.

Soon came an upheaval in Ellington's relationship with Irving Mills. One day, according to one report, Ellington asked to see Mills's books. He walked into the office, opened them, studied them for a while, and left without a word. Ellington had asked Mills to buy an expensive casket, worth $5,000, for his mother's funeral back in 1935. But, according to the story, Mills had bought a cheaper model. That was it; Ellington broke with Mills.

The two swapped their stock: Ellington gave up his share in Mills's publishing company in exchange for control of Duke Ellington, Inc. Ellington never commented publicly on why he split with Mills. It could have been the casket incident or something else Ellington spotted in the books, or lack of attention because of Mills's widening business interests. Or it might have been restlessness, or a desire to take more control of his affairs, or criticism in the black press over his relationship with the impresario. Harlem's Rev. Adam Clayton Powell, Jr., who later served in the United States Congress, railed that "Duke Ellington is just a musical sharecropper." And the *Pittsburgh Courier* complained, "No Negro writer has written the lyrics for any of Duke Ellington's melodies since he has been under the Mills banner. What's the matter,

Duke? House rules?" Mercer Ellington implied that his father no longer needed Mills: he said that Mills had taught Ellington the business and Ellington "grew up."

Even in his candid interviews with music critic and composer Carter Harman in the 1950s and 1960s, Ellington did not discuss his split with Mills. While Mills's fairness and honesty may have been a factor, it probably was not money itself that precipitated Ellington's shift in management—he seems to have been more interested in living and traveling in first-class fashion than in money per se. "There is no point now in debating who profited more from the association," Mercer wrote, "but it's clear that Irving served Ellington well in the formative stages of his career." The maestro wrote, "He had always preserved the dignity of my name. Duke Ellington had an unblemished image, and that is the most anybody can do for anybody."

Ellington now needed a new booking agent, and in April, he signed with the William Morris Agency, which had recently hired the crack band agent Willard Alexander away from the behemoth Music Corporation of America. Ned Williams was by now also with Morris, having left Mills, and he may have played a role in bringing Ellington on board. Soon, a young fellow named Cress Courtney took over from Alexander the day-to-day handling of Ellington.

Ellington made still another change. His music would no longer be published by Mills Music; he signed a three-year agreement with Jack Robbins, for whom he and Jo Trent had written the revue *Chocolate Kiddies* back in 1925.

In less than a year, Ellington would also sever his relationship with his record company, the Columbia/Brunswick/Vocalion combine. (Columbia had taken over Master and Variety records.) In January 1939, John Hammond was put in charge of jazz records at Columbia, and Ellington probably was uncomfortable. Ellington took his dismay with Hammond—and other critics—public in articles in the April and May 1939 issues of *Down Beat*, charging that by continuing to publish jazz criticism while producing records, Hammond had skewed his objectivity and entered into a conflict of interest. In addition to his growing antipathy to Hammond, Ellington may have been drawn to his new label, Victor, because it was better established.

. . .

Before their split, Mills arranged a return to Europe for the orchestra; and Ellington, who had long wanted to replay the continent, went along with the plans. The threat of war was everywhere by 1939; no one knew what would come next. The band left amid not only war jitters but controversy in the press. The American and British musicians' unions had been locked in a dispute, and until the end of the tour, no one was sure if Ellington's band would be allowed to play in England.

The orchestra set sail from New York on March 23, on the *Champlain*, with Ellington, thirteen instrumentalists, and singer Ivie Anderson. When the party landed in Le Havre seven days later, according to *Down Beat*, "hundreds of jitterbugs stomped and shouted at the dock." Rex Stewart recalled the scene and feeling: "There were a lot of people from all over France to meet us, members of the various 'hot clubs,' both fans and musicians, who all greeted us with such absolute adoration and genuine joy that for the first time in my life I had the feeling of being accepted as an artist, a gentleman and a member of the human race."

Again in Europe, Ellington and the orchestra were taken seriously as artists. The most significant aspect of his 1939 tour was that it gave Ellington a chance to perform almost exclusively for listeners. With the exception of one stage show, these were *concerts*—his most extensive concert circuit since his first European tour in 1933.

After holding a press conference in Paris, the orchestra played two concerts to packed houses at the new National Théâtre de Chaillot. At each session the musicians performed about thirty-eight numbers, according to press reports, for 2,800 enthusiastic listeners. "We were accorded an uproarious reception," Ellington wrote, "and were forced to play innumerable encores." The reviews were glowing. The Paris newspaper *Le Figaro* marveled, "By what orchestral imagination does one arrive at strange fluted sound effects, atmospheric vibrations with powerful humor!" *Variety*'s man in Paris reported that Ellington and his orchestra "wowed the Parisians." Ellington was feted by musicians and nightclub proprietors alike. His music was hailed by Jacques-Henri Levesque, a

Paris critic, as "related to the rhythm of the atom" and as revealing "the very secret of the cosmos." The poet Blaise Cendrars was ecstatic: "Such music is not only a new art form but a new reason for living." When Ellington moved on, he left a lasting legacy in Paris: thousands of old and new fans and greater interest in his recordings.

In Brussels they played a sold-out concert at the Palais de Beaux Arts. Antwerp greeted Ellington with a handsome twelve-page concert program as a measure of the great respect with which he was regarded there. That he wanted to emphasize his own compositions was obvious in the program: of the eighty-eight numbers listed as possible selections, he had written more than 80 percent. They ranged from the familiar *Creole Love Call* and *Mood Indigo* to the little-known *Blue Ramble* and *Dusk in the Desert* to his newest pieces, *Boy Meets Horn*, *King Dooji*, and *Jeep's Blues*.

The musicians traveled next to the Netherlands, where they appeared in The Hague, Utrecht, and Amsterdam at concerts organized by the Dutch magazine *De Jazzwereld*. They received considerable publicity, and the audience and press reaction was generally very favorable, although a correspondent for *Metronome* reported that the concerts "disappointed real fans a bit, owing to lack of new numbers and too commercial selection." Such an occasional off note notwithstanding, however, the musicians drew jazz aficionados in droves.

In the Netherlands—as at previous stops—the musicians sensed the impending war. Ellington's clarinetist, Barney Bigard, recalled their palpable nervousness. "As we were heading across Holland," he said, "we could see out of the train windows that they were putting machine-gun posts in all the haystacks and in the ditches. It was kind of scary I can tell you."

The next logical venue for Ellington and his ensemble would have been Germany, but the Nazis disliked black people and their music. Instead, the musicians were booked in Denmark and Sweden. To get there, however, they had to take a train through the northern part of Hitler's Germany. A mix-up on April 9 stranded them for six hours in Hamburg amid swarms of soldiers and officials in Nazi uniforms. Never ones to lose their senses of humor, though, the musicians set out in search of a hamburger joint. They

Théâtre MAJESTIC Theater
ANVERS - ANTWERPEN

D U K E
ELLINGTON
and his
FAMOUS ORCHESTRA

DONDERDAG 6 APRIL PRIJS 5 Fr.
JEUDI AVRIL 1939 PRIX

During Ellington's 1939 tour of Europe, he played concerts
almost exclusively and was treated to handsome program
booklets befitting a concert artist, like this one from the Théâtre
Majestic, Antwerp, Belgium, on April 6, 1939.

figured a city named Hamburg had to have decent hamburgers.
They were wrong.

In Sweden, the group embarked on an extensive fifteen-city tour
of the country with a one-concert detour to Oslo, Norway. Ellington's tour took him to smaller cities that had no doubt never seen
an American jazz group. As a result of the tour, Ellington was, in
the words of the Swedish Ellington aficionado Benny Aasland,
"really accepted throughout the whole country."

Ellington became inspired one night and exchanged his piano for
drums on Tizol's *Pyramid* and imitated footsteps with his fingers

instead of drumsticks. Reviews of his Swedish tour were extremely positive. "This is orchestral art of the highest order," wrote the theater and music critic of the Stockholm *Aftonbladet.* The Stockholm *Ny Dag* reported, "This presentation was a Jazz-Concert, the likes of which the people of Stockholm have never seen or heard its equal."

On April 15, the band took a night train from Jönköping to Stockholm. "The platforms of the railway stations, all along the route, were filled with people hoping to get a glimpse of the Duke," reported one newspaper. "He and his famous orchestra practically played all the way to Stockholm." Regarding their April 16 concert in Stockholm, one newspaper, *Nya Dagligt Allehanda,* wrote: "The enthusiasm of Duke's listeners knew no bounds. Following the program, they stamped, whistled, shouted so lustily the very walls and foundation of the Concert Hall quaked." Several critics commended the band for its musicianship and its avoidance of clowning and stage tricks. Wrote another newspaper, "Their refined appearance made a deep impression and was a decided contrast to those slovenly, indifferent, clowning orchestras, which belong in the cheap cabarets, and never have anything of musical quality to offer."

April 29 was a day Ellington would later describe as "the most exciting event in the trip." The occasion was his fortieth birthday —and from morning till night the Swedes proffered gifts worthy of a Duke. "I was awakened in my hotel by a 16-piece jazz-band," Ellington recalled, "which entered the suite of rooms serenading us with the Swedish equivalent of 'Happy Birthday.' " Flowers arrived all day long. And in the evening, during a birthday concert at the Konserthuset, celebrities paid tribute to him and the audience rose and sang the birthday song. Then "ten little girls dressed in white paraded onto the stage to sing 'Happy Birthday' in English." Fifteen-year-old Alice Babs was one of the singers, and some thirty years later, she would sing an important part in one of Ellington's large-scale compositions. Ellington offered a gift in return: he introduced a new composition entitled *Serenade to Sweden.* In an unusual move, Swedish radio broadcast Ellington's concert throughout the nation.

Ellington and his musicians would likely have enjoyed basking in such glory indefinitely. But, according to Barney Bigard and Rex Stewart, their tour was cut short because of the escalating threat of war. On May 2, Ellington sailed from Göteborg, Sweden, for London, where because of mutual distrust and competition between American and British performers the British Ministry of Labour still refused to let Ellington perform. Sorely disappointed, the band headed home without performing for their legions of British fans.

The musicians boarded the jam-packed *Île de France*, and on May 10 reached home—safe and relieved. Said Bigard, "I was never so glad to see that old Statue of Liberty." Ellington and his band—exhausted, in desperate need of shaves, but jubilant nonetheless—were met in New York by 500 fans, including Ellington's friend, prizefighter Joe Louis.

For European audiences, Ellington's tour was remarkable. By the mid 1930s, jazzmen Coleman Hawkins and Benny Carter were living in Europe, but Europeans rarely got to hear entire American jazz bands—many of the visiting American musicians appeared as featured soloists with local ensembles. Ellington went to Europe in 1933, 1939, and then not again until 1948—and in between these infrequent tours, Europeans had to content themselves with his recordings. Ellington's concerts gave listeners opportunities to experience the excitement that can only come when live performers

Ellington enjoyed a friendship with the boxing champion Joe Louis (at his side). Both were great cultural heroes, especially among African-Americans.

face responsive crowds. Many were the audience members who carried vivid memories of these war's-eve concerts with them the rest of their lives.

During his Spring 1939 sojourn, Ellington also felt temporarily freed from the racial prejudice he encountered in the United States. There was certainly racism in Europe—which could be detected, for instance, in several reviews of Ellington in Copenhagen newspapers—but the racism in Europe was much less overt, and Ellington basked in the greater freedom there. "Europe is a very different world from this one," biographer Barry Ulanov quotes him as saying. "You can go anywhere and talk to anybody and do anything you like. It's hard to believe. When you've eaten hot dogs all your life and you're suddenly offered caviar it's hard to believe it's true."

The tour was one of the highlights of his life to that point, and it inspired him musically. Europeans seemed more attuned to Ellington's growing genius as a composer, as demonstrated by the formal concert settings, the printed programs, and the glowing press reviews. The tumultuous reception Ellington received in Europe, together with the other changes he was making, would lead him to what some consider his most creative and illustrious three years, a period in which he would be exploring the possibilities of working with a partner in his career as a composer.

Essential Ellington, 1935–39

After the longer works *Symphony in Black* and *Reminiscing in Tempo* in 1934–35, Ellington continued to experiment with innovations (such as employing *two* bassists), and introduced showpieces or "concertos" for his

(continued)

star soloists, and a kind of chamber music performed by about seven of the usual fifteen players in the band. During the three and a half years ending in the spring of 1939, the orchestra enjoyed a period of exceptional stability. Wallace Jones replaced Arthur Whetsol on trumpet, and the bass changed hands several times, but otherwise the players' growing experience with Ellington and one another allowed the band to mature as a unit. Cornetist Rex Stewart first made his mark with Ellington then. Of the nearly two hundred records Ellington made for commercial release during this period, here are some of the most significant.

From 1936, *Echoes of Harlem,* one of the first of a series of showpieces for his star soloists, begins sparely with a loping, exotic ostinato rendered by Ellington and his two bassists. Cootie Williams dominates the piece with his beautifully constructed lead line on both muted and open horn, and his emotionally pungent blues work—especially in his artful bent, or "blue," notes. Deceptively simple, *Echoes of Harlem* offers numerous contrasts— in Ellington's orchestration (minor versus major, loping versus gently swinging beat, spare versus full accompaniment) and in Williams's playing (muted versus open trumpet, held notes versus short notes, etc.) and solidly integrates the soloist within the composition. With its haunting mood, *Echoes of Harlem* echoes persistently in one's head. The piece has been reissued on *Swing, 1930 to 1938* (ABC).

Clarinet Lament, the flip side of *Echoes of Harlem,* was Barney Bigard's "concerto." From the opening flourishes and the underlying harmonic basis (*Basin Street Blues*) to Bigard's almost entirely extemporaneous line —at times as filigreed as the wrought-iron balconies of New Orleans—the piece is steeped with the flavor of his native city. Bigard's liquid clarinet alternately swoops, slides, keens, glides low, soars majestically, and sings wistfully—perhaps of his Creole youth. *Clarinet Lament* is also available on *Swing, 1930 to 1938.*

(continued)

From Sonny Greer's dramatic opening percussion effects to the final un-resolved chord, *Caravan* (1937) paints an intriguing picture of some distant and exotic place. Its serpentine melody, credited to trombonist Juan Tizol and Ellington, conjures an image, perhaps, of a middle-eastern snake-charmer's trick, or a camel caravan undulating across the rolling sand dunes; yet at the same time, Tizol's inflections also bespeak his Latin Amer-ican roots. *Caravan* is one of the Ellington orchestra's first efforts con-sciously to incorporate influences from other cultures into its music. As Tizol renders the minor melody, Harry Carney and Cootie Williams offer aptly contrasting countermelodies and accents. After Bigard's eight bars, Wil-liams walks in with an inspired plunger-mute solo. Enriched by the soloists' syncopations, Greer and the two bassists set up a rhythmic juggernaut from beginning to end. This colorful, striking piece insinuates itself into the memory; it naturally became a hit and a standard of the jazz repertory. *Caravan* is available on *The Essence of Duke Ellington* (Columbia).

Ellington called *Azure* "a little dulcet piece which portrays a blue mood." Released originally on the flip side of *Caravan*, *Azure* evokes an entirely different mood—a quiet daydream, thoughts drifting in a cloudless blue sky. The wispy and muted voicings, based on those in *Mood Indigo*, create the illusion of lightness and airiness. The piece is striking harmonically, verging on atonality, and features low-keyed solos by Bigard and Carney. This is one of Ellington's gentlest, most delicate pastels or mood pieces. *Azure* is also available on *The Essence of Duke Ellington*.

In 1935, Ellington began to record between six and nine players from his fifteen-man band. Of these often overlooked small-group pieces, the most memorable from this period include Rex Stewart's showcase for his half-valve work, *Lazy Man's Shuffle* (1936), and *Back Room Romp* (1937), in which trumpeter Freddie Jenkins simulates a growl trombone. Barney Bi-gard contributed *Clouds in My Heart*, featuring Cootie Williams on open

(continued)

horn, the haunting *Caravan,* and the infectious *Stompy Jones* (all 1936). Cootie Williams made the good-time swinger *Downtown Uproar,* the inventively arranged *Diga Diga Doo,* and *Blue Reverie* (all 1937), with its wonderful wah-wah figures and clarinet filigree. And Johnny Hodges led the exotic *Pyramid,* the mournful *Jitterbug's Lullaby,* and the best-selling *Jeep's Blues* (all 1938). *The Duke's Men: Small Groups, Vol. 1* (Columbia) contains all these pieces except *Jeep's Blues,* which is included in *The Duke's Men: Small Groups, Vol. 2* (Columbia).

In 1938, Ellington expanded his 1927 classic *Black and Tan Fantasy* into two sides, awkwardly titled *Prologue to Black and Tan Fantasy* and *The New Black and Tan Fantasy.* Cootie Williams now plays Bubber Miley's growl part, while Ellington adds solos by Barney Bigard, Harry Carney, and Tricky Sam Nanton, and elaborates on the orchestral arrangement. Bigard's amazingly long, thirty-second, sirenlike glissando provides a hair-raising contrast to Nanton's muted solo. In reworkings such as this, Ellington continued to keep his older compositions fresh. This pair of pieces can be heard on *Braggin' in Brass* (Portrait).

Prelude to a Kiss (1938) ranks as one of Ellington's most esteemed ballads. It became best-known as a song (with lyrics by Irving Gordon and Irving Mills), though its chromatic melody has tripped up many a singer. Ellington, however, first recorded it as an instrumental. Trombonist Lawrence Brown and Johnny Hodges (on soprano saxophone) play the melody sentimentally, supported by Ellington's full, rich harmonies. *Prelude to a Kiss* is available on *Braggin' in Brass.*

Late in 1938, Ellington offered a witty commentary on the swing craze—the jaunty *Battle of Swing.* It comprises a miniature concerto grosso—Ellington's first. Only instead of facing off a soloist with the orchestra, he pits a quartet of his players against the rest of the band. The angular melodies,

(continued)

neatly disguised blues progression, and unison playing by the band, as Gunther Schuller has observed, presage Ellington's great *Cotton Tail* of 1940 and the 1940s bebop movement itself. *Battle of Swing* is on *Braggin' in Brass.*

From late 1938, *Blue Light* casts its subdued rays as if in a moody still-life painting. In the vein of *Mood Indigo*—but softer, slower, sparer, and more introspective—*Blue Light* features the same clarinet-trumpet-trombone trio offering a hushed melody. Bigard's enigmatic clarinet, Brown's creamy trombone, Ellington's dissonant piano solo, and his ingenious transformation of the blues progression as the piece's underpinning—all make *Blue Light* distinctive. *Azure* and *Blue Light* are but two of many pieces Ellington composed whose music and titles seem to reflect Ellington's early interest in painting and colors. *Blue Light* is included on *Braggin' in Brass.*

Composed on the eve of his departure to Europe, *Subtle Lament* (1939) is still another slow piece in the mold of *Mood Indigo*. Here, Ellington deftly transforms the old twelve-bar blues into something entirely new and personal. The piece offers a series of highly individual colors—including a trio of trombones and Bigard's fluid clarinet, and a hauntingly poignant solo by Stewart. In a number of places *Subtle Lament* delicately teases the listener's ears with harmonic ambiguity: is it major or minor? The work will be reissued in the CD series *The Chronological Duke Ellington.*

Premiered in Stockholm on Ellington's fortieth birthday, *Serenade to Sweden* radiates with the warmth the Swedes and Ellington felt for one another. Almost totally scored (there is virtually no improvisation), the piece features, in contrasting succession, Wallace Jones's muted trumpet, Nanton's wah-wah trombone, Harry Carney's husky baritone saxophone, and the ever-smooth Lawrence Brown's luminous solo. At the close, the chorus of saxophones glows as high and brightly as the aurora borealis or the Swedish midnight sun. *Serenade to Sweden* will be reissued in *The Chronological Duke Ellington* CD series.

SEVEN

*M*AKING

MASTERPIECES

•

1 9 3 9 — 4 3

ust before Ellington had departed for Europe, a twenty-three-year-old musician named Billy Strayhorn had come to look him up. The previous December, during an Ellington engagement at the Stanley Theater in Pittsburgh, Strayhorn had demonstrated some original songs to Ellington, and the older man, instantly impressed, had told him: "Why, young man, I'm going to bring you to New York, and you will be my lyric writer." In January, Strayhorn had shown up in New York, and Ellington put him to work. In March he contributed his first arrangement, *Savoy Strut*, for a Johnny Hodges small-group session, and his first song to an Ellington recording session—*Something to Live For*.

From that modest beginning was to grow an artistic partnership that would produce some of the musical high points of Ellington's life. If working with a composing partner was a problem, working with Billy Strayhorn was just the kind of problem Ellington needed.

While the orchestra was in Europe, Strayhorn moved in with Mercer and Ruth Ellington and the two men went through Ellington's scores, really studying them. Strayhorn began to crack the code to the master's style or—as the young man would later dub it —the "Ellington effect." Unlike Ellington, Strayhorn was schooled

After Ellington signed
with the William Morris Agency,
it issued this promotional
caricature of him.

Ellington and Billy Strayhorn (right),
sixteen years his junior, eventually
forged an almost telepathically
close musical relationship.

in the music of the European masters. "He had had enough training in composition to be able to appreciate Pop's work," wrote the younger Ellington, "and it was just a matter of having the instrumentation shown him for him to grasp the general principles." Strayhorn mentioned that he wanted to do some orchestrating, and pretty soon, he was collaborating with Ellington: five pieces from 1939 list them as cocomposers.

Starting modestly, Strayhorn soon became invaluable to his boss. Soon Strayhorn was playing the piano and arranging for a number of the band-within-a-band recordings and arranging pop songs such as *Chloë* for the orchestra. By 1941 he was writing original pieces such as *Take the "A" Train* and *After All*. He not only lightened Ellington's burden as provider of music for the orchestra, he contributed many ideas, particularly in harmony.

Strayhorn so mastered the Ellington style of composing that the two became uncannily close musical collaborators, yet in their personal lives they were opposites. While the handsome, six-foot-one-inch Ellington moved through life with dash and theatricality, a charismatic and imposing presence wherever he went, both charming and manipulating people, bedding many women along the way, the cherubic Strayhorn was short (five feet, three inches tall), shy, soft-spoken, bespectacled, modest, and homosexual. Despite their different personalities, they formed an exceedingly close musical and working relationship that would end only with Strayhorn's death. Ellington called him "always the most unselfish, the most patient, and the most imperturbable."

"Duke was a father figure, without a doubt, and certainly a better one than Billy's own father," asserted Lena Horne, who would become a close friend of Strayhorn's. "Their relationship was also very *sexual*. Don't misunderstand. It wasn't physical at all. But it was very, very sexual. Billy loved Duke and Duke loved Billy. The problem is, Duke treated Billy exactly like he treated women, with all that old-fashioned chauvinism. Very loving and very protective, but controlling, very destructive."

According to Mercer Ellington, the advent of Strayhorn led to the diminishing of the informal collaborations that had marked the creation and orchestration of some of Ellington's pieces. It was as if the formally trained Strayhorn, who had great sensitivity to the Ellington sound and understood its underpinnings and structure, complemented him perfectly, giving him a new musical soulmate with whom to collaborate, and making Ellington the composer somewhat more distinct from Ellington the bandleader. Strayhorn's arrival also created some jealousies: Juan Tizol, for years Ellington's music copyist, now refused to copy out music that Strayhorn had created. And yet, most of the orchestra grew to be affectionately protective of Strayhorn. They nicknamed him "Strays," "Weely," and—because of his youth, diminutive stature, and sweetness—"Swee' Pea," after the vulnerable baby in the comic strip *Popeye*.

Next, Ellington brought two more remarkable musicians into the orchestra. Jimmie Blanton was only twenty when he joined the Ellington band, about September 1939. (He always spelled his first name "Jimmie" in his autographs, though nearly everyone else has spelled it "Jimmy.") Ellington was probably drawn by his agility, unfaltering control of pitch, and masterful swing. Blanton revolutionized jazz bass playing by expanding the instrument's melodic role as accompanist and in solos, and by enriching the bass's sound through an outsized tone. Blanton loved nothing more than playing his bass; when not on the stand, it seems as if he was always practicing, grabbing a quick lesson from the classical music teacher in whatever town the band was playing, or hunting up a late-night jam session. "His amazing talent," Stewart declared, "sparked the entire band."

In October 1939, Ellington took Blanton into the recording studio and cut several remarkable duets, which—especially *Mr. J. B. Blues*—set listeners on their ears—and presaged impressive Blanton performances in 1940 and 1941, including *Jack the Bear, Ko-Ko, Sepia Panorama, John Hardy's Wife*, and *Cotton Tail*. Blanton played side by side with bassist Billy Taylor until January 1940, when the latter walked off the stand one night in Boston, saying, as Duke Ellington remembered it, "I'm not going to stand up here next to that young boy playing all that bass and be embarrassed."

Back in 1935 and 1936, tenor saxophonist Ben Webster had recorded and toured with Ellington briefly. In 1939, Ellington decided that he wanted to expand his saxophone section and could now afford it, and that the man he wanted was Webster. But Ellington faced a problem: Webster was playing in the band of Cab Calloway, his old Cotton Club colleague. Milt Hinton, who was playing bass with Calloway at the time, describes what happened. Webster, he recalled,

always wanted to play with Duke. . . . He would make his desires known that he wanted to play with Duke, and Duke being the very clever man that he was, told Ben, "I would love to have you in the band, but Cab's is my brother band and I can't take anybody out of his band. *But*, if you didn't have a job I'd have to give you one."

This started the chemistry in Ben and he started saving up his money. About six months later we hit Cleveland, Ohio, and Duke was going to play the Jeffrey Tavern in Chicago, so Ben put in his notice with Cab. Ben left and went to Chicago with no job. He went on the corners and told Duke, "Well, I'm unemployed." And Duke hired him.

The young Jimmie Blanton, seen here with singer Ivie Anderson, sparked the entire band with his rhythmic drive and influenced generations of bassists with his virtuoso playing.

Ben Webster, a passionate and romantic player of the highest order, became Ellington's first regular tenor saxophonist and contributed much during his few years with the orchestra.

The thirty-year-old Webster joined the Duke Ellington orchestra about December 1939.

Born in Kansas City, which developed a thriving jazz scene, Webster had studied at Wilberforce University, took up the saxophone about 1930, and after moving to New York in 1934 played with the orchestras of Fletcher Henderson, Benny Carter, and Cab Calloway. Webster played with an unfocused pitch, powerful rhythmic swing, versatility, passion, and intensity. On slow ballads, his breathy sound pulsated with deep-seated feeling; he was a romantic saxophonist of the highest order, spinning elegant melodies. A strong individualist on and off the bandstand, he was capable of terrible, even violent, fits of anger. Yet he could be as sweet as a honeydrop. His emotions were just below the surface, and they were always evident in his playing. Webster brought the tenor saxophone to new prominence in the Ellington orchestra, and from then on, the Ellington sound always included five saxophonists, most of whom doubled on clarinet. "Ben was inspired and he inspired us," said Harry Carney, "so that we worked together and tried to improve the section. We used to rehearse all alone, just the sax section."

The extroverted and passionate Webster was a great soloist, whether on romantic ballads or hard-driving tunes, and is considered, with Coleman Hawkins and Lester Young, as a top swing-era player on the tenor saxophone. Ellington began to feature him immediately, and Webster would figure prominently in several immortal recordings, notably *All Too Soon*, *Conga Brava*, and *Cotton Tail*, all in 1940.

Webster took a parental interest in young Blanton: "Ben would watch over the kid he nicknamed Bear like a mother hen," wrote Rex Stewart. The two newest players—Blanton from St. Louis and Webster from Kansas City—brought increased rhythmic drive, the kind for which Count Basie and the "southwest" jazz musicians were famous—to the Ellington sound. And, as Harry Carney put it, "Every time there was an addition to the band, the new instrumentalist seemed to give Duke new ideas and something to draw from and add in his writing." That was because, as Ellington said in 1942, "we write to and for the individuals in the band, not the instruments." These new players did indeed stimulate his composing.

When a new player came in, the others had to make room for him, not just literally but psychologically and musically. This led to constant petty jealousies, cliques, and frictions, since those already there tended to resent the newcomers. Ellington typically gave his new arrivals solo space almost immediately, which exacerbated the tensions. And the audience was not always welcoming of new talent. At first, Lawrence Brown and Rex Stewart had been resented by some longtime fans; the same thing happened when Ben Webster joined the band, and in the 1950s, with Paul Gonsalves.

Feuds between band members became common. Bigard and Brown wouldn't speak with each other, nor would Brown to Ellington, according to Stewart. Even Stewart got caught up in such conflict: he and Cootie Williams would not talk to one another for two years. And yet overall, Stewart declared, "An unbelievable *esprit de corps* held the Ellington band together for those many years. In a way, this was phenomenal, especially when one considers that we came from such divergent backgrounds with disparate degrees of musical training, heritage, and cultural environment. But we all learned to cleave together, think alike and play together as Duke's band."

This was a time of renewal and growth for Ellington; around 1940 he even stopped drinking heavily. Now living with a beautiful new woman, Evie Ellis; armed with a new arranger and second pianist, a virtuoso bassist, and an expanded and strengthened sax section; expectantly signed with a new publisher, new agent, and, soon, a new record company; and buoyed by memories of the dignity and acclaim he was accorded in Europe, Ellington led his orchestra into one of its golden periods. "After our very successful European tour," Stewart recalled, "the band started hitting on all cylinders like a wonderful musical juggernaut."

By 1939, swing was truly a national craze, especially for young people. Record sales rose 51 percent over those in 1938, due largely to swing, and three fifths of the records went right into the ever-more-popular jukeboxes. New swing bands seemed to be forming left and right, and in October 1939 *Down Beat,* until then a monthly, doubled its frequency to semimonthly. There were bobby soxers, zoot suits, and "jive" or "hep" talk—Cab Calloway even published a *Dictionary of Jive.*

Upon returning from Europe, Ellington's first engagements under the William Morris banner included a performance at the World's Fair in Flushing, New York, full weeks and split-weeks at theaters in New York City, Boston, and elsewhere, and a series of one-night dances at northeastern and midwestern ballrooms. *Variety* and *Billboard* reported strong box-office grosses. The orchestra's usual fee in 1939 was $5,550 per week, which would rise a year later to $6,500, but that would put it only in the middle bracket of name bands.

During a hectic schedule of touring to theaters and ballrooms, Ellington's new, exclusive contract with Victor went into effect on February 22, 1940. It contained an extraordinary provision: no other black band would be recorded for issue on the prestigious, full-priced (seventy-five cents per disc) Victor label (Victor's subsidiary label, the thirty-five-cent Bluebird, would continue to release Fats Waller, Earl Hines, and Erskine Hawkins). Victor allowed Ellington to choose his own material, thus freeing him from some of the commercial constraints he operated under with Mills. For his part, however, Ellington denied his commercialism had been due to Mills:

> That's all bunk! I am commercial because I've got to be. The support of the ordinary masses for the music from me, which they like, alone enables me to cater for the minority of jazz cognoscenti, who certainly, on their own, couldn't enable me to keep my big and expensive organisation going.

Ellington, as bandleader and practical businessman, always maintained a delicate balancing act between the general musical public, on the one hand, and jazz aficionados, on the other. In later years, when many jazz big bands could no longer sustain themselves economically, it would be the silver-haired couples who had come of age during the swing era dancing to *Sophisticated Lady* that would keep the Ellington orchestra going. During this period, Ellington the bandleader wooed wide audiences by featuring frequent vocals (besides Ivie Anderson, Herb Jeffries sang with the band from 1939 to 1942), utilizing theatricality during stage shows, and continuing to perform his past hits.

By 1939, a dispute was brewing between radio stations and the primary performing-rights organization, the American Society of Composers, Authors, and Publishers. The result was a ban, beginning January 1, 1941, on the broadcasting of music written by composers affiliated with ASCAP. This posed a serious problem for Ellington, who had been an ASCAP member since 1935. The ban meant neither new works composed by him nor his vast repertoire of existing pieces—from *Mood Indigo* to *Jeep's Blues*—could be aired during the first part of 1941. He solved this problem, with characteristic ingenuity, by turning to Strayhorn and his son, Mercer, neither of whom had yet joined ASCAP. Strayhorn would write *Day Dream* and *Passion Flower* for the Hodges small band, and *Take the "A" Train, After All, Chelsea Bridge,* and others for the big band. These new compositions established him as a composer in his own right.

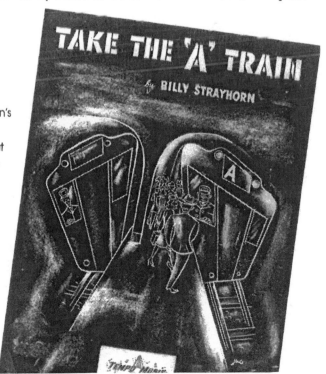

The sheet music for *Take the "A" Train,* which became a hit and Ellington's signature tune from 1941 on. Strayhorn said that in the lyric he was writing subway directions.

Twenty-year-old Mercer Ellington, then a saxophonist and later a trumpeter, had formed his own band late in 1939, making a debut in Harlem described by *Down Beat* as "wobbly," and the band was short-lived. Late in 1940, the elder Ellington took his son on as an arranger and composer. In 1941, the younger Ellington contributed four notable works to the Ellington repertoire: *Moon Mist, Blue Serge, John Hardy's Wife,* and *Things Ain't What They Used to Be.* This stint with the orchestra, however, would not last long: in 1943 he would be drafted into the armed services. (Years later, he would return to the Duke Ellington orchestra.)

In 1941, Ellington hired another behind-the-scenes musician, a Boston-bred pianist and conductor named Tom Whaley, to serve as the band's main copyist. Except for an absence in 1950, he would remain with Ellington until Ellington's death. Other than Ellington and Strayhorn, Whaley would be the person closest to Ellington's music.

Then, on September 14, 1942, Ellington brought on a new, lyrical trumpet player. "Shorty Baker came into the band, and we made it four trumpets," Ellington said. "It was another device opportunity, you know, when you change the size of a section, it changes the shape and the sound, too." The band was now sixteen instrumentalists strong. The following year, the trumpet section would grow to five players, the band to seventeen instrumentalists.

It was the original instrumentals composed by Ellington (and a few each by Strayhorn and Mercer Ellington) that propelled Ellington from one glorious recording session to another. Many things distinguish the music of this period. When Webster joined, there was written-out music initially for only four saxophones, none for him, and he had to find a fifth note that would work, while avoiding the jealously guarded parts of the other saxophonists, who kept accosting him, "Hey, you've got my note!"—and this process resulted in some rich, original, and dissonant chords.

Moreover, Ellington's music was marked by increased rhythmic drive and instrumental virtuosity brought by Blanton and Webster, inspired solos from other players, expanded harmonic choices introduced by Strayhorn, consistently high musical quality, presaging of bebop and other musical developments to come, and numerous musical explorations and innovations. With breathtaking originality, Ellington broke more and more new ground. Examples can be found in every decade, but in this period they abound. The early 1940s band, as Raymond Horricks put it, had "a lust for life; it hit harder musically, bit deeper emotionally and swung more animatedly . . . than any Ellington band that preceded it." From a composer's point of view comes this assessment by Gunther Schuller: beginning in March 1940 with *Jack the Bear* and *Ko-Ko*, "the best of the Ellington band's performances for some years are marked by an astonishing economy, even simplicity of means, a feeling of all non-essentials having been trimmed off, and a sense of inevitability that signifies true mastery." Not that all, or even most, of Ellington's music was understood by the public. *Down Beat* assessed an Ellington performance in May 1940: "It was a great show although—as usual—about 60 percent of the band's most impressive work sailed over all but a few heads."

Another reason for the current high quality was the maturing of not only Ellington but also the orchestra. The band that Ellington had taken to Europe was a seasoned group with an average age of thirty-four, and an unheard-of average of ten years' experience with the leader, more than in any other major band. Even with the personnel changes in the months following his return to America, the average tenure was an impressive eight years. This kind of stability was highly unusual: most bands suffered frequent change-overs in personnel (Goodman's turnover was legendary).

But by offering steady work, good travel arrangements, spot-lights and superior salaries for his stars, by providing inspiration and challenges, and by employing clever psychology, Ellington as bandleader had maintained considerable loyalty. "Duke is a great guy to work for," said Ben Webster. "He understands musicians better than any leader. He's quick to judge a man's ability accurately, and he can write a piece or a concerto for him that will fit that individual man." The steadiness of personnel enabled the musicians to get to know Ellington's and their colleagues' styles, and allowed the composer to learn thoroughly each player's strengths and weaknesses. The stability showed in his music. This was a period in which both of Ellington's careers, reinforcing each other, were reaching high points.

A salient factor in producing the distinguished music of this period was, of course, that Ellington employed some of the world's top players. His saxophone section was justly famous. As *Down Beat* indicated perceptively in September 1940, Johnny Hodges, Harry Carney, Barney Bigard, and Jimmie Blanton were without peer on their instruments; Ben Webster, Cootie Williams, and Rex Stewart were remarkable players; and the band enjoyed three great trombonists—Juan Tizol, Lawrence Brown, and Tricky Sam Nanton. And Ellington was able to keep them stimulated with the rich and varied music he (and Strayhorn) composed with them in mind.

The recording engineers at Victor managed to capture the Ellington sound with a richness and fidelity unprecedented in its previous recordings. "Not only is the music superb," pronounced *Down Beat* in reviewing *Jack the Bear*, "but the recording, technically, is perfect. Balance and surface reach a new peak with this release." Among other things, Blanton's bass was captured beautifully. Ellington was evidently particular about both the musical and sonic aspects of the recordings. According to Vincent Liebler, who engineered some of the Victor sessions, "Duke was very elegant and very nice, and very, very fussy about recording. His sessions would go on and on and on. All day and far into the night. He'd work over some arrangement, particularly the small-group things under Hodges and Williams, on the piano with one or two of his musicians while the rest of the guys just sat around smoking."

With the recording of *Cotton Tail* in May 1940, Ellington opened a window on the future, predicting developments to come in jazz. "It changed the face of jazz," Gunther Schuller has written, "and foretold in many ways where the music's future lay." The rhythmic inflections, melody line, and overall daring of the piece point ahead, and in the ending of *Subtle Slough* (1941) and the angularity of *Main Stem* (1942), Ellington would continue to help lay the foundation for what would soon become known as bebop. In addition, *Cotton Tail*, Schuller has found, "particularly in its execution, let in a gust of spontaneity, of freshness, of flexibility, which the Ellington band was never to lose again and which offered a whole new way of integrating composition and improvisation."

During this time and throughout his career, Ellington continued to prove wrong the common notion that improvisation is the sine qua non of jazz. In addition to solos that were conceived by Ellington and scored as melodies for the soloist to embellish and personalize, sometimes the musicians were more or less forced to repeat the solos they themselves created. For instance, Ben Webster found that after *Cotton Tail* became a sensation in 1940, audiences would demand that he reproduce his celebrated solo from the Victor record, note for note.

Just as Ellington was integrating Blanton and Webster into his band came the sad news that, in January 1940, Artie Whetsol, Ellington's old friend and first trumpeter, had died of a brain disease. That fall came the sudden departure of one of Ellington's leading players. Benny Goodman, recovering from back surgery, was reorganizing his band, wanted a headliner, and made an offer to Cootie Williams. The Ellington orchestra was playing in Chicago in October, and one night, Ellington wrote, Williams "took me for a ride all around Chicago in his car. He wanted to tell me that he had a very lucrative offer to go with Benny Goodman for a while." Generously, Ellington told Williams, "Well, go ahead on. You've got a chance to make money. And make a name for yourself." And the leader even helped Williams negotiate his salary with Goodman.

Williams left the first week in November, and according to *Down Beat*, "was almost in tears as he bade Duke and the Ellington gang goodbye." But, besides a raise to $200 per week, Williams said later, he was drawn by the Goodman beat. And his new boss was to spotlight him regularly in the Goodman sextet. The departure of Cootie Williams, an eleven-year veteran with Ellington, stunned the jazz world and was commemorated in Raymond Scott's mournful recording *When Cootie Left the Duke*.

Many were skeptical that Ellington could adequately replace Williams—one of the greatest all-time masters at playing both growl and open (unmuted) trumpet. Using his keen eye, ear, and instinct, Ellington chose in Williams's stead an obscure Chicago musician named Ray Nance, a veteran of the orchestras of Earl Hines and Horace Henderson. Whether on open or muted trumpet, fast or slow, sweet or hot, Nance played with style, lyricism, and

Taking Cootie Williams's chair in 1940, Ray Nance (playing violin) brought such varied gifts as trumpeter, violinist, singer, and dancer that he earned the nickname "Floorshow."

warmth. A versatile entertainer, the twenty-six-year-old Nance not only played trumpet, but also played violin, sang, even twirled his trumpet and danced in Ellington's performances—thus prompting the maestro to nickname him "Floorshow." With coaching from Tricky Sam Nanton he took over the growl chair from Williams, and also brought crowd-pleasing showmanship and a brand-new color to the Ellington palette—the violin. Beginning in 1942 with *Moon Mist*, Ellington would showcase Nance's crisp and swinging fiddle sound. Nance reminded many of Freddie Jenkins—they were both diminutive, irrepressible trumpet players, but Nance was more versatile and showmanly. "Ray Nance was a cocky kid," recalled Sonny Greer, "and we called him the Captain. He was always ready when asked—'Just a minute, I'll be right with you.' "

Meanwhile, Johnny Hodges was carving out a new area for himself, the result of his passionate playing on ballads such as Strayhorn's *Day Dream* and *Passion Flower*. Especially when he played such pieces, many women found him irresistible. As the wife of a fellow musician reportedly cautioned her husband, "Don't leave me alone around Johnny. When I hear him play, I just want to open up the bedroom door." Hodges's reaction to his success was down to earth: he pressed Ellington for a raise. "Money was a game they both played well," Stanley Dance revealed. "Sometimes, when Hodges had played an especially fine solo on a number to which he had originally contributed, he would turn to Ellington in full view of the audience, while the applause thundered, and mime the counting of dollar bills."

By the early 1940s, Johnny Hodges was the leading "star" musician in the Ellington orchestra. Strayhorn began writing luxuriant ballads for Hodges, whom Charlie Parker admiringly called "the Lily Pons of the alto" saxophone.

. . .

According to Mercer Ellington, his father had definite ideas about race relations, though in public he preferred to make them subtly rather than overtly. In February 1941, Ellington, performing at Casa Mañana, a ballroom in Culver City, near Los Angeles, happened upon a chance to do that. At a late-night jam session at the home of screenwriter Sid Kuller, an idea was born when he exclaimed, "Hey, this joint sure is jumping." "Jumping for joy!" Ellington responded from a piano across the room. "Jumping for joy! What a great idea," Kuller replied. "A Negro musical—*Jump for Joy* starring Duke Ellington."

Ellington may have been attracted to the idea of writing this work to make a stand on racial discrimination, to make some money, and to apply his creative powers in a new medium, musical theater. In fact, he had long been interested in writing a musical. In 1933, *Fortune* reported that "Ellington spends his spare moments writing a score for a Negro musical show to be produced next season by John Henry Hammond Jr." While that show never came to fruition, Ellington continued to aspire to write one. In 1936, the *Chicago Defender* reported that "the dream of Duke Ellington is a musical with an entire Negro cast. He has been working on the synopsis and score for several months."

Jump for Joy, as Patricia Willard has written, "evolved into a grand emancipation celebration in dance, sketch, and song. It aimed at banishing forever the stereotypical eyerolling, dialect, and shuffling gait" that was the standard way African-Americans were depicted in theatrical and motion-picture entertainment. A collective of writers worked with Ellington, who wrote all the music and some of the lyrics; most of the lyrics were written by Sid Kuller and the gifted songwriter Paul Francis Webster. Financing of $52,000 was scraped together, and the show opened on July 10, 1941, at the gaudy, awe-inspiring Mayan Theater in downtown Los Angeles. After it opened, the show was in constant flux—a pattern Ellington had often followed in tinkering with his orchestrations: he, in fact, was always engaged in the process of creating.

The show, in Willard's words, was "upbeat, satirical, topical, socially aware, ebullient, and . . . abidingly hip." Ellington, in

Jimmie Blanton, Ellington, and singer Herb Jeffries stand in the orchestra pit during *Jump for Joy,* Ellington's pioneering "civil rights" musical of 1941.

fact, called it "the hippest thing we ever did." The program booklet had a glossary to translate the show's jive. A year after the show closed, Ellington credited it with "creating that American phenomenon, 'The Zoot Suits with the Reet Pleat.' "

Jump for Joy offered romance between Dorothy Dandridge and Herb Jeffries in *The Brown-Skin Gal in the Calico Gown,* Ivie Anderson's heart-rending *I Got It Bad (and That Ain't Good)* (which became a hit record, selling hundreds of thousands of copies), bluesman Joe Turner shouting the lovesick *Rocks in My Bed,* humorous and hopeful commentary in *Uncle Tom's Cabin Is a Drive-In Now,* and biting social protest in *I've Got a Passport from Georgia* "and I'm sailing for the U.S.A.," which the producers reluctantly removed after receiving death threats.

Probably the first big-time musical to portray blacks in a non-stereotyped way, *Jump for Joy* was a source of great pride for African-Americans. One of the cast of sixty, Avanelle Lewis Harris, said, "Everything, every setting, every note of music, every lyric, meant something." Ellington got the comics to remove their usual burnt-cork makeup, and, as he wrote later, "comedians came off stage smiling, and with tears running down their cheeks." Among unanimous rave reviews, the *Los Angeles Tribune*, a black weekly, wrote, "In *Jump for Joy*, Uncle Tom is dead. God rest his bones."

The show, however, folded on September 27, after eleven weeks and 101 performances, dashing hopes it would tour the nation. Whether the demise was the fault of the show's unevenness resulting from fifteen cocreators, the strong competition from touring national shows in nearby Los Angeles theaters, or *Jump for Joy*'s strong, positive images of black people and its protest, however subtle, of white racism—the fact is the show was no longer profitable. That it folded and never made it to Broadway was one of the regrets of Ellington's life. Denied a Broadway run and an original-cast album, *Jump for Joy*, however socially pioneering, exuberantly appealing, and teeming with inventive and moving moments, had short-lived impact.

Ellington spent most of 1941 on the West Coast. Late in November, he secured an opportunity to perform in five short movies, Soundies, being made for the nation's 4,000 "nickel-in-a-slot" viewing machines, kind of an early video jukebox found in theater and hotel lobbies, bars, and restaurants. The band recorded *Cotton Tail*, *Flamingo*, *I Got It Bad*, *Bli-Blip* (the last two from *Jump for Joy*), and *C-Jam Blues*. While production values are low, the music is excellent, and these are among the few films of Webster performing with the Ellington orchestra. They remain among Ellington's most significant films.

Elsewhere in Hollywood, Ellington was subjected to a disappointment by the director Orson Welles, who had hired the composer to develop a section on early jazz for a feature film to be called *It's All True*. Welles put him on a retainer of $1,000 per week, and Ellington had begun writing the music when the mercurial Welles decided to drop jazz from the movie. As Hollywood had yet to portray jazz authentically in a feature film, Welles's original idea had created high expectations; the disappointment in the jazz community was widespread. Ellington, however, did receive a consolation: he walked away with $12,000 for very little work. (Incidentally, Welles reportedly said that, other than himself, Ellington was the only genius he had ever known.)

In September and October 1942, Hollywood would again beckon, this time offering a prime spot in *Cabin in the Sky*, an all-black musical fable which starred Ethel Waters, Louis Armstrong, Lena

The 1942 MGM movie *Cabin in the Sky* offered Ellington and the orchestra several numbers.
Here Rex Stewart (cornet), "Bubbles" (dancer John W. Sublett), Ellington,
Lawrence Brown (trombone), and dancer Buck Washington pose for the publicist's camera.

Horne, and others. Directed by Vincente Minnelli, and beautifully photographed, the film gave the Ellington orchestra two numbers —his *Goin' Up* (featuring Lawrence Brown preaching a trombone "sermon" with the dancers "amening") and Mercer's *Things Ain't What They Used to Be*—to which the Whitey's Lindy Hoppers showed their sensational stuff. The movie, however, except for Ellington, was in some ways a throwback to the handkerchief-wearing black stereotypes of the past. In *Reveille with Beverly,* a series of swing bands and pop singers—Count Basie, Bob Crosby, Frank Sinatra, the Mills Brothers—were strung together with a little wartime plot about a female radio deejay. With Betty Roché singing the lyrics, the Ellington orchestra performed *Take the "A" Train* aboard a train that seemed to be moving. Only Hollywood got it wrong: instead of a New York City subway train it was a passenger train zipping across country. Though the performances are enjoyable, neither film enlarged Ellington's reputation. He was paid well, however: for *Reveille,* the musicians received "union scale" wages of $60 for three hours' recording, while Ellington was paid somewhere between $4,000 and $8,000.

Creating a stream of pieces required Ellington, and increasingly Strayhorn, to devote considerable energies to composing and re-hearsing. Sometimes Ellington composed against recording studios' glass windows, on night trains or day coaches, on late-night buses (with a band member holding up a nonstop series of matches), and in other rather unorthodox settings—as Henry Blankford discovered when he found Ellington at his hotel composing songs for *Jump for Joy.*

> Duke was in the bathtub. Beside him was a stack of manuscript paper, a huge container of chocolate ice cream, a glass of scotch and milk, and Jonesy. Jonesy was his valet, and his job was to keep adding warm water and let out cooling water to maintain a constant temperature in the tub for the Maestro. And Duke was serenely scribbling notes on the paper and then calling to Billy Strayhorn. Billy would take the notes and play them on the beat-up old upright piano in Duke's room. Duke would listen and then write more notes, which he would give to Strayhorn. The band seemed to be all on the

same floor of the hotel—like a very long railroad flat—and the sound
of Strays at the keyboard was like some kind of signal. Pretty soon
you'd hear Ben Webster playing a line, then Ray Nance would start
tooting from somewhere down the hall, Sonny Greer would come in
with his sticks, and the music would start to form . . . Duke writing
more and more notes for Sweetpea . . . Jonesy keeping the water
just right . . . and about four or five hours later, two more songs for
the show were finished.

Occasionally, Ellington would arrive home at dawn, and write an
entire score before going to bed. As the Duke Ellington papers at
the Smithsonian Institution reveal, he often jotted down musical
ideas on backs of envelopes, hotel stationery, and other scraps of
paper. His mind seemed to be endlessly fertile. Ellington was once
asked where he got his ideas from. "Ideas?" he replied. "Oh man,
I got a million dreams. That's all I do is dream, all the time."

Some of his ideas took shape at his all-important rehearsals.
"The secret of Duke Ellington," wrote *Metronome*'s editor, Doron
K. Antrim, "is contained in one word: *rehearsal* . . . for every hour
of actual performance there are at least two hours of intensive
rehearsal." When they worked at the Kentucky and Cotton clubs,
the band got used to playing till three or four A.M., and Ellington
would call rehearsals till sunrise. The band would normally sleep
during the day. This was the pattern they generally followed in
succeeding years. If Ellington called a rehearsal for two o'clock he
would typically arrive at three, fellow musician Lionel Hampton
wrote in 1930, "but the boys know it, so they mentally add an
hour."

"If Duke Ellington has an idea for a tune," Antrim wrote, "the
men sit in with him until he finishes it, accepting criticisms and
suggestions from each." Ellington would go through a piece section
by section—first the saxophones, then trumpets, next trombones,
telling each player what to play for four measures. Each player
would play his notes and then the section would try it. Then an
entire sixteen bars would be practiced in this manner before the
whole band would try it. Ellington would have everyone repeat
what they'd played a number of times so as to memorize it.

Meanwhile, Juan Tizol might be writing down notes of what
everyone was playing, thereby creating a rough score. Ellington

Regarded as the world's greatest saxophone section, Ellington's saxmen rehearse:
Barney Bigard, Ben Webster, Johnny Hodges, Otto Hardwick, and Harry Carney.

would take the score home and tinker and polish it. The next night, the band would play the piece again. Throughout the entire process, there would be considerable give and take and lively discussion. Ellington, as Barney Bigard recalled, "was an open-minded man . . . I mean if we would come up with a good suggestion, anyone in the band that is, he would generally take it. He would at least try it out. If you took a chorus and played a little piece of improvisation that he liked, he would take it out and score it to make up a whole new tune." In this process, again, composer and bandleader were one.

"Changes and improvements are constantly made," continued Antrim, "until the finished arrangement is not only written but perfectly memorized. Then, and not until then, is the number ready for stage, radio, and recording." Even at the studio, however, Ellington would typically continue to revise. The result might be that section D would be played before section A, and E before B. Thus the resulting recording might have an order totally different from the musicians' scores and parts.

As Ellington was composing a growing body of highly original compositions, he was also composing a life that was as personal, distinctive, and colorful as his music. "Ellington is a highly original man in almost every aspect of his personality," declared Rex Stewart. "His clothes, his music, and his speech quickly display this originality. . . . The facets of personality emerge stronger than they do in the majority of men. . . . Almost every aspect of his personality is noteworthy."

"Ellington," added Stewart, a keen observer of human nature, "is the most complex and paradoxical individual that I've ever known." Stewart found him to be "a composite of each character quality and its exact opposite. He is both generous and stingy; thoughtful and inconsiderate; dependable and irresponsible; etc."

Besides the seeming contradictions, Ellington struck many as enigmatic; as Stewart wrote, "the more you know him, the more you realize that you don't really know him at all." "He lives a good deal within himself," agreed Sonny Greer. "There's a private side to him which only he knows." Ellington's inner privacy went beyond that of the entertainer maintaining an onstage persona and an offstage life; it went beyond the theatrical mask that a Bert Williams would wear for white audiences; with Ellington it went deeper. Ruth Ellington spoke of her own brother wearing "veil upon veil upon veil." "Edward did seem somewhat of a mystery sometimes," observed his friend in later years, the photographer Gordon Parks, "even to himself. And that's probably the way he wanted it. It wasn't his thing to be thoroughly understood. Those who knew him didn't try—they just sat back and enjoyed him. And there was plenty to enjoy: he was generous, kind, intelligent and entertaining. But his inner life and feelings were as personal to him as his music. He guarded them with a passion. Anyone who pried too deeply was cleverly rebuffed."

There are some things about Ellington, however, that are clear.

Ever image-conscious, and aware of ragtag negative stereotypes of blacks and of low-life images of jazzmen, he'd insist on a natty appearance for the band. He would often change stage clothes a number of times a day, and sometimes had the band do the same. Ellington reportedly owned 150 suits and over a thousand ties; his shirts, hats, and shoes were custom made. "He loves flash in dress," the *Chicago Defender* reported in 1937. "He combines the most atrocious colors and other well dressed men follow his leads." On the other hand, Stewart felt "his clothes were avant garde but not flashy or flamboyant. He knew full well that the audience will see you before they will hear you. I remember his favorite shirt, which he invented. It became known as a 'Barrymore roll' because of the long rolled collar. We all were fascinated by his original wardrobe."

In rehearsal, he normally wore a sport shirt or sweater and a porkpie hat with the brim turned up. Backstage, it was something else again: Ellington would relax in dubious old bathrobe and slippers, a stocking cap bedecking his head.

Ever since his mother's death, and until the day he died, he wore around his neck a little crucifix his sister, Ruth, had given him. He read the Bible daily, and said, "I've had three educations—the street corner, going to school, and the Bible. The Bible is the most important. It taught me to look at a man's insides instead of the cut of his suit." And yet, according to Stewart, "rarely did he forget or forgive anything."

A hypochondriac, he'd have four physical examinations a year, pop seven vitamins a day during the winter, and reportedly suffered a phobia of serious illness. He disliked fresh air: upon entering a room, he would typically close all the windows. He was said to dislike the country—grass reminded him of graves, and he refused to wear green clothes because they were the color of grass. Among his other phobias were flying and wearing clothes with loose or missing buttons, which he thought brought bad luck.

Uninterested in sports as an adult, he was something of a reader —he owned 800 books on black history, and had underlined passages about Denmark Vesey and Nat Turner, both leaders of violent slave rebellions. At one time his favorite movie actress was Mae West, and he was known to slip out of theaters where he was playing, between shows, to sit in on a western or action movie. He

Ellington greets a visitor backstage in his dressing room outfitted with stage makeup, changes of outfit, and a piano.

liked to get massages, and sometimes, with his privacy protected by a screen, even conducted magazine interviews during such sessions.

Ellington hated to hurry or be hurried, was often late to rehearsals and performances. "It is no secret among theatre folk," *The Afro-American* complained in 1937, "that the Duke is one of the most irresponsible men in show business. Whenever he is playing an engagement one or two of his bandsmen follow him around to make sure he gets on the stage on time." Ellington found train travel a sanctuary, because, as he put it, "Folks can't rush you until you get off."

His sleeping, eating, and romancing habits were legendary. Known for his energy, he could go for days with little or no sleep, and usually didn't go to bed till morning. But when he fell asleep, it often took an hour of great effort for someone to wake him. His road manager, Jack Boyd, lived in fear of Ellington's nodding off at an inopportune time. Once, sleepily getting off a train in San Francisco, he ended up in a van of prisoners bound for San Quentin. The guard would not let him off—till Boyd came to the rescue.

His appetite was enormous—one report had him eating thirty-two hot dogs in a single evening. A typical dinner might include a steak, then another, a lobster in butter, two orders of French fries, a salad, a bowl of tomatoes, coffee, and a custom-designed dessert beginning with slices of three different cakes, topped with scoops of three different varieties of ice cream, each set off with a different topping. Then, really stimulated, he might order pancakes, waffles, ham and eggs, and biscuits. Astonishingly he was able to keep his weight to 210 pounds.

The unabashed charm of his youth was by now polished to a sparkle: "Duke drew people to him like flies to sugar," observed

Ellington suavely charms a group of admiring women.
His sister said it was "shocking" the way some women threw themselves at him.

Sonny Greer. Above all, Ellington had a way of captivating women. Reaching a blond secretary on the telephone, he'd open with "Hello—is this the beautiful department?" Or he'd walk over to a woman and unashamedly offer one of his oft-used lines: "Whose pretty little girl are you?" or "Gee, you make that dress look pretty" or "My mother always told me to gravitate toward beauty, so I had to come and see you" or "I never knew an angel could be so luscious" or "I'm so jealous of your frock because it's closer to you than I will ever be." Ellington seemed to have not only a large appetite for food but also for feminine beauty and sexual relations, taking, in fact, an aesthetic delight in women. He regarded women "as flowers," his sister said in a Smithsonian interview, "each one lovely in her own way. And they absolutely adored him. Just was shocking—how the women—really shocking—I couldn't believe it, the way the women kind of fell on their faces in front of him."

Whether female companionship detracted Ellington from his life's work in music, or, on the contrary, enriched it is a question that is impossible to answer with any degree of certainty. One of his friends and lyricists, Don George, felt it was the latter. "It's all in there, and that's what makes it great. . . . His richness of experience is what gives the music its potency. Nobody wrote music and had a band that colorful and that tragic and that swinging, with all the other things in there, because nobody lived a life like Duke Ellington."

Amid the distraction and disorder of constant travel, rehearsals, performances, recording sessions, broadcasts, and dealings with people new and old, Ellington, perhaps in self-defense, worked to maintain a customary cool and calm. As one observer noted, "He craves peace," and hated to argue with his players, whether about an advance in salary or overtime pay. "Why should I knock myself out in an argument about fifteen dollars when in the same time I can probably write a fifteen-hundred-dollar song?" he asked. Moreover, Ellington the psychologist knew that an argument could easily lead to a less-than-satisfactory performance.

A writer might do his best work only at a favorite desk, a sculptor at her own studio, a composer at a special piano. That Ellington could turn out dozens, even hundreds, of inspired compositions while crisscrossing the nation, often in the musical equivalent of a politician's whistle-stop tour, is astounding. It took an individual of enormous purpose, flexibility, and calm to enable his creative juices to flow and flow and flow.

In 1941 and 1942, the band continued producing critically acclaimed records, despite rocky times. During a nine-month period, Ellington would lose no fewer than four performers. In the course of *Jump for Joy*, Jimmie Blanton, it was clear, had become increasingly ill. Suffering from tuberculosis, he finally had to leave the Ellington orchestra around November 20, 1941, and died seven months later. Ellington wired the money for a casket with 500 flowers for the funeral. Blanton was replaced by Alvin "Junior" Raglin, a twenty-four-year-old whom Ellington had found playing in a local nightclub. Raglin was a capable player, but the orchestra was diminished by the loss of the virtuoso Blanton.

After Pearl Harbor, things were never the same for the big bands: World War II created multiple difficulties for Ellington and his company. Their Pullman cars had been commandeered; the train coaches were so jam-packed that often the players were forced to sit in aisles; gasoline and automobile tires were in short supply, and so travel generally became dicey and difficult. Shellac for records was in short supply; and the number of musicians and ready fans was being reduced by the military draft.

Barney Bigard had grown soul-weary of traveling: "In all of my years these were the most confusing years," he related. "Your head stays in a permanent muddle because of the traveling. In fact all of the things happening here that I am telling are not in particular order; they just happened somewhere in the 'road' years." And, as the war progressed, he felt, "it seemed that things got worse by the day."

Not only tired of constant touring, Bigard also wanted to settle in Los Angeles to be with his wife-to-be, Dorothe. He departed the band around July 7, 1942. "When I told him I was leaving," he recalled, Ellington "just looked at me and didn't say a word." Bigard's departure after fourteen extraordinary years with Ellington was widely lamented, and it left a gaping hole in the orchestra's sound. Ellington first approached another New Orleans clarinetist,

Edmond Hall, but was turned down. Instead Ellington ended up hiring Chauncey Haughton, an east coaster whose style was a far cry from Bigard's and Hall's; by early 1943, however, Haughton would be drafted.

The same month that Bigard quit, Ivie Anderson resigned. The reason she gave publicly was wanting to settle in Los Angeles with her new husband. Now she would live in Los Angeles, manage Ivie's Chicken Shack—just off the main stem of African-Americans, Central Avenue—and sing occasionally in local clubs. But Anderson had suffered shortness of breath from asthma for years, and there was speculation that she was also quitting Ellington for health reasons. Her stage presence and moving delivery, sharpened after twelve years with Ellington, would be missed by many. She would be replaced in time by Betty Roché, one of Ellington's better choices in singers.

Herb Jeffries also chose to remain in Los Angeles. His position would be filled for six months by the now-forgotten Jimmy Britton. Southern California, with its sunny clime and somewhat less rigid race relations, was enticing more of the Ellington circle. In mid 1942, Juan and Rosebud Tizol moved their home from New York to Los Angeles.

"The backgrounds Duke wrote for individual talents not only showed them off to the best advantage," Sonny Greer declared in the 1960s, "but also made them feel comfortable. The art of presentation is engrained in him, and when musicians moved out on their own, or into another band, they soon found out it wasn't the same." In fact, Ellington brought out the best in his players, and in almost every case, musicians who left Ellington never achieved the heights they did while playing in his orchestra.

As if the departure of some of his stalwarts were not enough of a setback, on August 1, 1942, the American Federation of Musicians, ruled by union boss James Petrillo, enjoined its musicians to cease recording for record companies. Except for a few transcription recordings intended exclusively for radio stations, Ellington was forced to stop making records for sale to the public indefinitely. Thus not only did his (and his players') income drop, but also exposure for the band and its new compositions, too.

At the end of 1942, Ellington's contract with Robbins Music expired. As early as mid 1941, Ellington had decided to take the most forceful step of his career in bringing his business affairs under his control: he founded his own publishing firm, Tempo Music Company, which became affiliated with ASCAP at the end of 1942.

There certainly was precedent: Irving Berlin, to cite one famous example, had been his own publisher since 1913. But relatively few black tunesmiths had managed to create and successfully operate their own publishing firms (W.C. Handy and Clarence Williams were among the rare few who did, beginning in the 1910s). Normally, a composer's or songwriter's work came out through a Tin Pan Alley firm, nearly all of which were white operated. In establishing Tempo, Ellington struck a blow for his own creative and financial control, and set another example for artists to operate their own firms. Later, many other jazz musicians—for example, John Lewis, Charles Mingus, and John Coltrane—would follow Ellington's lead in establishing their own imprints, part of a small but significant movement toward decentralization of the music industry and greater economic power for creative artists.

Since at least 1930, there had been press reports that Ellington was thinking about a major concert piece. "I'm going to compose a musical evolution of the Negro race," he told a reporter in 1931. "I've been going to do this for five years, but somehow or other I've always kind of put it off." Newspaper reports described it at various times as a suite in five parts, a musical, a "saga," an operetta, an opera called *Boola*, and a symphony. An account in 1933 reported its five movements would be: *Africa, Slaveship, The Plantation, Harlem*, and a finale. He read books and spoke with experts: "He is always telephoning around for authentic information," a newspaper noted in 1938, "about slave ships, the civil war, cotton and the two Johns—Henry and Brown."

When, late in 1942, his manager, William Morris, secured him a debut at Carnegie Hall, Ellington decided to premiere the piece there. In December 1942, he began working in earnest on this major work and completed it in about six weeks. The concert was set for Saturday, January 23, 1943, and preceded by "National Ellington Week," a publicity gimmick which succeeded in garnering stories in *Time, Newsweek,* and the *New York Times.* An expectant crowd—including such celebrities as Eleanor Roosevelt and Leopold Stokowski—filled Carnegie and spilled onto the stage. Ellington was presented a plaque signed by thirty-two eminent musicians, including Walter Damrosch, Leopold Stokowski, Arthur Rodzinski, Roy Harris, Fritz Reiner, Kurt Weill, Aaron Copland, Marian Anderson, Jerome Kern, William Grant Still, Earl Hines, Count Basie, Paul Robeson, and Benny Goodman. It was, as Ellington admitted, "a very hectic night," and the composer was so nervous he walked on stage without the music.

The focal point and highlight of the three-hour-long concert was *Black, Brown and Beige: A Tone Parallel to the History of the Negro in America*—the longest (forty-four minutes) and most ambitious work of Ellington's career. The piece is a programmatic tone poem. A twenty-nine-page narrative sketch gives a fuller picture of the story line that Ellington had in mind in writing *Black, Brown and Beige.* It describes in Ellington's hand the story of an ageless African named Boola. He is ripped from his community, imprisoned—degraded, frightened, exhausted, and starving—on a slave ship, where in "the adjoining cabin a woman is screaming—a symphony of torture." The composer, however, dropped these first two movements—*Africa* and *Slaveship*—with all the pain and suffering they entailed. Perhaps this was due to a lack of time, or perhaps by his innate patriotism and a desire, especially during wartime, to emphasize positive aspects of American pluralism.

"The first thing the Black man did in America was WORK," wrote Ellington in his scenario, "and there the Work Song was born . . . a song of burden." *Work Song* became the first section of the opening movement *(Black),* followed by *Come Sunday.* Boola finds a Bible, painfully teaches himself to read it and then "he had something to live for—something to work for—something to sing for." Ellington continued, "Come Sunday, while all the Whites had gone into the church, the slaves congregated under a tree. Huddled together, they passed the word of God around in whispers. . . . He must enjoy the sweet suffering of this profound internal upheaval of love and joy in silence." "Good souls praying and singing faithfully," Ellington wrote, "without a word of bitterness or revenge—'I forgive my past suffering, just let my people go.' " *Black* concludes with a section called "Light." "The desire for freedom motivated their songs," wrote Ellington, "inspired their heroes—real and legendary, actions, policies, and efforts, fight for or with anybody, chain breaking."

The scenario continues with the second movement, called *Brown*, which, Ellington wrote in his memoirs, "recognized the contribution made by the Negro to this country in blood." In the handwritten scenario, Boola tries unsuccessfully to enlist on the American side during the Revolutionary War. "When things were darkest for the states, there came great warriors from the West Indies." A jangling *West Indian Dance* celebrated the contribution of 545 black soldiers from the island of Santo Domingo (later Haiti) to the battle of Savannah during the Revolutionary War. Some slaves got their freedom, but Boola's servitude continued. During the Civil War, he joined the Union army and "jumped for joy" with the Emancipation Proclamation—illustrated musically with a joyous *Emancipation Celebration* that is tinged with sorrow because the older folks, who had worked all their lives "and earned the right to sit down and be taken care of" were worried. In the third section of *Brown*, called *Mauve* or *The Blues*, Ellington writes, "Boola was *the* hero of San Juan Hill," but was caught up in a love triangle. The only vocal section, *The Blues* was sung by Betty Roché, in free rhythm to the accompaniment of dark orchestral colors and a feeling of unresolved mourning.

The third movement, *Beige*, covers the twentieth century, when, Ellington wrote, there was "swift progress." The scene moves to Harlem, full of hope, promise, and irony, as symbolized by the advent of World War II. This movement, ironically, is the least effective section. Evidence suggests that Ellington was rushing to complete this part, and it sounds more like a pastiche of themes than an integrated whole—in short, not fully realized.

The title *Black, Brown and Beige* suggests a historical progression not of skin colors but, metaphorically, of the increasing integration of people of African descent and their culture into American society. In this work, Ellington was recounting a saga, a heavily programmatic piece which is more meaningful and moving if you know the story: despite cruel and degrading treatment at the hands of some whites, the people in this narrative hold on to their faith and find life's joys along with self-esteem. Ellington tells a story that is troubling, powerful, and hopeful, of a people forgiving, affirming, and without bitterness. Covering considerable historical and emotional ground, *Black, Brown and Beige* is, by turns, painful, angry, patriotic, wistful, mournful, celebratory, brooding, ironic, bemused, reverential, assertive, and proud.

As music, however, the tone poem is also uneven, showing Ellington—heretofore primarily a brilliant miniaturist—struggling with large form. The third section, especially, revealed one of his weaknesses: he did most things at the last minute. "I couldn't work without a deadline," he once confessed. "If I retired to some luxurious home by the sea, you know what I'd write? Nuthin'!"

The concert was a financial success, grossing $7,000, and netting $5,000 for Russian war relief. Some of the criticisms of *Black, Brown and Beige* were harsh: Paul Bowles in the *Herald Tribune* called it "formless and meaningless . . . a gaudy potpourri . . . corny . . . trite. . . . The whole attempt to view jazz as a form of art music should be discouraged." There was some favorable reaction, too, but few reviewers—positive or negative, jazz or classical—seemed to really understand the piece, in part because probably few knew much about black history.

Prior to the premiere, Ellington told *Down Beat*, "If a sincere interest and intellectual discernment are not notably factors of the New York audience reaction, it will be a great disappointment to me and a deterrent to the ambition of all progressing American composers." His sister, Ruth, recalled that after the negative reviews to *Black, Brown and Beige*, he "sort of withdrew and was very quiet." "I believe its nonacceptance," writes Gunther Schuller, "discouraged Duke from trying similar extended compositional challenges—at least for a while. In crucial ways it interrupted the flow of his creative momentum."

Black, Brown and Beige never achieved a regular position in Ellington's repertoire. And except for a concert five nights later in Boston, and another a month later in Cleveland, Ellington never again performed the entire work. He never commercially recorded the entire piece, either, and a "live" recording of the Carnegie concert—with somewhat scratchy, uneven fidelity—was not issued to the public until 1977. He did, however, continue to feature cer-

An advertising handbill for Ellington's debut performance at Carnegie Hall, January 23, 1943, when he premiered the ambitious *Black, Brown and Beige*, which he called "a tone parallel to the history of the Negro in America."

tain sections of the work, and recycled parts of it into newer pieces. Fifty years later, analysts are still grappling with *Black, Brown and Beige* and its place in the Ellington canon and American culture. Now that the scores and sketches are accessible at the Smithsonian, more knowing assessments of this milestone will be possible.

And so, with his debut at Carnegie, Ellington passed a turning point: after working in New York for twenty years, having made more than 700 commercial recordings and selling nearly 20 million records, creating music of a kind never heard before, and having been acclaimed in some of Europe's leading concert halls, he was finally given an opportunity to perform at the United States' foremost *concert hall*. This event and the scope of *Black, Brown and Beige* altered his reputation and patterns of composing and performing. In addition to his other mantles, from now on, he would wear that of concert artist.

Since returning from Europe, Ellington had given up heavy drinking, taken firmer control of his business by creating his own publishing company, added two significant players, begun a soulfully deep collaboration with Billy Strayhorn, made dozens of acclaimed recordings, pioneered a civil rights musical, and was now, at long last, beginning to realize an important dream—to establish himself as a concert artist in his native land.

At the same time, the loss of Cootie Williams, Jimmie Blanton, Barney Bigard, and Ivie Anderson, the critical brickbats for *Black, Brown and Beige*, and especially the uncertainties of the recording ban and the war—no one knew how long either would last and what their costs might ultimately be—all cast shadows on the future of Ellington's composing, performing, and recording; in short, on his musical life.

Essential Ellington,

1939–43

On the heels of the European triumph, and the additions of arranger Billy Strayhorn, the bass virtuoso Jimmie Blanton, and the powerhouse tenor saxophonist Ben Webster, Ellington and his highly seasoned players now entered into a period of making what are widely considered to be dozens of masterworks. Here are twenty-some, culled from the more than a hundred recordings intended for commercial release. Unless otherwise noted, the following recordings can all be heard on the three-CD set *The Blanton-Webster Band* (Bluebird).

The exuberant *Sergeant Was Shy* is celebrated for a succession of virtuosic breaks featuring Bigard's clarinet, Stewart's cornet, and Nanton's trombone. The piece is built on the harmonic progression to *Bugle Call Rag*. It will be reissued in the CD series *The Chronological Duke Ellington*.

Revitalized by Webster and Blanton, the Ellington band made an auspicious debut on Victor in March 1940 with *Jack the Bear*, a showcase for

(continued)

---

the bass virtuoso Jimmie Blanton. The work, named for a Harlem bass player, also features striking orchestral effects and memorable solos by Bigard, Harry Carney on alto sax, and Nanton. The piece is on *Beyond Category*.

From its opening tom-toms to its final crescendo, *Ko-Ko* (1940) fascinates with its drama, reportedly depicting slaves' frenetic dancing in New Orleans's legendary Congo Square. The jungle effects of Ellington's Cotton Club days here become a deeper part of the musical structure, and, as in a bolero, each successive blues chorus builds in intensity. *Ko-Ko* includes memorable solos by Tizol, Nanton, Ellington, and Blanton, but it's the orchestral writing, especially, that makes it unique. Melodically and harmonically sophisticated, emotionally and intellectually stimulating, *Ko-Ko* ranks as one of Ellington's most esteemed recordings. It's on *Beyond Category*.

Concerto for Cootie (1940), also included in *Beyond Category*, is one of Ellington's foremost "concertos" and Cootie Williams's most celebrated single recording. The master of contrast, composer Ellington provides three unlike themes (the first of which, fitted with lyrics, became a hit song in 1943 as *Do Nothin' Till You Hear from Me*). Playing successively on muted, open, and growl trumpet, alternately poignant, sweet, bluesy, sorrowful, and exaltative, Williams showcases his remarkable range of sounds and moods.

The forward-looking, fast-swinging *Cotton Tail* (1940) is built upon a series of variations on the chord progressions of Gershwin's *I Got Rhythm*. Ben Webster's inspired improvisation became one of his most famous and enduring. *Cotton Tail* has dozens of rewarding aspects—right up to the ending, with its exceptional control of dynamics. *Cotton Tail* has been reissued on *Beyond Category*.

From the banner year of 1940 also came the tone poem *Dusk*, reminiscent of *Mood Indigo*, but darker. Rich sonorities never before heard in music,

(continued)

haunting solos by Rex Stewart and Lawrence Brown, the overall spareness and feeling of melancholy make *Dusk* memorable. It is available on *Beyond Category*.

On the classic ballad *All Too Soon* (1940), trombonist Lawrence Brown offers Ellington's theme ravishingly, with Hardwick's alto sax obbligato floating delicately above. Then tenorman Webster rhapsodizes sensuously on the melody, while muted brass slip in a contrasting, gentle riff.

The loose, eminently danceable *In a Mellotone* (1940) is a showcase for contrasting call-and-response patterns. In the first chorus, the saxophones are answered variably by the trio of trombones; in the second, Cootie Williams's intensifying solo is punctuated by the saxes. Johnny Hodges climaxes the piece with an increasingly bluesy chorus.

When it was released, the Ellington-Blanton duet *Pitter Panther Patter* (1940) amazed many listeners with its virtuosic bass playing. Blanton here transforms the bass into a *melody* instrument, providing contrast and counterpoint to Ellington's piano line. The recording can be heard on *Solos, Trios, and Duets* (Bluebird) and on *Beyond Category*.

The small-group sessions, now on Victor, came to an end in September 1941, but before that fifty-four recordings were made. Highlights include four Hodges vehicles—Strayhorn's harmonically rich ballads *Day Dream* and *Passion Flower*, the swinging *Squaty Roo*, and the bluesy *Things Ain't What They Used to Be*—along with three recordings under Stewart's name: the mournful *Mobile Bay* (made in tribute to Cootie Williams on evidently his final day with the band), the jaunty *Linger Awhile*, and the hip *Subtle Slough*. All are available on *The Great Ellington Units* (Bluebird).

Warm Valley (1940) describes a scene not geographical, but rather anatomical; Ellington was inspired by thoughts of a reclining woman. This sensuous piece is a concerto for Hodges—a complete master of both

(continued)

emotional and technical musicianship, and unmatched as a player of warm, lyrical, romantic melody.

Seemingly a casual piece, *Across the Track Blues* (1940) is Ellington's carefully worked out elaboration of that classically simple and soulful form, the blues, with Bigard, Stewart, and Brown contributing solos in their distinctive styles. Ellington's blues sounded unlike anyone else's.

Take the "A" Train is a showcase for trumpeter Ray Nance and orchestra, and marked Billy Strayhorn's breakthrough as a composer. This compelling dance number became a big hit, and Ellington adopted it as his orchestra's signature tune from 1941 until the end of his life. There was also a version with lyrics—Strayhorn said he was writing subway directions—but this is the classic "A" Train. It's available on *Beyond Category*.

Mercer Ellington's structurally complex *Blue Serge* (1941) conveys throughout a mood of darkness and brooding, enhanced by Nanton's sobbing trombone, Webster's shadowy saxophone, and the ensemble's somber harmonies and voicings.

From *Jump for Joy* came the hit *I Got It Bad (and That Ain't Good)* (1941). Singing the vernacular lyric (by Paul Francis Webster) that for a change begins to approach the quality of Ellington's music, Ivie Anderson gave the song one of her most affecting performances on record. She is matched by Johnny Hodges's sensuous, sliding, singing lines; indeed, *I Got It Bad* is one of *his* most lyrical and elegant ballad recordings.

Billy Strayhorn's melancholy tone poem *Chelsea Bridge* (1941) uses Debussyan harmonies and high, light sonorities. The piece represents another example of how, only two years after joining the Ellington orchestra as arranger, Strayhorn had mastered "the Ellington effect" of orchestration and enriched it with his own training in European classical music.

(continued)

With its succession of swinging soloists, *C-Jam Blues* (1942) sounds like an informal jam session, building through five solos. Then in the sixth and seventh choruses, composer Ellington engulfs Bigard's clarinet in dramatic orchestral figures that bring the piece to a climactic close.

Mercer Ellington's wistful *Moon Mist* (1942) features Ray Nance's alluring violin, and also offers affecting solos by Hodges and Brown and delicate and lovely orchestral voicings. *Moon Mist* can be heard on *Beyond Category*.

With its angular melody and rhythmic phrasing, *Main Stem* (1942) presages the bebop revolution to come. Ellington drew on two well-known jazz traditions—the blues and riff-based tunes—to create something new and exciting. He contrasts soloist after master solist—Stewart, Hodges, Nance, Bigard, Nanton, Webster, and Brown—punctuated by jabs from the orchestra. For soloists *and* ensemble, *Main Stem* is a triumph.

Climaxing Ellington's Carnegie Hall debut in 1943 was *Black, Brown and Beige*—his most ambitious work, inspired yet uneven. Its most memorable sections are *The Blues, Emancipation Celebration,* and *Come Sunday*. The hauntingly ethereal *Come Sunday* is one of Ellington's most ravishing melodies, played luminously by Hodges, who stretches from each phrase every nuance of tender and reverential feeling, drawing instant, awed applause from the audience. The entire concert can be heard on *The Duke Ellington Carnegie Hall Concerts, January 1943* (Prestige).

The Ellington orchestra was recorded often on location, but rarely as memorably as on *Fargo, North Dakota, November 7, 1940* (Vintage Jazz Classics). Two and one half hours of music have been reissued as a two-CD set, documenting a typical night's dance, pieces that were twice as long as the versions he recorded commercially—thus allowing the soloists to stretch out—and a number of fine solos, including Jimmie Blanton's on *Sepia Panorama* and Ben Webster's on *Stardust.*

EIGHT

•

Composing

FOR CONCERTS

•

1943 – 51

llington faced an unsettling period after 1942, a period when he confronted huge problems of personnel changes and new musical competition, when his career as a bandleader thrived for a time as he received increasing recognition, and when his career as a composer found new outlets in writing for concerts.

The period ahead, in fact, the next thirteen years, would bring Ellington many highs and lows. A boost came from the publicity surrounding his Carnegie Hall debut on January 23, 1943, and when he repeated the program five days later at Symphony Hall in Boston, despite the year's worst blizzard, a capacity audience of 3,000 jammed the hall and 1,200 were turned away. When he performed the program again at Cleveland's Civic Auditorium on February 20, a record-breaking crowd of 7,200 turned out.

On April 1, Ellington opened at The Hurricane, at Fifty-first and Broadway, his first nightclub engagement in New York in five years. He and his orchestra were booked for an initial six weeks; so successful was the engagement that they ended up performing for nearly six months. With wartime travel especially wearing, he and his players must have been relieved to settle into one location for a while.

Alternating with a six-piece white dance band, Ellington performed for dancing from 7 P.M. to 4 A.M., and played floor shows at 8 P.M. and 12:30 A.M. He made a flamboyant entrance: he was lowered from the ceiling, on a platform draped in satin, performing on an upright piano. The Ellington orchestra played every night except Monday, and was featured in six nightly broadcasts a week: typically a 10:45 to 11:00 P.M. broadcast, and on Sunday nights, a thirty-minute broadcast, at 7 P.M., called *Pastel Period,* in which Ellington played his mood pieces (for example, *Moon Mist*), which were seldom heard in public.

With the union-dictated ban on making records dragging on, Ellington's only record-making during the embargo was an occasional session to cut sixteen-inch transcription discs intended exclusively for broadcast by disc jockeys, who were coming into

Ellington entertains dancers at The Hurricane in New York,
where the orchestra played for nearly six months in 1943. Their national radio broadcasts
from the club gave his band a terrific boost in popularity and earning power.

prominence at radio stations. These discs and the radio remotes from The Hurricane became especially important in keeping his name and sound before the public. The exposure from The Hurricane broadcasts gave his band a terrific boost in popularity and thus earning power.

Financial records for the Ellington orchestra from 1943 to 1944 provide a rare glimpse inside the orchestra's financial workings and reveal, among many things, the lift given him by The Hurricane. These records, together with a few previously published figures, show that in 1939, Ellington grossed $160,000 but just broke even. In 1940, he took in $185,000, but a jump in his payroll ate up some of the increase in income. In 1941, he earned $135,000, and reported a loss of $1,500 for the year. In 1942, Ellington was paid anywhere from $700 to $1,200 for a one-nighter; for the year Duke Ellington, Inc., grossed $210,000, but netted a mere $4,000.

Ellington evidently was paid at least $3,000 per week at The Hurricane, but, according to one report, he actually lost $18,000 on the engagement, yet felt it was worthwhile because of the Broadway location and the excellent radio exposure, free of charge, and the publicity.

Then, after leaving The Hurricane in October, and going to New York's Capitol Theater, Ellington was reportedly paid more than $8,000 per week. By late 1944, Ellington could command between $1,000 and $2,260 for a one-night dance—nearly double the figure from 1942. At long last, Ellington found a place among the best-paid bandleaders.

Yet his income was offset by high expenses. His payroll increased 66 percent during the period from 1942 to 1944. During this time, Ellington's weekly payroll—including his instrumentalists, singers, touring dancers, road manager, valet, and Billy Strayhorn—ran between $2,000 and $2,500, sometimes as high as $3,000. In July 1942, he was paying salaries to twenty-two people, and in November 1944 that number had climbed to twenty-nine, including his new brother-in-law, Dan James, who was helping to run Tempo Music Company.

Salaries, in fact, were by far Ellington's biggest expense. He paid his players according to a formula known only to him, based perhaps on some combination of the player's last salary before joining

Ellington, star status, seniority within Ellington's orchestra, negotiating persistence and ability, frequency and seriousness of offers to jump to other bands, solo and ensemble-playing abilities, and showmanship, as well as contributions to arrangements, compositions, performances, and recordings.

The financial records confirm that Ellington paid Johnny Hodges more than anyone else, occasionally even more than he himself drew. And Hodges's salary kept escalating. In early 1942, for example, he was making $125 per week. In July, he was making $140, and by May 1943, $160. By late October 1943, he was paid $175 a week and by late December $190. For Victor recording sessions in early 1942 each player was paid $30 to cut three tunes—except Hodges, who commanded $50.

Rex Stewart was second-best paid during most of the this time. In late November 1943, he was getting $160; Otto Hardwick, $150; the newly hired trumpeter Taft Jordan, $140; Juan Tizol, $135; the new clarinetist Jimmy Hamilton, Lawrence Brown, Billy Strayhorn, and trumpeter Shorty Baker, who joined in September 1942, $125; Sonny Greer, $120; and the others $110 or less.

Each week the pay for each player went up and down, depending on how many days the band worked, if they played extra shows, and if they made records. The business records reveal that Hodges was not alone in receiving raises. At a time of war-fueled inflation, a draft-induced shortage of veteran musicians, and rising fortunes for his orchestra, Ellington kept raising the salaries of other players, though not as dramatically as Hodges's. In a 1989 interview Jimmy Hamilton recalled that if a player did not say anything about a raise, Ellington wouldn't bring it up, either. Thus, those who got raises were those who asked for them.

Ellington, Strayhorn, and the road manager and valet got steady salaries, no matter how much or little the band played. (Ellington said in 1943 that Strayhorn "writes when he feels like it, and perhaps it is because he can wait for inspiration to strike him, that what he turns out is good.") Ellington's salary was $250 per week plus $100 expenses, until 1944, when his salary doubled to $500 per week, plus $100 expenses. In 1993 dollars, on an annual basis that would be close to $250,000, including expenses. He was doing well, though not getting rich.

Everyone was paid in cash, and road manager Al Celley, who took over from Charles "Jack" Boyd around 1944, said in a 1989 Smithsonian interview that he packed a .45-caliber pistol because of all the money he was carrying around. (In June 1944, when the band's instruments were stolen from a Toronto nightclub, Celley said, he brandished the gun and forced their return. Celley also claimed that Ellington carried a pistol, too, and knew how to use it.)

A 1944 year-end financial statement prepared by the accounting firm of Frendel, Brown & Co. showed Duke Ellington, Inc., had an income of $405,000 (twice the gross reported just two years earlier, confirming that Ellington's marketability was rising) and expenses of $394,000, which yielded a profit of just $11,000. His expenses are summarized in the following table:

DUKE ELLINGTON, INC.

Statement of Operations for 1944

Expenses and Deductions

Payroll—Band	$119,000
Payroll—Acts	14,300
Payroll—Vocalists	11,400
Payroll—Staff	33,300
Salary—Duke Ellington	26,500
Advertising and publicity	15,100
Fares, baggage transfers, gratuities, etc.	78,300
Commissions	43,300
Arranging and copying	16,300
Union tax	500
Telephone and telegraph	1,500
Choir expenses	1,600
Photos	1,000
Uniforms and costumes	9,900
Xmas expenses	3,000
Repairs of instruments	1,400
Employees hospitalization & medical expenses	1,800
Accounting & executive expense	6,500
Legal	500
Insurance	1,200
Stationery & supplies	100
Interest	300

Miscellaneous expenses	1,400
Social Security tax	1,000
Unemployment insurance taxes	3,000
Other taxes	500
Depreciation—automobile	300

$395,000

NOTE: All figures are rounded to nearest hundred dollars, and the total many not add because of rounding. The "choir expenses" included payments, the day after Christmas, of $200 to Ellington's uncle George, $50 to Mrs. Laura Ellington, and $100 to a Gloria Dickman.

"He spends money lavishly," claimed one report in 1944, "supports a good many hangers-on, lends money freely, gets it back infrequently, and is usually broke when the weekly pay day rolls around." The financial records contain hints to support this assertion. An occasional payment to Sonny Greer ($100) for "arrangements" shows up on the list of "Petty cash paid out." In fact, Ellington was probably either lending the money to Greer or helping him out in a scrape. An expense summary for December 1944 shows Ellington sending $50 a week to his long-estranged wife, Edna, and $10 a week to former band member Freddie Jenkins. But both Al Celley and Jimmy Hamilton, in separate Smithsonian interviews, agreed that Ellington was unconcerned about money. He did not seem to think about it very much, Hamilton said; he was thinking about composing music. On occasion, perhaps when thinking more as a bandleader/businessman than as a composer, Ellington was known to get upset about finances—perhaps confirming that he liked money as much as the next person—but mostly, to maintain his cool, he avoided discussing money matters.

As Tempo Music Company settled in, one big difference became obvious: it was not going to offer much of its music to the public as sheet music. Mills and Robbins had both issued a stream of song sheets, piano editions, and collections of Ellington's music. Tempo would publish very few pieces. This was part of a long twentieth-century trend: the decline of sheet music. As musical literacy decreased, the public decreasingly made its own music (or did it without reading music) and increasingly relied on professionals—through records, radio, and, soon, television—for its music. Tempo would derive most of its income not from selling sheet music to the public but rather, like most other publishers, from collecting royalties from the sale of recordings of its compositions. Thus, during the post–World War II period, one looked in vain for sheet music to most of Ellington's pieces. The only written version of most of these pieces was in the Ellington orchestra library—completely unavailable to the public until 1988, when his archive was acquired by the Smithsonian Institution.

The years of 1943 and 1944 were prosperous ones for Ellington the songwriter. In the first half of 1943, *Don't Get Around Much Anymore* became a hit via radio, sheet music, and record (in a version by the Ink Spots). Ellington was astounded when he received a royalty check from RCA Victor for $22,500. *Do Nothin' Till You Hear from Me* in 1943, and *I'm Beginning to See the Light* in 1944, also became popular.

Despite these successes, some hits back in the 1930s, and one in the 1950s, Ellington did not achieve the degree of popularity he wanted as a writer of songs. Gunther Schuller has posited three reasons: that Ellington was not a "natural" writer of pure melody that could stand on its own—most of his "tunes arose out of their harmonies"; that his melodic choices tended toward "sinuous," large intervals that limited their appeal to singers and listeners; and that he used "such sophisticated harmonies that . . . the average listener would be left aurally far behind."

In addition, Ellington's songs mostly don't equal the quality of his instrumental works because he conceived many of his songs *as instrumentals* and the words were added later, sometimes as a decided afterthought. Thus the songs don't necessarily form the unified wholes that can result when a lyricist and composer work hand in glove, or when one person writes both words and music. Finally, Ellington rarely met his match among lyricists, and some of the lyrics suffer from triteness, awkwardness, or forgettability.

. . .

As the war raged on, it affected Ellington both positively and neg-
atively. By 1944, many of the biggest stars in Hollywood would join
the army and go off to war—Clark Gable, Robert Taylor, Jimmy
Stewart, Mickey Rooney, along with directors Frank Capra, William Wyler, John Huston, John Ford. Many musicians—including
Jack Jenney, Buck Clayton, Jay McShann, Mel Powell, Willie
Smith, and Jimmy McPartland—were drafted, and bandleaders
such as Artie Shaw, Claude Thornhill, Bob Crosby, and the ill-
fated Glenn Miller would serve abroad. Ellington had been expecting to take a physical examination for the draft around January 15,
1943, but potential induction was halted by a government edict in
December 1942 against conscripting men over the age of thirty-
eight. The forty-two-year-old Ellington, like Count Basie, then just
thirty-eight, remained a civilian throughout the war. A number of
Ellington's men, however, received calls from their draft boards.
Ray Nance was rejected. In May 1943, Lawrence Brown went to
the West Coast and waited six weeks for his call, which ultimately
didn't come. Several players, however, were drafted out of the
orchestra, including Barney Bigard's replacement Chauncey
Haughton, trumpeter Wallace Jones, as well as Mercer Ellington.

As a civilian, Ellington did his patriotic part by performing ben-
efits for Russian war relief and the Joint Anti-Fascist Refugee Com
mittee and for savings bond rallies, and playing for soldiers at
military bases such as Fort Dix, New Jersey. In January 1944,
however, Ellington refused to play for a whites-only USO show at
the Great Lakes Naval Training Base (north of Chicago) unless also
allowed to perform for 8,000 black trainees stationed there.

While some of the popular songs that appeared during the war
offered themes of patriotism or jingoism, most were, in the words
of Charles McGovern, "love ballads of separation and fantasy."
Ellington's only directly war-related recording was *A Slip of a Lip
(Can Sink a Ship)* in July 1942, written by Mercer and Luther
Henderson, with Ray Nance singing the vocal good-naturedly. Perhaps the most visible things Ellington did were to make transcription discs of more than seventy-nine half-hour programs for the

Armed Forces Radio Service, cooperate with the issuing of other special records for servicemen called V-Discs, and, beginning in April 1945, participate in a series (of about forty-eight shows) of fifty-five-minute network radio programs called *Your Saturday Date with the Duke*, sponsored by the U.S. Treasury Department as a means of selling war bonds. As a result of his work for the Treasury Department, road manager Celley said, he was usually able to secure a bus for the band during the war.

Because shellac was in short supply, Ellington's records, like so many others, became harder to purchase in the United States and abroad. Leonard Feather reported in November 1942 that "American swing records are still at a premium; disks that sell here for thirty-five cents are retailed [in London] at one dollar. Chief American favorites are Goodman, the Dorseys, Duke Ellington, Jimmie Lunceford. . . . A national poll revealed Ellington as British fans' No. 1 favorite—they still remember the sensation he caused on his British tour" of 1933.

The changes in personnel which had stepped up in 1942 became more frequent in 1943. Some of the positions became almost revolving doors. Jimmy Britton left, and, in mid-May, was replaced by the blind singer Al Hibbler. Chauncey Haughton was drafted on April 10, 1943. A big blow came in August 1943, when tenorman Ben Webster left to take a solo job on Fifty-second Street. Then, for three years in a row, a major voice would depart. On April 21, 1944, longtime valve trombonist Juan Tizol would leave to join Harry James's band (with a raise), and Tizol's family, on the West Coast. Around September 12, 1945, Ray Nance left to form his own group; he would, however, return in seven months. On December 17, 1945, cornetist Rex Stewart would leave, upset with "a new member of the Ellington organization," whom he wouldn't name, "who was harassing me," and formed his own sextet. And on July 20, 1946, trombonist Tricky Sam Nanton would be felled by a cerebral hemmorhage, a jolting loss because he was the first musician to die while with Ellington, and his sound was so strikingly original. Also in April 1946, in a dispute with Ellington reportedly over a woman, veteran alto saxophonist Toby Hardwick walked off the stage during a performance at the Howard Theatre, in Washington, D.C., leaving the orchestra, and, subsequently, the music business.

After 1942, Ellington never again regained the stability of personnel that graced his band during the 1930s and early 1940s. There was great turnover: sometimes a "chair" in his orchestra would change three times a year. The turnover among singers, particularly the women, during the 1940s was especially frequent. Between 1943 and the end of 1950, fifteen different trumpeters worked in Ellington's band. There were various reasons: the draft, salaries and other allures of other bands, some conflicts with Ellington, and increasingly, as the 1940s wore on, the difficulties Ellington faced in keeping his band going. The discontinuities made Ellington's job, and that of the players, more difficult. Yet characteristically, Ellington seemed to take the comings and goings in stride. In the ensuing years, some of his best veterans would leave and some would remain, and some marvelous new instrumentalists would join the fold. But for now, at least, Ellington and his fans could count on the inimitable Johnny Hodges, the unmatched Lawrence Brown, and the trademark sound of Harry Carney.

One of the most gifted players to join during the mid- to late-1940s was the twenty-five-year-old clarinetist Jimmy Hamilton, who joined in April 1943 and would remain twenty-five years. A veteran of the bands of Lucky Millinder and Teddy Wilson, Hamilton boasted virtuosic technique and superb fluency. Taking Ben Webster's old chair, tenorman Al Sears would play from mid 1944 to the end of 1948. The twenty-three-year-old Oscar Pettiford, who extended Jimmie Blanton's innovations and made the bass a genuine solo instrument, played with Ellington from November 1945 to March 1948. The high-note trumpet specialist William "Cat" Anderson worked with the orchestra from September 1944 until May 1947: "One note higher," quipped *Variety*, "and only a dog could hear him." Russell Procope, who played able lead alto saxophone and, more impressively, clarinet in the New Orleans style, joined in April 1946 and would stay until the end. The "musical chairs" brought audible changes in the Ellington sound, perhaps none more than the loss of Bigard's woody clarinet, echoing back to New Orleans and all that it symbolized, and the addition of Jimmy Hamilton, with his clean, modern sound, minimal vibrato, and classically trained technique. Compare, for instance, the hot Bigard in *Harlem Airshaft* (1940) with the cool Hamilton in *Fugue-a-Ditty* (1947).

Some writers have asserted that partly because of the loss of such great individualists as Bigard, Webster, Stewart, Tizol, and Nanton, Ellington's music suffered a marked falloff after the halcyon days of the early 1940s. A biography of Ellington written by James Lincoln Collier and published in 1987 went so far as to paint Ellington's musical life after about 1943 as one long decline. Among younger critics, on the other hand, Stanley Crouch has argued that Ellington later "went on to deepen the clarity and conception of his craft, very nearly creating something every decade that was superior to all high points in his previous work." Which period of Ellingtonia a critic likes best has often been a matter of generation: those who discovered Ellington during the early 1940s, typically as they were coming of age, have tended to argue for the primacy of his music from that period. Some who discovered him around 1960 gravitated toward his music of *that* period.

Unquestionably, the Ellington sound was altered by changes in the orchestra's personnel. Part of Ellington's genius, however, was the way he would write pieces to bring out the strengths of his players, and he always continued to do that, but it generally took time for him to learn a player's capabilities before he could compose just the right pieces for him. So perhaps after 1942 there was not so much a falling off as a leveling off, at a time when new styles of jazz would offer innovations and excitement and thus grab considerable attention. The loss of markedly original voices, the instability of personnel combined with Ellington's switches in record companies, some lapses in taste, and changes in the music audience and business so that his artistic successes came far less often now: in the early 1940s, Schuller has argued, the forgettable Ellington recording was the exception, while in the late 1940s it was the rule. Ellington would, however, make many more "masterpieces" in later years.

In retrospect, Ellington's musical creativity intensified through a twenty-year-long arc from the beginning of the Cotton Club engagement (1927) through 1947. Recordings, the best datable evidence, dipped sharply in quantity in 1931 (because of the depression), in

Ellington poses in February 1942 outside a record-shop window display in Washington, D.C. His records were now being issued in albums containing multiple discs and colorful covers.

quality and quantity in 1935 (after his mother's death), and in quantity in 1943–44 (because of the recording ban). Judging from recordings again, 1940 was the musical peak of this arc, and then beginning in 1948 there was a relatively fallow period, though even during it Ellington produced some sparkling and enduring music. (Later, Ellington would enjoy another, somewhat shorter period of concentrated creativity, from 1956 to about 1968.) If after 1942, Ellington the composer did not produce eminent works as frequently as during the prior two years, Ellington the bandleader was enjoying greater success and more accolades.

During World War II, in the midst of personnel changes, Ellington was receiving greater recognition through awards and honors. As is so often the case with an artist who has been ahead of his public, it took several years for even knowledgeable jazz fans to catch up with Ellington's remarkable work of the early 1940s. Ellington had been winning band polls in the African-American newspaper the *Pittsburgh Courier* since 1931, but finally he began winning polls truly national in scope. This represented a lag between artist and audience—by rights he should have been winning polls during the 1940–42 period, and before that, too.

Before 1944, Ellington came in no higher than second in *Down Beat*'s readers' polls, though Hodges had earned first place. In 1944, Ellington, Hodges, and Carney took top honors. In 1945, Ellington took first place as bandleader and arranger in *Esquire*'s poll, while Hodges won on alto, and Brown, Carney, and Strayhorn took second place in their categories. In 1946, Ellington swept the *Down Beat* poll, copping first place in both "swing band" and "sweet band" categories, and he continued to beat out all other bands in 1947 and 1948.

In 1943, Ellington was presented the Page One Award by the New York Newspaper Guild and invited to deliver a lecture at Harvard University's Music Department on "Negro Music in America," illustrated at the piano. As the result of Carnegie Hall's legitimizing role, the hoopla stirred up by William Morris, the radio exposure from The Hurricane, and his song and record hits, Ellington was becoming more and more popular in mainstream America. *The Saturday Evening Post* published a big story called "The Duke of Hot," replete with color pictures, in its issue of August 7, 1943, and *The New Yorker* ran a detailed three-part profile, "The Hot Bach," in its issues of June 24, July 1, and July 8, 1944. By 1945, there were about seventy-five Ellington fan clubs across the United States, and in Europe, study groups had formed to audition and discuss Ellington recordings. However, when a biography by Barry Ulanov came out in 1946, Ellington was annoyed. "I'm not old enough to be historical, and I'm too young to be biographical," he argued. "Biographies are like tombstones. Who wants one?"

With this rise in popularity would come a rise in musical stature, when the band increasingly would be presented as a concert orchestra. Despite the mixed reviews that had greeted *Black, Brown and Beige*, Ellington's Carnegie Hall debut had been a commercial success and enabled him to establish an essentially annual series of return appearances at Carnegie. Ellington seems to have broken through some kind of barrier. From then on, he would increasingly play concerts at Carnegie or other esteemed halls in the East.

Ellington was not only a concert artist, of course, nor would he ever be one exclusively. But he relished the concert stage, as he told the *The Afro-American* in December 1943:

> On the basis of my experience, concerts are the best medium for trying out new musical ideas on audiences. All the other channels have some disadvantage. Records give you a good balance and plenty of rehearsal, but you can't get the audience reaction on the spot.
>
> Regular theatre dates have the disadvantage that part of the audience expects a vaudeville show, with singers and dancers and acts, plus a movie, so that the band is limited in time and the type of material it can play.
>
> Dance dates get the band swinging ideally, but when you have to play for dancing, it's impossible to play numbers at certain tempos, or to include changes of tempo during a number. In a concert hall, you don't get any of these disadvantages, because you know that everyone is there to listen to the music and nothing else.

Ellington's move into the concert realm was part of a long-term evolution in the kind of venues he played, and in the degree and nature of audience participation. Like other nightclubs, the Kentucky Club ignored the proscenium of the theatrical stage, and thrust the audience into close proximity with the performers. There, Ellington and Greer moved their instruments among the customers. At the Cotton Club, the floor show was surrounded by tables of customers. In general, the physical setup of nightclubs and cabarets provided an intimacy and a feeling of participation that were among their chief allures.

As Ellington's career progressed, his options increased. When he first began in the mid 1910s, he had played primarily for dances in dance halls—a very participatory kind of musical event. Next he began playing in cabarets, and, in the late 1920s, in vaudeville shows. Then in the early 1930s, he started performing for stage shows, on a big stage between movies. Finally, he began playing concerts. Each change of venue brought the music—for itself—more definitely into central focus.

After his debut at Carnegie Hall, Ellington played an increasing number of American concerts. In 1946, he was advertised as playing for St. Louis's "first real jazz concert."

Ellington kept moving toward making listening to his music central to his audience's experience. Yet, ironically, given the multi-genre character of musical events in ancestral Africa and the participatory nature of much African-American music, by reducing distractions this evolution also reduced direct participation by the audience. It separated the audience from the musicians physically, sonically, and psychically, and minimized the historically strong relationship between his music and the ritual of public dancing. Writing music for concert audiences—mostly white—carried other drawbacks. Some of his concert music has a self-conscious, occasionally pretentious, quality—for example *A Tonal Group* of 1946. "To be smart or 'arty' was in a sense to compromise," asserts Stanley Dance, "but an underlying commercial necessity for Ellington was, from first to last, the maintenance of his instrument, his orchestra. . . . It became harder to stir [the audience] without resorting to exhibitionism, novelty, and constant variety."

These were the heaviest prices Ellington paid in becoming more of a concert artist and composer for concerts. Concerts, however, typically brought in a lot of money (sometimes more than $5,000 a night); generated publicity; offered the occasions to bring out unusual and memorable works (*On a Turquoise Cloud* of 1947, for example) ill suited to dances and nightclubs but well suited to concert stages; created the deadlines Ellington needed to compose more ambitious works; and provided a kind of legitimation for someone whose music was still undervalued by the classical music establishment. Ellington may have felt a more deep-seated drive to perform concerts, too. As we've heard Ruth Ellington observe, his parents taught him that he could be as good as anybody else, on the same level as anyone. And perhaps he believed that his music, which increasingly crossed or defied categories, ought to be able to be heard in all categories of performance venue. Throughout his career, he would maintain the two basic kinds of venues that represented, or served, the two basic and continuing facets of his careers—dances for the bandleader and concerts for the composer.

Having a band that had to work constantly, most of the time on the road, made it difficult to steal away the time to compose, especially for the longer, more ambitious works. Ellington and Strayhorn were notoriously last-minute with their parts for the band, as Jimmy Hamilton attested. "Duke and Strayhorn never had anything ready," he said. "Never was ready. Right up to the day you're gonna do it." Partly Ellington lacked time to be leisurely about composing—he usually was racing to a deadline; partly he was by temperament a procrastinator; and partly he "never liked to close a chapter on anything," as Hamilton commented. A later member of the orchestra, Clark Terry, said that Ellington "wants life and music to be always in a state of becoming." He was wrapped up in the process of creating, refining, tinkering, and perfecting. As a result, some of the performances recorded at Carnegie Hall sound underrehearsed.

Ellington performed six further Carnegie Hall concerts on a more-or-less annual basis, ending in 1948. The concerts included a mix of short instrumentals and songs, old and new, and typically a medley of his hits. The most noteworthy aspect, however, was the new instrumental works he composed for these occasions: short "concertos" or showpieces for star soloists, and longer suites.

In his concert of December 11, 1943, he premiered *New World a-Comin'*, a sort of piano concerto, nearly fifteen minutes long, inspired by Roi Ottley's book of the same title optimistically predicting a better life for African-Americans after World War II. Ellington wrote in his memoirs that he had "visualized this new world as a place in the distant future where there would be no war, no greed, no categorization, no nonbelievers, where love was unconditional, and no pronoun was good enough for God." The piece, however, would not be issued by a major record company for many years; and it was not until 1970 that Ellington, at the piano, would record a version with symphonic accompaniment by the Cincinnati Symphony Orchestra.

At Ellington's third Carnegie concert, held on December 19, 1944, he offered showpieces for Hodges, Brown, and Hamilton—respectively *Blue Cellophane*, *Frantic Fantasy*, and *Air Conditioned Jungle*, as well as an Ellington-Strayhorn collaboration, the four-part *Perfume Suite*, which shows signs of Strayhorn's classical training.

Carnegie concert number four, on January 4, 1946, offered two notable premieres—the wordless vocal feature *Transblucency*, which Ellington sprung on singer Kay Davis, Hodges, Brown, and bassist Oscar Pettiford at the concert, with no notice, and the somewhat self-conscious classically oriented *A Tonal Group*.

By the time of the fifth program, the audience had expanded to warrant two nights of concerts, on November 23 and 24, 1946. Ellington introduced features for Harry Carney (*Golden Feather*, named for the critic Jane Feather, blond wife of critic Leonard Feather), Brown (*Golden Cress*, for Jackie Courtney, blond wife of Ellington's manager Cress Courtney), and Hamilton *(Flippant Flurry)*, and the *Deep South Suite*. A social commentary on the southern racial situation, the suite's four movements are replete with a biting contrast of the difference between the chamber of commerce image *(Magnolias Dripping with Molasses)* and reality *(Hearsay)*, irony *(When Nobody Was Looking)*, and good humor

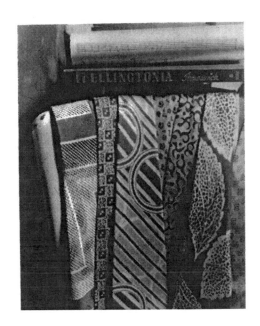

In the 1940s, Ellington continued to dress fashionably, even to set styles. Here a selection of his ties drapes a chair in the dressing room of New York's Hurricane club, 1943.

(Happy-Go-Lucky Local). Ellington recalled that William Morris, Jr., whose firm managed him, "was for out-and-out protest, but as with *Jump for Joy,* I felt it was good theatre to say it without saying it. That is the art." It is unfortunate that with the exception of the last section, *Happy-Go-Lucky Local,* the *Deep South Suite* was never recorded for release to the public.

At the sixth affair, on December 26–27, 1947, besides more "concertos," Ellington unveiled the remarkable *The Clothed Woman* and the twenty-seven-minute *Liberian Suite,* commissioned to celebrate the centennial of the nation of Liberia, which had been established by black Americans returning to their ancestral continent. The suite comprises a six-movement series of vehicles for singer Al Hibbler (he opens with the delightful *I Like the Sunrise*), for tenor-saxman Al Sears, for Jimmy Hamilton, for Ray Nance on violin, for Sonny Greer's timpani, and finally, for Carney, Nance (on trumpet), and Tyree Glenn on trombone. While there seems to be a consensus that the first two or three movements are the strongest, critical opinion remains divided on the work as a whole.

The seventh and final appearance in this series was on November

13, 1948. Besides more vignettes for his soloists, the concert included the first documented public performance of *Lush Life*, Billy Strayhorn's harmonically rich, rubato, theatrical art song, with his sophisticated lyrics of jaded loneliness, and a variegated program piece called *The Tattooed Bride*.

"The annual Carnegie Hall concerts were really a series of social-significance thrusts," Ellington wrote in his memoirs, "or so I and many other people came to regard them." He had established the commercial and artistic viability of concerts by African-Americans and had offered some pieces—notably *Black, Brown and Beige, New World a-Comin'*, and the *Deep South Suite*—that offered commentary on black history and the contemporary racial situation and expressed subtle but real protest as well as hope. In 1944, entrepreneur Norman Granz introduced "Jazz at the Philharmonic," a series of concerts (long jam sessions, really, played by all-star musicians) at Los Angeles's Philharmonic Hall, and after 1945, concerts were increasingly common. "By 1950," Ellington wrote, "everybody was giving concerts, and even a concert at Carnegie Hall no longer had the prestige value it had had in 1943, but our series there had helped establish a music that was new in both its extended forms and its social significance." And by 1950, partly through the concerts given by Ellington, his musicians (and others, too) were enjoying an additional measure of respect within American society.

One way to view the repertoire that Ellington introduced and performed at his concerts is that increasingly in the 1930s and '40s, he was not interested in composing jazz. He wanted to compose *music*. By writing concert works that were intended exclusively for listening, by extending the lengths of his works, by drawing sometimes on European forms or techniques, by creating unheard-of sonorities, Ellington (while acknowledging his many debts to jazz tradition) seemed almost to be asserting his independence from jazz, declaring his uniqueness.

As an examination of the newly available Ellington scores at the Smithsonian reveals, many of Ellington's longer (concert) works left little room for improvisation. This raises a question (one, it must be understood, which Ellington, with his contempt for categorizing, would have been uninterested in): if, as often contended, improvisation is the sine qua non of jazz, what does that make Ellington's music? Despite the lack of improvisation in a considerable number of works, he did employ the instrumentation of a jazz orchestra; excepting a few such as Tizol, all his musicians came from jazz backgrounds; Ellington manipulated the language of jazz; and he performed in typical jazz venues. While he found the term *jazz* too limiting, Ellington also found himself in the role of explaining and defending it. "Expressive jazz requires as much scholarship," he wrote in 1947, "as much musicianship, as any other kind of music. In addition, it requires a peculiar awareness of form and of the human thoughts and feelings those forms express."

However, in scope, innovations, colors, dynamics, narrative and programmatic storytelling, length, control of the musical process, and range of expression, Ellington went beyond the jazz category. In a published rebuttal to a 1943 attack on jazz by Winthrop Sargeant, the music editor of *Time*, Ellington mentioned some of the emotions he was working to express in his music: "But it was when Mr. Sargeant remarked that jazz doesn't encompass such emotions as tragedy, romantic nostalgia, wonder, delicate shades of humor, etc. that I felt badly. Either Mr. Sargeant stuck his neck out, in making such a statement, or we did, in trying to write music that expressed these particular emotions." And yet, despite his originality, brilliance, and public esteem, Ellington was restricted to working in jazz venues because of racial and cultural prejudice, his need to make a living, and the historic undervaluing of anything smacking of pop, jazz, dance, vaudeville, ballroom, cabaret, and nightclubs. Even if he wanted to, he could not make a living playing solely or even mostly concerts, so his bread and butter consisted of dances, stage shoes, and smoky nightclubs.

Other than continuing to revise *Black, Brown and Beige* over the next decades, and writing a few scattered works, Ellington the composer would from now on avoid grappling with truly large and integrated compositional forms; instead, his long works would typically take the form of suites, a series of loosely related "movements." One of Ellington's long-held goals seems to have been to express himself in a grand musical form, such as symphony or opera, but if that was a goal, he would never achieve it. While Ellington has been criticized for this lack, one should realize that this kind of musical architecture historically had no precedent in African music (African music was based on shorter, iterative forms); rather they were imported to America from Europe; and this raises questions about ethnocentrism. Ellington was faced with many who failed to understand the underlying nature of African (and thus African-American) music and tended to judge it by European standards. And there were many who underrated conciseness and economy of expression, in which hardly a note is inessential—the kind of succinctness which Chopin achieved in his nocturnes, Joplin in his rags, and Ellington in such pieces as *Blue Light, Ko-Ko,* and *Dusk.*

After Victor and Columbia finally caved in to the musicians' union in November 1944, Ellington resumed recording for Victor on December 1—his first commercial discs in sixteen months. He made a few inspired pieces such as *Transblucency* and then in September 1946, when his Victor contract expired, perhaps desiring to have more freedom to record experimental pieces, he switched to the small label Musicraft. There he made a brief series of memorable recordings such as *Happy-Go-Lucky Local,* but company financial problems cut the recordings short after just two months, and finally, in August 1947, Ellington went back to Columbia (his enemy, John Hammond, had left in 1943), where he would remain until the end of 1952. However, just four months into this contract, the American Federation of Musicians again struck the record companies, and Ellington had to cease making records until April 1949. In the meantime, there was new competition.

During the recording ban of 1942–44, a group of young, mostly black players—led by Dizzy Gillespie, Charlie Parker, Thelonious Monk, and Kenny Clarke—had been experimenting in Harlem and in 1945 made their first important recordings. Employing angular melodies, asymmetric phrases, heightened rhythmic complexity, a faster melodic rhythm, sometimes dizzying tempos, and extended harmonies, they introduced a music that was intended far less for dancing than for listening in small clubs. In contrast to much of Ellington's music, in many cases the new style was "pure" or abstract music with no overt programmatic references. Initially known onomatopoetically as "rebop" or "bebop," it finally took the shortened label "bop."

The bebop musicians worked independently from previous career paths (entertainer, dance musician); they relied for their livelihoods on an intense circle of jazz fans to an extent that a musician of Ellington's generation would have found uncomfortable. Now, led by African-American musicians searching for their own music not co-opted by the (white-controlled) music industry, many younger jazz players rebelled against swing and its commercial aspects and took up the new, startlingly different bop, which was clearly a non-European "concert" music—that is, intended for listening.

The advent of bebop was a watershed in American music, and presented a striking contrast to all previous styles of jazz-related music. Though such Ellington recordings as *Cotton Tail* and *Main Stem* had, to an extent, helped pave the way for bop, the new music posed challenges to Ellington, too. Would he try to master the new language of bop and transform his composing and performing style? No, he chose to go his own separate path. But that meant that, as the new style gathered adherents, it was the musicians of bop who were seen as advancing the artistic vanguard. Previously, Ellington (and a few other musicians) had adopted the roles of experimenter, innovator, and leader; the changed music world must, at some level, have been disconcerting to him.

The musical changes were partly a result of societal events. World War II brought more than a million blacks into uniform, and fighting abroad for freedom raised the expectations of returning servicemen. Hundreds of thousands of blacks had moved north and west to work in war plants, and they helped support a style of black popular music that would in 1949 be dubbed "rhythm and blues." What became known as R&B was really a diversified group of styles. Sung by the likes of singer-saxophonist Louis Jordan and his Tympany Five, the vigorous blues shouter Wynonie Harris, and others, R&B was decidedly accessible, dominated by singers and later by electric guitars, offered a strong dance beat, and was fresh.

The general pop music world was changing markedly. Exempt from the 1942–44 recording ban, popular singers, despite the wartime shortage of shellac used on records, were making some records and gaining in popularity. This development, and the growing wartime rush of singers to leave the big bands that had heretofore employed them and strike out on their own (Frank Sinatra and Perry Como in 1942, Dick Haymes in 1943, and Jo Stafford and Peggy Lee in 1944) helped create an era of the "big singer." All these changes in musical taste—singers, R&B, and bebop—combined with other factors to push the big bands into a sharp decline, effectively ending the big-band era. In November and December 1946, eight of the bands disbanded either permanently or temporarily, including Benny Goodman, Harry James, Woody Herman, Tommy Dorsey, Benny Carter, and Les Brown. The reasons are numerous: higher salaries (raised during the war); stiff competition from singers; growing interest in the new bebop and rhythm and blues; a short-lived postwar boom in moviegoing; and preoccupation among returning servicemen with settling down and starting families. And television was a distant threat as well, though at that time, few really understood that.

Ellington's audience, too, was distracted by competing music or pursuits; and most younger listeners, some of whom in previous years would have become fans, were attracted to more accessible vocal sounds or fresher and newer music. From then on Ellington would never have a vast audience of young people; his audience would age with him.

In the face of postwar swing, the emerging bebop, popular song, rhythm and blues, as well as classical composition (which was heading in a number of directions including serialism, atonalism, post-Webernism, *musique concrète*, and, soon, electronic music), Ellington, at his best, continued to go his own musical way. In this sense, he was self-contained enough to inhabit his own musical world, to deserve his own musical category (or none at all). In 1970, Stanley Dance would aptly title his compilation of interviews with Ellington and his players *The World of Duke Ellington*.

Despite his success in the band polls, Ellington experienced a series of disappointments. Again stretching himself beyond his "safe" boundaries, in 1946, he teamed with lyricist John LaTouche to write an updated version of John Gay's classic *Beggar's Opera* of 1728, in which MacHeath (played by Alfred Drake, who had created a stir in *Oklahoma!*) would become a modern American gangster. Titled *Beggar's Holiday*, it opened at New York's Broadway Theater on December 26, 1946. The remarkable accomplishment of *Beggar's Holiday* was social: its cast, chorus, dancers, and production team were biracial, with no stereotyped distinction between black and white.

Brooks Atkinson of the *New York Times* praised Ellington and the "eloquent score, brisk ballets and a cast of dancers and singers who are up to snuff. . . . He has not written a pattern of song hits to be lifted out of their context, but rather an integral musical composition that carries the old Gay picaresque yarn through its dark modern setting." The *New York World-Telegram* called the work "more opera comica than musical comedy." But other reviews were negative, and after 14 weeks and 108 performances, the show closed, the victim also of a weak libretto, uneven casting, insufficient revision, an overblown budget, a cavernous theater inimical to the intimacy of Ellington's music, and stiff competition from new shows—*Finian's Rainbow* and *Brigadoon*—as well as older ones still running. Once again Ellington was denied the satisfaction of a cast album, and most of the dozens of songs he wrote for the show dropped into total obscurity.

In 1948, the musician's union dictated another ban on making records, which would last all year. During the previous ban, Ellington had made transcription records for broadcast by radio stations, but not so this time. Then, when the strike was over, Columbia, in no hurry because pop singers now dominated the record market, took another eight months before returning him to the studio. Thus Ellington was out of commercial recording studios until September 1949—an unprecedented period of twenty months. During this hiatus, Ellington accepted an offer to return to scenes of triumph and to tour England, as well as Paris, Antwerp, Brussels, Geneva, and Zurich, for six weeks in June and July 1948. The British musicians' union refused to allow his band to join him, so he took only the quadruple-threat Ray Nance and the coloratura soprano Kay Davis, and they played as a "variety" act.

. . .

Between 1947 and 1950, there were only a few highlights for Ellington as he struggled to survive in both his careers. Ben Webster returned to his tenor saxophone chair in November 1948, but left after just seven months. Ellington's strong showing in magazine polls continued; he made his first long-playing (LP) record, *Masterpieces by Ellington*, for Columbia in 1950; and was featured in three motion pictures: a seven-minute Paramount short, released in 1947, called *Date with Duke*, imaginatively combining live action of the Ellington band with animated puppets in a performance of his *Perfume Suite*; in 1949, a fifteen-minute Universal short, *Symphony in Swing*, with high production values; and in 1950, another Universal production, the fifteen-minute-long *Salute to Duke Ellington*. Significantly, this would be Ellington's last motion-picture short, at a time when big bands and Hollywood were both in economic decline.

In June 1949, not long after Ellington celebrated his fiftieth birthday by appearing on his first television show, *Adventures in Jazz*, in New York, *Down Beat*'s Mike Levin published a harsh denunciation: "His reputation shredded, Duke should disband." He called the band "sloppy, disinterested . . . dreary and tired. . . . The band has played badly almost consistently. When it hasn't been technically lacking, it has not had the indefinable quality of spirit which distinguishes a creative band from one playing for salaries. . . . Duke seems tired and dejected." He also criticized Ellington's recording of *Singin' in the Rain* as "trash-worthy of any studio band. From Ellington we used to get much better than this." One reader added his complaint that at a recent performance, one trumpeter had actually fallen asleep on the stand.

Ellington must have been hurt and angered by the story, especially since the magazine previously had lavished so much praise on him, and the editor then was Ned Williams, a former promoter of Ellington's. A controversy arose and many rushed to his defense. Bandleader Charlie Barnet, an ardent admirer of Ellington, admitted that the band's performances were uneven—had always been —and wrote that many of Levin's charges were true, but they applied to the surviving big bands as a group, not just to Ellington's. The times were indeed dispiriting, as some of the top ball-rooms were dropping big bands and others were nearly empty, and nightclubs were drawing poorly. And the road travel was exhausting: the bands were constantly on the move, and only a handful of big band musicians (other than leaders) lasted more than a few years in this kind of life; most got out and went into studio work or teaching or some other line of work. "When I left Duke [in June 1947, after just four years,]" Taft Jordan recalled, "I was so tired I slept almost a whole year. I'd had too much road. For a long time I actually slept two or three times a day, and not cat naps, but for two or three hours. I hadn't realized how tired I was while I was out there." Ellington and his remaining veterans such as Hodges, Greer, and Carney (guitarist Fred Guy left in 1949 and Ellington never replaced him) had now been touring for eighteen years, and the cumulative strain must have taken its toll on the fifty-year-old maestro and made it impossible to maintain a consistently high level of inspiration and performance.

The late 1940s were difficult for Ellington, who was facing a decline in the ballroom and nightclub business for big bands, falling sales of jazz records generally (complicated by a confusing war of the record speeds, when consumers faced three different formats—33⅓ rpm, 45 rpm, and 78 rpm), reduced recording opportunities for himself, resulting financial pressures, and continued problems with the stability of his personnel. Sonny Greer suffered increasing drinking and health problems, and Ellington had to tour with a second drummer, Butch Ballard, as backup. Perhaps tired, perhaps just uninspired, perhaps missing the deadlines of recording sessions, Ellington the bandleader slipped into programming mostly his old hits like *Mood Indigo* and *Sophisticated Lady*, and his arrangements of current pop hits. As a composer he was equally adrift, needing to worry more about survival. The end to both careers may have seemed in sight in January 1950 when his long-time friendly rival, Count Basie, was forced to break up his band and tour instead with only a seven-piece group.

In the midst of these tough times, Ellington acted. He returned to the fans who had earlier rejuvenated him and took his band

After a hiatus caused by World War II
and its aftermath, Ellington resumed
touring abroad in the late 1940s.
During a 1950 tour of Europe, a group
of fans welcomes him to Rome.

Ellington had long sought an audience with the U.S. president and
finally received an opportunity on September 29, 1950,
when he presented the score of his new work *Harlem* to
President Harry S. Truman, at the White House.

abroad—the first European trip for the entire orchestra in eleven
years. After arriving at Le Havre on April 4, 1950, they played
seventy-four concerts in seventy-seven days in France, Belgium,
Holland, Switzerland, Italy, Denmark, Sweden, and West Germany, returning to the United States on June 30. Though not all
the audiences were happy with Ellington's selection of tunes, the
concert tour (as in 1933 and 1939) gave him inspiration, and now,
on the return voyage, he wrote an important fourteen-minute work,

which had been commissioned by Arturo Toscanini for the NBC Symphony Orchestra and which came to be called *Harlem*. The piece would be recorded in 1951. Ellington sought, and on September 29, was, at last, given the honor of a meeting with the president, Harry S. Truman, at the White House, where the composer presented Truman a manuscript copy of *Harlem*. The piece was premiered by the Duke Ellington orchestra in a benefit concert for the NAACP at New York's Metropolitan Opera House on January 21, 1951. Papers in the Harry S. Truman Library reveal that in November 1950, Ellington wrote the president, the man who had ordered desegregation of the military, about the concert, whose proceeds, Ellington noted, "will be used to help fight for your civil rights program—to stamp out segregation, discrimination, bigotry and a variety of other intolerances in our own American society." Someone in the White House underlined the word *segregation*, and after the final paragraph, in which Ellington asked the president if his daughter, Margaret Truman, a classical singer, would serve as honorary chairwoman of the event, somebody wrote an emphatic "*No!*" in inch-high letters, underlined twice.

Within a matter of weeks after the NAACP concert at the Met, a bombshell struck the Ellington orchestra and the musical world: Johnny Hodges, Lawrence Brown, and Sonny Greer, who among them had seventy years with Ellington, were leaving en masse to form a combo (along with ex-Ellingtonians Al Sears and Joe Benjamin) under Hodges's leadership. They had worked out the details in secret, even had themselves measured for new band uniforms in advance of a booking at the Blue Note in Chicago on March 9, 1951.

Evidently Hodges left for a number of reasons: he did not feel well enough compensated, impresario Norman Granz was urging him to leave (and had already begun recording Hodges for his label Clef), he liked to stretch out in a combo setting, he was not terribly happy with some of Ellington's compositions ("We didn't like the tone poems much," he grumbled), and perhaps his ego played a role, too, for the new band would be known as Johnny Hodges and His Orchestra.

Jam-a-Ditty and *Fugue-a-Ditty,* which made up two of the three movements of *A Tonal Group.* The enthusiastic *Jam-a-Ditty: Concerto for Four
Jazz Horns* is a concerto grosso for Taft Jordan's trumpet, Lawrence Brown's
trombone, Harry Carney's baritone sax, and Jimmy Hamilton's clarinet,
while the cool, measured *Fugue-a-Ditty* offers one of Ellington's rare excur-
sions into studied counterpoint, with Hamilton, Carney, and trombonist
Claude Jones doing a fugue. Both are available on *Duke Ellington and
His World Famous Orchestra* (Hindsight).

Ellington's lengthiest portrayal of trains was part of the *Deep South Suite*
(1946). The six-minute-long *Happy-Go-Lucky Local* is as remarkable in its
way as was *Daybreak Express* thirteen years earlier. One of his most successful pictorial or programmatic pieces, the *Local* is a different train than
the *Express,* as it bounces, toots, wails, chugs, clanks, clangs, and rocks. It's
featured on *Happy-Go-Lucky Local* (Musicraft); a slightly longer version is
on *Duke Ellington and His World Famous Orchestra.*

In 1946, Ellington began to extend the tradition of wordless vocalizing he
initiated in 1927. *Transblucency (A Blue Fog You Can Almost See Through)*
features counterpoints of Kay Davis's wordless vocal with Lawrence Brown's
silken trombone and Jimmy Hamilton's flawless clarinet. It's on *Black, Brown
and Beige* and *Beyond Category.* The next year came the unhurried, airy
On a Turquoise Cloud. By combining Kay Davis's soprano voice with
Jimmy Hamilton's clarinet, Ray Nance's plucked violin, and Harry
Carney's bass clarinet, Ellington, with spare voicings, created exquisite
tonal colors. Lawrence Brown's mellow muted trombone contributes to
the daydreaming mood. The piece is available on *The Complete Duke
Ellington, 1947–1952, Vol. 2.*

Probably his foremost composition for piano, *The Clothed Woman* (1947)
reaffirms Ellington as a witty experimenter, in this case with European modernist techniques: the piece begins and ends in virtual atonality and free
rhythm, next offers a bit of angular, minimal melody. Then a surprise—a

(continued)

completely different, toe-tapping middle section that suggests the Harlem piano of Willie "The Lion" Smith (it's based on Smith's *Spring Air* of 1939). Then, Ellington puckishly returns to the modern beginning. It's on *The Complete Duke Ellington, 1947–1952, Vol. 2.*

Air Conditioned Jungle is a "concerto" for the smooth, urbane clarinet of Jimmy Hamilton. With bassist Oscar Pettiford leading the brisk tempo, Hamilton impresses with his technical virtuosity, unpredictable, tigerlike leaps of melody, and witty surprises. In contrast to Ellington's jungle pieces of the 1920s, *this* jungle is a very cool place. A version from 1947 is found on *The Complete Duke Ellington, 1947–1952, Vol. 2.*

Based on the first theme of *Concerto for Cootie* (1940), *Do Nothin' Till You Hear from Me* became a song hit in 1943. Bob Russell's lyric—Philip Furia calls it "probably the slangiest pledge of romantic fidelity ever written"—does justice to Ellington's melodious theme. A version recorded in 1947 features Al Hibbler's distinctive vocal, Ray Nance's wry comments on wah-wah trumpet, and, as contrast, Lawrence Brown's creamy trombone.

The economical Ellington wrote the catchy song *Don't Get Around Much Anymore* (1942) by again recycling an earlier instrumental, *Never No Lament* (1940), and wedding it to a terse, vernacular lyric by Bob Russell. It was on the best-selling song charts for sixteen weeks in 1943. A 1947 rendition has a vocal by the earthy Al Hibbler, Hodges gliding through the melody—by stretching out the highest note he heightens the feeling of yearning for a lost lover—and Ray Nance providing a bluesy contrast to the lyric Hodges. It and the previous piece have been reissued on *The Complete Duke Ellington, 1947–1952, Vol. 2.*

One of Ellington's first long-playing (LP) records, *Masterpieces by Ellington* (1950), featured two memorable pieces. The composer took advantage of the extra playing time to extend *Mood Indigo* to fifteen minutes, with

(continued)

each of the seventeen choruses a variation on the now-classic theme. His updating of the almost twenty-year-old piece showed it to be a still-fresh evergreen in the hands of this resourceful and inventive composer-arranger: this version goes through several meters (one section is in waltz time), three keys, and effective contrasts in sonorities, densities, and timbres. What variety Ellington and Strayhorn could manage from the sixteen-piece orchestra and from a familiar short song! *The Tattooed Bride*, twelve minutes long, is a piece of program music about a man on his honeymoon who finds his wife wears a tattoo. Built on the manipulation of a four-note motif, the piece, like this *Mood Indigo*, offers varieties of mood, tempo, and colors. *The Tattooed Bride* is considered by some critics as one of Ellington's most effective extended works, and together with the transformed *Mood Indigo* showed him (and Strayhorn) in command of forms other than miniatures. Listening to either piece is akin to the feeling of going through the tension, change, and release of a several-act play. *Masterpieces by Ellington* has been reissued, along with a 1947 recording of *The Liberian Suite*, as *The Complete Duke Ellington, 1947–1952, Vol. 5* (CBS).

NINE
PLAYING
FOR TIME
1951–56

he jolting departures of his stars Johnny Hodges, Lawrence Brown, and Sonny Greer stirred speculation that
Ellington was "going to retire, that he was 'losing'
eight more musicians," wrote *Down Beat*, "that he
would 'settle down in Hollywood' to write music for movies, and numerous other rumors." To these Ellington responded, "Absolutely ridiculous." And then as a bandleader he
went to work attacking this serious new problem.

He moved with dispatch to replace the defecting trio of players.
He knew that his old valve trombonist Juan Tizol, then with Harry
James's band, wasn't working year-round, so he offered him steady
employment. And two more of James's men—drummer Louie Bellson and alto saxophonist Willie Smith—came along. A veteran of
the bands of Jimmie Lunceford, Charlie Spivak, and Harry James,
the forty-year-old Smith was less a soloist than Hodges, but one of
the top sax-section leaders. The precise and driving twenty-five-
year-old Bellson, other than Juan Tizol the first white player to join
the Ellington orchestra, had established a reputation with Benny
Goodman and Tommy Dorsey, and was soon said by *Down Beat* to
be lifting the band "into more enthusiastic blowing than they have
known in years."

Faced with the departure of three key players, Ellington raided the Harry James orchestra for drummer Louie Bellson, alto saxophonist Willie Smith (3d from left), and ex-Ellingtonian Juan Tizol (not pictured). Holdovers Jimmy Hamilton, the virtuoso clarinetist and saxophonist, at left, and Harold "Shorty" Baker, the sweet-toned trumpeter, at right, flank the newcomers.

The jazz press dubbed the move the "Great James Robbery," and it was indeed a coup for Ellington: each of the trio was a superb musician, and Bellson especially brought a new sparkle to the orchestra. Ellington also hired thirty-year-old Britt Woodman, who proved as versatile as any Ellington trombonist. Tenor saxophonist Paul Gonsalves, formerly with Dizzy Gillespie's band, was another new player. He had actually joined the band in September 1950, at the age of thirty. From Boston by way of Providence, Rhode Island, he was nicknamed "Mex," but was really of Cape Verdean extraction. Gonsalves memorized many of Ben Webster's solos and played with virtuosity, drive, individuality, and, especially on slow numbers, unfocused pitch. Like Ben Webster, Gonsalves became famous for his driving solos but was at his peak as a player of breathy, romantic ballads.

About his triple loss, Ellington appeared both wry ("I'm a young bandleader starting out all over again," he said) and philosophical: "There is no such thing as a 'replacement' in my band. A new musician means for us a new sound and the creation of new music, which he, and he alone, can properly express." There were several noticeable changes in Ellington's repertoire: he retired some of Hodges's old features such as *Jeep's Blues*, *Magenta Haze*, and *Day Dream*. Greer had never gone in for drum solos, not normally even for drum features, but now, some new pieces showcasing Bellson were introduced, several written by the drummer himself: *The Hawk Talks*, *Ting-a-ling*, and his solo vehicle, *Skin Deep*. Willie Smith, however, left after only a year, before Ellington had an opportunity to determine how to write for him.

Accompanied by Bellson, the band seemed rhythmically tighter and more propulsive. But without Hodges, the Duke Ellington orchestra just didn't sound the same. Yes, baritone saxist Harry Carney was continuing to anchor the band, Ellington continued to color from his piano, Tizol and his distinctive, thin trombone tone were back, showman Ray Nance was carrying on, and trombonist Quentin "Butter" Jackson was maintaining the plunger style of Tricky Sam Nanton. Yet in all the years of Ellington's music making, Hodges ranked as his single sine qua non player: without him the Ellington sound simply was missing an elegant, fundamental, irreplaceable ingredient.

The defection of his three stalwarts must have deeply wounded Ellington, especially given the passion he had for loyalty. "He likes to feel loyalty reciprocated," wrote Stanley Dance in 1959. "His own so often abused, he remains deeply considerate of the sensitivities of others. Thus a musician not found suitable for the band leaves because 'he needs to study a little more.' The language is customarily nuanced to avoid giving pain or offence." Yet Ellington revealed no bitterness about the men who jumped ship. On the contrary, recalled Al Celley, Ellington kept Greer on the payroll for many years. And Ellington did not stand in the way when several of his players joined Johnny Hodges in small-group recording sessions for Norman Granz's labels, which produced some remarkable small-group jazz as well as one rocking, rhythm and blues-flavored moderate hit: *Castle Rock*, recorded in March 1951.

That November, Ellington hired two new, younger trumpeters.

Willie Cook, twenty-eight, was nicknamed "Ool-Ya-Koo" after a record made by Dizzy Gillespie, with whom he had previously worked. Clark Terry, age thirty, had previously played with the bands of Charlie Barnet and Count Basie. Terry would become known for his excellent technique, considerable versatility, and good humor. The new younger players gave Ellington his first substantial coterie of modernists, musicians who had come up during the bebop era. And his newer players, generally, were technically well trained and (unlike Hodges) good readers. Inevitably, these new players introduced bop-tinged ideas in their solos, and Ellington would occasionally incorporate their ideas into his arrangements, but he didn't substantially alter his basic decision, which he must have reached some years back, to continue in his own direction. The band now had several cliques—the older players like Carney and Tizol, and the younger players. There was a kind of a third group whom the band referred to as the "air force," for their penchant for flying high on drugs: Gonsalves, Cook, singer Jimmy Grissom, and, at times, Ray Nance. Ellington, older and more reluctant to get into hassles, now typically turned a blind eye to these problems, and others such as drinking, showing up late for performances, and lack of proper stage dress. As Dance observed in 1959, "He is famous for his blind eye—and his deaf ear—a fact which has infuriated critics for at least twenty years."

Under the management of Associated Booking Corporation, from July 1951, the orchestra continued to find work, though most of its gigs were now one-nighters. Widespread racial discrimination continued to make finding places to eat on the road quite difficult. Al Celley, the road manager, would typically go into the restaurant and ask if they would serve the band. By the late 1950s, he said, things would get better, at least in the North.

Now the band no longer traveled by railroad; Ellington probably could not afford to rent the private Pullman cars and didn't want the comedown of sitting in regular railroad coach cars. Instead, the entourage normally went by rented bus, while Ellington usually preferred traveling by car. Beginning at some point after World

War II, Ellington would often ride in Jimmy Hamilton's car, and in 1949, Hamilton said, Harry Carney bought an automobile and from then on, whenever it was feasible, Ellington would ride with Carney. They'd have long stretches of silence, which is just the way the maestro wanted it, so he could think and create. When he had traveled on trains, Ellington had sometimes sat by himself and ruminated or composed; other times he had joined the men in poker games and bull sessions.

The reason he traveled by car was perhaps a desire to stay away from inquiries and squabbles about salaries; or a self-defense against Cat Anderson's kleptomania (there are stories of his regularly rifling his bandmates' things on the bus); or a celebrity's superior stance; or a need to carry on a less hectic, inner conversation, to think in peace. He would tell music critic Carter Harman in 1956 that musical ideas came when he traveled. "You know, long stretches. Better in the car than in a bus because in the bus, with the band, you know, there's so much shit goin' on all the time. You know how they are." Ellington laughed. "Eighteen maniacs, you know, and it's quite a thing." "Harry and I don't talk much," Ellington would say to Nat Hentoff, "so I can just dream and write." Whatever the considerations, his switch to riding by himself was a sure sign that he was no longer one of the guys, but rather seemed to be growing increasingly aloof.

In advance of a one-nighter, a performance at the Mosque Auditorium in Richmond, Virginia, on January 28, 1951, the local chapter of the NAACP threatened to picket in protest that the audience would be segregated. Ellington angrily canceled the engagement, calling the boycott of him "appalling" and complaining it hurt all the members of his orchestra. When, in a subsequent interview with the *St. Louis Argus*, Ellington was quoted as saying the African-Americans "ain't ready" to fight segregation, there was a huge uproar in the black press. DUKE ELLINGTON'S VIEWS ON JIM CROW SHOCK NATION: MAESTRO SAYS "WE AIN'T READY YET," ran a headline in *The Afro-American*. In a three-page rebuttal, Ellington denied having made the statement, defended his commitment to civil rights, took a slap at the NAACP by complaining it was "too bad that Southern Negroes picketed only Negro artists," called for a nationwide, professionally organized campaign against racial segregation, rather than the current one led by part-timers or volunteers, and said "much more can be done." This conflict caused a major though temporary disruption in the normally very favorable, prideful coverage he received in the black press.

Finding enough work for the "new" band was becoming more difficult. In the early 1950s, as suburbs were growing rapidly, there seemed to be fewer and fewer nightclubs, which were typically located in city centers, interested or able to book Ellington. The small combos (typically quartets, quintets, and sextets) were much less expensive: they not only employed far fewer musicians but often no singers, no separate arrangers and copyists—since their arrangements were often not written down, and some of them dispensed with road managers. And combos were the fashion then. Of those clubs that did engage Ellington, the Blue Note in Chicago's

Musical "parts" from the Smithsonian's Duke Ellington Collection reveal how Ellington personalized his music. He wrote not for instruments but for specific players: here Ray (Nance), Jimmy (Hamilton), Butter (Quentin Jackson), and Rab (Johnny Hodges, "Rabbit").

Loop, for example, paid him $5,000 for a week's work in 1954—about what he had been making twenty-three years earlier, when his band and staff were smaller and the cost of living was 43 percent less. In addition, some of his old performing venues were dropping music or going out of business.

Competition from television and changing demographics and tastes were forcing more of the vaudeville houses to close. For example, in September 1952, Ellington played the Earle Theater, Philadelphia's last vaudeville house, where he had periodically performed since at least 1934, for the final time before it was demolished. In October 1953, Ellington played New York's Paramount Theater, but a month later it dropped live acts and converted to a CinemaScope movie policy. This left, as *Down Beat* wrote, "only the Palace and Radio City Music Hall featuring stage presentations in midtown" Manhattan. (He would continue to perform periodically at theaters in black neighborhoods—Harlem's Apollo Theatre, Washington's Howard Theater, and Chicago's Regal Theatre.) Understandably, then, to keep the band going Ellington turned to more one-night stands—concerts and dances. But by 1952, the famous Atlantic (New Jersey) City Steel Pier, where Ellington had played many times for dancing, had noticed that big bands were attracting only about one third their former draws.

Yet his fame was not suffering. The magazine that most faithfully covered Ellington and his engagements, *Down Beat*, made an unprecedented move and devoted its entire issue of November 4, 1952, to him, on the occasion of the twenty-fifth anniversary of his opening at the Cotton Club. Dozens of notables, ranging from Arthur Fiedler and Milton Berle to Deems Taylor, Frank Sinatra, and Cole Porter, paid tribute to him, and Billy Strayhorn contributed a brief, perceptive article in which he coined a now-celebrated phrase, "the Ellington effect." "Each member of his band," he wrote, "is to him a distinctive tone color and set of emotions, which he mixes with others equally distinctive to produce a third thing, which I like to call the Ellington effect. Sometimes this mixing happens on paper and frequently right on the bandstand. I have often seen him exchange parts in the middle of a piece because the man and the part weren't the same character."

. . .

While performing in Los Angeles, the Ellington orchestra was invited to make a series of short films for television, sort of early, unelaborate music videos—without choreography or special effects. The company making them, Snader Telescriptions, made 751 films between 1950 and 1952, and eventually they were seen in almost every television market in the United States. Ellington made seven of these "videos," each one about four minutes long; five offered old standards from the 1920s and 1930s—*The Mooche*, *Mood Indigo*, *Sophisticated Lady*, *Solitude*, and *Caravan*; and there were two recent pieces—*V.I.P.'s Boogie* and Bellson's *The Hawk Talks*. These films were shown for years on television stations, and have now found their way to videocassette.

By 1950, 95 percent of households in the United States had radios. Television, until then a novelty for the well-to-do, started to penetrate into more and more homes, jumping from 9 percent of households that year to 65 percent by 1955 and to 87 percent by 1960, dramatically reducing radio listenership. The rapidly growing popularity of television transformed American entertainment. As advertising dollars migrated to television, radio stations offered fewer of the expensive live broadcasts of music and greatly increased their playing of recordings. By 1950, as millions of Americans tended to their new babies and suburban homes, movie attendance was at "a 1933 low." "By mid-1951," concluded authors Joseph and June Csida, "every television city, without exception, reported decreases ranging from twenty percent to forty percent in movie attendance. Movie theatres were closing in these same cities."

These changes meant that Ellington had fewer opportunities to disseminate his music on American radio, that Hollywood would no longer come calling on him to make band "shorts," and that he'd better get himself on television. At the time he appeared on a TV program called *Music '55*, Ellington wrote an article in which he proclaimed high hopes for the medium: "The future of big band existence in the entertainment industry, I firmly believe, is closely associated with television."

But it was not to be. Radio's replacement by television as the primary means of home entertainment meant, in fact, a decline in exposure for Ellington. In the United States, television has never been as interested in the kind of music Ellington played as radio was. It was a matter of demographics and economics: by the time TV was making a real mark, there were several other kinds of music that were more popular, especially among the younger generation, and the medium wanted to reach the widest possible audience. Television was broadcasting in the original sense of that word, while, with the boom of new radio stations after World War II, radio often "narrowcast" to target audiences. American television generally gave jazz short shrift, allowing it some exposure in the 1950s and 1960s, less after the 1970s.

It is probably safe to say, however, that Ellington fared as well on television as any black bandleader or instrumentalist, though certainly far poorer than pop or rock singers. A number of his early appearances were without his orchestra, where he'd appear as a pianist or a nonperforming celebrity (as on *What's My Line?*, a popular mystery-guest show). Though the sea change in popular taste and the rise of youth culture meant that music on TV was dominated by young performers, Ellington's longevity may have been an asset in securing the modest exposure he did receive, since he now had household name recognition and an armload of standards and old hits; and there was his charm, which proved to be thoroughly telegenic. However, with one notable exception in 1957, television would not be a medium for Ellington to advance any new musical ideas; rather it served to keep him and his most familiar pieces before the fickle public. He may have made a few converts, but probably TV served primarily to sustain the audience he already had—a holding action.

Besides television, during the 1950s Ellington would actively pursue two other new means of disseminating his music: the long-playing record and, by 1956, the outdoor festival.

The 33⅓-rpm long-playing record, or LP, introduced in 1948 by Columbia, was being accepted throughout the industry by 1950. Ellington's very first twelve-inch LP, *Masterpieces by Ellington*, 1950, took advantage of one of three qualities of the medium that were challenges and opportunities: no longer could two single tunes make up a record; now it took many, and that raised the need for

Ellington bends one of the new
vinyl long-playing records.
The LP gave Ellington a new set
of challenges and opportunities.

consistency. Second, the greater overall playing time eliminated
the three-minute limit of previous 78-rpm records, and Ellington
was quick to seize the chance to write and record longer pieces—
such as *Harlem*—to exploit this potential. (Most of his extended
works, however, would lie in the future.) And finally there was the
opportunity, and soon the expectation, to create *themes* for albums.
This Ellington would do, for example, in *Ellington '55* and in 1956,
in *Historically Speaking—The Duke*, both albums looking back on
earlier music.

The LP coincided with technical advances in sound recording
and reproduction known as "high-fidelity" (his *Ellington Uptown
in Hi-Fi*, 1951–52, was a favorite test record for hi-fi salesmen),
and thus Ellington's records made in the early 1950s sound generally better than earlier ones. (The LP disc, hi-fi, and a boom in
FM radio would also provide a great boon to classical music, which,
after 1948, enjoyed a tremendous growth in symphony orchestras
in the United States and in attendance at classical music concerts.)

The producer of *Masterpieces by Ellington* and *Ellington Uptown in Hi-Fi* was George Avakian, who told the author in 1992, "I never had too much to do with Duke's dates other than make sure he got what he wanted. He was always either very well prepared, or developed new ideas quickly in the studio in his patented way: 'You do this, and they'll do that; let's try it.' . . . All sessions were relaxed, and Duke was never upset or ruffled. What a pleasure! If Strayhorn was there, things were even easier."

In early 1953, Ellington secured a release from his contract with Columbia Records, his label for the last five-plus years, and signed with Capitol, once an industry upstart (founded in 1942 by songwriter Johnny Mercer and two others) and known for its vigorous promotion and cultivation of relations with disc jockeys. Ellington's recordings probably had been selling far fewer copies than ten years ago, and the reason he gave publicly for the switch was that Capitol was interested in promoting his music. At his first Capitol session, on April 6, 1953, Ellington introduced a new instrumental, *Satin Doll*, that in time became a jazz staple, and after Johnny Mercer and Billy Strayhorn outfitted it with lyrics in 1958, something of a pop standard, too.

However, though Ellington recorded more than ninety pieces for Capitol, and they were sonically excellent, the association with the label would produce only two LPs of much substance. Under producer Dave Dexter, Ellington even recorded such forgettable tunes as the *12th Street Rag Mambo*, *Bunny Hop Mambo*, a mambo built on *St. Louis Blues*, and a *Tyrolean Tango*. Writing in 1976, Dexter blamed the whole thing on Ellington: " 'I want a hit, Dave,' " Dexter recalled Ellington saying. "Other bands make hits. I want to hear Ellington records in the jukeboxes, and on the radio, and playing over the p.a. systems in shops and markets." Continued Dexter, "We got together at the time of the mambo craze . . . Duke said he wanted to tackle a mambo too."

Ellington was yearning for a hit; the last hit singles of his career probably had been *I'm Beginning to See the Light* in 1945 and *The Hawk Talks*, from 1951, which received some jukebox play. However, despite his efforts and the collusion of Capitol, Ellington would have no real hits during his association with the label. These examples of Ellington's lapses of taste should be seen not as disappointing work by a composer-orchestrator, but rather as attempts by a bandleader to keep his orchestra going. The mambo was a fad at this time, and there was a vogue for novelty songs. Ellington evidently hoped to cash in on this trend as a means of economic survival. Bandleading was a business, and the early 1950s were a low point for big bands generally. Ellington was struggling to generate the income he needed to maintain his orchestra.

"It's a matter of whether you want to play music or make money," he asserted. "I like to keep a band so I can write and hear the music next day. The only way you can do that is to pay the band and keep it on tap 52 weeks a year. If you want to make a real profit, you go out for four months, lay off for four and come back for another four. Of course, you can't hold a band together that way and I like the cats we've got. So, by various little twists and turns, we manage to stay in business and make a musical profit. And a musical profit can put you way ahead of a financial loss."

A record company and producer more strongly in tune with Ellington's genius might not have gone along with recording such drivel as *Bunny Hop Mambo*, but Capitol was never much inclined toward jazz, except for Stan Kenton. Ellington's years with Capitol, as Dan Morgenstern has observed, coincided with an industrywide transition from singles (78s and 45s) to LPs. Ellington's records for Capitol were singles-oriented, containing would-be hits.

Along with the album *Ellington Uptown*, one of his musical highlights of the early to mid 1950s was a Capitol LP he made at the piano, with only bass and drums as accompaniment, recorded in 1953, and released as *The Duke Plays Ellington* (later retitled *Piano Reflections*). He had first recorded a couple of piano solos in 1928, and over the years, made a few more solos, duets with either Jimmie Blanton or Billy Strayhorn, or trios with his bassist and drummer. But with its fifteen pieces, *The Duke Plays Ellington* was his most extensive recording of piano solos to date.

These and other recordings suggest that as a pianist he was both overshadowed by his orchestra and neglected by the press and public, partly because he wore so many different hats. On stage, as Dick Katz has noted, Ellington might appear during one evening as conductor, composer, arranger, announcer and master of ceremonies, as well as pianist-accompanist. With feigned modesty Ellington called himself "the piano player in the band." He was, after all, primarily a bandleader and composer, only secondarily a pianist.

Yet the piano, had been and always would be vital to Duke Ellington—both as composer and bandleader. He often composed at the keyboard: "You know how it is," he said once. "You go home expecting to go right to bed. But then on the way, you go past the piano and there's a flirtation. It flirts with you. So, you sit down and try a couple of chords and when you look up, it's 7 A.M." When entering a room, he'd often head straight for the piano. Usually his hotel room had a piano; in later years, he traveled with a portable Wurlitzer electric piano. And Ellington wielded the piano as a great telegraph, sending signals to his band. "You would never guess out front the amount of signaling that Duke does on the ivories," wrote one observer back in 1938. Rather than counting or stomping off the beat, Ellington employed the piano to set the tempo; sometimes instead of announcing the next tune, he would play the piano to identify the piece to the band; and he even used the piano to call his players back to the stand after intermission—his riffs became known as the "band call."

Ellington was generous to his musicians; unlike Benny Goodman, he featured his own playing sparingly, especially on recordings. Ellington would even sit out for a chorus or occasionally for an entire piece. Sometimes he used the piano almost more as a conductor's baton than as a major instrument. Typically he led his men at, from, and with the piano, feeding them ideas, rhythmically energizing them like a dynamic drummer, and superbly accompanying their solos. "As a band pianist he was just great," testified Bigard. "That is, once you got used to his chords. He would make the weirdest chords on practically any number." Ellington often played piano introductions, which became increasingly inventive, and in performance, long and meandering (at nightclubs oftentimes he was, in fact, shrewdly filling in till wayward players returned to the stage); some of these introductions became separate pieces (the prelude to *Rockin' in Rhythm* spun off into *Kinda Dukish*).

If his piano playing generally took a back seat to his two main careers, Ellington was still a fine instrumentalist. His piano sound was deep and resonant, his touch remarkable, his use of all registers of the piano exceptional. "I have never encountered a pianist, jazz or classical," averred Gunther Schuller, "who could command at once such purity of tone *and* range of dynamics and timbres as Ellington." His style was versatile, ranging from Harlem rent-shouts and down-home blues to poetic prefaces and impressionistic interludes, often laced with dissonant clusters of notes. He could jump instantly from elegant to earthy. And as the years passed, his very personal style of piano playing became more creative and impressive.

Though his piano album was exceptional, the ever-present critics, whom Ellington publicly disdained as a group, were complaining that his best work lay fifteen years in the past. Wherever he went, people wanted to hear *Sophisticated Lady* and other songs he had written twenty years before. During the 1951–56 period, Ellington seemed to be glimpsing few new musical horizons. Needing to devote great attention to keeping the band going, his composing seemed to stagnate, and he premiered only one major new work: *Night Creature*, which he and the Symphony of the Air introduced at a concert at Carnegie Hall on March 16, 1955. Scored for Ellington's orchestra and symphony orchestra, the piece showed up on a few more of his concerts, but it was not recorded until 1963, when Reprise Records put it out on the LP *Symphonic Ellington*, its effect delayed by eight years. It is one of Ellington's better-regarded large works, however, and it is a shame that it wasn't issued at the time he introduced it. But Capitol Records, at least under producer Dexter, would not likely have been interested in a long "art" piece.

From 1951 to 1956, Ellington made no theatrical motion pictures, enjoyed no renewing overseas trips. Rather, he was primarily struggling to hold the band together, and perhaps biding his time till he could stage a comeback. He accepted jobs paying less money than he wanted and needed, continued to perform one-nighters, even took one gig that was far beneath his gifts and stature. For six weeks in the summer of 1955, Ellington was reduced—undoubtedly out of financial necessity—to the demeaning role of accompanying a water show with ice skaters, called the Aquacade, in Flushing, New York, during which he played only a medley of his hits, then was excused while another conductor led his band, augmented by strings. For the duration of the engagement, he had to let four players go because they were not members of the New York City musicians' local. "It just seemed like a stupid, senseless gig," said Clark Terry in a Smithsonian interview, "but it was regular employment."

What kept him going at times like this? Ellington's creativity *had* to find an outlet—it's what made him tick—he had to have his band to hear his music. While his work as a composer was in some ways paramount, leading a band was the expression of a lifelong need to perform before an audience. He loved putting on a show, being theatrical, relished the high-wire aspects of improvising and performing, the element of controlling his realm, the challenge of winning the next audience—they were truly in his blood, and he was compelled to perform. He would have been miserable if he had retired from composing or bandleading. And without his band he couldn't have written: he couldn't have composed inspiredly in a vacuum, couldn't have written nameless parts for faceless trumpets, trombones, and saxophones. He had to write for characters —the men behind the horns, those whose musical style, personality, strengths and weaknesses he knew.

"The only reason we're still in it is mainly artistic interest," he said in 1956. "We're not one of those people who stay in the business only so long as business is good. We stay in it 52 weeks a year. . . . The fun of writing and participating in music is the motivating force that keeps us going on and on. It has nothing to do with money. . . . I enjoy solving problems."

Ellington had a gift for seeming to make the best of bad situations: during the Aquacade gig, he used his free time to go off and continue working on a musical play he had been pursuing since at least 1952, originally called *Mr. and Mrs. Lane*, then retitled *The Man with Four Sides* (that is, a square). It was rich in clever vernacular verse, but Ellington was ultimately unable to find a backer and it was never produced.

Then, just when Ellington needed a boost, his chance came. Lawrence Brown left Hodges's combo, and it began breaking up. Who approached whom is not clear, but Ellington brought Johnny Hodges back into the band. Hodges, like several others before and after, returned to what Norman Granz, in a Smithsonian interview, called "the protective womb." "I've heard the band members say," said Ruth Ellington Boatwright in another Smithsonian interview, " 'When you leave Duke Ellington, there's no place else to go.' "

The shy and undemonstrative Hodges had found showmanship simply not his forte, the grind of band leading very tiresome. "That was my main reason to give it up," he revealed. "It was too much. Duke has people to worry for him. You have to rush and get the tickets and get the money and go to the union and pay the tax and all of that kind of stuff." Hodges returned on August 1, 1955, marking the beginning of the saxophone section that stayed together and intact longer than any other. At the same time that Hodges rejoined the orchestra, a new drummer, Sam Woodyard, joined. Though erratic, like Greer, he proved to be one of Ellington's best drummers, driving and inspiring the band with his unflashy but empathetic playing; he would remain longer with Ellington than any other drummer except Greer. In composing for the band, Ellington took full advantage of Woodyard's varied talents, including drumming with his bare hands.

The return of Hodges heightened the division of the band into two camps—the older players (especially Carney, Tizol, and Hodges) and the younger (Terry, Cook, Gonsalves, Britt Woodman, and bassist Jimmy Woode, who was recruited in 1955)—that reflected generational, musical, and social differences. Yet Ellington and his players seemed to have been energized by the addition of Hodges and Woodyard, and soon the orchestra's fortunes would pick up. Before that, however, the 1955 *Down Beat* Readers' Poll would give the Ellington orchestra only a fourth-place rating, with just one sixth the votes of the winner, Count Basie. And in January 1956, Ellington suffered the indignity of a review in the *Toledo Blade*, by the paper's classical music critic, that attested to the struggle his music was still facing for acceptance. "What I heard last night seemed a carnival of uncouth and ugly sound . . . perhaps . . . vulgarity is permissible anywhere."

When Ellington's contract with Capitol Records came up for renewal at the end of 1955, he quit the label, even though he did not have another contract in waiting. He nevertheless recorded an album for Columbia in January 1956 with singer Rosemary Clooney that revealed a revitalized band. A hint of what the new year of 1956 might bring came about the same time, when *Time* published an approving article on Ellington. In May, *Saturday Review* ran an article by Whitney Balliett, and then, after persistent suggestions from Ellington's publicist, Joe Morgen, the editors of *Time* decided to run a cover story on Ellington, only the sixteenth American-born musician to be honored, but more than twenty-five years after he had established a national reputation and thirty-one years after his contemporary, George Gershwin, was given this national stamp of recognition. The magazine's music editor, Carter Harman, went to Las Vegas in April to interview Ellington. A tape of their interview, now at the Smithsonian, has Ellington, clearly eager for a comeback, shrewdly telling Harman, "I think it would be better for you —well, for me, too, of course, if we don't get, uh, too historic. . . . I mean, it would do me a hell of a lot more good if—if the reason for the goddamned thing is—has to do with now." While performing in San Francisco in June, Ellington sat for Peter Hurd's cover portrait, now preserved in the Smithsonian's National Portrait Gallery.

Then came one of those rare and pivotal moments, a classic example of luckily "being at the right place at the right time." In 1954, a young Boston entrepreneur named George Wein had inaugurated an outdoor jazz festival in Newport, Rhode Island, a summer retreat for wealthy New Yorkers and Bostonians. The festival had garnered considerable media attention, and Ellington had worked the 1955 edition but only as an M.C. This time, Saturday night, July 7, 1956, the entire band would perform. While waiting to take the stage, Ellington calmly discussed music and the outlines of a proposed contract with Columbia Records' producer Irving Townsend.

Given the impending *Time* story, Ellington knew the stakes were high that night. He had prepared for this night by composing a new work for the festival. But at his opening set of his performing debut at Newport, four of Ellington's players were absent. It was a poor start. After three hours of waiting to go back on, Ellington was growing testy. "What are we—the animal act, the acrobats?" he grumbled to Wein, referring to vaudeville exit acts.

Jeep's Blues by Johnny Hodges, before the fans would let him and his men go home, at 1 A.M.

The crowd-pleasing *Diminuendo and Crescendo* was more a triumph of showmanship than music; still, the performance, whose swing and energy reaffirmed the dance element in Ellington's music, caused a sensation not only among the crowd but also among the press. The word was out: Duke Ellington was back, and he was hot. When *Time*'s cover story appeared on August 20, people assumed it was sparked by Ellington's festival grand slam, which simply added luster to the legend of Newport and the magic of that midsummer midnight. Ellington had survived the most difficult period in his career, hung in there till he could regain the indispensable Hodges, and now, after so many setbacks and problems, stood on the verge of a winning streak again. Newport had created a turning point for Ellington; his wit and irony showing, in later years he would say, "I was born in 1956 at the Newport festival."

Essential Ellington,
1951–56

From the time Hodges deserted the Ellington orchestra early in 1951 until he returned in August 1955, none of Ellington's recordings can be considered quintessential. Aside from *Harlem*, written in 1950 before Hodges quit, Ellington created only one significant extended work (which was not recorded until 1963), and with the particular exception of a series of piano pieces, composed little of longevity. A few recordings made during Hodges's absence, however, are memorably strong. New players such as Louie Bellson, Willie Smith, Clark Terry, Paul Gonsalves, and the returning singer Betty Roché made their mark on records now. After Hodges's return,

(continued)

Ellington's (and the band's) inspiration heightened, as the record (and records) will show.

Monologue (Pretty and the Wolf) (1951), written by Ellington and Jimmy Hamilton, is played by only the reeds, bass, and drums; the real star, though, is not the minimal music but rather Ellington's narration. In just two minutes, he relates an amusing allegory of a girl from the country who meets a smooth character from the city. Ellington's fanciful, ironic commentary on the sexes reveals something about his attitudes, and encapsulates his urbane, smooth-spoken public persona. It's available on The Complete Duke Ellington, 1947–1952, Vol. 3 (CBS).

The highlight of the LP Ellington Uptown in Hi-Fi, recorded in 1951–52, is the fourteen-minute Harlem, also known as A Tone Parallel to Harlem. This kaleidoscopic, marvelously descriptive tour of Harlem, led, as it were, by the footsteps of bassist Wendell Marshall, passes by folks working and shopping, fighting for equal rights, festively parading, mourning at a church funeral, and includes other honest, affirmative glimpses of everyday life. Much shorter and tighter than Black, Brown and Beige, Harlem, with its three well-integrated themes, is regarded by a number of observers (including, reportedly, the composer himself) as Ellington's best extended work, and he chose to perform it fairly frequently at concerts. It has been called "every bit as much a miniature masterpiece as is Rhapsody in Blue." Reissued as simply Ellington Uptown (Columbia), the album also features extended arrangements of evergreens The Mooche, Perdido, Take the "A" Train (with a boppish scat vocal by Betty Roché), and a new Louie Bellson drum vehicle, Skin Deep.

In 1953, Ellington went into the studio with just bass and drums and recorded a remarkable album of seven old and eight new piano numbers, The Duke Plays Ellington, since retitled Piano Reflections (Capitol). Most exceptional are the spare, modern B Sharp Blues, the dissonant, wistful

(continued)

Melancholia, the measured, solemn *Retrospection,* and especially the intimate, prayerlike *Reflections in D.* As Mark Tucker has observed, these last three pieces "form a link between earlier mood pieces . . . and the sacred music of the '60s" and are virtually impossible to categorize musically.

In *Ellington '55* (actually recorded in 1953 and 1954), the orchestra made an album of classic Ellingtonia and pieces associated with other leading bands. Besides stirring renditions of his own *Rockin' in Rhythm* (1931) and *Happy-Go-Lucky Local* (1946), there is the lightly swinging *One O'Clock Jump,* an uncharacteristic but satisfying style switch into the classic Basie mode. This Capitol record is currently out of print.

From February 1956 comes an album called *Historically Speaking—The Duke* (Bethlehem), a thirty-year retrospective of a dozen Ellington and Strayhorn originals, from *East St. Louis Toodle-Oo* (1926) through the new *Lonesome Valley* (1956). With Johnny Hodges back in the fold, and drummer Sam Woodyard propelling the rhythm, the band sounds energized and tight. A brisk reading of *In a Mellotone* has striking solos by Hodges and Ray Nance.

In the early hours of July 8, 1956, the Ellington orchestra was captured live in a performance at the Newport Jazz Festival that became legendary. There are just three numbers on the LP *Ellington at Newport* (Columbia): the newly written *Newport Jazz Festival Suite; Jeep's Blues,* with Hodges whispering, moaning, and wailing a consummate, moving blues—the musical zenith of the Newport Festival; and the fourteen-minute *Diminuendo and Crescendo in Blue,* with the famous Gonsalves solo and the band driving the crowd wild. Though not typical Ellingtonia, the best representation of his genius as a composer, or a musical highlight of the Ellington oeuvre, this *Diminuendo* is nonetheless an exciting performance and a career milestone, and no Ellington library would be complete without it.

TEN

$\mathcal{R}$ENEWING
CAREER AND
CREATIVITY

•

1 9 5 6 – 6 5

fter the lows of the late 1940s and early to mid 1950s, Ellington must have felt good indeed to receive the adulation of the crowd at Newport, the prominence of the *Time* cover story, and the prospect of a record deal with Columbia. Perhaps Ellington had vowed all along ultimately to be vindicated for keeping his band together despite tough times and musical sacrifices. One evident result of his reversal in fortunes was that he determined to trim down, managing to shed thirty-five pounds in 1956. Soon his Columbia album *Ellington at Newport* would be released and become his best-selling LP ever, reportedly eventually selling in the hundreds of thousands, a virtually unheard-of feat at that time for music considered to be jazz. Columbia would reissue *Ellington at Newport* in simulated stereo and would thereafter record Ellington (and all its other artists) in genuine stereo to offer the latest in sound reproduction. Ellington was ready to tackle new problems, achieve new heights.

Ellington's sudden success relaunched his rocket on a high trajectory of visibility. But in the summer of 1956, no one knew how far or high the rocket would travel, if it would breach new musical

In Columbia Records' Irving Townsend, who supervised most of Ellington's late-1950s records, he found a savvy and sympathetic record producer.

space, if indeed it would stay aloft or instead drop back to earth, weighed down by high salaries, changed demographics and popular taste of the ever-more-powerful youth culture, and the burden of Ellington's past. Since the 1930s, he was always competing creatively with his younger self, and he was always dogged by two questions: How does the current band compare with past editions? How would his next work stand up to his past works? Perhaps as a result, Ellington, as Billy Strayhorn disclosed, "hates talking about the old bands and old pieces." Instead, Ellington preferred to look ahead to the next piece, and if he asked himself questions about his upcoming work, they were likely to be: What problem will have to be solved? Will the piece make a satisfying new statement? Will it find an audience and help bring in money to keep the band going?

That seminal night at Newport, Columbia producer Irving Townsend approached Ellington about a deal—a three-year recording contract, with normal royalties, and an advance of $1,000 for each piece he recorded. Presumably, Columbia also offered to pay the musicians scale—the standard fees set by the musicians' union. Ellington, wary of record companies, warned him, "Record companies don't like me." It was a sad admission for someone whose records had once sold very well. But the maestro, quickly calculating that a typical recording session of three or four pieces could pay his band's salary for a week, said he wanted his money up front.

"But my loot comes from publishing," Ellington told Townsend. "We have to make new music. Don't talk to me 'bout no *Sophisticated Lady*." Ellington was serving notice that he wanted to record not only his own pieces, which he had always done, but *new* pieces, which, unlike his pre-1942 material, would be published by his own Tempo Music Company and bring him the composer's half *and* the publisher's half of the royalties, in other words, double the royalty income.

The Columbia contract was important to Ellington. It offered him three years of recording stability and a more prestigious label than Capitol (especially under Columbia's president, Goddard Lieberson, who was committed to bringing the public new works by American composers). And in evident contrast to Capitol, Columbia was willing to invest the time and money in recording more than one "take" of a piece, when necessary, to get it right.

Perhaps it was another stroke of Ellington's lifelong luck with finding a "friendly advisor," at a critical moment, that Irving Townsend was assigned to Ellington, for the composer seemed to have found a new advocate and confederate in the producer. The thirty-five-year-old Townsend, a former professional-musician-turned-writer, had an intelligent mind and empathetic ear and, by his own account, great admiration for Ellington as a composer. Townsend seemed to understand Ellington as well as if not better than any producer with whom he worked.

Now rearmed with Johnny Hodges (playing better than ever), equipped with a strong drummer, gliding on the triumph of showmanship and excitement at Newport and the *Time* cover story, gearing up to tackle new musical problems, and teamed with a savvy producer at Columbia, Duke Ellington was going into a rebound, a second great creative period.

Recognizing that Ellington wanted to write new compositions, and yet knowing there was a greater market for the familiar and commercial, Townsend faced a problem. How would he keep his employer, with its ever-present profit motive, happy and yet satisfy Ellington? Probably with Ellington's collusion, he hit upon a solution: have Ellington make both commercial LPs *and* more artistic LPs. He and Ellington would balance art and commerce, the old and the new, the familiar and the fresh, and the comfortable with the challenging. The idea worked. Though never again would one of Ellington's records sell as briskly as *Ellington at Newport*, the strategy would keep Columbia executives satisfied; in 1959 Columbia and Ellington would renew their contract for another three years.

Maintaining what was undoubtedly the most expensive band of its day put constant financial pressure on Ellington; thus he was eager to make records. During his Capitol contract, Ellington had been in the recording studio periodically, but now, at Columbia, he went much more frequently. From July 1956, when the contract began, until July 1962, when it would expire, Columbia would record twenty LPs' worth of material: that's an average of one LP every three and a half months, which meant that Ellington and Strayhorn were writing or arranging a new piece or movement nearly every week just for Columbia. In addition, Ellington recorded more than 150 pieces during this period for other projects.

The regularity of recording gave Ellington his needed deadlines, and the increased opportunity to record supplied economic incentive to compose (so he would receive composer royalties from record sales) and perhaps stimulated his thinking, too. "The man," said Strayhorn, "is a revelation. He's continually renewing himself through his music." However, creating this quantity of music while leading the band in constant and increasingly wide-ranging travels, appearing on television, composing for motion pictures and other special projects, all the while striving to keep the orchestra afloat, made it very difficult for Ellington to be consistently inspired. George Avakian, who as director of popular music for Columbia in the 1950s produced occasional records of Ellington's and was Townsend's boss, told the author, "Except for 'commissioning' *The*

Newport Festival Suite, I never suggested repertoire because that was impossible with such a busy touring band. Duke had to record what he had in his active book, or had rehearsed on the road before coming to town." (This meant that Ellington frequently worked out new compositions on the road, often trying them out on unsuspecting audiences at dances, concerts, and nightclubs.) There were bound to be disappointments with all this activity; but on the whole, the Columbia years would be a distinguished period for him.

Beginning in 1956, and for perhaps the next fourteen or fifteen years, Ellington would compose with renewed zeal, inquisitiveness, and inventiveness. His later works seemed, as Peter Watrous has put it, "the compositions of a man eager to share the knowledge gained from years on the road in all possible social settings. Once heard, this music colors a listener's musical experiences indelibly. It isn't possible to know the depth and density of American music without having heard it."

Columbia, however, did not serve as Ellington's patron, nor did any other institution on a regular basis. Mid-twentieth-century America did not offer Ellington musical patronage from church or state. And while American composers in the European tradition had symphonies, foundations, and universities to support them, as an African-American and a "jazz" musician, Ellington found he received commissions from neither foundations nor universities, only rarely from a symphony. Instead of Columbia or other record companies paying him specially to compose new works, he *used* the recording sessions as opportunities to compose *self*-commissioned pieces.

The pattern of mixing commercial with artistic records began immediately after the release of *Ellington at Newport*. His next recording for Columbia was based on an idea he had been thinking about since at least 1941, when he had conceived of it for Orson Welles's never-completed film *It's All True* and its planned segment on the history of jazz. On that July night at Newport, when Ellington met Irving Townsend, the producer asked the composer what kind of new music he had in mind to create. As Townsend told it, Ellington asked him, "Did you know that a drum is a woman?" Unwilling to take the bait, Townsend responded, "Is that the first album?" "Man, that's not only the first album," laughed Ellington, "that's the mother of all albums. That's the story of Madam Zajj."

Recorded in September 1956, *A Drum Is a Woman* is a suite with narration, in four parts, weaving an allegorical story of Madame Zajj ("jazz" more or less spelled backward), who's born on a Caribbean isle, goes (in the second part) to New Orleans, journeys (in the third) to New York, and finally, in a fanciful projection into the future, travels to the moon. In each location, Zajj meets a man named Joe, whom she affects, and then leaves him behind for the next man named Joe. Townsend considered it one of Ellington's "most self-revealing works" for he "saw himself as the one 'Joe' that Madam Zajj could not leave behind." The critical response was decidedly mixed; some called *A Drum Is a Woman* pretentious —they failed to catch its humor and wit.

CBS, the television network of Columbia Records' parent company, aired a revised and expanded version, with dancing by Talley Beatty and Carmen de Lavallade, on May 8, 1957, as part of

Ray Nance, masked as in New Orleans's Mardi Gras, plays trumpet before the CBS cameras in the 1957 television production of Ellington's *A Drum Is a Woman.*

the *U.S. Steel Hour*. This hourlong special was one of American television's first programs performed exclusively by African-Americans. Though the show was broadcast live, at least some of the music was prerecorded; eyeing the script boards instead of the camera, Ellington appeared rather indirect and distant instead of charming and engaging. The program was not viewed favorably by most jazz fans, who would have preferred less dancing and narration, more of the soloists.

Whatever the critical reaction, Ellington was committed to expanding his composing horizons, to moving "beyond category." On July 20, 1956, the Ellington orchestra had performed a concert at the Stratford, Ontario, Shakespeare Festival, and the festival had commissioned him to compose a piece fitting for performance at the 1957 festival. In fact, Ellington premiered this work, *Such Sweet Thunder* (sometimes called *The Shakespearian Suite*), on April 28, 1957, at a concert at New York's Town Hall and then performed it at Stratford the following September. Ellington and Shakespeare: at first it must have seemed a somewhat surprising match to some. Ellington wrote mostly about twentieth-century American and African-American themes, sometimes of women and love, sometimes of feelings, moods, and personal memories. Now he was turning to the pinnacle of English literature, from more than three hundred years ago?

It should not have surprised anyone, however, given Ellington's thirst for challenges. The Bard and the Duke, moreover, had a number of commonalities. Shakespeare was an actor as well as a dramatist; Ellington was a performer as well as a composer. Shakespeare wrote about a range of human experiences; so did Ellington. Shakespeare had a keen understanding of human nature, led a fertile and productive artistic life, and expressed a range of emotions and values; so did Ellington. One of Shakespeare's greatest strengths was the richness of his characterizations; one of Ellington's was the richness of the musical characters he hired and the way he enhanced their individuality. Shakespeare wrote for all levels of society, from royalty to pauper; so did Ellington. Shakespeare wrote not for publication but for performance: only half of his writings were published during his lifetime, and then mostly in "corrupt" quarto editions. Likewise, Ellington never wrote for publication, but rather for performance—whether live, on record, or on film. Few of his pieces were published during his lifetime, and those that were bore poor resemblance to the originals.

As did Shakespeare, Ellington deployed his players like great actors on a stage. For nineteen years, Shakespeare was part owner of a repertory company (Lord Chamberlain's Men, which became The King's Men) and wrote *only* for that company, in fact, for particular thespians—like Richard Burbage (who played Hamlet, Richard III, Lear, and Othello), Will Kempe, and John Heminges. Likewise, Ellington had *his* own repertory company—for fifty years —and wrote almost exclusively for its players—Hodges, Nanton, and Bigard, and the others. Shakespeare's plays have outlived the actors for whom they were conceived. Ellington's music may, as the centuries pass, attain the same achievement.

Ellington's *Such Sweet Thunder* was a very personal statement of how the maestro interpreted the Bard, and it was hailed by most critics. Certain of its movements, such as *Star-Crossed Lovers*, Ellington often performed in concert. *Such Sweet Thunder*, though, pointed up a problem inherent in the suite format. Originally a series of dance movements in the same or related keys, the suite frees its composer from having to come to grips with large-scale architecture, but it presents another problem—the challenge of creating consistency among the various movements, especially, as in this case, when there are as many as twelve movements. Composing large collections of character pieces was quite characteristic of the European Romantic tradition—e.g., Schumann's *Carnaval* and Mussorgsky's *Pictures at an Exhibition*—which Ellington may have absorbed along the way and Strayhorn almost certainly did.

A number of reasons have been suggested for the fact that Ellington and Strayhorn were to write more and more suites. They were encouraged by the long playing time of the LP record and by a desire, perhaps, for titles of "suite," which carried more prestige than earlier titles such as *Saturday Night Function*, *Jive Stomp*, or *Jumpin' Punkins*. They may have chosen the suite over longer, truly extended forms, since the format allowed them greater ease in highlighting the various soloists in the band, was a logical extension of the shorter song length, and made it easier to divide the work between them, especially as Ellington was traveling incessantly and Strayhorn was often in New York composing. When separated, they would confer often by phone, Ellington typically calling Strayhorn (and anyone else he wanted to reach) in the middle of the night. "They continued to write and arrange music, just as they had for many years, but under new headings," wrote Ellington's close observer, Stanley Dance. "So far as they were concerned, there was nothing pretentious about this, although Ellington was ever adept at putting his public on!"

With *Ellington '55*, Ellington had created an LP with a theme: looking back on music of the past. With *A Drum Is a Woman*, he pioneered what later became known as "concept" albums: whether a series of pieces or one long work, such an album entailed, at its best, music conceived, written, and played for record release and organized around a unified theme. Though it lacked the narration and lyrics of *A Drum Is a Woman*, Ellington's *Such Sweet Thunder* was another concept album.

In March of 1956, while he was still unaffiliated with any record label, Ellington had taken his orchestra into the Universal recording studio in Chicago, one of his favorites, and recorded several pieces under his own "steam." If evidence was needed of his insatiable need to create, revise, and experiment, here it is. His creativity would come faster than the record companies were willing to act and so over the next seventeen years, he would privately record more than three hundred pieces in order to preserve his inspirations. These sessions also served as means for maintaining the band's musical discipline, trying out new ideas in workshop fashion, and securing a chance to hear the results. These recordings, which came to be called "the stockpile," in a number of cases surpass the ones he was making for the record companies. These stockpile sessions would become available to the public only after Ellington's death.

While Ellington intimates knew of the stockpile, Ellington had for decades maintained another, hidden storehouse—unexplored ideas that he kept in his long memory. He would harbor ideas for years, sometimes decades, waiting for his chance to bring them out. He did not seem to be daunted if no one else thought the ideas good—he would hang on to them and bide his time. For instance, as we have seen, he had been thinking about a long piece on the history of black people in America since the late 1920s; it saw fruition in 1943 as *Black, Brown and Beige*. Then, when the critical reaction was, at best, mixed, he kept coming back to the piece, or parts of the piece, until finally, in March 1965, he would record it privately, getting in his last word on how he thought it should sound. Sometimes Ellington's use of earlier material amounted to shrewd and thrifty recycling; sometimes it was revision or transformation; and sometimes it was a matter of retaining a concept in his mind until a favorable moment arose.

After serving as producer for several of Ellington's LPs, Townsend observed that the maestro, keenly aware of the permanence of records, "takes records more seriously than anyone I have ever recorded." Townsend found that Ellington was at the peak of his creativity in the recording studio, where he could exercise a high degree of control over his musicians and music. He would always come prepared—usually with written-out parts—but would make revisions throughout the session. Rarely would Ellington be satisfied with just one take. He would, however, usually arrive late at the studio. "He has nurtured the reputation he has made for always being late," Townsend observed, "because it allows him the freedom to time his entrance to suit his sense of drama. . . . In our years of recording together, I've known Duke to arrive an hour early, two hours late, and at every point between these two extremes. I have never known him to arrive anywhere at the wrong moment."

But recording was only part of the orchestra's life. As the fame of the Newport Jazz Festival spread, it was inevitable that other cities would want to establish their own such events. In 1958, Monterey, California, began its jazz festival, one which Ellington would play six times. Festivals became one of Ellington's most visible venues. With the rare exception such as Tanglewood and Ravinia (near Chicago), he was usually confined to playing *jazz* festivals. Soon the festival format would catch on, and summer would become the time for jazz festivals throughout the United States and eventually abroad. The festival was an extension of the concert idea, and reinforced the emergence of jazz as an art form for listening; although some outdoor festivals had a decidedly social aspect, too.

There were some competitive feelings among festivals. At one of the Monterey festivals, Ellington was preparing to go on stage when Jimmy Lyons, the festival's producer, approached him and asked him, whatever he performed, to please not play the piece Ellington had written for that *other* festival. Ellington went on stage and promptly proceeded to perform *Newport Up*. The independent Ellington got advice from many, listened to a few, and followed practically no one.

Meanwhile, Ellington was involving himself in various means of keeping his music before the public. Edward R. Murrow, American television's most respected journalist, who had a high reputation for fairness to blacks, was host of a weekly program called *Person to Person*, and on March 15, 1957, he interviewed Ellington. In a thirteen-minute segment, Ellington was seen in his apartment overlooking the Hudson River, as he answered questions, pointed out some of his awards and an original oil painting he called *Satin Doll*, and played a bit of piano.

About this time, there were press reports that Ellington had written twenty-one new songs for a forthcoming Broadway play about South Africa—variously reported to be titled *Saturday Laughter* or *The Man Below*. But it never came to fruition Ellington seemed to be ever seeking new challenges. "I'm so damned fickle," he was once quoted as saying. "I never could stick with what I was doing —always wanted to try something new."

In October and November 1958, the Ellington orchestra returned to Europe for nearly fifty days of concerts in England, Scotland, France, Belgium, Holland, Sweden, Norway, Denmark, Germany, Austria, Switzerland, and Italy. The orchestra's first performance in Britain in twenty-five years was made possible because a U.S.–British agreement in March 1956 enabled exchanges of each other's musicians. The concerts were critically well received.

During the trip, royalty met royalty when Ellington was introduced to Queen Elizabeth and the Prince of Edinburgh at the

Leeds Festival in Yorkshire. Ellington and the queen charmed each other, and the meeting made quite an impression on him. Within two months of his return, he had written a piece in her honor, for which he took the unheard-of and wonderfully romantic step of pressing but a single copy, which he had sent to Buckingham Palace. He consistently refused to release the record the rest of his life. It was only in 1976, after his death, that *The Queen's Suite* was issued to the public.

In January and February of 1959, the Ellington orchestra went to Miami Beach to perform a revival of *Jump for Joy* at a theater-restaurant called Copa City. Ellington and Strayhorn had worked with Sid Kuller to update the lyrics, written seventeen years earlier, for the changed musical and social sensibilities of the era of the civil-rights movement. But the show lost $100,000 and closed after twenty days. Once again, Ellington's hopes in musical theater were dashed, but he continued to push himself.

In April of 1959, Ellington would turn sixty years old. Wanting to mark this milestone in a special way, Strayhorn, Mercer Ellington, Townsend, and Arthur Logan got together and decided on a big project. Ellington's music was a mess, and for many pieces there were not even lead sheets. Strayhorn quietly got busy on the music, and they brought trombonist and copyist John Sanders into the conspiracy, hiring him to transcribe music from thirty years of recordings. After several months of backbreaking effort, they assembled a massive collection of the maestro's music, organized into twenty-four impressive, leather-bound volumes. When they presented it to Ellington, "He made polite noises and kissed us all," said Logan, "but, you know, the son of a bitch didn't even bother to take it home." Ellington was not interested in dwelling on or preserving his past; and "he thought," as Logan's wife, Marian, said, "that having all the music catalogued and copied meant that his life was over, and he wasn't ready for that." The finality of assembling his corpus upset him, as Don George observed: "He wanted nothing in his life ever to be that complete and final." He wanted the creative process to be ongoing. Through the foresight of Mercer Ellington, however, the volumes and their seven-hundred-some pieces of music are now safeguarded at the Smithsonian.

. . .

In 1959, for the first time in twenty-five years, Ellington was asked to write the score for a motion picture. As had happened so often in Hollywood, jazz was again linked with crime, for this was a murder mystery set in a small town on the upper peninsula of Michigan. *Anatomy of a Murder* starred Jimmy Stewart as the pros-

Royalty meets royalty: when they met in the fall of 1958,
Queen Elizabeth and Duke Ellington charmed each other.

ecuting attorney, Ben Gazzara as the accused murderer and Lee Remick as his wife. Ellington had a small acting role, his first in thirty years, as "Pie Eye," a piano player who got to speak four sentences—a total of fifteen words. In addition, he "ghosted" at the piano for Jimmy Stewart. The soundtrack was performed by the full Ellington orchestra, a small group from within the band, and Ellington as solo pianist. His music was edited considerably to fit the requirements of the movie, but the score is first rate. That November, the Columbia soundtrack album earned three Grammy Awards.

The following year, he received another film commission, this time to write the music for *Paris Blues*. Filmed in the City of Light, this picture starred Paul Newman and Sidney Poitier as expatriate American jazzmen and Louis Armstrong in a cameo appearance as trumpeter "Wild Man" Moore. For *Paris Blues*, Ellington composed in Hollywood during November and December 1960, then flew to Paris for three weeks, during which the band was given time off, and Ellington composed and played a bit. "It was," he said, "the closest thing to a vacation I'd ever been able to think about." Though the jazz press found the movie's story disappointing, it applauded Ellington's music, especially the underscore or background music, which was nominated for an Academy Award.

While in Paris, he was commissioned to compose a musical score for a revival of *Turcaret*, a comedy by Alain-René Lesage from 1709; the score consisted of interludes, mostly briefer than thirty seconds, between the dialogue, recorded by a band under Ellington's direction and reproduced during the play by means of a tape recorder. *Paris Blues* and *Turcaret* were among the first (and few) times that Ellington composed for an ensemble other than his own orchestra.

His feud with the NAACP long ago patched up, on September 11, 1959, Ellington was presented the organization's Spingarn Medal, for "the highest or noblest achievement by an American Negro during the preceding year or years." Normally indirect about civil rights, occasionally Ellington took a very public stand. On February 22, 1960, after giving a concert at Johns Hopkins University in Baltimore, Ellington went to the Blue Jay restaurant because twice that day black students had been refused service. He was

Director Otto Preminger overlooks Billy Strayhorn and Ellington as they compose their masterful score for *Anatomy of a Murder*, 1959, Ellington's first film score commission in twenty-five years.

Ellington pauses during a 1961 recording session in Paris for his score to the film *Paris Blues*.

Returning to the Ellington orchestra in 1962, Cootie Williams resumed his role as master soloist in the "growl-and-plunger" style.

also refused; it made newspaper headlines. On September 5, 1961, he canceled an engagement in Little Rock, Arkansas, after the NAACP informed him that seating at the club would be segregated. The next two nights, he played the Music Halls of Dallas and Houston, after ensuring that the audiences would be integrated, which they were for the first time in those auditoriums' history.

Ellington had enjoyed a rather stable lineup in his orchestra, but in the fall of 1959 a period of reshuffling began. First, the sweet-toned trumpeter Harold Baker, who had rejoined the band in 1957 for his fourth stint, left in September 1959 to lead his own group. Then, when the orchestra spent about a month abroad, in September and October 1959, playing concerts in France, Holland, Sweden, Denmark, West Germany, Austria, and Switzerland, where they were an artistic success, Clark Terry and Quentin "Butter" Jackson left the orchestra to remain in Europe with Quincy Jones's revue *Free and Easy*. (Terry would remain forever grateful for his years with Ellington, saying that he had learned so much it had been like attending the "University of Ellingtonia.")

Then, as Hodges had done four years earlier, in May 1960, Lawrence Brown, who had been doing studio work in New York, returned to the security of Ellington's protective nest after an absence of nine years. His rejoining gave the Ellington orchestra a lift, and restored to the Ellington sound one of the greatest lyric trombones of all time.

Trumpeter Willie Cook left in December 1961. Eventually, in early September 1962, he was replaced by Cootie Williams who, now somewhat streamlined and diminished—though still powerful —as a soloist, returned to the fold after twenty-two years away. Williams and Cat Anderson didn't get along at all; they sat at opposite ends of the trumpet section, their backs psychologically turned to one another, and were known as "bookends." "And a couple of times," recalled Jimmy Hamilton, "they got in a scuffle on the bus and we had to break it up."

Despite the recent turnover, there were still five players who had been with the orchestra thirty years earlier—Ellington, Carney, Hodges, Williams, and Brown—all still vital musicians, plus six others with considerable experience with the Ellington sound: Strayhorn (twenty-three years), Nance (twenty-two), Hamilton (nineteen), Procope (sixteen), Anderson (thirteen), and Gonsalves (eleven). So Ellington remained blessed with a contingent of seasoned players. At the same time, many close followers felt that as more musicians with formal training joined, the orchestra's sum total of individuality declined. In the earlier days, musicians had often been self-taught or schooled on the bandstand, and had come up at a time when jazz and big-band traditions were just being formed, so there was a lot of latitude and variety among individual styles. Later musicians could often read music better, but were not necessarily as original as the early Ellingtonians, Miley, Bigard, Stewart, Nanton, and Hodges.

For his performance on September 24, 1960, at the third annual Monterey Jazz Festival, Ellington and Strayhorn composed a piece based loosely on area writer John Steinbeck's novel *Sweet Thursday*. Ellington and Strayhorn punningly dubbed their new work

Suite Thursday. At the recording session the next month in Los Angeles, Hodges became ill and had to be flown to New York City, where he was treated for an ulcer. Saxophonist Paul Horn was brought in to substitute for Hodges. Even without Hodges, *Suite Thursday* is considered one of Ellington's most successful works of his later years.

In about January of that year, Ellington undertook an unusual musical project. He and Strayhorn began adapting and arranging Tchaikovsky's popular *Nutcracker Suite* for the Ellington orchestra, and they commenced recording it in May. Other than three-minute popular songs, this was their first adaptation of music from outside the Ellington orchestra. Soon they applied the same approach to Edvard Grieg's *Peer Gynt Suites Nos. 1 and 2*, but the *Nutcracker* was more of a popular and critical success than *Gynt*. *Peer Gynt* was initially paired with *Suite Thursday* and issued by Columbia as *Swinging Suites by Edward E. and Edward G.* Many of Ellington's LPs were controversial, but critical opinion was especially divided over the *Nutcracker* and *Gynt* adaptations. "What esthetic pleasure does Duke find in caricaturing these relative lightweights?" asked John McLellan of the *Boston Traveler.* "For that is what these amount to, really—amusing caricatures of some not very important music." The British critic Eddie Lambert, on the other hand, found that the *Nutcracker* "is transformed into jazz with affection, skill, and humour, while the scoring lacks nothing in richness of texture and tone colour."

Why did Ellington and Strayhorn adapt the Tchaikovsky and Grieg suites? To set and meet a challenge? As part of the time-honored traditions of ragging or jazzing the classics, to make Tchaikovsky and Grieg hip, to make them swing? To "signify" in Henry Louis Gates, Jr.'s sense of creating "repetition with a signal difference"? To fit within the tradition in classical music of (re)orchestrating another composer's music? To grab a piece of academic-classical respectability? Because Ellington needed music for a record date and he could not produce enough original music? (This seems most unlikely, given Ellington's flow of creativity during this period and the number of pieces he recorded for his stockpile.) Was it at least partly to put people on? If so, it would not take anything away from the results, because Ellington would have wanted anything he recorded to possess style and quality.

Whatever the motivation for these adaptations, by this time in his life Ellington was highly practiced at the put-on. Miles Davis said once, "Duke puts everybody on." In an unpublished rumination, probably from March 1967, comes this uncensored and revealing declaration from the maestro: "To be a great bull-shitter is great, but to be a great bull-shitter and wear a diffusing veneer *over* the bullshit is the ultimate."

Ellington exemplified an urbane version of the trickster, an often-heroic archetype that has a long tradition in myth and folklore of many cultures, including European (Reynard the fox), African (Ananse the spider), and African-American folklore, where he's taken many forms, from animal tricksters such as the wily Br'er Rabbit, to human ones such as John of the John and Master (or John and Boss) tales, and such outlaw badman heroes as Stackolee and John Hardy. The trickster embodies many qualities, including deception, shrewdness, control, elusiveness, hope, and irony.

In a candid, unpublished, tape-recorded interview Ellington laughingly said, "I'm not a bank robber. I'm a sneak thief." "I may be a heel," his former associate Leonard Feather quoted him as once saying, "but I hate for people to think so." Dizzy Gillespie told of sitting in on an Ellington recording session, probably *Ellington Jazz Party*, in 1959. "I just happened along one day with my horn and we blew and they taped it and they put it out. And when I got no money, I mentioned it, very gently, to Duke, and he smiled and he says, 'Well, Diz, I can't pay you what you're really worth.' Whee, was that a cunning, elegant man! So I smile and I say, 'Don't give it no mind, Duke. Just so long as you *pay* me!' And maybe a year later, he did."

The trickster in Ellington was also operating when he attempted to charm his way into the reluctant White House of Herbert Hoover, offered highly exaggerated flattery to a music publisher or an attractive woman, used the typical sardonic banter or veiled sarcasm that caught his conversationalists off guard, or suavely and mockingly proclaimed everywhere he performed, "We love you madly"—which his audiences ate up. Being a trickster was part of the streetwise survival Ellington had learned early on; it was partly

Ellington's music was broad enough to encompass Dizzy Gillespie, the great exponent of bebop, and they recorded together several times.

a way of achieving control and attaining his goals, partly a self defense against the outside world, a way of outwitting everyone else. The secret, exclusive aspect of it related, also, to the jazz-man's traditional insider or hip behavior.

Not wanting to reveal much of his personal self or thoughts, Ellington disliked direct questions. "I don't find it too annoying to have people around who talk incessantly," he confided in those unpublished ruminations mentioned above. "It's when they start asking direct questions, and I—to keep from feeling that I am being rude—must dig into my brain and use valuable thought to make an answer to meaningless questions, and still try to say keep quiet without saying it."

His characteristic lack of directness found a parallel in his rela-tionships with his family, musicians, and close friends. He was always keen to protect his privacy. His estranged wife, Edna, said, "Duke . . . is a lonely man. He masks his emotions. Never wants you to know how he actually feels." His players found him rather distant, too. One of his veterans told Nat Hentoff, "He kids around with us but if you get too close to him, he'll make a joke or put you on, and edge away."

In an insightful analysis, Irving Townsend suggested that Ellington operated his private world with an inner circle of Ruth, Mercer, and their families; then a middle circle of tight friends Strayhorn, Dr. Arthur Logan, and band members and their wives; and then outer circles consisting of business associates, new and old girlfriends, and friends scattered through many nations. Rarely did he allow people in different circles to come together at the same time. Rather, he preferred to reveal only parts of himself to people in the various circles. Just as he called several compositions tone "parallels," that was how he interacted with his friends: on a parallel, "never quite touching, never far apart." In Townsend's view, only a whole convention of people who "knew" Ellington, each revealing their understanding of the enigma, could begin to piece together an accurate portrait of him.

There are reports that Evie Ellis (who was often erroneously referred to as "Mrs. Duke Ellington") very much wanted Ellington to marry her, but he consistently refused, saying to divorce Edna would be too expensive. In March 1959, when *Ebony*, the *Life* magazine for black America, discovered that Edna was living in Washington and prominently ran an interview with her, Ellington was furious. His cover had been blown and his privacy punctured.

Sometimes, not even Ellington could find ways to work the band's problems out within the group. In February 1961, for instance, there was a rare and sudden public scandal in the Ellington orchestra itself. During an engagement at the Riviera Hotel's Starlight Room in Las Vegas, Ray Nance, Paul Gonsalves, Willie Cook, and new trumpeter "Fats" Ford were arrested on charges of narcotics possession. Ellington must have been deeply embarrassed when the story went public; he put up $2,500 in bail. Nance and Gonsalves went to trial; the latter was acquitted, but Nance was sentenced to sixty days in jail because in 1956, he had been convicted on similar charges in New York City, where he was given a suspended sentence. For years after this incident, Las Vegas night-clubs spurned Ellington. Only by securing gigs in Reno and agree-ing to a substantial cut in pay was he given reentry into the casino capital.

Ellington drew on his psychology to deal with the ever-present problems of running a band. Though normally the most lenient and calm of bandleaders, sometimes he was piqued by a player's drink-ing or other offense, and the maestro, the master of indirection, clever psychology, and manipulation, would exact an unusual kind of punishment. "He would call upon the culprit," recalled Town-send, "to stand for endless solos (I have watched Duke keep Paul Gonsalves or Hodges or Cootie thus in front of the band), calling out every number that featured him, meanwhile lavishing high praise upon him, encouraging calls of 'Encore!' from the audience over the breathless protests of the victim." But the men could turn the trick back on Ellington: sometimes, averred Hamilton, a player who wanted to play more would *act* drunk so that Ellington would call on him. Once, during a recording session, Ellington swiftly responded to Gonsalves's problem in another way. "The band tried several takes on a tune," reported an eyewitness, photographer Ted Williams. "Paul Gonsalves kept botching it. Duke, in the con-trol booth, pushed the talk-back switch on the console and said, 'Paul Gonsalves. You're wanted on the telephone in the hall.' Gon-salves left the studio, and Duke called to the other musicians, 'Lock that door!' And then he kicked off a tempo, and Duke got his take."

Besides usually outwitting troublesome band members, Ellington at this stage in his life could deal deftly with nearly any kind of person, virtually any situation. The jazz singer Jon Hendricks tells of an instance in which Ellington demonstrated, through his use of clever psychology, his ingenuity at turning something unpleasant into "something delightful." Once in 1963, between sets at the Basin Street East, Hendricks and Paul Gonsalves were hanging out in Ellington's timeworn dressing room, when they heard a couple arguing outside the door. The husband, a longtime Ellington fan and member of the Duke Ellington Society, wanted to meet Elling-ton, but his wife wanted to go back to her hotel, as they had to leave the next morning to return to their home in Cleveland.

Ellington . . . said hello to the man very warmly. And the man said, "This is a great honor," and Duke said, "No, the honor is all *mine!*" And his wife was standing there with her jaws very tight, and very tense—not at all enjoying this. And the guy introduced . . . his wife, and Ellington says, "Oh, Florence, it's lovely to meet you. Let me show you something beautiful," and he took her hand and led her into the dressing room. And so I look at Paul as if to say, "Something beautiful. Where is it? Why haven't we seen it?" And Ellington stood her in front of the mirror. And she stood in front of the mirror, and a whole metamorphosis took place. First she began to flush, from her neck around to her ears, and into her face, and as her face flushed, everything softened, her eyes softened and got misty, and she relaxed her look, and she seemed to sink down about an inch and relax, and she became *beautiful*—as she was naturally. And it was miraculous. And so then, she must have gotten a good look at herself, 'cause she walked back and said, "Thank you very much, Mr. Ellington." . . . And it was amazing. It was a real metamorphosis. And it was magic, too. It was pure magic. And if I hadn't seen it, I wouldn't have believed it.

Ellington charmed individuals and audiences alike through his quick wit, polished manners, and musical use of language. "Part of the explanation for Ellington's verbal charm," Carter Harman has observed, "is that he intuitively . . . applied his musical impulses to his speech. Graceful phrases rose to his lips like bubbles in champagne. He enriched word-meanings by an extraordinary range of pitches, inflections and rhythmical patterns, practically singing his words."

Ellington continued to be busy making music and records in a variety of contexts. In 1961, he made an LP for Columbia called *Piano in the Foreground,* with only bass and drums as accompaniment, highlighting his gifts as a pianist. On January 4, 1962, he played his first concert as a solo pianist, at the Museum of Modern Art in New York. But there were some musical disappointments, too, for example, an LP containing his arrangements of a short-lived, Columbia Records–backed Broadway musical called *All American* from 1962 that remains one of his lesser efforts.

During the late 1950s and 1960s, seeming more confident and

Ellington and Count Basie meet in a recording studio to make a collaborative album with their orchestras.

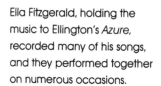

Ella Fitzgerald, holding the music to Ellington's *Azure*, recorded many of his songs, and they performed together on numerous occasions.

expansive, Ellington made a number of notable, though not always well-rehearsed, collaborative recordings. Besides the disc with Rosemary Clooney in early 1956, there were albums with Ella Fitzgerald in 1957, and in 1959 with Johnny Hodges and a small group that featured Ellington's piano playing and proved that, at age sixty, he had emerged as a jazz *soloist* of the first rank.

In 1961, the Ellington and Basie orchestras recorded an album together, and Ellington sat in with Louis Armstrong and his band, which quickly adapted to Ellington standards. Then after Ellington's contract with Columbia Records expired in mid 1962, which Ellington implied was due to his dissatisfaction with Columbia's promotional commitment, he proceeded to make three more collaborative albums of note. First, in August 1962, he met the tenor-saxophone master of swing, Coleman Hawkins, for a record. Then, in September, he teamed up with several leading lights of the

Ellington's collaborative LPs included one with the saxophone modernist
John Coltrane, in 1962.

younger generation, first recording with John Coltrane and each
other's rhythm sections. Finally, and perhaps most successfully
among his collaborations, *Money Jungle* was made with two modernists who idolized Ellington: the fiery bassist-composer Charles
Mingus and the bebop drummer Max Roach. Recording a new
piece of his called *Fleurette africaine*, Ellington felt, "was one of
those mystic moments when our three muses were one and the
same."

That November, Frank Sinatra threw a press party to announce
that Ellington had signed with the singer's eighteen-month-old record label, Reprise, and would serve as head of A&R (artists and
repertoire) for its jazz series. Sinatra gave Ellington carte blanche
to record what he wanted to. The next day, the orchestra began
recording a number of tunes associated with other big bands, issued as *Will the Big Bands Ever Come Back?* and *Recollections*

of the Big Band Era. Striving for popular success, Ellington in 1964 recorded his interpretations of music from the Walt Disney movie *Mary Poppins*, and a few of these numbers found their way into the band's regular repertoire. *Ellington '65* and *Ellington '66* offered remakes of non-Ellington pop hits such as *Hello, Dolly!* and *Moon River*, along with another remarkable Ellington transformation, *Never on Sunday*, which marches, then swings. For Reprise Ellington also recorded an exceptional album called *Afro-Bossa*.

Meanwhile, the year 1963 was a truly eventful one for the United States—at once prideful and painful. Protests in Birmingham, Alabama, and elsewhere culminated when 200,000 people marched in Washington, D.C., on August 28, 1963, and helped pave the way for landmark legislation—the Civil Rights Act of 1964 and the Voting Rights Acts of 1965. While Martin Luther King, Jr., was in Washington galvanizing the nation with his celebrated "I Have a Dream" speech, Duke Ellington was in Chicago celebrating a range of black heroes including Mary McLeod Bethune, Countee Cullen, Florence Mills, Jesse Owens, Medgar Evers, and King himself. That year marked the centennial of the Emancipation Proclamation, and in commemoration, a Century of Negro Progress Exposition was organized in Chicago. Ellington was invited to participate, and responded with *My People*, a musical theater production for jazz band, choir, four singers, and tap dancer. During the eighteen days of the exposition, there were twice-daily performances at the Arie Crown Theater, McCormick Place, which seated five thousand people. Funds were insufficient to hire the Ellington orchestra, so a group comprising local musicians and nine Ellington alumni played the accompaniment.

The roots of *My People* could be found in the musical pageants that Ellington heard as a young man in Washington. The music was based on the dichotomy between the blues and the spiritual, the secular and the sacred, and borrowed from *Black, Brown and Beige* —another instance of Ellington's returning for material to his reservoir of original repertory. *David Danced Before the Lord*, an accelerated version of the haunting theme *Come Sunday*, featured the sight and staccato sound of tap dancer Bunny Briggs. Though Ellington said that the work had "only about one minute of social protest" and asserted it was entertainment, the production in fact included Ellington's declaration that "the foundation of the United States rests on the sweat of my people," and concluded with two very timely pieces: *King Fit the Battle of Alabam'*, about the confrontation in Birmingham between the police and civil-rights marchers led by Martin Luther King, Jr., and the universalist *What Color Is Virtue?—What Color Is Love?* During the rehearsals, Ellington had an opportunity to meet King. The two embraced as if they had known each other all their lives, and the civil-rights leader sat in on a rehearsal of *King Fit the Battle*. The production of *My People* was hailed as impressive; as a recording, however, *My People* did not fare as well critically, though *David Danced* is quite effective on disc.

At about the same time, Ellington again involved himself with Shakespeare, this time writing the underscore, or background music, for a production of *Timon of Athens* at the Shakespeare Festival in Stratford, Ontario. The music was played by six Canadian musicians. The composition received mixed reviews, and was never recorded for release during Ellington's lifetime. Still, whether for release or not, Ellington continued to broaden and refine his musical vision. His body of compositions also continued to gain him fame and, to a degree, fortune.

By the 1960s, some of Ellington's earlier song hits had become standards of the jazz and popular song repertoire—especially *Don't Get Around Much Any More*, *Sophisticated Lady*, *Satin Doll*, and *C-Jam Blues*. As a result of his and especially others' recordings and broadcasts of these evergreens, he was earning impressive royalties. In 1961, for example, he earned about $79,000 in royalties; adjusted for inflation, that would have been nearly $370,000 in 1993. The Ellington business records at the Smithsonian also reveal that Hodges continued to pull down the highest salary of any band member—more than $20,000 in 1961 ($93,000 in 1993 terms), which was 50 percent higher than the next-highest-paid members, veterans Lawrence Brown and Harry Carney, and more than three times the salary of drummer Sam Woodyard.

U.S. record sales were climbing rapidly, from $377 million in

1956, to $862 million by 1965, a 229 percent increase in nine years. Most of the growth was due to the phenomenal popularity of rock music, heightened when the Beatles invaded the United States in February 1964. As the youth culture became more dominant in the music business, and as Elvis Presley, the Beatles, and a host of others in their twenties grabbed a greater and greater portion of record sales and radio airplay, Ellington, more than a generation older than they, had to work harder to maintain his audience and bookings. One of his responses was to return to the scene of some of his greatest receptions—Western Europe, and then to extend his overseas touring to new frontiers.

The year 1963 would see Ellington travel abroad more than he would in any other year—a total of 174 days, almost half the year. In January 1963, the Ellington orchestra traveled to Europe for its second longest foreign tour to date: sixty-one days in Western Europe, including ten days of recording sessions in Paris, Stockholm, Hamburg, and Milan, and TV programs in London and Stockholm. The concerts in Paris were recorded and issued as *Duke Ellington's Greatest Hits* (Reprise) and *The Great Paris Concert* (Atlantic), showing Ellington in especially fine form as a band pianist. Also, with symphony and opera orchestras of Paris, Hamburg, Stockholm, and Milan, the Ellingtonians made an album called *The Symphonic Ellington* that finally realized his dream to record *Night Creature*, his composition from 1955, which Capitol and Columbia had been unwilling to record because of the costs of hiring more than one hundred musicians to play music out of Ellington's "category," which, everyone knew, was jazz. Despite a terrible winter, the concerts were thronged and the newspapers full of glowing praise. This trip may rank as the most successful foreign tour of Ellington's life.

Then, in September, the Ellington orchestra flew out of New York for its first tour of India and the Middle and Near East, sponsored by the U.S. State Department. The orchestra wound its way through Jordan, Pakistan, India, Ceylon, Iraq, Iran, and Lebanon. On September 9, the opening night of the tour in Damascus, the Ellingtonians drew 17,000 Arabs and Westerners to what was called "Syria's first big band jazz concert. The applause," reported *Variety*, "was mixed with Arabic yells of 'Ash al Duke' (long live

Duke)." The tour was so successful that CBS television sent out a five-person film crew on November 20 to travel with the orchestra for the remaining fourteen weeks.

At a press conference in Delhi, Ellington was verbally accosted by a man who, in a series of confrontational questions, seemed determined to disparage the United States. Ellington hoodwinked his challenger with a jive answer, then, when the questions turned to race relations in the United States, he frankly admitted to serious problems, praised Martin Luther King as "the representative of an oppressed race of people," and also defended America's freedom of the press and its people's determination to succeed. Among his other qualities, Ellington was a patriot.

When the band got to Amman, Jordan, Ray Nance left, reportedly for drug or behavior problems. Eventually he was replaced by trumpeter Herbie Jones. According to Jimmy Hamilton, the reason was behavior problems. On the trip, serious friction developed be-

Ellington observes a sarod player and ensemble in India in 1963. During his travels, Ellington kept himself open to musical impressions.

tween Nance and roommate Cootie Williams. Nance may have felt threatened by the newly returned Williams, whose place he had taken back in 1941. In Amman, during the playing of the national anthem, everyone except Nance stood up. Faced with this embarrassing show of pique, some of the veteran players and Ellington held a meeting and decided Nance ought to go home.

During this tour, Hamilton recalled in a Smithsonian interview, the musicians got tired of being ushered around from one official function to the next. He felt that the band was performing too much for dignitaries and the "little" people were not getting a chance to hear them. Sometimes, to get out of attending an official function, he'd play sick. Then came the awful news from Dallas that President John F. Kennedy had been assassinated. The State Department canceled the rest of Ellington's tour—though not those of the Los Angeles Chamber Orchestra or the Clarion Concerts Chamber Orchestra, touring elsewhere abroad. This unequal treatment caused some bitterness among the Ellington players.

Ellington was soon off on another foreign tour. In February 1964, the band undertook a month of concerts in Western Europe, making TV broadcasts in London, Milan, and Paris, including a notable appearance in London on the inaugural program of the BBC's *Jazz 625*, this one featuring Duke Ellington in concert. Ellington aspired to TV exposure; writing in 1957, Leonard Feather had said that Ellington had long dreamed of getting his own television program. Why not? Musical entertainers such as Tennessee Ernie Ford, Dinah Shore, Nat King Cole, Lawrence Welk, the Dorsey Brothers, had their own shows. But it was not ever to be. American television largely ignored Ellington's kind of music, and rarely gave it more than middlebrow treatment. Yet abroad it was a different story: in England, Canada, France, Japan, Denmark, Sweden, and elsewhere, Ellington and his music were televised with decidedly more care and respect. There were memorable performances, beautiful production values, intelligent interviewers; but none of this material ever made its way to American viewers.

One of the results of the eye- and ear-opening tour of the Middle and Far East was that Ellington and Strayhorn became inspired to compose something based upon their reactions to the orient. *Impressions of the Far East*, comprising four movements, was evidently premiered during the band's tour of Europe in early 1964. By June, when the band visited Tokyo for the first time, Ellington, Strayhorn, and Jimmy Hamilton evidently had written *Ad Lib on Nippon*. This piece would be added to *Impressions* and, with the addition by 1966 of five more movements, would be renamed *The Far East Suite*. The three-week trip was captured on film by CBS TV crews and was broadcast as *Duke Ellington Swings through Japan*, in Walter Cronkite's series *The Twentieth Century*.

In 1964, when road manager Al Celley resigned because of failing eyesight, Mercer Ellington quit his job as a disc jockey at the Harlem radio station WLIB to join the Ellington band as road manager and trumpeter on December 17. The managing job was difficult, given the small army of people who had to be moved around the globe and the difficult personalities of several of the players. "As a road manager, I was a combination psychologist, mathematician, and private detective," he said. "In order to get everyone on the bus or plane in the mornings, I had to keep track of who everybody had shacked up with the night before. . . . What made the job really difficult was that I was riding herd on the men who had helped to raise me: Cootie Williams, Johnny Hodges, Harry Carney."

In late January and February 1965, the orchestra returned to Europe for its tenth tour, this time of France, Denmark, Sweden, Germany, Switzerland, and England. Ellington's esteem among jazz aficionados and critics there continued at a high level: in February, the annual *Melody Maker* Critics' Poll gave Ellington honors as Musician of the Year, and winner in the Big Band, Arranger and Composer categories. In the Readers' Poll, he took the same honors.

Ellington was on his way to becoming the most honored composer America had produced, yet there was one important award he had not yet received: the United States' most prestigious musical honor, the Pulitzer Prize in Music, given to an American composer annually since 1943 by the trustees of Columbia University. The prize was established for a "distinguished musical composition . . . in any of the larger forms, including chamber, orchestral, choral, opera, song, dance, or other forms of musical theater." The three-member music jury had recommended unanimously to the fourteen-member advisory board that Duke Ellington be given a *special* prize for his forty years of contributions to music, but their recommendation was rejected by the board. Two of the three music jury members then resigned in protest, and the brouhaha made newspaper headlines.

Many were aghast and furious, and criticism of the Pulitzer decision was widespread. The *San Francisco Chronicle* called it "an appalling insult"; Aaron Copland said, "It's *very* too bad. . . . He's deserved it for so long." Critic Nat Hentoff indignantly titled an article in the *New York Times Magazine* "This Cat Needs No Pulitzer Prize." In rejecting a prize for Ellington, the Pulitzer Prize board demonstrated bias against a music with an inescapable African heritage expressed through musical structures drawing heavily on oral traditions. The Pulitzer rejection of Ellington was, as cultural critic Jonathan Yardley has observed, "a confession, however unwitting, of the cultural establishment's hostility to the new and the different and the unsanctioned. It was a narrow-minded judgment by a narrow-minded group of men. . . . [Ellington] put on a brave front, but he more than anyone else knew the true value of his music and he badly, if not desperately, wanted it accepted for what it was: the great American music, the true voice of his country, a total body of work that was neither jazz nor classical but something that drew strength from both and emerged, triumphantly, sui generis." With characteristic irony veiling his real feelings, Ellington, in a well-publicized response, said simply, "Fate is being kind to me. Fate doesn't want me to be famous too young." To *Newsweek*, he added, "It doesn't matter. All I do is compose music. I can't afford to get bugged. . . . I must not let it destroy my musical integrity."

Perhaps in response to the embarrassment many felt about the Pulitzer rejection of Ellington, on August 2, New York's acting mayor Paul Screvane presented the composer with the city's Bronze Medal for his outstanding contributions to New York City's life and the world of music. And in its August 1965 issue, *Esquire* named Ellington one of the "hundred best people in the world," though probably more because of his personality, charisma, and familiar popular songs than for his instrumental compositions: still relatively few people recognized him as the master composer-orchestrator he was.

Those who had known Ellington a long time could observe changes in his countenance and personality. While in former years, he impressed many as looking ten years younger than his age, now in his mid-sixties, Ellington was showing his age. "His transition from Washington and Room Ten to command performances for royalty was a long and arduous trail," wrote Rex Stewart in 1965, "speckled by the various joys and sorrows of life. And even Ellington is not exempt from the immutable law of change. He grows grander but more introspective. He has apparently learned to give more of himself in public but less in private.

"The strain of constantly being on stage," continued Stewart, "has taken its toll, the hassles with band personnel, with bookers, with schemers and parasites who attempt to pinch a bit off the top. These all have caused the famed bags under his eyes to grow baggier. The hail fellow, well met, who was a buddy to his boys is no longer there—and understandably so." Ellington gamely referred to the bags under his eyes as "an accumulation of virtue," but in a 1992 Smithsonian interview, Artie Shaw revealed that Ellington once told him he was tired of the problems of leading a band, and that he kept it going because it was the only way to hear his compositions.

Perhaps more mindful of his mortality as the result of his age and occasional hospitalizations, perhaps glimpsing the end of his life, Ellington became more spiritual as he aged. In his unpublished writings, for instance, he declared, "The greatest thing one man can do for another man is pray for him." A famous credo of his was that "Every man prays in his own language, and there is no language that God does not understand."

In 1965 came the opportunity to make a larger musical statement about his spirituality than ever before and to break down more barriers. Grace Cathedral, San Francisco's new Episcopal landmark, commissioned him to write a liturgical work to be performed there as part of the building's yearlong consecration celebration.

When the piece was premiered on September 16, 1965, it made newspapers across the country. His *Concert of Sacred Music* was mostly a compilation of earlier ideas from *Black, Brown and Beige* and *My People*, and included the 1943 piano feature *New World a-Comin'*. The newly written, fifteen-minute opening section, *In the Beginning, God*, inspired by the first four words in the Bible, and musically a progression of climaxes, would win a Grammy Award in 1966 as best original jazz composition. Besides the Duke Ellington orchestra, the performers included the Herman McCoy Choir, the Grace Cathedral Choir, singers Jon Hendricks, Esther Marrow, and Jimmy McPhail, and tap dance artist Bunny Briggs.

This was not a Mass, Ellington pointed out, in which the composer addresses God; rather, as Gary Giddins has observed, Ellington was addressing the people by bringing the Cotton Club revue to the church. This indeed was not the intimate music of some recording-studio pieces such as *Mood Indigo* or *Azure*, but a big, entertaining religious-musical spectacle designed to fill cavernous cathedrals, as was Handel's *Messiah*. Critical opinion was again divided. Presumably basing their judgments solely on the recordings, critics such as the Englishman Max Harrison found the *Concert of Sacred Music* and Ellington's later efforts along this line "commonplace" and "embarrassing." As with other works of Ellington's, many critics could not seem to accept music that did not fit neatly into a category, whether dance-band music or jazz. On the other hand, other critics such as Raymond Horricks found the *Concert of Sacred Music* "a most remarkable religious synthesis . . . of Western Christianity . . . with African roots and Pantheism, gospel singing, the chronicles of the Bible, the aspirations of the New Testament and, not least, the extra problems faced by mankind in our modern society."

While in San Francisco preparing for the Sacred Concert, as it came to be called, Ellington was followed around by a film crew from KQED. Jazz critic Ralph J. Gleason, the show's producer, said that Ellington "really directed the whole thing." The resulting two programs, *Duke Ellington: "Love You Madly"* and *A Concert of Sacred Music*, received high praise when broadcast in June 1967 on National Educational Television, and *"Love You Madly"* won an Emmy Award. When the *Concert of Sacred Music* was repeated

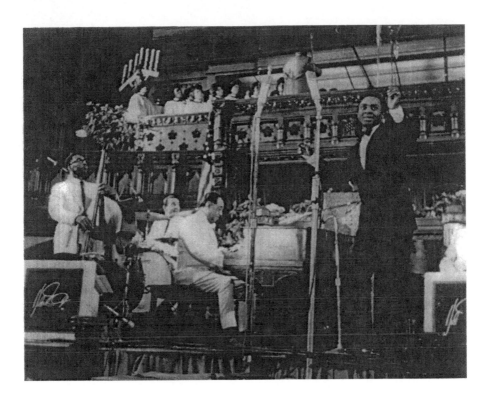

The Ellington orchestra accompanies dancer Bunny Briggs, in its *Concert of Sacred Music,* at New York's Fifth Avenue Presbyterian Church, December 26, 1965. This religious-musical spectacle represented breakthroughs for both Ellington and the church.

twice on December 26 (with Brock Peters replacing Jon Hendricks) in New York's Fifth Avenue Presbyterian Church, it made headlines again, and was recorded for release on RCA Records. The sacred music concert turned out to be good for business, as television took quite an interest in the work and Ellington was asked to repeat the performance in a number of U.S. and British churches.

Ellington felt the *Concert of Sacred Music* was "successful beyond my wildest dreams." The Sacred Concert represented two breakthroughs, one for Ellington, the other for the church. Typically categorized as a practitioner of jazz—which was considered highly secular—Ellington broke through the walls he hated, to a new spiritual area of musical endeavor that he would continue pursuing the rest of his life.

Traditionally in the African-American community there has been a rather rigid distinction made between sacred religious music—

spirituals and gospel—and secular music—blues and jazz—though musically there has been great interchange. For the church, where some were scandalized by the very idea of jazz in a church, it was also a departure from the musical norm. "Duke Ellington's concert provoked deep discussion of what constitutes sacred music," said Rev. Bryant M. Kirkland, minister of the Fifth Avenue Presbyterian Church. "Many discovered a new spiritual exaltation in the modern idiom."

And so in this period Duke Ellington, after having relaunched himself in 1956 at Newport, made triumphant appearances and globetrotting tours, brought back the masters Lawrence Brown and Cootie Williams, managed to keep his band going in the age of rock music, wrote a number of acclaimed works and made upward of five hundred recordings. He enjoyed new media acclaim and felt the painful Pulitzer rejection, and continued to move across categories in the evolution of his own musical world. Throughout this period, Ellington exhibited extraordinary productivity, especially for a man in his fifties and sixties—a time in life when most people are slowing down and preparing for retirement. In the years ahead would lie an armload of honors, a few musical glories, and a series of final losses as Duke Ellington finally had to face a problem he could not solve—human mortality.

Essential Ellington, *1956–65*

Revitalized by the return of Hodges, the new drummer Sam Woodyard, the triumph at Newport, the *Time* cover story, and the new contract with Columbia, Ellington renewed himself. When Lawrence Brown returned in 1960

(continued)

and Cootie Williams in 1962, the orchestra sounded more Ellingtonian than it had in years. The late 1950s and early 1960s, with more than five hundred recordings, would comprise the first and greater part of Ellington's second grand arc of creativity and productivity. During this period, he exploited the LP as a recording medium and plunged confidently and repeatedly into the domain of concert music, creating works of heightened rhythmic invention, imagination, and detail, and textural and melodic richness. Toward the end of this period, he wrote the first of several liturgical works he called sacred concerts. Unless otherwise specified, the following recordings are all available on Columbia/CBS/Sony.

Beginning in March 1956, Ellington took his band into the studio and made recordings at his own expense—"the stockpile," he called it. In late 1956, at one of these sessions, the orchestra recorded the catchy *Satin Doll*, which since its publication in 1953 was becoming a jazz standard. In 1958, Ellington finally was matched with a worthy lyricist, Johnny Mercer, who, along with Billy Strayhorn, contributed lyrics to *Satin Doll*. Ellington, however, typically performed it as an instrumental. This rendition, featuring Paul Gonsalves and issued on *The Private Collection, Vol. 1* (Saja), is relaxed, and the disc introduces a half dozen other short works. Another version of *Satin Doll*, one on *The Great Paris Concert* (Atlantic, 1963) featuring Ray Nance, has bite.

A Drum Is a Woman (1956), which made up an entire LP record, is a satirical history of jazz, narrated by Ellington. It takes Madame Zajj from the Caribbean, to New Orleans, Harlem, and the moon. The four pieces that make up Section II, set in New Orleans, are the strongest part. After a pensive introduction on unaccompanied clarinet, *New Orleans* offers a festive, Mardi Gras–like parade. In the masterful character sketch *Hey, Buddy Bolden*, the legendary trumpeter is evoked by Clark Terry, who tunes up, mightily calls his flock, offers a virtuosic cadenza and a traditional blues, and then, in the climax, trades half bars with Ray Nance as they explore

(continued)

how many ways one can play an A by varying the rhythm and inflection. *Carribee Joe* is evocative and exotic, with notable instrumental voicings, and *Congo Square* offers sensuous, minor-key chords in an undulating rhythm supporting Ellington's story of a pretty girl arousing erotic passions in the crowd. Though as spoken and sung drama, *A Drum Is a Woman* now seems dated and perhaps the whole is somewhat less than the sum of its parts, still, as music *A Drum Is a Woman* ranks as one of Ellington and Strayhorn's most ambitious, fanciful, and exuberant works, skillfully scored, and effectively performed by the instrumentalists.

Its forty-seven minutes filling an LP, *Such Sweet Thunder* (1957) has twelve varied movements in which Ellington's players portray and at times caricature characters and ideas from Shakespeare, with moods ranging from grave to romantic and stately to puckish, though eschewing the deeply tragic. While marred by a hastily written last movement, *Such Sweet Thunder*, also known as *The Shakespearean Suite*, is one of Ellington and Strayhorn's most imaginative works. The movements include the lush *Star-Crossed Lovers*, uniting Johnny Hodges's sensuous Juliet with Paul Gonsalves's warm Romeo; *Lady Mac* waltzing in ragtime; Clark Terry's merry Puck in *Up and Down;* the deliberate and foreboding *Sonnet for Caesar;* and the boppish, rhythmically intricate, evocative portrait of Hamlet, *Madness in Great Ones,* with Cat Anderson blowing *his* top. Ellington the inventive master dramatist shines in this album.

A product of Ellington's continued interest in making small-group recordings was the LP *Happy Reunion,* recorded in 1957 but not issued until 1985. The highlight is the slow, spare, haunting plaint, *Where's the Music?,* suffused with the spirit of a down-home church. Scored for just four lead instruments (plus piano, bass, and drums), the emphasis here is on varied densities and interweaving melodic lines. Jimmy Hamilton and Johnny Hodges keen the melody, Hamilton and Clark Terry call and respond to one another, and Ellington punctuates more wails with percussive piano

(continued)

clusters. As Stanley Dance aptly observes in the album notes, "There's no performance quite like this one in the whole canon of Ellington's music."

Nearly all of Ellington's best work was instrumental. Of interpretations of his songs, however, one of the most notable albums came in 1957 with *Ella Fitzgerald Sings the Duke Ellington Songbook* (Verve), the first and best of their collaborations. While Fitzgerald is perhaps too sunny to be the definitive interpreter of Ellington songs, she brings much to this album, including her lovely and warm voice, splendid rhythmic sense, and improvisatory gifts as a superb natural melodist. She recorded half the album with the Ellington orchestra (sounding somewhat underrehearsed), the other half backed by a small group including Ben Webster, playing strikingly. The thirty-eight pieces on this three-CD set include the expected Ellington songs, new pieces such as the *E and D Blues* and the sixteen-minute instrumental *Portrait of Ella Fitzgerald*, and unexpected mutations such as a recomposed *Caravan* and Fitzgerald scatting a new melodic line in the instrumental *Rockin' in Rhythm*.

Ellington's first motion-picture sound-track commission in twenty-five years came in 1959 with *Anatomy of a Murder*. Among the highlights of the recording (beautifully remastered for CD by Rykodisc) are the elegant and languorous *Midnight Indigo*, featuring highly unusual musical textures of celeste, bass clarinet, and tightly muted trumpet; the call-and-responsive *Flirtibird*, the leitmotif of the female protagonist (Lee Remick), with Hodges's wailing alto; the unhurried *Almost Cried* (a slow version of *Flirtibird*) with Shorty Baker's sweet-toned trumpet, both romantic and wistful; the aptly named *Grace Valse*; the tantalizingly short *Sunswept Sunday* with its haunting opening, reverential mood, and plaintive Hamilton clarinet theme; and Cat Anderson's closing *Upper and Outest*. Incidentally, the rocking main theme, *Anatomy of a Murder*, was later turned into a song, with lyrics by Peggy Lee, known as *I'm Gonna Go Fishin'*. As in *Such Sweet Thunder*, here Ellington again demonstrates the many possibilities of a jazz orchestra

(continued)

using conventional instrumentation (plus, in this case, celeste). The twelve pieces that make up *Anatomy*'s suite of mostly related themes are brilliantly composed and orchestrated, well rehearsed, impeccably played, and make an effective sound track.

During the late 1950s and early 1960s, Ellington recorded as a piano soloist more often, with a style now emotionally deeper and more forceful. Teaming with Hodges in small-group sessions in 1959, Ellington demonstrated, at age sixty, his piano prowess in such pieces as *Weary Blues, St. Louis Blues,* and his *Stompy Jones* on two discs Verve issued as *Back to Back* and *Side by Side,* moving critic G. E. Lambert to proclaim "a newly arrived jazz soloist of the highest calibre." Three years later, Ellington paired with admirer and bassist Charles Mingus and drummer Max Roach on the album *Money Jungle,* with Mingus and Roach prodding Ellington into vigorous, sharp-edged playing, on *Caravan, Money Jungle,* and other pieces. The impressionistic *Fleurette africaine (African Flower)* offers virtuoso high-note bass playing by Mingus and a lovely, hypnotic Ellingtonian melody. The recording, reissued on Blue Note, is marred throughout by muddy sound.

The Queen's Suite, dedicated to Queen Elizabeth, was recorded in 1959 at Ellington's expense, and pressed in a single copy, which Ellington sent to Buckingham Palace. Only after his death was the piece released to the public (*The Ellington Suites,* Pablo). Unusually, the work has virtually no improvisation. While it breaks no new ground, undoubtedly the highlight (and the movement Ellington performed most often) is the reflective *A Single Petal of a Rose,* scored for piano supported only by bowed bass, and played rubato. Ellington said *A Single Petal* "represented wonder." Its arpeggiated melody is one of his loveliest and most luscious; this singular piece is another that defies categorization.

Suite Thursday (1960) is a jaunty work composed equally by Ellington and Strayhorn in tribute to John Steinbeck's low-comedy novel *Sweet Thursday,*

(continued)

set around the Cannery Row fisheries of Monterey Bay, California. The outer movements have as their basic formal structure the blues, perhaps the only new musical form produced in twentieth-century America, one which Ellington was ever adept at exploring and personalizing. All four movements share a foghornlike descending minor-sixth interval which Ellington was using perhaps more for programmatic than structural purposes. The third movement, *Zweet Zurzday*, evokes the Monterey wharf—boats, foghorns, and dockside activity. The final movement, *Lay-By*, features Ray Nance alternating between bowed and pizzicato violin, ending with Harry Carney prolonging a low D on the baritone saxophone like a boat in the fog, and Nance irrepressibly plucking out the main interval.

Afro-Bossa (1962–63), the best of the records Ellington made for Frank Sinatra's Reprise Records, is marked by unusually rich rhythmic patterns, extensive use of percussion instruments, and robust playing by Hodges. Highlights include an updating of the evocative and plaintive *Pyramid* of 1937, with Lawrence Brown playing Juan Tizol's part and a strong solo by Cootie Williams; and the unique *Bonga: Empty Town Blues,* which conjures a strange image of a "deserted border town," as the liner notes put it, with a trio of wah-wah trumpets punctuated by menacingly darting, ghostly figures from clarinetist Jimmy Hamilton and trombonist Buster Cooper.

Other notable recordings from this fertile period include *Idiom '59*, a three-part suite highlighting the clarinets of Russell Procope and Jimmy Hamilton and Clark Terry's fluegelhorn (available on *Festival Session*). The spare *Blues in Blueprint* (1959) opens with bass clarinet, bass, and finger snapping, and proceeds on its calypso-flavored way (on *Blues in Orbit*). Hodges and the luxuriant orchestral backdrop given him on *Arabesque Cookie [Arabian Dance]* are the high point of the good-humored, sometimes witty, sometimes irreverent adaptations by Ellington and Strayhorn of Tchaikovsky's *Nutcracker Suite* and Grieg's *Peer Gynt Suites* (reissued, with *Suite Thursday*, as *Three Suites*). *Recollections of the Big Band Era* (1962–63, Atlantic),

(continued)

offers *Minnie the Moocher* with Cootie Williams making his trumpet "talk" as he growls out Cab Calloway's famous vocal line, and a truly remarkable Billy Strayhorn arrangement of Stan Kenton's *Artistry in Rhythm,* which with inventive rhythms, textures, and instrumental interplay, transforms the piece into something stunningly new. *The Great Paris Concert* (1963, Atlantic), one of Ellington's best live recordings, has Cootie Williams in fine form, Ellington the band pianist shown to excellent advantage, and well-vetted renditions of *Star-Crossed Lovers* and *Suite Thursday.* Also from 1963, *The Symphonic Ellington* (Trend) is notable for *Night Creature,* especially its second movement; *Mood Indigo* is a highlight of *Duke Ellington Meets Coleman Hawkins* (1962, MCA). *Duke Ellington's Concert of Sacred Music* (1965, RCA) presents the joyous *Ain't But the One* and three moving versions of the haunting theme *Come Sunday*—one by singer Esther Marrow, a second spotlighting Johnny Hodges's alto sax, and a faster, third version, titled *David Danced before the Lord with All His Might,* featuring the percussive taps of dancer Bunny Briggs. *The Private Collection, Vol. 10* (Saja) contains Ellington's revised version, from 1965, of *Black, Brown and Beige,* now streamlined by four minutes and enhanced in several places. It turned out to be the composer's final word on his magnum opus.

ELEVEN

*A*CHIEVING

FINAL GLORIES

•

1 9 6 6 – 7 4

The creative period that Ellington rekindled in the mid 1950s was by 1966 at or past its peak. Yet, as if sensing his mortality, Ellington perhaps viewed his major problem as ensuring that the last chapter of his life was a fitting close to his astounding career as bandleader and composer. Even as he would face more losses, some of them devastating, he would maintain his band, and his fertile mind and restless energy would enable him to produce many more compositions and records. Ellington continued to perform "live" and to make recordings both for his growing stockpile and for record companies, though he was now and would remain without a long-term association with a major label. During this time, Johnny Hodges's playing seemed to be getting better—more silken, assured, and expressive—as he got older.

The "ecumenical Ellington," as Stanley Dance dubbed him, repeated the *Concert of Sacred Music* on February 21, 1966, at the Cathedral of Coventry in England, and in November 1966 at Temple Emanuel in Beverly Hills, and eventually, about fifty times. On December 5, 1966, Ellington returned to his hometown to perform the Sacred Concert at the famous Constitution Hall. Reflecting traditional religious views of sacred and secular music, the 250-

Johnny Hodges continued to refine and improve his playing as he got older. Here Ellington holds up a piece of new music for Hodges to perform.

member Baptist Ministers Conference of Washington, however, went on record "refusing to endorse the concert." Some complained his music was too "worldly." His publicist, Joe Morgen, said, "This is the first time a thing like this ever happened to him. He's 67 and he's upset. This is his hometown, and these are ministers criticizing him." The show went on, though the house was not much more than half full.

In 1966, Ellington resumed an association, albeit short-lived, with RCA Records, which had recorded much of his best-regarded, most brilliant work from his earlier years. Strayhorn and Ellington continued to compose in their unique partnership, and that year, the two composers took the five movements they had written for *Impressions of the Far East* and added four more. When recorded for RCA, this nine-part work was now retitled *The Far East Suite* and ranks as one of their best late works. The suite was another sign of Ellington's creative use of new experiences as a basis for his music; wherever he was, he was always on the lookout for material he could transform into something personal and artistic.

Still willing to take artistic and financial risks to explore many musical forms, he again tried his hand at musical theater. Since 1962, Ellington had been working on a musical based on the 1930 Marlene Dietrich movie *The Blue Angel*, with its locale changed from Berlin to New Orleans. After numerous delays, tryouts in Toronto and Detroit, and major overhauls, *Pousse-Café* finally premiered on March 18, 1966, at New York's Forty-Sixth Street Theatre. Despite a book by Pulitzer Prize–winning Jerome Weidman and famous leads (Theodore Bikel and the French star Lilo), the show was met with thunderous disapproval: "POUSSE-CAFÉ" CALLED DISMAL DISASTER read a typical headline. The ineffectual show, which failed to exploit New Orleans's color and atmosphere, closed after just three performances, even before Ellington had a chance to see it.

One problem Ellington never solved was that of adapting his style to the musical theater in a way that would draw a sustained audience and give him the hit he wanted so badly. Many of his harmonies and textures were perhaps too intimate and sophisticated for the musical theater, where they normally are supposed to serve the melody, words, dancing, and action. His writing for the stage was infrequent and so squeezed by his other responsibilities that he was not really able to hone his skills. And Ellington wrote inspiredly when composing for individual players, not for unfamiliar musicians in a Broadway-pit orchestra. Largely for this reason, *Jump for Joy*—his first musical and the only one for which his own band played—was musically his most successful.

Though now going on sixty-seven, Ellington showed few signs of slowing down. Indeed, in most respects he was still a robust man. In 1964, while recounting his life for a book of memoirs with Carter Harman—a collaboration which soon fell apart—Ellington had told Harman that he was a sexual intercourse "freak," perhaps both a confession and, given his age, a boast. His conversations confirmed to Harman what other intimates had long known: behind the elegant Ellington the public knew there was an earthy Ellington who loved to tell long, dirty jokes of his own creation. The seemingly contradictory aspects of Ellington—sacred and profane, religious yet philandering, debonair and raunchy, charming but private—in fact coexisted as facets of a complicated whole.

In January and February 1966, Ellington made another tour of Europe. In April, the orchestra went to Africa to perform in the first World Festival of Negro Arts in Dakar, Senegal, where they played *La plus belle africaine*, a new composition which was well received. In May, the orchestra made its second tour of Japan; in July they played the south of France, captured for an album, *Ella and Duke at the Côte d'Azur*, and for a film, *Duke Ellington at the Côte d'Azur*.

The long-estranged Edna died in 1966 and was buried in Washington. Evie, his companion since 1939, said she hoped that Ellington, now freed from marriage, would finally marry her. He did not and, in fact, never would. "She felt very exploited," Mercer Ellington said, "and worried that she wouldn't be taken care of if he died, because he didn't believe in wills. She acquired a reputation as a grump, which enabled Ellington to use her as a shield. If he invited someone over and then changed his mind, he'd send her to the door to chase them away. The next time he ran into them, he'd act like Mister Sunshine and ask them why they hadn't shown up, giving the impression that she kept people away from him because she wanted him all to herself." While Ellington and Evie would always maintain a joint residence, he spent little time there because of his travels, and Evie became more lonely. There were other women in his life, most notably Fernanda de Castro Monte, about eight years younger than Evie and twenty years younger than Ellington. A former singer, this striking blond spoke five languages and, as Norman Granz said, was "a very cultured woman." Everyone in the band called her The Countess or Contessa, and she often traveled with Ellington, looking after him and helping translate.

Billy Strayhorn, Ellington's only true musical partner, was ill. In 1965, as Ellington was preparing to premiere the Sacred Concert at Grace Cathedral, Strayhorn had to undergo surgery for cancer of the esophagus. There would be more such painful operations ahead, and he would no longer travel with the orchestra. Instead, he and Ellington kept up their link by telephone and, it seemed, telepathy. For instance, once when Ellington and Strayhorn were three thousand miles apart, they separately went to work on *In the Beginning, God.* When Strayhorn sent his manuscript to Ellington, he found that the two pieces began and ended on identical notes, and most of the key melodic idea was also identical. "They were that simpatico," said Marian Logan, recalling their "extraordinary relationship."

By early 1967, Strayhorn had dwindled to just eighty pounds, and he spent much time in New York hospitals. His food had to be minced, liquefied, and sipped through a straw. While he no longer traveled with the band, he kept on composing, even from his hospital bed, where he revised a much earlier work and titled it *Blood Count,* sending it over from the hospital for a performance at Carnegie Hall, one he could not attend. His old friend Lena Horne

Billy Strayhorn with Ellington at the piano. The death of Strayhorn was the most profound musical loss Ellington ever sustained.

tended to "Swee' Pea" faithfully and lovingly. Then, the night of May 31, 1967, cradled in Lena Horne's arms, he succumbed to the ravaging tumor. He was only fifty-one. Ruth reached Ellington in Reno and broke the terrible news. After crying and banging his head on the wall, Ellington sat down and wrote a short tribute to his friend, which read, in part, "Poor little Swee' Pea, Billy Strayhorn, William Thomas Strayhorn, the biggest human being who ever lived. . . . His greatest virtue, I think, was his honesty, not only to others, but to himself. . . . His patience was incomparable and unlimited. He had no aspirations to enter into any kind of competition, yet the legacy he leaves, his *oeuvre*, will never be less than the ultimate on the highest plateau of culture. . . . God bless Billy Strayhorn."

Because Strayhorn had been such an extraordinary source of collaboration, feedback, and friendship, it was the most devastating death Ellington had ever faced other than that of his parents. Strayhorn's funeral services were held on June 5, 1967, at St. Peter's Lutheran Church in New York City, officiated by Pastor John Gensel, who maintained a special ministry to the jazz community. Flowers had been sent by twenty organizations and individuals, including Louis Armstrong and Arthur Logan, who had been Strayhorn's doctor. In accordance with his wishes, his body was cremated and the ashes scattered in the Hudson River by the Copasetics, a show-business club in which Strayhorn had been active. Within three months the Ellington orchestra began recording a powerful, moving tribute to Strayhorn, called . . . *And His Mother Called Him Bill*. In the spring of 1969, Ellington became the sole proprietor of Tempo Music Company by paying $100,000 to Strayhorn's estate for the 10 percent share that he had owned.

July 31, 1967, marked an ominous day for the Ellington orchestra. In order to accept a five-week engagement at the Rainbow Grill atop the sixty-fifth floor of New York's Rockefeller Center, one for which he was paid to bring in only an octet, Ellington had to let half the band go temporarily. Taking a small group to the Rainbow, and putting the rest of the band on hiatus, would become an annual event—a tacit admission that in the band business, as one of his standards, written by Mercer, said, "things ain't what they used to be."

In 1965, the Ellington orchestra performed at the White House Festival of the Arts. The following year, Ellington was presented with the President's Gold Medal on behalf of Lyndon Johnson and in November 1968 was appointed by President Johnson to the National Council on the Arts. During the Johnson years he went to the White House seven times for official functions or to perform. Even a change in presidents brought no decline in recognition by the White House.

In 1969, Leonard Garment, a former clarinetist with Woody Herman, and then an attorney serving as a key aide to President Nixon, teamed with the Voice of America's Willis Conover and several others to arrange for a special White House celebration of Ellington's seventieth birthday. Ellington was asked to submit a list of fifty people he wanted invited. The joint Ellington–White House guest list included, besides the expected politicians, musicians Count Basie, Billy Taylor, Dizzy Gillespie, Benny Goodman, Mahalia Jackson, Richard Rodgers, and Harold Arlen; Ellington friends Arthur Logan and Stanley Dance, critic Leonard Feather, producer George Wein, director Otto Preminger, the Smithsonian Institution's Secretary S. Dillon Ripley, the Voice of America's Willis Conover, and *Ebony* publisher John Johnson. Ellington's sister, Ruth, and his son, Mercer, and his wife and three children also attended.

In a remark that became often quoted, Ellington said, "There is no place I would rather be tonight except in my mother's arms." Nixon winningly declared, "In the royalty of American music, no man swings more or stands higher than the Duke." Ellington kissed Nixon twice on each cheek. "Four kisses?" asked the president. "Why four?" "One for each cheek," Ellington replied. Nixon was momentarily dumbfounded. The climax of the evening came when Nixon presented Ellington with the Presidential Medal of Freedom —the nation's highest civilian honor. The medal was the supreme recognition the U.S. government could offer Ellington, and it must have gone a long way to compensate for the disappointment of the Pulitzer rejection.

This was the White House into which, historically, most black people had entered through the servants' quarters, including Ellington's father when he had helped serve at special functions. This

In a White House ceremony on April 29, 1969, at which he was presented the Presidential Medal of Freedom, Ellington prepares to kiss President Nixon twice on each cheek.

At the White House ceremony, Ellington jams beside Willie "The Lion" Smith, his onetime mentor, for whom he had years before written two musical portraits.

was the White House of Abraham Lincoln, who had freed Ellington's ancestors. The White House of Woodrow Wilson, who set back the cause of people of color. The White House of Lyndon B. Johnson, who had signed into law the most sweeping civil-rights legislation since Reconstruction. It was an evening that may have seemed to Ellington rich in meanings, associations, ironies, as well as sweetness. As ovations go, it was the capstone of his career. And it symbolized the unifying power of music to bridge all gaps and to bring the races together "beyond category."

Ellington took the microphone and said, "I am reminded of the

four freedoms Billy Strayhorn created for our sacred concerts—
the four major moral freedoms by which he lived, and I use those
four major moral freedoms by which Strayhorn lived as a measure
of what we ourselves should live up to." Ellington described
those freedoms as: "freedom from hate, unconditionally; freedom
from all self-pity (even throughout all the pain and bad news);
freedom from fear of possibly doing something that might help another more than it might help himself; and freedom from the kind
of pride that could make a man feel he was better than his brother
or neighbor." The applause was thunderous. Ellington sat at the
piano next to his old mentor, Willie "The Lion" Smith, wearing his
trademark derby hat and at seventy-one, still of nimble fingers.
After the Nixons went to bed, there was a jam session and dancing
till 2 A.M.

The overdue but emphatic recognition by the American royal
court must have touched Ellington deeply. Nixon's praise of Ellington's stature in American music was a reminder that the maestro,
with all due respect to Aaron Copland, Samuel Barber, and others,
was in fact the grand old man of American music, the dean of
American composers, though the White House uncharacteristically
seemed to be ahead of the cultural establishment in recognizing
this fact.

Now, despite the American cultural establishment's slowness to
accord Ellington the full recognition he deserved, honors were rolling in from many quarters, validating Ellington as not only a national but an international treasure. In 1967, the West African
Republic of Togo had issued a commemorative postage stamp in
Ellington's honor, to be followed by another from Chad in 1971.
Ellington was receiving honorary doctorates seemingly left and
right—a total of nineteen, including those from St. Louis University, Columbia, Yale, Brown, and Howard universities. In addition
to the jazz poll awards he had been receiving since the 1930s,
Ellington would win eleven Grammy Awards, the National Academy of Recording Arts and Science's Lifetime Achievement Award
and Trustees Award, keys to cities in the United States and abroad,
mayoral proclamations, medals, and so on—more than three
hundred such items are part of the Ellington Collection at the
Smithsonian. In 1971 the Royal Swedish Academy of Music elected

By the late 1960s, Ellington's trophies and awards filled an entire room. At top left: *Down Beat* awards; atop piano: *Esquire* statuettes and Grammy Awards.

Ellington clutching one of the seventeen honorary doctorates he was awarded.

him to membership, the first nonclassical composer to be admitted in its two-hundred-year history; in November 1973 Haile Selassie, the ruler of Ethiopia, presented him with the Emperor's Star; and that same year President Georges Pompidou and the government of France gave him *its* highest award, the Legion of Honor. No American composer had ever been so widely honored, nationally and internationally, as Duke Ellington. Though he might have professed to be too busy to worry about his place in the cultural hierarchy, this must have been important to him, as indicated, for one thing, by the extensive list of his honors he chose to include in his memoirs, where it occupies fifteen pages.

Ellington entered into occasional collaborations, such as another record with Ella Fitzgerald called *Ella at Duke's Place*, which was released in 1966. In December 1967, he recorded an album with Frank Sinatra for Reprise Records with arrangements by Billy May tailored more to Sinatra than to the Ellingtonians. That same year, Ellington was featured in a notable television program, the hour-long "On the Road with Duke Ellington," filmed over the course of six months and broadcast as part of NBC's *Bell Telephone Hour*, a respected musical showcase. And in 1968 he composed a work called *The Degas Suite* as the soundtrack for a motion picture that was never completed because the producer ran out of money.

As meaningful as awards and recognition were to him, they were not enough. He also wanted to make spiritual contributions, for he took religion seriously. Reflecting traditional religious views of the sacred and the secular, Ellington had told Carter Harman some years before, "I am that way about, about God . . . I don't know whether the words are good enough . . . and I don't use any pronoun. And I'm very—very serious about that . . . I won't play the *Saints Go Marching Home* [sic]. It's . . . a fear . . . I just don't think it has a place in jazz, that's all. Sometimes people keep insisting and I just tell them, I say, 'I just don't believe in playing hymns in jazz, that's all.' " But he felt it was entirely acceptable to write new music for performance in churches, and the success of the *Concert of Sacred Music* encouraged him to begin another, more ambitious work to express his spirituality. By 1967, he had begun working on a second liturgical piece, this time writing virtually the whole thing from scratch. The *Second Sacred Concert* was premiered at New York's Cathedral of St. John the Divine on January 19, 1968. Before an audience of six thousand people, the Ellington orchestra, augmented with singers Alice Babs, Tony Watkins, and others, and three choirs totaling a hundred voices, and directed by Tom Whaley, presented the 155-minute program.

"I regard this concert," Ellington would write in 1973, "as the most important thing I have ever done." He promptly repeated the work in Connecticut, then in Minneapolis at the Hennepin Avenue Methodist Church, and elsewhere. In February, he recorded it, at his own expense, for the small label Prestige Records. Soon he would perform it in Paris, Stockholm, Barcelona, and Orange, France. The work was generally very well received; *Down Beat* gave the recording "all the stars in God's heaven." Ellington felt gratified when a girl came up to him and said, "You know, Duke, you made me put my cross back on!"

He also made sure he kept his band working. In September 1968 came the Ellingtonians' first tour of South America and Mexico, and in June 1969, they went briefly to the Caribbean. In October 1969, they went to Europe, under the auspices of George Wein, for a seventieth birthday tour. This trip was grueling—thirty-two cities in just thirty-five days, often requiring two performances in one day, but a big success. In Paris, there was a belated birthday party, and *Le Figaro* produced a special Ellington edition. In January 1970, the orchestra went to the Far East: besides Japan, a host of new countries for them—the Philippines, Hong Kong, Singapore, Thailand, Taiwan, Australia, and New Zealand.

He continued to keep up a vigorous schedule of travel. "He often said," Marian Logan remembered, "that New York was his mailbox—where he received his mail, but he never stayed any length of time. . . . His home was on the road in hotels, and he made them as comfortable as could be for him. . . . And he stayed in suites and hotels all over the world. And that was his life. He loved it." "I'm a hotel man," Ellington declared to Carter Harman. "I like living in hotels. I'd like to live in the best fuckin' hotel I can live in, in the best suite, and just live there and order food, and never eat in the dining room." He had always liked the privacy of hotel rooms, the royal treatment of room service, and the lack of the hassles he used to encounter in restaurants still segregated in the 1950s in places like Las Vegas.

On the road, whether in the United States or abroad, he continued to keep in touch with his sister and close friends via the telephone. He loved phones—"telephonitis," Marian Logan dubbed it. "He would call from . . . India or any place." Typically he would reach Arthur Logan in the middle of the night and ask him, "How do I feel today?" His friend, the photographer Gordon Parks, noted, "If a telephone rang within ten yards of him he went for it." Ellington said, "I'm a telephone freak, the greatest invention since peanut brittle. The only way to keep me from answering one is to padlock my lips. Even then I'll try sign language." Ellington preferred to lie down when he talked on the telephone, as a way, Townsend said, of "avoiding useless and enervating irritation."

It was fortunate he loved travel, hotels, and long-distance communication for he had to travel continually if he wanted to maintain a year-round, full-time orchestra. And by this time, almost all bookings were short-term for high-priced musical groups.

But maintaining the orchestra was difficult in more ways than one. In the late 1960s, Sam Woodyard was fighting illness and was in and out of the drummer's chair. Turnover was high: between April and September 1967 there were at least five different drummers with the orchestra. Meanwhile, other members of the orchestra were periodically ailing. In December 1967, Lawrence Brown was hospitalized in New York for a heart condition, and Cootie Williams underwent surgery. In April 1969, Johnny Hodges would suffer a heart seizure and leave the band for two months.

The Ellington octet went back to the Rainbow Grill in May and June 1968. That July, clarinetist Jimmy Hamilton, not part of the octet, left Ellington after twenty-five years. His replacement was Harold Ashby, a tenor saxophonist who idolized Ben Webster. Now the clarinet duties would fall mostly to Russell Procope, who maintained a style on that instrument much closer to Bigard's woody New Orleans sound than to Hamilton's more "legitimate" style.

It's significant that for inspiration for one of his last important works, Ellington would turn back to the roots of jazz in New Orleans, mother lode of America's greatest secular music. *The New Orleans Suite* premiered April 25, 1970, at the New Orleans Jazz Festival. Each of the suite's five parts described a palpable part of the area's heritage—such as *Bourbon Street Jingling Jollies.* Two days later, back in New York, the orchestra recorded those first five movements. Within three weeks, Ellington had written another four movements, tributes to Sidney Bechet, Louis Armstrong, Wellman Braud, and Mahalia Jackson. For the Bechet piece, Ellington wanted Hodges to play soprano sax—something he had not done for Ellington in thirty years. The canny maestro began plotting how he could get Hodges to revive his soprano for the recording date that would be an Ellington celebration of African-American secular music that just might rival his sacred suites.

Then came the news that "Rabbit" had dropped dead while at his dentist's. Two days later the band had to go ahead and record the rest of the suite without Hodges. Ellington said of Hodges, "Johnny is not replaceable. Because of this great loss our band will never sound the same." As difficult as it had been to lose Hodges in 1951, there had always been the possibility and hope that he would return. Now that the sine qua non player was gone forever, Ellington would have not only a different but a diminished band. And yet his original instrumental textures and voicings, the growling brass, the special voice of Harry Carney down there in the bottom, and the maestro's distinctive stylings at the piano—all these continued to define an unmistakable Ellington sound.

In September 1971, under George Wein, the orchestra made an extensive tour of Europe, beginning with five weeks in the Soviet Union, arranged by the U.S. State Department, and despite the difficult existence jazz had led in the USSR, the concerts were a smash success, with sell-out crowds, tickets selling for eight times their face price, and adulation galore. Concerts in Britain, France, the Netherlands, Belgium, Poland, Hungary, Romania, Austria, Denmark, Norway, Sweden, Italy, Germany, and Spain followed, and from there the band flew directly to South America, where, again under State Department auspices, they played in Brazil, Uruguay, Argentina, Chile, Peru, Ecuador, Colombia, Venezuela, Puerto Rico, Panama, Nicaragua, and Mexico. In January 1972,

Paul Gonsalves Jams with Ellington and Russian musicians under a silhouette of Lenin in Leningrad. The Ellington orchestra created great excitement among Eastern bloc musicians and audiences during its 1971 tour.

the Ellingtonians made another tour of the Far East and Southeast Asia: Japan, Taiwan, the Philippines, Hong Kong, Thailand, Burma, India, Ceylon, Singapore, Malaysia, Indonesia, Australia, and New Zealand.

Lawrence Brown had left the Ellington orchestra in January 1970 for good, bitter about Ellington's ego and his salary, and retired from the music business. Cat Anderson departed in January 1971 to make a career playing in recording studios. Turnover increased in the 1970s, but Ellington soldiered on.

Ellington continued to take every challenge, tackle every interesting musical problem he could. In 1970, the American Ballet Theater commissioned a forty-four-minute ballet Ellington called *The River*, which was choreographed by Alvin Ailey and premiered at the New York State Theater at Lincoln Center on June 25. That year, New York's public television station WNET commissioned Ellington to complete a one-hour comic opera he had been occasionally working on since the 1950s—initially as a feature for Lena Horne—called *Queenie Pie*. In 1972, Ellington, now seventy-three, hired conductor Maurice Peress to help in orchestrating the singers' parts.

Ellington continued to perform all around the country, and abroad, too—though not at quite such a killing global pace as before. His last performance at the Monterey Jazz Festival was in 1970, when he premiered the *Afro-Eurasian Eclipse*, which was filmed as part of a documentary called *Monterey Jazz. Eclipse* was inspired by the tour of the Far East; and written in recognition of Marshall McLuhan's opinion that "the whole world is going oriental," as Ellington was fond of quoting.

One of *Eclipse*'s movements, *Acht O'Clock Rock*, written three years earlier, represented a response by Ellington to the terrific popularity of rock music, which was disdained by many jazz musicians but had seeped into jazz here and there. In 1969, Miles Davis had taken his band electric, but Ellington never got more electric than the occasional electric-piano piece. *Acht O'Clock Rock* was about as close as he got to rock music, though he had helped pave the way for the music through his rhythmically propulsive pieces dating as far back as the 1930s, including such strong back-beat dance numbers as *Rockin' in Rhythm* and *Happy-Go-Lucky Local*.

With the loss of some of his stars, the turnover in personnel, and the aging of other players, Ellington increasingly was carrying the show with his public personality and stage presence, now polished to a fine level of smoothness, cliché, and charm. After 1971, he made a number of recordings but was glimpsing few new musical horizons, though there were occasionally new kinds of engagements which kept things interesting for the band. From July 17 to July 21, 1972, Ellington and the orchestra took on the highly unusual role of teachers, en masse. During what was declared as

"Duke Ellington Week" at the University of Wisconsin, Madison, the band taught classes and workshops, as well as played concerts. Still this was not new artistic ground, but rather more a matter of passing on the heritage while there was still time. Now in his seventies, having watched aging players' illnesses, having seen Strayhorn and Hodges die, he was glimpsing more clearly his own mortality. But death was a subject he hated talking or thinking about, so much so that he refused to prepare a will.

For some years, Sam Vaughan, an editor at Doubleday, had been pursuing Ellington to write his memoirs. Ellington continually resisted the offer of a $10,000 advance against future royalties. Then Nelson Doubleday himself, excited after hearing the band perform, offered a $50,000 advance. "Sold," exclaimed Ellington. In 1968, Ellington received $25,000 of the advance. But then the work had to begin. Ellington began jotting down ideas and paragraphs on pieces of paper, hotel stationery, and other miscellany, and Stanley Dance deciphered his handwriting and assisted in piecing together a book, which was published in the fall of 1973 as *Music Is My Mistress*. Ellington did not write a true autobiography; rather he offered anecdotal, generous remembrances of over a hundred people, some breezy historical narrative, and, predictably, limited self-revelation. He took an almost uniformly positive tone—the literary equivalent of his conceit "We love you madly"—and there's hardly a negative word in the book: little about the gangsters at the Cotton Club, nothing about Jim Crow, the feud with the NAACP, drinking, drugs, disputes, or other unpleasantness within the band. Key women in his life—Edna Ellington, Mildred Dixon, Evie Ellis, Fernanda de Castro Monte, and other romantic liaisons—are absent as well. It was another protective veil for the ultimately private man who spent his life before the public.

During 1973, Ellington devoted almost all his composing energies to the third Sacred Concert. When asked why he was taking so long, he replied, "You can jive with secular music, but you can't jive with the Almighty." From October through December 1973, the orchestra performed in Europe, with a brief side trip to Ethiopia and Zambia. In London, they gave a Royal Command Performance for Queen Elizabeth II. Then, on October 24, at London's Westminster Abbey, Ellington premiered his *Third Sacred Concert*, in a performance sponsored by the United Nations. This piece was quieter, more serene than the previous two. "It is illuminating," Gary Giddins wrote touchingly, "not least for showing how Ellington coped with the insoluble problem of having outlived his band." Cootie Williams was not on this tour, Paul Gonsalves was taken ill suddenly, and Ellington knew the orchestra was not nearly as strong as in earlier times. So, he gave it a supporting role and focused the piece on Alice Babs, Harry Carney, and his own piano playing. The program was a mixed success, but Alice Babs again sang impressively.

If he had outlived his band, he was ever more aware of his own mortality. In September, Ben Webster died, and on November 25, Ellington suffered another death in the "family" when friend and physician Arthur Logan died in a fall from a bridge: his widow said he was pushed by two men who "rolled" him. Ellington was highly distraught. "If ever he lost a friend," said Mercer, "it was Arthur. I saw him affected by Billy, but nothing like with Arthur." Now, Ellington told Marian Logan, "I'll never get over this, I won't last six months." In January of that year, Ellington had been hospitalized in Los Angeles for eight days because of influenza and fatigue. Dr. Logan diagnosed the deeper reason Ellington had been feeling and looking tired and weak. A lifelong smoker, the maestro had contracted lung cancer, and it was rapidly spreading through his body. He must have known that he did not have long to live, but he kept this knowledge from the members of the orchestra. Instead, he kept on creating, conducting, and touring. There was so much more music in him.

In March 1974, he had to leave the band, then touring the Midwest, and return to New York, where he checked into the Harkness Pavilion of the Columbia Presbyterian Hospital. Though confining him to a hospital bed, his cancer, infecting both lungs, could stop neither his creativity nor his ambitions. With his electric piano by his bed, he continued to work on *Queenie Pie*; held discussions with Mercer about *The Three Black Kings*, a ballet suite; and made decisions about which portions of the Westminster Abbey recording of the *Third Sacred Concert* he wanted released. On his seventy-fifth birthday, selections from the Sacred Concerts were performed at New York's Central Presbyterian Church, but Ellington was too ill to attend. He had typically sent out his Christmas cards in mid-year, to avoid the rush, and in recent years had created his own designs. In mid-May, he sent out his last such greeting: on a rich blue background, it carried these words in gold letters:

L
GOD
V
E

On May 15, Paul Gonsalves died, and on May 18, Tyree Glenn, who had played trombone for Ellington from 1947 to 1951, and again in 1971, also died. No one had the heart to tell Ellington. He developed pneumonia and then, at 3:10 A.M. on Friday morning, May 24, 1974, he succumbed. It had been almost exactly the six months he had predicted to Marian Logan.

Expressions of loss and tribute poured in. President Nixon observed, "The wit, taste, intelligence and elegance that Duke Ellington brought to his music have made him, in the eyes of millions of people both here and abroad, America's foremost composer. His memory will live for generations to come in the music with which he enriched his nation." Gunther Schuller remarked, "For me, he was always in the pantheon of great musicians along with Bach and Beethoven and Schoenberg." Ella Fitzgerald said simply, "It's a very sad day. A genius has passed." And Dinah Shore offered this: "When someone like Duke Ellington dies, we haven't lost him. Every time I sing one of his songs, I realize how lucky I am and how lucky we all are to have his exquisite talent to draw joy and sustenance from."

For a brief time, Paul Gonsalves and Tyree Glenn and Ellington were laid out in the same funeral home. Some 65,000 people came to view Ellington's body, and to accommodate them, the mortuary kept its doors open around the clock. People shook his hand, kissed him, left mementos in the coffin.

His funeral, held at the cavernous Cathedral of St. John the Divine, on Memorial Day, May 27, was thronged by 10,000 people, while police kept back 2,500 who stood outside and listened via

Ellington's casket lies in state at New York's Cathedral of St. John the Divine
on May 27, 1974. More than twelve thousand mourners mobbed the funeral, at which music
from his *Second Sacred Concert* was played.

loudspeakers. Most of the mourners were ordinary people, black
and white, who came by foot, subway, or bus. Stanley Dance delivered a dignified and moving eulogy. Father Norman O'Connor, a
friend of Ellington's who helped officiate at the service, said,
"Duke, we thank you. You loved us madly. We will love you madly,
today, tomorrow, and forever." Slowed somewhat by arthritis, Ella
Fitzgerald stood up and sang Ellington's *Solitude* and the old funeral hymn from New Orleans, *Just a Closer Walk with Thee*.
Count Basie wept, tears streaming down his face. There were other
musical performances, and as the mourners receded, Johnny

Hodges's saxophone, accompanying Alice Babs singing *Heaven* and *Almighty God*, descended ethereally from a tape recording of the second Sacred Concert, bringing many to more tears. Ellington was buried next to his mother and father at Woodlawn Cemetery in the Bronx, where he had purchased fourteen plots for the Ellington family.

Now, finally, in death, Ellington could be in his mother's arms again. And if there is a music heaven, Ellington must have had an extraordinary reunion, for so many of his musicians had predeceased him: Bubber Miley, gone for forty-two years, Artie Whetsol, Tricky Sam Nanton, Ivie Anderson, Rex Stewart, Wellman Braud, Billy Strayhorn, Jimmie Blanton, Ben Webster, Willie Smith, Johnny Hodges, Otto Hardwick, Tyree Glenn, and Paul Gonsalves.

His suave style, sardonic banter, wily ways, restless creativity, enormous energy and productivity, dignity and example and vision and music making, all ended. But while Edward Kennedy Ellington was gone, his story would not end with his death. Indeed, it would continue to evolve.

Essential Ellington,
1966–74

Though after losing Strayhorn in 1967 and Hodges in 1970, Ellington's inspiration seemed to fall off, he nonetheless managed to compose a number of striking works. Here are some of the most memorable of his final recordings.

What began in 1964 with the four movements of *Impressions of the Far East* developed by 1966 into the nine movements of *The Far East Suite* (Bluebird), a forty-four-minute musical travelogue of the Near, Middle and

(continued)

Far East. These are not mere snapshots, however, but tone paintings of Ellington's and Strayhorn's impressions filtered through the blues and other musical resources they had been using for decades. Like John Coltrane's album *A Love Supreme,* this work pays homage to modal melodies and other Asian musical influences, but where Coltrane makes his tribute apparent, Ellington and Strayhorn make it transparent. *Isfahan* (where, Ellington wrote, "everything is poetry") has Hodges in one of his most lyrical ballad performances, while Jimmy Hamilton depicts a mynah in the humorous *Bluebird of Delhi.* The ominous *Agra* and the dance-inspired *Depk* are harmonically and rhythmically advanced, while the mysterious *Amad* includes a "call to prayer" by Lawrence Brown. The eleven-minute *Ad Lib on Nippon,* an extended piece within the suite, opens with Ellington toying with the listener's sense of time and harmony as he pays a slyly disguised blues seemingly out of tempo, shifts scene several times, and concludes with superb, virtuosic clarinet playing by Hamilton; as they did often, Ellington and Strayhorn deceptively make the movement sound mostly improvised. *The Far East Suite* ranks as one of the most carefully ordered, singular suites in the Ellington canon. One of the final collaborations of Ellington and Strayhorn, the suite is regarded by some as their best work since the early 1940s.

The death of Billy Strayhorn in 1967 was more traumatic to the Ellington orchestra than that of anyone else in the history of the organization. They recorded their tribute . . . *And His Mother Called Him Bill*—comprised solely of Strayhorn and Ellington-Strayhorn compositions—just three months after his passing. Rarely did the entire band play with such heartfelt passion, and the album is widely considered one of Ellington's best. This Bluebird disc—superbly recorded, arranged, and performed—includes premiere recordings of two Strayhorn compositions: *Blood Count,* which Hodges, in one of his supreme performances, makes an intense and anguished dirge, and the swinging, pungent *Charpoy.* (These, the Ellington music manu-

(continued)

scripts at the Smithsonian reveal, actually date from the 1940s: the former was titled *Blue Cloud* and the latter *Anal Renrut*—Lana Turner spelled backward.) Hodges solos movingly on the ballads *My Little Brown Book, After All,* and the resplendent *Day Dream.* Feeling the magnitude of Strayhorn's loss, the band plays with an edge of deep sorrow and stinging anger even in exuberant, celebratory pieces like *U.M.M.G.* and *Smada.* Showing his bereavement, Ellington ends *Midriff* with angry, thunderous clusters of piano notes that sustain and slowly fade out.

If *...And His Mother Called Him Bill* seemed to be undergirded by the spiritual strength of Ellington, Hodges, et al., Ellington's *Second Sacred Concert* (1968, Prestige) lifted his spirituality onto a stage for all to witness. Though its lyrics (written by Ellington) are uneven, this work, unlike the first *Sacred Concert,* consists entirely of new material. Ellington considered the piece his supreme achievement and paid for its recording. Among the highlights are *Heaven* in free rhythm and then a bossa nova rhythm, sung by the extraordinary Swedish coloratura soprano Alice Babs, whose lovely, clear voice can soar into the highest spires of any cathedral. Beginning sparely and building in volume, *Almighty God* features Babs, bassist Jeff Castleman, and Russell Procope on clarinet. Cootie Williams "talks" and growls his trumpet masterfully through Ellington's tribute to Pastor John Gensel, *The Shepherd (Who Watches over the Night Flock). T.G.T.T. (Too Good to Title)* has Ellington atypically playing electric piano, accompanying in dulcet tones Babs in a wordless vocal, with a melody that goes up and down, from heaven to earth, and ends in the City Celestial.

Recorded in 1968 but not issued until twenty-one years later, *The Private Collection, Vol. 9* (Saja), offers fresh arrangements of the familiar Ellington standards *Sophisticated Lady,* featuring Johnny Hodges; *Just Squeeze Me* (Harold Ashby); *Mood Indigo* (Hodges and Harry Carney); and *In a Sentimental Mood* (Paul Gonsalves). Most notable are his new compositions

(continued)

written after Strayhorn's death: *Knuf* ("funk" spelled backward); the sunny *GigI* (used in his ballet *The River*); the moody, mysterious *Reva;* and the slow, soulful *Elos.*

In 1970 Ellington honored New Orleans as a source of inspiration with a somewhat underrehearsed yet notable tribute recording, *The New Orleans Suite* (Atlantic). It comprises five movements interpreting aspects of Crescent City life, and four portraits celebrating Louis Armstrong, Wellman Braud, Sidney Bechet, and Mahalia Jackson. On his last recording session, made just before his sudden death, Johnny Hodges wails *Blues for New Orleans,* while organist Wild Bill Davis and the band rock the beat. Cootie Williams pays affectionate homage to his hero in *Portrait of Louis Armstrong,* and the exuberant *Second Line* conjures a band marching, parading, and swinging its way through city streets. A showcase for Harold Ashby's searing tenor saxophone, *Thanks for the Beautiful Land on the Delta* is an intense and spiritual experience. The *New Orleans Suite* is rich with essences—hearty melodies, striking rhythms, and evocations of this seminal city.

TWELVE

*E*LEVATING

ELLINGTON

•

1974 —

he Duke Ellington story now depended on the living. The key players would be his son, Mercer, the mass media, the U.S. government, and an earnest band of apostles scattered around the world. Through the efforts of these forces, Ellington would gradually find a place of higher value in the cultural pantheon.

Meanwhile, with the death of Ellington, Harry Carney had lost his reason for living: four months later, on October 8, he was dead. Evie would die of cancer within two years, on April 7, 1976, and be buried beside Ellington in Woodlawn Cemetery. One by one, the pioneers and collaborators dropped: Ray Nance would go in 1976, Freddie Jenkins in 1978, Barney Bigard in 1980, Russell Procope, Cat Anderson, and Irving Townsend in 1981. Sonny Greer would survive until 1982, Juan Tizol and lyricist Paul Francis Webster until 1984, Cootie Williams and Irving Mills until 1985. Lawrence Brown and Sam Woodyard lived until 1988.

On the day of his father's funeral, Mercer Ellington picked up the reins of the Duke Ellington orchestra and took the band off to Bermuda to play an engagement for International Business Machines (IBM). Some were surprised at the lack of a hiatus, but Mercer told the *New York Times*, "The Duke would have wanted it that way." In fact, his father had pledged to the president of IBM that the orchestra would perform in Bermuda, with the maestro or without him. "I discovered when we got there that we were in danger of losing our way," Mercer recalled in 1986. "There were new men coming into the band, and the men who knew his music by heart were on the way out. . . . What I had to do was restore the library, by hiring arrangers to transcribe older pieces from records. . . . Through the process, I began to catch up with him. I'm still catching up with him." It was a difficult job, as Krin Gabbard observed in 1989: "No matter how closely he recreates the original recordings of his father, as many critics will condemn Mercer for not measuring up as will chide him for producing slavish imitations."

In the ensuing years, Mercer Ellington continued to lead the Duke Ellington orchestra, bringing back some early Ellington works that his father had rarely performed in his later years. Though few of Duke Ellington's players remained, the orchestra made several commercially successful recordings, notably *Digital Duke*, and in the 1990s was continuing to perform in the United States, Europe, and Japan.

The late-seventies Broadway fad for revues of black songwriters (*Eubie!*, *Ain't Misbehavin'*) stimulated the production of *Sophisticated Ladies*, a Broadway revue of Ellington's songs mixed with some instrumentals. With the music under the nominal direction of Mercer Ellington, the show opened on March 1, 1981, starring Gregory Hines, Judith Jamison, and Phyllis Hyman. Mercer conducted the Ellington orchestra during most of the show's two-year run and a number of its later revivals, but the creative control belonged to others. "What I objected to about the show was that there was a bit too much Broadway in it," he said. "The music wasn't the star of the show, the way it should have been. The dancing and the staging took precedence." Though some jazz critics sniffed at it for emphasizing Ellington the writer of popular songs rather than the instrumental composer-orchestrator, and the musical was a patchwork of existing songs rather than a wholly conceived composition, the show finally achieved for Ellington something he was unable to do himself: a Broadway hit.

Mercer Ellington worked to complete his father's nearly finished opéra bouffe *Queenie Pie*, and it was premiered in Philadelphia at the American Musical Theater Festival in the fall of 1986, followed by a month's run at the John F. Kennedy Center for the Performing Arts in Washington, D.C. Mercer insisted that the cast be racially mixed. "Every show my father was ever involved with was racially integrated," he asserted, "and this one will be, too, if I'm going to have anything to do with it." *Queenie Pie* was based vaguely on Madame C. J. Walker, the Harlem hairdresser who became a millionaire by selling beauty products. In the story, Queenie Pie is threatened by a new arrival and rival from New Orleans, Café

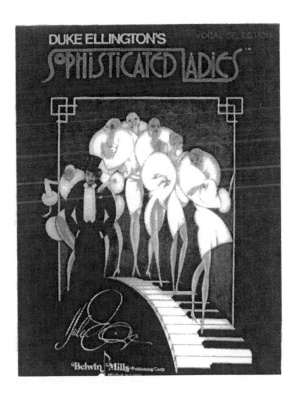

The vocal score for the musical revue *Sophisticated Ladies,* which opened in 1981 and finally gave Ellington what he never achieved in his lifetime: a Broadway hit.

O'Lay. One observer felt that the story, perhaps paralleling Ellington's own experiences, dealt "with a mature and successful person coming to terms with a younger generation, asking the question, What is timeless and what is ephemeral?" The music was rich in its diversity, and offered echoes of earlier Ellington, including *Harlem* and *A Drum Is a Woman*. "Ellington Lite," is what the critic Francis Davis called the work. "But," he continued, *"Queenie Pie* affirmed that even minor Ellington can be pretty wonderful."

Meanwhile, interest in Ellington steadily gathered momentum. Several books were published in the 1970s, notably Mercer Ellington's *Duke Ellington in Person: An Intimate Memoir*, with Stanley Dance, which came out in 1978, and candidly revealed the pain as well as pleasure that Mercer experienced in his relationship with his father. By 1984, Gary Giddins had reckoned that fifty hours of previously unreleased Ellington recordings had been brought out in the decade since his death. That same year, Mercer Ellington, now married to a Danish woman, donated six hundred tapes of unissued Ellington ("the stockpile") to Radio Denmark, and the Republic of Mali issued a pair of stamps for Ellington and his contemporary Sidney Bechet, who had once played in his orchestra.

Around 1986, a dozen years after his death, the Ellington renaissance was moving into high gear. That year, the U.S. Postal Service issued a commemorative stamp in Ellington's honor, RCA Records finally reissued Ellington's glorious early 1940s work on a four-record set called *The Blanton-Webster Band*—about which record producer Steve Backer noted, "Despite their size [and price], the boxes are selling at the pace of single albums"—and the Australian sound engineer Robert Parker began restoring 1920s and 1930s records of Ellington, which when issued on BBC Records beginning in 1987 struck many as never having sounded as vibrant and rich. That same year, New York's Lincoln Center began an annual series of concerts of Ellington's music, performed by a jazz repertory orchestra under the artistic direction of Wynton Marsalis and the baton of David Berger. In 1987, the first of the "Private Ellington" recordings—drawn from his stockpile—were issued to the public, and by 1988, the boom in compact discs had caused a stream of Ellington reissues to begin, which would become a flood, within five years totaling some four hundred CDs and growing. That same year saw the publication of two books on Ellington, one by James Lincoln Collier and another by Peter Gammond.

In 1988, the Public Broadcasting System presented a two-hour television documentary, *A Duke Named Ellington*; a joint American-Russian production of *Sophisticated Ladies* played in Moscow, where the cast posed with Raisa Gorbachev; and in 1989, it played the Kennedy Center in Washington. In 1989, Ellington's star had risen to the point that Famous Music Corporation paid a reported $8 million to Mercer Ellington to buy most of his rights to his father's music.

In the 1990s, interest in Ellington continued to grow, as more books, recordings, broadcasts, and concerts explored and cele-

Mercer Ellington (second from right) with daughter Mercedes at the 1986 unveiling of a U.S. postage stamp honoring Duke Ellington.

brated his musical riches. Singer Bobby Short was raising funds for a statue of Ellington to be erected in New York's Central Park, though controversy arose about the sculptor's plans for nine nude women who would be holding Ellington and his piano aloft. In 1991, the Public Broadcasting System aired another biographical TV documentary on Ellington, *Reminiscing in Tempo*.

One of the most important developments for the Ellington legacy was the acquisition by the Smithsonian Institution of the Ellington archives. After the transfer in 1988, the museum moved to establish an active program of disseminating the collection to the public. The availability of the collection to researchers, teachers, and musicians made possible performances of previously unavailable music in a number of leading concert halls, and helped a Chicago theater mount a 1991 revival of *Jump for Joy* that included five numbers, long thought lost, which were discovered in the archive and fleshed out from lead sheets. As researchers began poring through the music, they began to understand more of Ellington's compositional methods and style—for example, the previously inscrutably dense voicings at the end of his aptly titled *Mystery Song* from 1932. And a comparison of manuscripts reveals that while Strayhorn evidently composed in a straightforward linear fashion, Ellington seems to have sometimes manipulated his passages, sections, and phrases, reordering them until he got the desired result, almost as if these units were a child's wooden alphabet blocks. Further discoveries about his compositional process and style, the chronology of his arrangements, the degree to which solos were improvised, and other matters await researchers.

Then in 1991, the U.S. Congress established the Smithsonian Jazz Masterworks Orchestra which, under the batons of the composer-conductor-educators David Baker and Gunther Schuller, presented concerts and broadcasts of Ellington's music, in part drawing on the archive. In the 1990s, two decades after his death, Ellington seemed to be much larger than life. Judging from the increased interest and respect accorded him by such arbiters of culture as the *New York Times*, the *Washington Post*, Carnegie Hall, Lincoln Center, the Smithsonian Institution, and the Kennedy Center, Ellington seemed to be commanding his biggest comeback yet.

. . .

But if the American concert hall and museum, two of the fundamental definers of an ordered, canonical culture, were giving Ellington more recognition, another of the cultural referees, the university, has been far slower to respond. Only as he approached his seventh decade did Ellington begin receiving honorary degrees. Over the years, American music education at the college and university level has resisted broadening its studies beyond "classical" works—especially for the symphony and opera—from the nineteenth century and before, overwhelmingly from Europe. "Until very recently," observed Austin B. Caswell in 1991, "becoming musically educated in America, whether as listener, performer, or composer, meant putting one's own culture aside and adopting another."

"I'm hardly surprised that my kind of music is still without, let us say, official honor at home," Ellington told writer Nat Hentoff in 1965. "Most Americans still take it for granted that European music—classical music, if you will—is the only really respectable kind." He added angrily, "What we do, what other black musicians do, has always been like the kind of man you wouldn't want your daughter to associate with." Though the situation has improved somewhat in subsequent years, in the 1990s Ellington's pained observation holds largely true.

As Ellington's centennial and the twenty-first century both approach, he still has found no meaningful place in the offerings of most college and university music departments. In fact, Ellington's music is taught in only a minority of American colleges and universities and then usually only in jazz courses—not in music history, musicology, music theory, composition, or orchestration. Most American college textbooks on music or Western music fail even to mention Ellington. Were it not for cultural gerrymandering, Ellington would have found his rightful place in the academic and cultural pantheon; but the categories based on race, instrumentation, and venue that Ellington found so confining still haunt his music and restrain his legacy.

In truth, musicologists, accustomed to basing their analyses and judgments on written notations, have been stymied by the almost total lack of published music during Ellington's lifetime and after. Finally, in the 1990s, there is an effort to address the great lack of his published music with the national publication series called Jazz Masterworks Editions.

One of the thorniest problems facing any analyst of Ellington is that his music was constantly and deliberately in a state of flux. "As long as something is unfinished," he once said, "there's always that little feeling of insecurity. And a feeling of insecurity is absolutely necessary unless you're so rich that it doesn't matter." Because he hated the finality of writing endings, constantly tinkered with his pieces as his taste, players, venues, and eras changed, and frequently rerecorded his compositions in different versions, Ellington left not a fixed edition of many of his compositions but an evolving trail of variants. He was a man wrapped up as much with the process as with the finished product.

As a composer Ellington had his limitations. When it came to securing lyric writers, he rarely, if ever found someone as gifted as he. Working to deadline, he left things until the last minute, and thus some pieces did not achieve their potential. He was sometimes given to clichés, and when he wrote prose or poetry into his works, the words could become overblown. As a bandleader, his gift for finding and developing gifted instrumentalists was partly offset by frequent poor judgment in choosing singers. Then there was the need to be commercial that sometimes caused lapses in musical taste. And partly because of a lack of discipline, in later years especially, his band's performances were uneven.

One of Ellington's strengths, however, was his ability to grow artistically: he shaped his music to fit the times, changes in personnel and venues, and the direction of his artistic muse. Brilliant and influential as they were, once Louis Armstrong and Charlie Parker had perfected their styles, they stuck with and elaborated on them. In contrast, Ellington kept on evolving, partly by remaining open to new sounds, influences, and ideas. Charles Ives, the great iconoclast, turn-of-the-century American composer, had heeded his father's advice to "stretch your ears." Ellington heeded Will Marion Cook's advice to find his *own* way, which evolved during the course of his career. Ellington seems to have been driven to tackle new problems, to create new sounds, right up to his death. As a result of his artistic growth, Ellington's work of the 1970s sounded differ-

A page of manuscript, from the Smithsonian's Ellington papers,
for his memoirs, *Music Is My Mistress*.
It includes a telling assertion at bottom: "If jazz means
anything it is freedom of expression."

ent in many ways from that of the 1920s—yet it was all identifiably Ellingtonian.

Among the many problems Ellington solved, reconciling improvisation with composition was one of his greatest achievements. As the British historian E. A. Hobsbawm, writing under the nom de plume Francis Newton, observed in 1958:

> He is the man who first recognised and solved the unbelievably difficult problem of turning a living, shifting and improvised folk-music into composition without losing its spontaneity. Anyone can use jazz devices in orthodox composition or leave cadenzas blank for solo improvisation. Nobody but the Duke (in a peculiarly anarchically controlled symbiosis with his musicians) has produced music which is *both* created by the players *and* fully shaped by the composer. He has been so unique and so far ahead of his time that even jazz musicians sometimes fail to appreciate his originality, surprised to find some revolutionary device of modern jazz anticipated in the early 1930s.

As a composer-orchestrator, Ellington founded no school, cloned no single-minded imitators: his art, like that of Picasso and Frank Lloyd Wright, was too personal for that. And it was too complex to be easily copied. "Stan Kenton," said the conductor-arranger André Previn in the 1950s, "can stand in front of a thousand fiddles and a thousand brass and make a dramatic gesture, and every studio arranger can nod his head and say, 'Oh, yes, that's done like this.' But Duke merely lifts his finger, three horns make a sound, and I don't know what it is!" But Ellington nonetheless influenced a range of pianists, composers, and orchestrators. His influence is everywhere: for example, in the elegance that other orchestras strove to emulate; in the miniature tone poems and the range of expression that some other bands sometimes offered; in the vocalizing of instruments and the instrumentalizing of vocals; in the compositions of Charles Mingus and Wynton Marsalis, to name just two; and in the greater respect that African-American and jazz musicians are now accorded. And some of his players were highly influential—for example, Bubber Miley, Harry Carney, Lawrence Brown, and Jimmie Blanton, to cite just four.

Writing in 1987, the critic Francis Davis found, "Ellington's in-

fluence has never been greater." It wasn't just that his compositions continued to be recorded by mainstream jazz musicians and
now by iconoclastic avant-gardists; or that the growling, speech-
influenced work of his brass players had been taken to new lengths
by trumpeters like Lester Bowie and trombonists like Steve Turré;
or that Ellington's style of composition and orchestration had pro-
foundly influenced composer Charles Mingus, and through him,
David Murray, John Carter, Henry Threadgill, and others. The
1980s were "Ellington's decade," wrote Davis, "because visionary
jazz composers are taking up his unfinished task of reconciling
composition and improvisation." Just as Charles Mingus had taken
up this concern in his epic *Epitaph* (unfinished at his death in 1979
and later completed by Gunther Schuller), a younger generation of
composers such as Abdullah Ibrahim in his 1982 mixed-media
opera *Kalahari Liberation*, John Carter in such works as *Castles of
Ghana*, and Anthony Davis with his 1985 opera *X*, based on the life
of Malcolm X, were striving to integrate the predetermined with
the spontaneous in works small and large.

Ellington was a great exemplar of an African-American aesthetic
that calls for, rather than replicating exactly what is given you,
finding your own voice as a means of expressing your individuality.
One way Ellington did this was in his choice and use of instruments. As an orchestra leader, Ellington could have chosen to
feature violins and other bowed string instruments. This would
have given him a smooth sound. But he did not want an ever-
smooth sound because it was too European for him. He generally
valued the African-American tradition of percussiveness, of sharp
musical attack, and these sounds are easier to achieve on brass
instruments, percussion instruments, and piano than on violins.

The way Ellington deployed the instruments also reflects this
African-American aesthetic. He was constantly searching for new
ways of using the instruments: Wellman Braud's percussive slap
bass, Tricky Sam Nanton's talking trombone, Bubber Miley's
muted growls, and Rex Stewart's half-valve effects on cornet indelibly personalized their instruments. And Ellington found ways of
combining instruments to produce new tonal colors, like the ex-

traordinary blend on *Mood Indigo* (1930), or *On a Turquoise Cloud* (1947), or so many others. In these ways, Ellington was fulfilling the aesthetic's manifesto of being his own person, having his own sound, creating his own style.

Ellington managed to create an orchestra that sounded unlike any other. He selected players for their distinctive voices, learned to downplay their weaknesses and emphasize their strengths, wrote to highlight them singly (as in *Concerto for Cootie* and *Clarinet Lament*) and in various combinations. Through these means, and by composing highly unusual and innovative works for them to play, he produced a unique music. After Billy Strayhorn joined the band and learned Ellington's ways, he helped the master continue —even extend—that singular sound.

Thus Duke Ellington and his players rank as some of the greatest individualists of the twentieth century. Ellington and his band achieved the highest expression of the African-American aesthetic tenet that values creating a distinctively personal sound, name, appearance, or style.

In fact, Ellington—an original and singular person in language, dress, music, and overall style—went beyond individualism. He created a new type of music, sui generis. He created his own category. He was in a class beyond Benny Goodman, Jimmie Lunceford, Tommy Dorsey, and the other big-band leaders of the 1930s and 1940s, few of whom were composers and orchestrators of much import, and none of whom had his originality. And Ellington stands well outside the circle comprising Aaron Copland, Charles Ives, Virgil Thomson, and other composers writing American-accented "classical" music in the European tradition. By the 1930s, Ellington was already developing his own kind of American art music, highly reflective of the cultural diversity of his native land.

Though Ellington's music was deeply rooted in the African-American life he experienced in his native Washington, D.C., and in Harlem, his art is quintessentially American in its integration of the primary colors—European, African, and American—that form the rainbow culture of the United States. He often composed on American themes that affirmed the dual cultural identity of being simultaneously an American and an African-American, celebrated such American cultural heroes as Bert Williams, Louis Armstrong, and Martin Luther King, Jr., and affirmed his own and his people's struggle for complete citizenship.

Ellington's sound grew out of his experiences and those of his multihued company of players in urban, twentieth-century America. Like so many others—including Scott Joplin, George Gershwin, Bill Monroe, Sarah Vaughan—Ellington was searching for what it meant, as a musician, to be an American. Leopold Stokowski once reportedly asked Ellington what he was "striving for in music." Replied Ellington, "I am trying to express American music as I hear it and know it." Ellington wanted to sound like a twentieth-century American. To do that he had to create something new, in the spirit of his forefathers and of other Americans who were busily developing their own modern idioms and institutions. Duke Ellington did not want to sound like anyone else; he wanted to sound like himself.

Perhaps no one deserved the phrase "beyond category" more than
Edward Kennedy Ellington himself.

Ellington represented the full flowering of a truly American orchestral idiom, a music more comprehensive of the diverse cultural groupings in America than any other, at once reflecting and transcending its day, seemingly timeless in its best moments of inspiration and beauty and feeling. "I don't think anybody has achieved a higher aesthetic synthesis of the American experience than Duke Ellington expressed in his music," critic and novelist Albert Murray has written. "Anybody who achieved a literary equivalent of that would be beyond Melville, Henry James and Faulkner."

"Duke Ellington is the quintessential American composer," Murray has argued, "because it is his body of work more than any other that adds up to the most specific, comprehensive, universally appealing musical complement to what Constance Rourke, author of *American Humor: A Study of the National Character*, had in mind when she referred to 'emblems for a pioneer people who require resilience as a prime trait.' Nor can it be said too often that at its best an Ellington performance sounds as if it knows the truth about all the other music in the world and is looking for something better. Not even the Constitution represents a more intrinsically American statement and achievement than that." Ellington's music summarized the American experience, with its diverse cultural streams, its pain, pleasure, pride, dreaming, vitality, hope, and yearning for freedom.

Yet beyond being American, Ellington's music is joyously and positively human. What could be more affirming than to celebrate individuality; to unite differing musical personalities into a synergistic ensemble; to communicate a range of human emotions from anger and sorrow to awe, humor, hope, love, and joy; and to express timeless values such as dignity, reverence, and freedom?

For generations of Americans and legions of listeners around the world, his music has resonated with cultural and personal appeal and identity. In a century rife with mass production, uniformity, predictability, hopelessness, impersonality, derivativeness, categorization, and artificially synthesized music, Duke Ellington in his life and music affirmed the personal, the human, the heartfelt, the hopeful, the unique, the inventive, and the individual as eloquently as anyone. Perhaps that is why his singular music and exceptional life continue to move and inspire so many people.

Notes

Works and sources frequently cited in the text are identified by the following abbreviations.

Allen Walter C. Allen, *Hendersonia: The Music of Fletcher Henderson and His Musicians; A Bio-Discography*. Jazz Monographs no. 4. Highland Park, New Jersey: Walter C. Allen, 1973.

Bigard Barney Bigard, *With Louis and the Duke: The Autobiography of a Jazz Clarinetist*, ed. Barry Martyn. New York: Oxford University Press; London: Macmillan, 1985.

Boatwright Ruth Ellington Boatwright, interview by Marcia Greenlee, New York City, August 18, 1989, DEOHP.

Bordman Gerald Bordman, *American Musical Theatre: A Chronicle*. 2nd ed. New York: Oxford University Press, 1992.

Boyer Richard O. Boyer, "The Hot Bach," in Peter Gammond, ed., *Duke Ellington: His Life and Music*. London: Phoenix House, 1958, pp. 22–60. Originally published in *The New Yorker*, Part 1 (June 24, 1944), pp. 30 34, 37–38, 40, 42, 44; Part 2 (July 1, 1944), pp. 26–32, 34; Part 3 (July 8, 1944), pp. 26–31.

Bushell Garvin Bushell as told to Mark Tucker, *Jazz from the Beginning*. Introduction by Lawrence Gushee. Ann Arbor: University of Michigan Press, 1990.

Calloway Cab Calloway and Bryant Rollins, *Of Minnie the Moocher and Me*. New York: Thomas Y. Crowell, 1976.

Calloway papers Cab Calloway papers, Special Collections, Mugar Library, Boston University, Boston, Massachusetts.

Collier, *Ellington* James Lincoln Collier, *Duke Ellington*. New York and Oxford: Oxford University Press, 1987.

Collier, *Goodman* James Lincoln Collier, *Benny Goodman and the Swing Era*. New York: Oxford University Press, 1989.

Crow Bill Crow, *Jazz Anecdotes*. New York and Oxford: Oxford University Press, 1990.

Csida and Csida   Joseph and June Bundy Csida, *American Entertainment: A Unique History of Popular Show Business*. New York: Watson-Guptill Publications, 1978.

Dance, "Ellington"   Stanley Dance, "Duke Ellington," in the booklet notes for the three-record set *Giants of Jazz: Duke Ellington*, Time-Life Records TL-J02, 1978, pp. 3–33.

Dance, "Hodges"   Stanley Dance, "Johnny Hodges," in the booklet notes for the three-record set *Giants of Jazz: Johnny Hodges*, Time-Life Records TL-J19, 1981, pp. 3–29.

Dance, "Impressions"   Stanley Dance, "Impressions—Firsthand and Secondhand," in *Duke Ellington: His Life and Music*, ed. Peter Gammond, pp. 15–21. London: Apollo Press, 1958.

Dance, *World*   Stanley Dance, *The World of Duke Ellington*. New York: Charles Scribner's Sons, 1970. Reprint. New York: Da Capo, [1981].

Davis   Francis Davis, *Outcats: Jazz Composers, Instrumentalists, and Singers*. New York: Oxford University Press, 1990.

DEC   Duke Ellington Collection, Archives Center, National Museum of American History, Smithsonian Institution, Washington, D.C.

DEOHP   Duke Ellington Oral History Project, Archives Center, National Museum of American History, Smithsonian Institution, Washington, D.C.

DEPS   Duke Ellington Publicity Scrapbooks, Duke Ellington Collection, Archives Center, National Museum of American History, Smithsonian Institution, Washington, D.C.

Ellington/Dance   Mercer Ellington with Stanley Dance, *Duke Ellington in Person: An Intimate Memoir*. Boston: Houghton Mifflin; London: Hutchinson, 1978. Reprint. New York: Da Capo, 1979.

Ellington/Harman   Duke Ellington, interview by Carter Harman, Carter Harman Collection, Archives Center, National Museum of American History, Smithsonian Institution, Washington, D.C.

Ellington, *Music*   Duke Ellington, *Music Is My Mistress*. Garden City, New York: Doubleday, 1973. Reprint. New York: Da Capo, 1976.

Erenberg   Lewis A. Erenberg, *Steppin' Out: New York Nightlife and the Transformation of American Culture, 1890–1930*. Westport, Connecticut: Greenwood Press, 1981. Reprint. Chicago: University of Chicago Press, 1984.

Fabricant   Solomon Fabricant, *The Output of Manufacturing Industries, 1899–1937*. New York: National Bureau of Economic Research, 1940.

Feather   Leonard Feather, "Ella Meets the Duke," *Playboy*, November 1957, pp. 38–40, 68, 71–72, 77.

Furia   Philip Furia, *The Poets of Tin Pan Alley: A History of America's Great Lyricists*. New York: Oxford University Press, 1990.

Gault   Lon A. Gault, *Ballroom Echoes*. Wheaton, Illinois: Andrew Corbet Press, 1989.

George Don George, *Sweet Man: The Real Duke Ellington*. New York: G. P. Putnam's Sons, 1981.

Giddins, "Notes" Gary Giddins, "Notes on the Music," in the booklet notes for the three-record set *Giants of Jazz: Johnny Hodges*, Time-Life Records TL-J19, 1981, pp. 30–52.

Gleason Ralph J. Gleason, *Celebrating the Duke: and Louis, Bessie, Billie, Bird, Carmen, Miles, Dizzy, and Other Heroes*. Boston: Little, Brown, 1975. "The Duke," pp. 153–266.

Green, *Secret City* Constance McLaughlin Green, *The Secret City: A History of Race Relations in the Nation's Capital*. Princeton, New Jersey: Princeton University Press, 1967.

Green, *Washington* Constance McLaughlin Green, *Washington: Capital City, 1879–1950*. Princeton, New Jersey: Princeton University Press, 1963.

Greer Sonny Greer, interview by Stanley Crouch, New York City, January 23, 1979, Jazz Oral History Project, Institute of Jazz Studies, Rutgers University, Newark, New Jersey.

Hamilton, DEOHP Jimmy Hamilton, interview by Marcia Greenlee, Christiansted, St. Croix, U.S. Virgin Islands, March 26, 1991, Duke Ellington Oral History Project, Archives Center, National Museum of American History, Smithsonian Institution, Washington, D.C.

Hamilton, Yale Jimmy Hamilton, interview by Kate Setlow, St. Croix, U.S. Virgin Islands, August 28, 1983, Oral History, American Music, Yale University, New Haven, Connecticut.

Hentoff Nat Hentoff, "This Cat Needs No Pulitzer Prize," *New York Times Magazine*, September 12, 1965, pp. 64–66, 68, 70, 72, 74, 76.

Hobson [Wilder Hobson], "Introducing Duke Ellington," *Fortune* 8 (August 1933), pp. 47–49, 90, 92, 94, 95.

Hughes Langston Hughes, "Our Wonderful Society: Washington," *Opportunity* 5 (August 1927), pp. 226–27.

Jewell Derek Jewell, *Duke: A Portrait of Duke Ellington*. London: Elm Tree Books; New York: W. W. Norton, 1977.

JOHP Jazz Oral History Project, Institute of Jazz Studies, Rutgers University, Newark, New Jersey.

JWJ James Weldon Johnson Collection, Beinecke Library, Yale University, New Haven, Connecticut.

Morgenstern, *Early Ellington* Dan Morgenstern, booklet notes for the sound recording *Early Ellington*, RCA Bluebird 6852-2-RB, 1989.

Morgenstern, "Notes" Dan Morgenstern, "Notes on the Music," in the booklet notes for the three-record set *Giants of Jazz: Duke Ellington*, Time-Life Records TL-J02, 1978, pp. 34–48.

Murray Albert Murray, "Storiella Americana as She Is Swyung: Duke Ellington, the Culture of Washington D.C. and the Blues as Representative Anecdote," *Conjunctions* 16 (1991), pp. 209–19.

Nye   Russel B. Nye, "Saturday Night at the Paradise Ballroom: Or, Dance Halls in the Twenties," *Journal of Popular Culture* 7 (Summer 1973), pp. 14–22.

Schuller, *Early Jazz*   Gunther Schuller, *Early Jazz: Its Roots and Early Development*. New York: Oxford University Press, 1968.

Schuller, *Swing Era*   Gunther Schuller, *The Swing Era: The Development of Jazz, 1930–1945*. New York: Oxford University Press, 1989.

Shapiro/Hentoff   Nat Shapiro and Nat Hentoff, eds., *Hear Me Talkin' to Ya*. New York and Toronto: Rinehart, 1955. Reprint. New York: Dover Publications, 1966. "Ellington Plays the Piano, but His Real Instrument Is His Band," pp. 224–38.

Simon   George T. Simon, *The Big Bands*. Foreword by Frank Sinatra. 4th ed. New York: Schirmer Books, 1981.

Smith   Willie "The Lion" Smith with George Hoefer, *Music on My Mind: The Memoirs of an American Pianist*. Introduction by Duke Ellington. Garden City, New York: Doubleday, 1964. Reprint. New York: Da Capo, 1978.

Sommer   Sally Sommer, "Social Dance," in *The Reader's Companion to American History*, ed. Eric Foner and John A. Garraty, pp. 263–64. Boston: Houghton Mifflin, 1991.

Stearns and Stearns   Marshall and Jean Stearns, *Jazz Dance: The Story of American Vernacular Dance*. New York: Macmillan, 1968.

Stewart, *Boy*   Rex Stewart, *Boy Meets Horn*, ed. Claire P. Gordon. Ann Arbor: The University of Michigan Press, 1991.

Stewart, *Jazz Masters*   Rex Stewart, *Jazz Masters of the Thirties*. New York: Macmillan; London: Collier-Macmillan, 1972.

Stratemann   Klaus Stratemann, *Ellington Day by Day and Film by Film*. Copenhagen: JazzMedia, 1992.

Tucker   Mark Tucker, *Ellington: The Early Years*. Urbana: University of Illinois Press, 1991.

Ulanov   Barry Ulanov, *Duke Ellington*. New York: Creative Age Press, 1946. London: Musicians Press, 1947. Reprint. New York: Da Capo, 1975.

West   Hollie I. West, "The Duke at 70," *Washington Post*, April 26, 1969, Style Section.

Williams   Martin Williams, *The Jazz Tradition*. 2nd ed., rev. New York: Oxford University Press, 1983.

Yale   Oral History, American Music, Yale University, New Haven, Connecticut.

PREFACE

Page

17   *"I have two careers"*: Ulanov, p. 274.

17   *"My biggest kick in music"*: Max Jones, " 'It Was a Challenge,' Says Duke," *Melody Maker*, January 14, 1961, p. 5.

1: ENJOYING A CAPITAL CHILDHOOD, 1899–1913

Page

21 *"Edward, you are blessed"*: Ellington, *Music*, p. 15.

22 *"I was pampered and pampered"*: Ibid., p. 6.

22 *Edward Ellington devoutly loved*: Ibid., p. 12.

22 *"Because . . . no one else"*: Ibid., p. x.

23 *"He said that when"*: Boatwright.

23 *"He raised his family"*: Ellington, *Music*, p. 10.

23 *"father kept the house"*: Michael Dolan, "Duke Slept Here," *The Washingtonian*, May 1989, p. 104.

23 *"were the lighter complexioned"*: Stewart, *Boy*, p. 34.

24 *he even had his*: Tucker, p. 23.

24 *"a woman of rigorous"*: Ulanov, p. 3.

24 *many old-line families*: Theodore Hudson, personal communication, December 12, 1992.

24 *a warm, close relationship*: Jerome I. Sashin, "Duke Ellington's Life Seen as a Prime Example of Affect Tolerance," *The Psychiatric Times*, November 1988, p. 35.

24 *Edward had twenty-eight cousins*: Boyer, p. 50.

24 *Both Daisy and J.E.*: Boatwright, p. 1.

24 *"I bust out crying"*: Boyer, p. 50.

26 *his first formal training*: Tucker, p. 23.

26 *Playing baseball on Sixteenth Street*: Ellington, *Music*, p. 10.

26 *"Washington was in the American League"*: Ibid., p. 9.

26 *"putting on a show"*: Tucker, p. 23.

27 *"The shows were very good"*: Ellington, *Music*, p. 23.

27 *"how all levels could"*: Ibid., pp. 17, 23.

27 *"full of love"*: Tucker, p. 24.

28 *period from 1897 to 1901*: Rayford W. Logan, *Betrayal of the Negro. From Rutherford B. Hayes to Woodrow Wilson*. New York: Collier Books, 1965, p. 74.

28 *In 1900, to serve*: Green, *Secret City*, p. 131.

28 *Between 1900 and 1909,*: Green, *Washington*, p. 210.

28 *Jobs in other fields*: Ibid., p. 211.

28 *Trade unions discriminated*: Florette Henri, *Black Migration: Movement North, 1900–1920*. New York: Anchor Press/Doubleday, 1975, p. 257.

29 *"I have recently spent"*: Green, *Secret City*, p. 173.

29 *"the undisputed center"*: Green, *Washington*, p. viii.

29 *"a higher standard of culture"*: Paul Laurence Dunbar, "Negro Life in Washington," *Harper's Weekly*, January 13, 1900, p. 32.

Ellington's Washington: Monumental, Ironical—and Inspirational?
Page
30 *"Washington is one of the most"*: Hughes, p. 227.
32 *"Never before, anywhere"*: Hughes, p. 226.
32 *a middle class:* Donald R. Kennon and Richard Striner, *Washington Past and Present: A Guide to the Nation's Capital.* 2nd ed. Washington, D.C.: The United States Capitol Historical Society, 1983, p. 45.
32 *"I don't know how many"*: Ellington, *Music,* p. 17.
32 *"the indisputable differentiation"*: Stewart, *Boy,* p. 34.
32 *Washington, D.C.—all them pretty girls:* Greer, p. 14.
33 *"everywhere you go"*: Hollie I. West, "The Duke at 70: Honor from the President," *Washington Post,* April 27, 1969, Style Section.
33 *"What one did"*: Theodore Hudson, personal communication, December 12, 1992.
33 *Jazz pianist Billy Taylor:* Tucker, pp. 24–25.
33 *"was a norm"*: Boatwright, p. 49.
33 *"The driving power"*: Ellington, *Music,* p. 45.
33 *"was born and raised among people"*: Murray, p. 212.
33 *They taught him and Ruth:* Tucker, p. 24.

2: STARTING A CAREER, 1913–23
Page
34 *M Street High School:* Sandra Fitzpatrick and Maria R. Goodwin, *The Guide to Black Washington: Places and Events of Historical and Cultural Significance in the Nation's Capital.* Introduction by Adele Logan Alexander. New York: Hippocrene Books, 1990, pp. 88–89.
34 *"a kind of rough high school"*: Ellington/Dance, p. 9.
35 *sale of pianos hit:* Fabricant, p. 319 notes that upright pianos reached their U.S. sales peak in 1909, player pianos in 1923, and grand pianos in 1925. See also John Edward Hasse, "Ragtime: From the Top," in *Ragtime: Its History, Composers, and Music,* ed. John Edward Hasse, p. 15. New York: Schirmer Books; London: Macmillan, 1985.
35 *"Back in those days"*: Ellington/Dance, p. 10.
35 *"We had two pianos"*: Dolan, pp. 104–5.
36 *"ragtime had an unspeakable connotation"*: Stewart, *Boy,* p. 28.
36 *Ellington was beginning:* Ulanov, p. 14.
36 *"I cannot tell you"*: Ruby Goodwin, "Meet the Duke," *The Bronzeman* 9 (August 1932), p. 20.
36 *"He was swinging"*: Ellington, *Music,* p. 20.
36 *"I played piano by ear then"*: "Ellington, at 14, Wrote First Song of Long List," *Buffalo Times,* June 18, 1933, in DEPS.
37 *"Oh, I was a great listener!"*: Ellington, *Music,* p. 26.
37 *Washington bred many fine pianists:* Ibid., p. 24.

37 *"Those ragtime pianists sounded"*: Ulanov, p. 14.
37 *took a job as a soda jerk:* Sanford Socolow, comp., "The Summer Job I Had as a Boy," *Esquire*, June 1958, pp. 55, 66.
37 *We had a piano player:* "Ellington, at 14."
37 *I began by tinkering:* "The Summer Job."
38 *"a pretty good 'hug-and-rubbin' "*: Ellington, *Music*, p. 20.
38 *Tried it on the sofa:* Brooks Kerr, telephone interview by the author, September 1, 1991.
38 *Edgar McEntree:* Ellington, *Music*, p. 20.
38 *"an elegant cat":* Ellington/Harman.
38 *"when you were playing piano":* Ibid., p. 22.
39 *less a completed composition:* Tucker, p. 41.
39 *His unsuspecting listeners:* Boyer, p. 51.
39 *These recyclings:* Tucker, p. 39.
39 *black artists' tradition of "signifying"*: Henry Louis Gates, Jr., *The Signifying Monkey: A Theory of African-American Literary Criticism.* New York and Oxford: Oxford University Press, 1988, p. 66.
39 *These ragtime and "animal" steps:* Stearns and Stearns, pp. 98–99.
39 *These percussive steps:* Sommer, pp. 263–64.
39 *To accommodate the mushrooming:* Erenberg, pp. 146–47, 153, 155–58.
40 *I don't think there were many:* Stewart, *Boy*, p. 33.
40 *Sometimes he would steal:* Ellington/Dance, pp. 20–21.
40 *His grades were average to poor:* Academic transcript for Edward Ellington, Armstrong Manual Training School, Washington, D.C., February 1914–January 1917.
40 *"There were a lot of great":* West, p. 10.
41 *"He was terrific":* Boyer, p. 51.
41 *"by men like James P. Johnson":* Ellington, *Music*, pp. 416–17.
41 *"Every time I reached a point":* Ibid., p. x.
41 *"He was my piano parent":* Ibid., p. 28.
42 *Perry and fellow pianist:* Tucker, pp. 45–46.
42 *"Brown had unbelievable technique":* Ellington, *Music*, p. 26.
43 *"Music is everything":* Ibid., pp. 212–13.
43 *Ellington still had much to learn:* Ulanov, p. 20.
43 *And Wooding fired him:* Ibid., p. 17.
44 *The latter tradition:* Edward A. Berlin, "Ragtime and Improvised Piano: Another View," *Journal of Jazz Studies* 4 (Spring/Summer 1977) pp. 4–10.
44 *The next year:* Tucker, pp. 53–54.
44 *"I played my first date":* Gwen Dobson, "Luncheon with . . . Duke Ellington," *Washington Evening Star*, April 23, 1971.
45 *"I can still see":* Stewart, *Jazz Masters*, p. 82.
46 *"disciplinary climate":* Ellington, *Music*, pp. 53–54.
46 *"a Washington pattern":* Ulanov, p. 13.

46 *By March of 1918:* Tucker, p. 53.
46 *Sometime in about 1918:* Ellington, *Music,* pp. 30–31.
46 *"All of a sudden":* George Hoefer, "Duke Ellington, Society Band-leader," *Washington Post Potomac,* May 20, 1962, p. 12.
47 *Other times, they would drive:* Ellington/Harman, April 1956.
47 *Playing for this stratum:* Mark Tucker, "The Early Years of Edward Kennedy "Duke" Ellington, 1899–1927," Ph.D. diss., University of Michigan, 1986, p. 124.
47 *"From then on":* Ellington/Dance, pp. 14–15.
49 *"When customers came":* Ellington, *Music,* p. 32.
49 *"There was too much pulling":* Davis, p. 6.
49 *"I was beginning to catch on":* Ellington, *Music,* p. 33.
49 *He found an ideal teacher:* Tucker, p. 61.
50 *"the whole thing suddenly":* Ellington, *Music,* p. 33.
50 *There were lynchings:* Arthur F. Raper, *The Tragedy of Lynching.* Chapel Hill: University of North Carolina Press, 1933, p. 481.
51 *"From the moment I was introduced":* Dance, *World,* p. 62.
51 *"In those days," Rex Stewart:* Stewart, *Boy,* p. 152.
51 *"had Black Bowie":* Ellington/Dance, p. 33.
52 *At the Howard, Ellington's band:* Tucker, pp. 65–66.
53 *"This was a wild area":* Stewart, *Boy,* p. 7.
54 *"There was a dance somewhere":* Stewart, *Boy,* p. 33.
54 *sounded great to us kids:* Stewart, *Jazz Masters,* p. 81.
55 *"You've got to listen":* Ellington, *Music,* p. 34.
55 *Then, probably on November 25, 1921:* Tucker, p. 74, citing *Chicago Defender,* December 3, 1921.
55 *Ellington, "scared stiff":* Ellington, *Music,* p. 34.
56 *"I took him out":* Shapiro/Hentoff, p. 228.
56 *"What I absorbed on that occasion":* Ellington, *Music,* p. 34.
56 *"Throughout his whole life":* Ellington/Dance, p. 26.
56 *"The jazz band battle":* Stewart, *Boy,* p. 33.
56 *"I can see the scene":* Ibid., p. 35.
57 *"Whenever we had a contest":* Shapiro/Hentoff, p. 228.
57 *"It was well dressed":* Ellington, *Music,* p. 35.
57 *"So I come in there and started":* Greer, p. 13.
57 *"Harlem, in our minds":* Ellington, *Music,* p. 36.

3: SEEKING SPECIAL SOUNDS, 1923–27

Page

61 *"The world's most glamorous":* George Hoefer, booklet notes to the three-record anthology *The Sound of Harlem,* Columbia C3L 33, 1964, p. [1].
61 *"I had never seen":* Calloway, p. 68.

61 *Between 1910 and 1920:* Cary D. Wintz, *Black Culture and the Harlem Renaissance.* Houston: Rice University Press, 1988, pp. 20, 22.

62 *"It is a Mecca":* James Weldon Johnson, *Black Manhattan.* New York: Alfred A. Knopf, 1940, p. 3.

63 *"Those of us in the music":* Calloway, pp. 105–6.

65 *"an announcement, an overture":* Arna Bontemps, "The Awakening: A Memoir," in *The Harlem Renaissance Remembered,* ed. Arna Bontemps, p. 5. New York: Dodd, Mead, 1972.

66 *The irresistible Charleston:* Sommer, p. 264.

66 *In 1923, New York City:* Allen, p. 116.

66 *"Dancing," wrote the Ladies Home Journal:* Nye, p. 19, and MacDonald Smith Moore, *Yankee Blues: Musical Culture and American Identity.* Bloomington: Indiana University Press, 1985, p. 86.

66 *"emblems of 1920s values":* Lewis A. Erenberg, "From New York to Middletown: Repeal and the Legitimization of Nightlife in the Great Depression," *American Quarterly* 38 (Winter 1986), pp. 761–63.

66 *Both periodicals answered:* Anne Shaw Faulkner, "Does Jazz Put the Sin in Syncopation?" *Ladies Home Journal,* August 1921, pp. 16, 34; Anne Shaw Faulkner, "Does Jazz Cause Crime?" *Musical Observer,* August 1924, p. 24.

66 *White religious periodicals:* Neil Leonard, *Jazz and the White Americans: The Acceptance of a New Art Form.* Chicago: University of Chicago Press, 1962, p. 34.

66 *"the music that somebody likes":* Ellington/Harman, May 27, 1964.

67 *Most of the Negro population:* Bushell, p. 19.

67 *"the glitter of more substantial":* Roi Ottley and William J. Weatherby, *The Negro in New York: An Informal Social History, 1626–1940.* Preface by James Baldwin. New York: Praeger Publishers, 1967, p. 292.

67 *"Americans shared a common perception":* Kathy J. Ogren, *The Jazz Revolution: Twenties America and the Meaning of Jazz.* New York: Oxford University Press, 1989, pp. 6–7.

68 *In the early 1920s:* Tucker, p. 140.

68 *"When I began my work":* Gunnar Askland, "Interpretations in Jazz: A Conference with Duke Ellington," *Etude,* March 1947, pp. 134, 172.

68 *The band sat on stage:* Tucker, p. 81.

68 *By day, they went around Harlem:* Ellington, *Music,* p. 36.

69 *"good-looking, well-mannered":* Smith, pp. 149–50.

69 *Ellington tagged along:* Ibid., p. 151.

69 *After the gig ended:* Tucker, pp. 84–85.

69 *was house-rent parties:* Ottley and Weatherby, *The Negro in New York,* p. 249.

70 *They would crowd a hundred:* Smith, p. 157.

70 *"In New York the gigs":* George, p. 44.

70 *Besides Ellington, the pianists:* Smith, p. 154.

71 *"We would embroider":* Ibid., p. 155.

71 *Growing out of ragtime:* Lawrence Koch, "Piano," in *The New Grove Dictionary of Jazz*, ed. Barry Kernfeld, vol. 2, p. 310. London: Macmillan Press, 1988; New York: Grove's Dictionaries of Music, 1988.

71 *"we were getting more bored":* Ellington, *Music*, p. 37.

71 *" 'Course," he would say:* Burt Korall, "The Roots of the Duchy," *Down Beat*, July 13, 1967, p. 21.

71 *"We got to Washington":* Boyer, p. 53.

72 *Leaving his family again:* Ellington, *Music*, p. 69.

72 *"It was summertime":* Ellington/Harman, April 1956.

72 *"A hundred-dollar bill":* Konrad Bercovici, quoted in Jervis Anderson, *This Was Harlem: A Cultural Portrait, 1900–1950.* New York: Farrar, Straus & Giroux, 1982, p. 172.

72 *The band, Ellington recalled:* Hentoff/Shapiro, p. 230.

72 *"We used to get about thirty dollars":* Ellington/Harman, April 1956.

72 *After getting established:* Collier, *Ellington*, p. 44.

72 *In 1923, New York:* Tucker, p. 91.

72 *In the summer of 1923:* Ibid.

73 *By this time, Ellington:* Ellington, *Music*, p. 70.

73 *In August 1923:* "New York News," *Pittsburgh Courier*, August 18, 1923, p. 10.

73 *There were probably very few:* Philip T. Rosen, *The Modern Stentors: Radio Broadcasters and the Federal Government, 1920–1934.* Contributions in Economics and Economic History, number 31. Westport, Connecticut: Greenwood Press, 1980, p. 113.

73 *In the summer of 1923:* Tucker, pp. 94–95.

73 *Elmer Snowden:* Ibid., p. 98.

74 *"that our music acquired":* Ellington, *Music*, p. 71.

75 *the bandstand was up:* Smith, p. 173.

75 *"one of them back-in-the-hole":* Greer, p. 54.

75 *The club could hold:* Morgenstern, "Notes," p. 14.

75 *"We paid quite a lot of attention":* Ellington, *Music*, p. 70.

75 *"This colored band":* Abel Green, "The Washingtonians," *New York Clipper*, November 23, 1923, p. 12.

75 *to finish at Armstrong:* Chester Nerges, "Blue Notes," *Chicago Defender*, local edition, August 1, 1931, p. 6.

75 *"Our band changed character":* Shapiro/Hentoff, p. 231.

76 *"three basic elements":* Ellington/Dance, p. 25.

76 *his "tonal character":* Ellington, *Music*, p. 70.

77 *Miley also played mellophone:* Tucker, p. 102.

77 *Ellington continued to try his hand:* Ibid., p. 103.

77 *Late in December 1923:* J. A. Jackson, "Picked Up by the Page," *Billboard*, December 22, 1923, p. 54.

79 *"I got most of my instruction"*: Boyer, p. 54.

79 *Cook, who after failing:* S. Frederick Starr, "Oberlin's Ragtimer: Will Marion Cook," *Oberlin Alumni Magazine* 85 (Fall 1989), p. 14. See also Marva Griffin Carter, "The Life and Music of Will Marion Cook," Ph.D. diss., University of Illinois at Urbana-Champaign, 1988.

79 *"First you find the logical"*: Ellington, *Music*, p. 97.

79 *The idea was:* Tucker, p. 106.

79 *In April 1924:* Ibid., p. 184.

80 *"business would get slack"*: Greer, p. 40.

80 *During this hiatus:* Tucker, p. 106.

80 *At the Kentucky Club:* Ibid., p. 116.

80 *Then after sending the band:* Ellington, *Music*, p. 72.

80 *"I was making good money"*: Greer, p. 20.

80 *"The Kentucky Club was something"*: Ibid., p. 19.

80 *"we . . . stayed open"*: Ibid., pp. 18–19.

81 *"Bechet and Bubber"*: Ellington, *Music*, p. 47.

81 *"Paul Whiteman would bring"*: Greer, p. 18.

81 *Also, the orchestra was one:* Dance, *World*, pp. 65–66.

81 *"The Washingtonians"*: Tucker, p. 118.

82 *"He had a big proposition"*: Ellington, *Music*, p. 71.

82 *They wrote at least four songs:* Tucker, p. 121.

82 *tour in Europe:* Horst P. Bergmeier, "Sam Wooding Recapitulated," *Storyville* 74 (December 1977–January 1978) p. 45.

82 *He said it made publisher:* Ellington, *Music*, p. 71; Ellington/Harman, April 1956.

82 *In any event, The Washingtonians:* Tucker, p. 136.

83 *While Ellington's group:* Ibid., p. 137.

83 *"Louis Armstrong, Don Redman"*: Ibid., p. 168.

84 *"a moderately accomplished"*: Ibid., p. 170.

84 *"Tricky possessed the gift"*: Stewart, *Jazz Masters*, p. 104.

84 *"got great pleasure from playing"*: Dance, *World*, p. 74.

84 *He opted not to hire:* Ellington/Dance, p. 66.

85 *"All these people were valuable"*: Ellington, *Music*, p. 108.

85 *"He knew your limits"*: Bigard, p. 63.

85 *"You can't write music"*: Boyer, p. 38.

85 *"You've got to write"*: Clifford A. Ridley, "The Duke's Dominion Was All of Music," *New York Post*, June 1, 1974.

85 *"like all who were close"*: Irving Townsend, "Ellington in Private," *Atlantic*, May 1975, p. 80.

86 *The Washingtonians opened on July 12:* Tucker, pp. 187–88.

86 *The tour proved successful:* Ibid., p. 190.

86 *Nuttings-on-the-Charles:* Gault, pp. 97, 190.

86 *"public dancing in America"*: Nye, p. 15.

86 *"Huge, brilliantly lighted"*: Ibid., p. 17.
86 *The most celebrated dance palaces*: Gault, pp. 13–27, 31–35, 36–40, 43–46, 49–51, 53–54, 139–40, 141–44, 148–50, 238–43, 283–89.
87 *The Washingtonians returned to New York*: Tucker, p. 194.
87 *In March 1926*: Allen, p. 169.
88 *"When I first formed"*: Ellington, *Music*, p. 419.
88 *It was probably in the fall*: Tucker, pp. 197–98.
89 *"We were very aggressive"*: Irving Mills, interview by the author, Palm Springs, California, February 2, 1984.
89 *"This was," said Ellington*: Ellington, *Music*, p. 73.
89 *While a number of Jews*: See Kenneth Aaron Kanter, *The Jews of Tin Pan Alley: The Jewish Contribution to American Popular Music, 1830–1940*. New York: Ktav Publishing House; Cincinnati: American Jewish Archives, 1982.
90 *Probably formalized by 1928*: Ulanov, p. 58; Tucker, p. 198.
90 *In addition, this arrangement*: Collier, *Ellington*, p. 70.
90 *"practically everything we wrote"*: Ellington quoted in Robert Levi, booklet notes to the Duke Ellington recording *Reminiscing in Tempo*, Columbia Legacy CK 48654, 1991, p. 6.
90 *"Those old Negroes"*: Duke Ellington, "My Hunt for Song Titles," *Rhythm*, August 1933, p. 23.
91 *Besides Brunswick*: Tucker, pp. 199–200.
92 *And his compositions were copyrighted*: Ibid., p. 200.
92 *"Our aim as a dance orchestra"*: Ellington, "My Hunt," pp. 22–23.
93 *Take any 1920s record*: Morgenstern, *Early Ellington*, pp. [7–8].
93 *"a very well-behaved"*: Ellington, *Music*, p. 111.
93 *"His massive tone"*: Ellington/Dance, pp. 65–66.
94 *"pulling the single strings"*: Ibid., p. 16.
94 *"Duke Ellington and His Washingtonians"*: Tucker, p.202, citing *Salem Evening News*, May 21, 1927.
94 *"taking the territory"*: W.E.B., *New York Tribune*, August 7, 1927, p. 20.
94 *Unless he had an afternoon gig*: Ibid.
95 *"Both in the orchestra pit"*: "Theatregoers Acclaim Clarence Robinson's New Revue, 'Jazzmania,' " *New York Age*, October 15, 1927, p. 6.
95 *Third, in November*: "Adelaide Hall Delights in 'Dance Mania' at The Lafayette Theatre," *New York Age*, November 19, 1927, p. 6.

Essential Ellington, 1926–27
Page
96 *"actually changed my life"*: Morgenstern, *Early Ellington*, p. [6].
97 *Evidently Bubber Miley*: Schuller, *Early Jazz*, p. 330.

4: COMPOSING AT THE COTTON CLUB, 1927–31

Page

98 *"Night Life is cut out"*: Ellington, *Music*, p. 63.

98 *In the fall of 1927*: Ulanov, p. 66; Bushell, p. 73.

98 *By banjoist Fred Guy's account*: John McDonough, "Reminiscing in Tempo: Guitarist Freddy Guy's Ellington Memories," *Down Beat*, April 17, 1969, p. 16.

99 *By Ellington's account*: Ellington, *Music*, pp. 75–76.

100 *"Be big or you'll be dead"*: Boyer, p. 55.

The Cotton Club, "The Aristocrat of Harlem"

Page

101 *Located on the second floor*: Edward Jablonski, *Harold Arlen: Happy with the Blues*. Garden City, New York: Doubleday, 1961. Reprint. New York: Da Capo, 1986, p. 53.

101 *"There were brutes at the door"*: Ibid., pp. 53–54.

101 *During Ellington's tenure*: Advertising flyer headlined "Breaking All Records!" New York: The Cotton Club, 1930. Calloway papers.

102 *"Entr'acte: Dance"*: Ibid.

102 *It was a huge room*: Calloway, p. 88.

102 *"The floor shows at the Cotton"*: Marshall Stearns, *The Story of Jazz*. 2nd ed. New York: Oxford University Press, 1958, p. 133.

102 *The job of chorus girl*: Stratemann, p. 10.

102 *"Them girls stopped the show"*: Greer, p. 67.

103 *The sets and costumes*: Calloway, p. 88.

103 *the spring 1929 review*: Abel [Green], "Cotton Club (Harlem)," *Variety*, April 3, 1929, p. 65.

103 *"50—most beautiful Creoles"*: Cotton Club advertising flyer, "Breaking All Records!" Calloway papers.

103 *"I can't say I was too much impressed"*: Shapiro/Hentoff, p. 235.

104 *Ellington's first Cotton Club revue*: Abel [Green], "Night Club Reviews: Cotton Club (New York)," *Variety*, December 7, 1927, pp. 54, 56.

104 *It is the foremost*: Ibid.

105 *When we got to the Cotton Club*: Dance, *World*, p. 67.

105 *"I am a man of the theater"*: Charles Fox, "Duke Ellington, *Flaming Youth*," in Max Harrison, Charles Fox, and Eric Thacker, *The Essential Jazz Records, Volume 1: Ragtime to Swing*, p. 191. Discographies, number 12. Westport, Connecticut: Greenwood Press, 1984.

106 *"Too weird"*: George Hoefer, booklet notes to the three-record anthology *The Sound of Harlem*, Columbia C3L 33, 1964, p. [30].

107 *Ellington "moved away"*: Mark Tucker, "Ellington's 'Jungle Music,' " in *Duke Ellington and New Orleans*, ed. Caroline Richmond, p. 14. Ascona, Switzerland: Festa New Orleans Music Productions, 1989.

108 *"the formal problem of jazz arrangement"*: André Hodeir and Gunther

Schuller, "Duke Ellington," in *The New Grove Dictionary of Jazz*, ed. Barry Kernfeld, vol. 1, p. 332. London: Macmillan Press; New York: Grove's Dictionaries of Music, 1988.

108 *"learned to exploit"*: Ibid.

109 *"prolonged workshop period"*: Schuller, *Early Jazz*, p. 348.

109 *"You know what?"*: Simon, p. 187.

109 Variety *dubbed them:* "Last of the Big Timers," *Variety*, February 22, 1928, p. 27.

110 *he was a light-skinned product:* "Duke's Clarinettist Barney Bigard," in *Duke Ellington and New Orleans*, ed. Caroline Richmond, p. 10. Ascona, Switzerland: Festa New Orleans Music Productions, 1989.

110 *read difficult parts easily:* Ibid.

110 *Bigard had a beautiful sound:* Ibid.; Lewis Porter, "Barney Bigard," in *The New Grove Dictionary of Jazz*, ed. Barry Kernfeld, vol. 1, p. 108. London: Macmillan Press; New York: Grove's Dictionaries of Music, 1988.

110 *" 'I want you to join my band' ":* Bigard, p. 45.

111 *"We were doing real good":* Ibid., p. 49.

111 *"A great organization man":* Ellington, *Music*, p. 54.

111 *Someone nicknamed him:* Chester Nerges, "Blue Notes," *Chicago Defender*, local edition, August 1, 1931, p. 6.

111 *by February 1928:* "N.B.C.'s 56 Network Stations," *Variety*, February 29, 1928, p. 57.

112 *Sales of radio receivers:* Fabricant, p. 573.

112 *Most such opportunities:* Morgenstern, *Early Ellington*, p. [8].

112 *"One of the hottest bands":* Abel [Green], "Radio Rambles," *Variety*, March 21, 1928, p. 69.

112 *"From the Cotton Club":* Greer, pp. 61–62.

112 *"Duke Ellington and his heated jazzpators":* Abel Green, "Ellington Subdued," *Variety*, March 21, 1928.

112 *"The band was becoming":* Bigard, p. 49.

113 *"People would ask me":* Ellington, *Music*, p. 82.

113 *"Charlie Johnson's Paradise Band":* Schuller, *Early Jazz*, pp. 269–70.

113 *In 1928, an exciting new dance step:* Sommer, p. 264.

113 *"a strutting step":* Pauline Norton, "Lindy," in *The New Grove Dictionary of American Music*, ed. H. Wiley Hitchcock and Stanley Sadie, vol. 3, p. 88. London: Macmillan Press; New York: Grove's Dictionaries of Music, 1986.

114 *"That idea of taking a residential":* "Is This Really Harlem?," *Amsterdam News*, October 23, 1929, p. 9. Reprinted in *Harlem on My Mind: Cultural Capital of Black America, 1900–1978*, ed. Allen Schoener, p. 79. New York: Dell, 1979.

114 *"That part was degrading":* Quoted in Robert Sylvester, *No Cover*

Charge: A Backward Look at the Night Clubs. New York: Dial Press, 1956, pp. 47–48.

114 *By 1929, there were:* "Is This Really Harlem?" in *Harlem on My Mind*, p. 80.

114 *"It is a glittering pageant":* Program brochure, *Cotton Club Show Boat.* New York: The Cotton Club, 1928. Calloway papers.

114 *a real production:* Advertising flyer, *Hot Chocolate.* New York: The Cotton Club, 1928. Calloway papers.

115 *"a snappy and colorful revue":* "The Supper Clubs," *New York Evening Post,* October 13, 1928.

115 *"weird chords that would come":* Bigard, p. 47.

116 *"Duke was a real good leader":* Ibid., p. 48.

116 *"Finally," Bigard recalled:* Ibid., p. 52.

116 *"The reason why [Ellington]":* Cootie Williams, interview by Helen Dance, New York City, May 1976, JOHP, p. 88.

116 *Miley, along with Nanton:* Abel [Green], "Disk Reviews," *Variety,* May 9, 1928, p. 77.

116 *As Martin Williams has observed:* Williams, p. 110.

118 *Variety found the show:* "Night Club Reviews: Cotton Club," *Variety,* April 3, 1929, p. 65.

118 *present to "the public a great":* Irving Mills, "I Split with Duke When Music Began Sidetracking," *Down Beat,* November 5, 1952, p. 6.

118 *Mills wanted to spotlight:* Tucker, p. 201.

119 *That summer:* Stratemann, p. 14.

119 *"a rare example of":* David Meeker, *Jazz in the Movies.* 2nd ed. New York: Da Capo, 1981, p. [unpaginated: see entry for *Black and Tan*].

119 *The motion-picture executives:* Ernie Smith, "Films," in *The New Grove Dictionary of Jazz,* ed. Barry Kernfeld, vol. 1, p. 376. London: Macmillan Press; New York: Grove's Dictionaries of Music, 1988

119 *On June 20:* Bordman, pp. 451–52.

119 *Through the recommendation:* Charles Schwartz, *Gershwin: His Life and Music.* New York and Indianapolis: Bobbs-Merrill Co., 1973, p. 178. Edward Jablonski, *Gershwin: A Biography.* New York: Doubleday, 1987, pp. 188–92.

122 *"Duke Ellington's colored jazz":* "Plays on Broadway: 'Show Girl,'" *Variety,* July 7, 1929, p. 47.

122 *"The guys were sitting":* Ellington/Dance, p. 45.

122 *It was probably foolish of me:* Advertising postcard headlined "Ziegfeld Is Angry!" New York: The Cotton Club, 1929. Calloway papers.

122 *the victim of heaviness:* Bordman, p. 453.

122 *"valuable in terms of both":* Ellington, *Music*, p. 77.

122 *"For their spot in this show":* Ellington/Dance, p. 45.

123 *"valuable lectures":* Ellington, *Music*, p. 98.

124 *"Had jazz not been so stanch"*: [Hobson], p. 90.
125 *On March 2, 1930*: "Duke Ellington to Make National Tour," *Chicago Defender*, June 28, 1930, p. 5.
125 *" 'The Black Berries of 1930' premiere"*: Lee Posner, "Clubs Around the Town," *New York Morning Telegraph*, March 5, 1930.
126 *"This was about the only time"*: Ellington, *Music*, p. 77.
126 *"Chevalier is aided"*: *New York Daily News*, quoted in Cotton Club advertising flyer headlined "Never Before!" New York: The Cotton Club, 1930. Calloway papers.
126 *The orchestra played*: Robert Garland, *New York Telegram*, March 31, 1930; program, *An Evening with Maurice Chevalier*, p.17, JWJ.
126 *"I didn't know"*: Unidentified clipping, Ellington vertical file, Institute of Jazz Studies, Rutgers University, Newark, New Jersey.
126 *Ellington was booked to play*: "At Harlem Theatres," *Amsterdam News*, April 30, 1930; "At Harlem Theatres," *Amsterdam News*, May 7, 1930.
127 Variety *found the band*: *Variety*, May 21, 1930.
128 *"Couple of ofays"*: Ulanov, p. 83.
129 *For* Check and Double Check: "Duke Asks $10,000 for 2d Picture," *Chicago Defender*, May 16, 1931, p. 5.
129 *Later, Mercer Ellington: Reminiscing in Tempo*, public television documentary produced by Robert Levi, 1991.
129 *"down so many darned barriers"*: Calloway, p. 106.
129 *But reportedly both Ellington and Edna*: Collier, *Ellington*, p. 102.
131 *"I came home from school"*: Davis, p. 6.
131 *"a citadel of stately"*: David Levering Lewis, *When Harlem Was in Vogue*. New York: Alfred A. Knopf, 1981, p. 217.
131 *"On Sugar Hill"*: A. Clayton Powell, Jr., "Powell Says Rent Too High," *New York Post*, March 28, 1935, reprinted in *Harlem on My Mind*, p. 137.
131 *"would be out there writing"*: Ellington/Dance, p. 28.
131 *"Hail the Conquering Hero"*: Table card headlined "Hail the Conquering Hero." New York: The Cotton Club, 1930. Calloway papers.
131 *"Those shows by Arlen"*: Calloway, p. 93.
132 *"Dorothy Fields wasn't really funky"*: Ibid., pp. 93, 96.
132 *"I had always considered myself"*: Ibid., p. 91.
132 *"Monster fall opening"*: Advertising flyer. New York: The Roseland Ballroom, 1930, in DEPS.
133 *"most profound change"*: Gilbert Osofsky, *Harlem: The Making of a Ghetto; Negro New York, 1890–1930*. New York: Harper & Row, 1966, p. 135.
133 *By late in 1929*: "Bandleaders Commercially Rated by Broadcasters for Air Values," *Variety*, November 27, 1929, p. 65.
133 *In September, Ellington landed*: Richard L. Baltimore, "Radio News and Programs," *Amsterdam News*, September 24, 1930, p. 10.

133 *aired popular entertainment:* Philip T. Rosen, *The Modern Stentors: Radio Broadcasters and the Federal Government, 1920–1934.* Contributions in Economics and Economic History, number 31. Westport, Connecticut: Greenwood Press, 1980, p. 116.

134 *"The first tune I ever":* Duke Ellington, "My Hunt for Song Titles," *Rhythm,* August 1933, p. 23.

134 *"The next day":* Ellington, *Music,* p. 79.

Ellington's Musical Sources: A Treasury of Traditions
Page

135 *"my strongest influences":* Ellington/Harman, May 30, 1964.

135 *"high-affect combinations":* Robert Ferris Thompson, *African Art in Motion: Icon and Act in the Collection of Katherine Coryton White.* Los Angeles: University of California Press, 1974, pp. 13, 22.

137 *"I don't believe a man":* Ellington, *Music,* p. xx.

137 *"symphonic devices":* André Hodeir and Gunther Schuller, "Duke Ellington," in *The New Grove Dictionary of Jazz,* ed. Barry Kernfield, vol. 1, p. 334. London: Macmillan Press; New York: Grove's Dictionaries of Music, 1988.

Essential Ellington; 1927–31
Page

142 *In* Old Man Blues: Schuller, *Early Jazz,* p. 350.

142 *As Gunther Schuller has asserted:* Gunther Schuller, "Duke Ellington as a Major American Composer," unpublished lecture presented to the College Music Society, Washington, D.C., October 27, 1990.

143 *"as close as an arrangement":* Morgenstern, "Notes," p. 38.

5: TAKING THE ROAD, 1931–35
Page

144 *Ellington took with him:* Bigard, p. 52.

144 *"what bus, train or boat":* Ibid., p. 52.

145 *Until this time:* Eric Townley, "Reminiscing with Cootie," *Storyville* 71 (June–July 1977), p. 172.

145 *had been sent over from the Grand Terrace:* Dance, "Ellington," p. 23.

145 *"bossing the poker game":* Stewart, *Boy,* p. 177.

147 *"His is a band":* Rob Reel, "Ellington Band, Corking Film on Bang-Up Bill," *Chicago American,* February 18, 1931; in DEPS.

147 *In the first show:* The Scribe, "S.R.O. Signs When Duke Plays in Loop," *Chicago Defender,* February 21, 1931, p. 5.

147 *Due largely to Ellington:* "Lacking Stage Name, Oriental Slides to $26,000 as Chicago with Vallee Leaps Up to $60,000," *Variety,* February 25, 1931, p. 68.

147 *After Chicago, they went:* "Ellington's Dance Tour," in DEPS.
147 *In Detroit:* "Records Fall with Duke at the Michigan," *Chicago Defender*, March 28, 1931, p. 5.
147 *"the biggest sensation ever":* "Duke Ellington Packs Palace; Special Show," *Peoria Journal Transcript*, March 29, 1931; in DEPS.
147 *After the Publix tour:* "NBC to Send D. Ellington on Long Tour," *Chicago Defender*, April 26, 1931, p. 5.
147 *"rush at you with":* W. Ward Marsh, "Duke Ellington Burns 'Em Up," *Cleveland Plain Dealer*, July 6, 1931; in DEPS.
148 *Back in Chicago:* "The Duke Ellington News," August 19, 1931, in DEPS.
148 *Ellington was seen:* Clifford W. MacKay, "Going Backstage with the Scribe," *Chicago Defender*, August 1, 1931, p. 5; Rob Roy, "Jack Ellis Gets the York Grand Tavern Roadhouse," *Chicago Defender*, August 13, 1932, p. 5.
148 *A long-standing enmity:* "Refuses Pleas That Clerical Error Is Cause," *Chicago Defender*, September 5, 1931, p. 5.
148 *"When the kidnapping party":* Joseph Kastner, "The Music in This Volume," in book accompanying the three-record set *The Swing Era: One More Time*, Time-Life Records STL 353, 1972, p. 56.
148 *"Being a married man":* "Duke Denies Masher Role," *Chicago Review*, August 26, 1931; in DEPS.
149 *"Handsome in his square shouldered":* John Del Valle, "Duke Ellington Here, Composes African Saga," *San Francisco Call-Bulletin.* [probably in February 1932], in DEPS.
150 *"We violate more laws":* Ibid.
150 *"My own music, if you wish":* "Ellington Talks About His Band; 'Got Rhythm,' " *Columbus Dispatch*, August 22, 1934, in DEPS.
150 *August of 1931:* "Colored Band Wins Over Publix Circuit," *Motion Picture Herald*, August 8, 1931, p. 168.
150 *During this period, Ellington:* "Off the Air," *New York World-Telegram*, October 17, 1931.
150 *But this absence from:* "Famous Dance Orchestra Has Been Engaged," *Indianapolis Times*, [n.d.], in DEPS.
150 *"I do not think":* unidentified article, *Bridgeport* [Connecticut] *Herald*, January 13, 1935, in DEPS.
151 *The African-American press:* "Where's Hoover's Picture," *Cleveland Gazette*, October 10, 1931.
151 *In Philadelphia, Ellington encountered:* "Ellington Flees Thugs," *Philadelphia Afro-American*, October 3, 1931; unidentified article with no source in DEPS.
151 *"he was accorded all of the respect":* "Duke Ellington Figths [*sic*] Jim Crow in St. Louis," [no source], December 1931, in DEPS.

151 *"received with overwhelming success"*: Aileen Eckstein, "Wave Lengths," *Pittsburgh Courier*, February 4, 1933, section 2, p. 6.

151 *By this time, Ellington's growing*: William H. Smallwood, " 'The Duke Comes to Town'—Huge Crowds Greet Him," *Washington* [?], October 2, 1931, p. 15; "Answering Fan Mail Costs Duke Ellington $50. Month," *Afro-American*, February 16, 1935, p. 9, both in DEPS.

152 *"trouble-shooter, office and personnel"*: Ellington/Dance, p. 36.

152 *"Two applicants for a guide"*: "Tidbits," *Los Angeles Examiner*, June 27, 1933, in DEPS.

152 *"Duke Ellington is notable"*: Constant Lambert, "Gramophone Notes," *New Statesman and Nation*, August 1, 1931, p. 150.

152 *Ellington won the contest*: Floyd G. Snelson, Jr., "Polls 50,000 Votes to Cop First Place; Henderson Second," *Pittsburgh Courier*, December 12, 1931, section 1, p. 1, section 2, p. 8.

152 *At an award ceremony*: "Ellington Is Presented with Courier Loving Cup; Record Crowd Out," *Pittsburgh Courier*, January 9, 1932, section 1, p. 1.

152 *"The supremest dandies"*: O. O. McIntyre, "New York Day by Day," *New York American*, July 4, 1933, in DEPS.

152 *Ellington grossed $5,000*: "Say Ellington Gets New Plan and Higher Pay," *Chicago Defender*, October 3, 1931, p. 5; "Ellington Playing 50-50 on Full Gross," *Variety*, September 22, 1931; unidentified article, *Chicago Review*, March 20, 1932; in DEPS.

153 *Victor Records had named it*: flyer in DEPS.

154 *"only occupy one side"*: Lambert, "Gramophone Notes," p. 150.

155 *"We do not use any"*: Duke Ellington, "My Hunt for Song Titles," *Rhythm*, August 1933, p. 23.

155 *In April 1931*: "Ellington's Arrangements Now Available," *Metronome*, April 1931, p. 45.

156 *going across country*: "Ellington's Music Troupe on the Coast," *Chicago Defender*, February 27, 1932, p. 1.

156 *"That a personality headed"*: "Ellington Band Hit at Debut," *San Francisco Call-Bulletin*, February 20, 1932.

156 *"thud-thud from an audience"*: Lloyd S. Thompson, "Ellington Band Wins Audience," *San Francisco Examiner*, February 20, 1932.

156 *In Los Angeles, Ellington's orchestra*: "Stage Parade for Duke Ellington and His Band," *Omaha Evening Bee News*, March 28, 1932.

156 MUSIC SCORCHES HEARERS: Philip K. Scheuer, "Music Scorches Hearers," *Los Angeles Times*, March 14, 1932.

157 " *'I don't know you'* ": Dance, *World*, p. 123; Howard Brown, "Duke Ellington Adds Two New Men to Band," *Chicago Defender*, May 21, 1932, p. 5.

158 *especially Don Redman*: Ellington/Dance, p. 63.

158 *"Negro bands like plenty"*: "Negro Musicians Set the Pace Followed by Dance Orchestras," *Cincinnati Enquirer*, June 5, 1932, in DEPS.

158 *"It wasn't our* thing": Dance, "Hodges," p. 15.

159 *Sometimes, I have pretended:* unidentified article, *Cleveland Press*, ca. June 12, 1932; in DEPS.

159 *Ellington mostly led:* article in the *Los Angeles Record*, March 19, 1932, in DEPS.

160 *In the old days, you know:* Ellington/Harman, April 1956.

161 *"his first triumphant bass-fiddle"*: Sid Olson, "The News Reviewers Say," *Salt Lake City News*, June 3, 1934; in DEPS.

161 *"the young folks danced"*: H. E. Cherrington, "Duke Ellington Edifies the Dale–De Mille Picture for Loew's Ohio," *Columbus Dispatch*, September 14, 1933; "A Moment's Chat," *Brockton* [Massachusetts] *Enterprise*, June 2, 1932; "Charmed! That's How Duke Affects Others," *Cincinnati Post*, June 4, 1932; "Duke Ellington's Trip Abroad Answers," *Kansas City Call*, June 23, 1933; "Albee," *Cincinnati Enquirer*, June 6, 1932; "Duke's Band Well Received," *Dayton News*, August 22, 1934; Frank Marshall Davis, "Duke Ellington, 'Just Plain Folks,' Likes Drinks, Cards and Movies," *Afro-American*, February 9, 1935, p. 9. All in DEPS except last article.

161 *"as one of the outstanding"*: Jerry Wald, "Not on the Air," *Evening Graphic*, June 18, 1932; in DEPS.

161 *"a type of music not noted"*: [Hobson], p. 48.

162 *In fact, Ellington often traveled:* "Ellington Revue Offered at Earle," *Philadelphia Record*, February 3, 1934; in DEPS.

163 *"I'll have to find out"*: [Hobson], p. 90; photograph caption, *Radio Art*, November 15, 1932, p. 19; "Better Than Symphony Says Grainger of Ellington," *Dallas News*, August 27, 1933; "Highbrows Bow to Duke Ellington," *Columbus Citizen*, August 22, 1934; all in DEPS.

164 *resourcefully inventive:* R. D. Darrell, "Black Beauty," *Disques*, June 1932, pp. 153–55, 157–59.

165 *"because it portrayed"*: "King of Jazz Wins New Honors," *Chicago World*, n.d., probably April 1933, in DEPS.

165 *As further indication:* "Ellington Gets School Award," *New York City Herald-Tribune*, January 7, 1933; in DEPS.

165 *"an idol of the jazz cult"*: [Hobson], p. 47.

165 *"Show business, as the current year"*: Sid Silverman, "What the Grosses Say," *Variety*, December 29, 1931, p. 1.

165 *By 1932, every aspect:* Lewis A. Erenberg, "From New York to Middletown: Repeal and the Legitimization of Nightlife in the Great Depression," *American Quarterly* 38 (Winter 1986), p. 763.

166 *At one point, more than eight hundred:* Stratemann, p. 52.

166 *The record industry's fortunes:* Russell Sanjek, *From Print to Plastic:*

Publishing and Promoting America's Popular Music, 1900–1980. Brooklyn: Institute for Studies in American Music, 1983, p. 17. Russell Sanjek, *American Popular Music and Its Business: The First Four Hundred Years, III: From 1900 to 1984.* New York and Oxford: Oxford University Press, p. 69. Csida and Csida, pp. 311, 314.

166 *In 1930, radio had:* Lawrence Lichty, "Radio," *International Encyclopedia of Communications,* ed. Erik Barnouw, vol. 3, p. 420. New York and Oxford: Oxford University Press, 1989. Fabricant, pp. 573–74.

166 *By 1934, more than 650: Radio Stars and Stations of 1934.* Harrison, New Jersey: RCA Radiotron Co., [1934], p. [16].

166 *That month, Mills:* "No Dough—No Duke," *Orchestra World,* March 1933, p. 11; in DEPS.

166 *He landed the Ellingtonians:* Unidentified clippings from March 1933 in DEPS.

166 *By April 1933: unidentified article, Waterbury* [Connecticut] *Democrat,* April 19, 1933; in DEPS.

167 *On opening night:* untitled clippings in DEPS.

167 *"put three trumpets":* unidentified article, *Los Angeles Examiner,* April 10, 1933; in DEPS.

167 *"an all star cast":* table card headlined "The Famous Cotton Club Presents . . . " New York: Cotton Club, 1933. Calloway papers. Advertisement headlined *"Cotton Club Parade," New York Evening Journal,* April 22, 1933.

167 *There were eighteen scenes:* Jim Haskins, *The Cotton Club.* New York: Random House, 1977, p. 86.

168 *"the biggest song hit":* "Two Big Song Hits at $200,000: Valley and Stormy Tell Story of Pop Song Selling Now," *Variety,* July 18, 1933, p. 63.

168 *The opening night drew:* Vivian M. Gardner, "Melody Club to Entertain Veterans," *Milwaukee News,* May 3, 1933; in DEPS.

168 *In May, the Ellingtonians:* Stratemann, p. 55.

168 *"Barbaric," "weird":* "Ellington Is Master of Barbaric Rhythms," *Brooklyn Times,* January 1, 1933; in DEPS.

169 *"inspires some to dance":* H.C.E., "Star Salon Slick Spot," *Columbus Journal,* December 30, 1932; in DEPS.

169 *Mills, continuing to seek:* "Mills Abroad to Sell for Mills and Duke," *Chicago Defender,* January 8, 1933, p. 5.

170 *"We are of the opinion":* "The Duke to Open at the Palladium on June 12th," *Rhythm,* June 1933; in DEPS.

170 *Arriving at London's Waterloo: Melody Maker,* June 10, 1933, p. 2.

170 *The orchestra members found:* Ulanov, p. 134.

170 *For two weeks they played:* Ibid., p. 137.

170 Rockin' in Rhythm: Ibid., p. 137.

170 *"This was a night"*: Duke Ellington, "Duke Tells of 10 Top Thrills in 25 Years," *Down Beat*, November 5, 1952, p. 7.

170 *"On the first day"*: "Duke Ellington's Success," *Billboard*, July 8, 1933, p. 10; but datelined "London, June 20"; in DEPS.

170 *After closing in London:* "Those Dusky Entertainers," *Kansas City Post*, July 9, 1933, in DEPS; unidentified article, *New York Enquirer*, July 2, 1933, in DEPS.

170 *And there was a round:* Arthur Johnson, "Dial Twists," *Boston Transcript*, August 19, 1933, in DEPS; Ellington/Dance, p. 60; "Jazz as I Have Seen It," part VII, *Swing*, September 1940, p. 9.

170 *Even before his arrival:* H. A. Overstreet, "Touching Tomorrow's Frontiers in Duke Ellington's Music," *Metronome*, October 1933, p. 31, in DEPS.

170 *Then, for a forty-five-minute:* Nick Kenny, "Editor Gives Radio Fans Lowdown," *New York Sunday Mirror*, July 23, 1933, in DEPS.

170 *Ellington's fees were:* Roger Doulens, "On the Air," *South Norwalk* [Connecticut] *Sentinel*, August 8, 1933, in DEPS.

171 *Overall, a reported 100,000:* "Duke Ellington Sets Records in London," *Chicago Defender*, August 12, 1933, p. 5.

171 *"The cream suits, orange ties"*: Ellington/Dance, p. 60.

171 *"With just one exception"*: S. R. Nelson, "Music of To-day: Ellington—and After: Art or Debauchery? Music of Revolt," *London Era*, June 21, 1933.

171 *"Is this music?"*: S. R. Nelson writing in the *London Era*, quoted in "Duke Ellington in London Moves Critic to Tears," *Denver News*, July 2, 1933; in DEPS.

171 *"When all arguments are finished"*: Ulanov, p. 138.

172 *"I received the thrill"*: "Concert and Dance Here on Tuesday," *Evansville Press*, September 17, 1933; in DEPS.

172 *Ellington the Amazing:* Kaspar Monahan writing in the *Pittsburgh Press*, July 20, 1933; in DEPS.

172 *I am not ashamed:* S. R. Nelson, quoted in "Duke Ellington in London Moves Critic to Tears."

172 *Ellington has yet stamped:* Nelson, "Music of To-Day."

172 *"His music has a truly"*: Boyer, p. 24.

173 *"The Palladium concert greatly"*: Peter Rush, "The Music of Duke Ellington: Some Impressions and Criticisms," *Tune Times*, September 1933, p. 27; in DEPS.

173 *"It was perhaps the most"*: J. A. Rogers, "Duke Ellington," *Amsterdam News*, August 9, 1933, in DEPS.

173 *"apart from the waltz"*: J. A. Rogers, "The Duke's Success Encourages Musicians," *Amsterdam News*, August 16, 1933, in DEPS.

173 *The orchestra also presented:* Edgar A. Wiggins, " 'Won't You Come Back?' Is Paris' Plea to Ellington," *Chicago Defender*, August 19, 1933, p. 5.

173 *"This was respect and knowledge":* Ellington/Dance, p. 61.

173 *"composure, wit, and innate dignity":* Ibid.

174 *"probably the first composer":* London Sunday Referee, quoted in unidentified article, *New York American*, August 7, 1933, in DEPS.

174 *"Ellington's visit has been":* C. L. Ricketts, "Reflections on the Duke's Visit: Some of the Things We Should Have Learned," *Melody Maker*, July 29, 1933, in DEPS.

174 *"the greatest impression":* Overstreet, "Touching Tomorrow's Frontiers." p. 31.

175 *With such a high standard:* Rush, "The Music of Duke Ellington," p. 27.

175 *"The main thing I got":* Ulanov, p. 151.

175 *"We were absolutely amazed":* Ellington, *Music*, p. 84.

175 " *'A musician should have'* ": Frank Marshall Davis, "Duke Ellington, 'Just Plain Folks,' Likes Drinks, Cards and Movies," *Afro-American*, February 9, 1935, p. 9.

176 " *'I won't go south,'* ": Ulanov, p. 152.

176 *"the first tour of a big":* Calloway, p. 122.

176 *"The trip was trouble":* Ibid., p. 123.

176 *"somebody shouted":* Ibid., p. 124.

176 *"It was tough traveling":* Pops Foster, *Pops Foster: The Autobiography of a New Orleans Jazzman,* as told to Tom Stoddard. Berkeley and London: University of California Press, 1971, pp. 159–60.

176 *Using new scenic equipment:* "Ellington Gets New Scenic Equipment for Appearance in Dallas," *Dallas News*, September 28, 1933, in DEPS.

176 *"something of an African Stravinsky":* "Higher Development of Jazz Expounded by Duke Ellington," *Dallas News*, October 1, 1933; in DEPS.

178 *"Duke was a big name":* Bigard, p. 69.

178 *"If you'd been a white":* Boyer, p. 43.

178 *Duke had the ability:* Bob Udkoff, interview with Bruce Talbot, London, ca. 1988.

179 *"You have to try":* Boyer, pp. 32–33.

179 *"I was but a young boy":* Ralph Ellison, "Homage to Ellington on His Birthday," *Washington Sunday Star*, April 27, 1969. Reprinted in *Going to the Territory*. New York: Random House, 1986, p. 220.

179 *a few years later:* Ibid., pp. 221–22.

180 *By early 1934:* Unidentified article, *Radio World*, March 3, 1934; in DEPS; "Duke Ellington Invading South for First Time," unidentified newspaper, July 1934; in DEPS.

180 *Sometimes they had a dining car:* Bigard, p. 68.

180 *once in a while Ellington:* Nat Hentoff, *Boston Boy.* New York: Alfred A. Knopf, 1986, p. 123.

180 *Approximately 7,500 persons:* unidentified *Atlanta Constitution* article, quoted in "Ambling About Among Amusement Artists," *Washington Tribune,* August 18, 1934; in DEPS.

180 *This trip also took them:* Ellington, *Music,* p. 115; Ellington/Dance, p. 68.

181 *According to records:* Memorandum from Lizzie McDuffy to Malvina Scheider, series 80.2, Eleanor Roosevelt papers, Franklin D. Roosevelt Library, Hyde Park, New York.

183 *In September 1934:* "Popular Musician Barred by Ministry," *Amsterdam News,* August 25, 1934; in DEPS.

183 *received Hollywood exposure:* Stratemann, p. 96.

183 *In December 1934, the orchestra went:* Stratemann, p. 124.

184 *"put into the dirge":* Edward Morrow, "Duke Ellington on Gershwin's 'Porgy,' " *New Theatre,* December 1935, p. 6. Thanks to Steven Lasker for bringing this article to my attention.

184 *it marked the first time:* Stratemann, pp. 122–23.

186 *Ellington, however, moved quickly:* Stewart, *Boy,* pp. 131, 156.

186 *In November 1934:* Stratemann, p. 116.

186 *Once a second bassist was added:* "Inside Stuff—Music," *Variety,* February 12, 1935, p. 62.

186 *At the end of May:* Stratemann, p. 130.

186 *on May 27, 1935:* "Mother of Ellington Is Buried Here," *Washington Tribune,* June 1, 1935.

186 *"His world had been built":* Ellington/Dance, pp. 68–69.

187 *"When my mother died":* Boyer, p. 58.

187 *"After my mother passed":* Ellington, *Music,* p. 86.

187 *can be seen as an effort:* Schuller, *Swing Era,* p. 78.

187 *"I have always been":* unidentified article about *Rude Interlude,* in DEPS.

187 *"Irving Mills had twice":* Ellington, *Music,* p. 86.

Essential Ellington, 1931–35
Page

189 *written and arranged it:* Walter Barnes, Jr., "Hittin' High Notes," *Chicago Defender,* August 8, 1931, p. 5.

189 *"famous as the expression":* Ellington, *Music,* p. 419.

189 *"They taught all winter":* Dave Penny, booklet notes to the Ellington recording *The Brunswick Sessions (1932–35), Vol. 3,* Jazz Information RBD 3003, 1989.

189 *"Sentimentally didactic:"* Furia, p. 257.

189 *"not entirely fitted":* Morgenstern, "Notes," p. 43.

190 *"Duke would lie there"*: Dance, *World*, p. 85.
190 *"anything that was being done"*: Schuller, *Swing Era*, p. 64.
191 *The piece sounds more modern:* Ibid.
191 *As Gunther Schuller has observed:* Ibid., p. 70.

6: SWINGING TO A DIFFERENT DRUMMER, 1935–39
Page
193 *"once this was the greatest band"*: Collier, *Ellington*, p. 196, citing *New Masses*, September 29, 1936.
194 *In August 1935:* Stratemann, p. 132.
194 *a new nightclub area:* See Edward Pessen, "The Kingdom of Swing: New York City in the Late 1930s," *New York History* 70 (July 1989): pp. 277–308.
194 *And across the nation:* Nye, p. 20.
196 *"Ellington's weird chords"*: Walter J. Dodd, Jr., "College Rhythm: Dartmouth," *Variety*, January 29, 1936, p. 45.
196 *Only new bands:* Ulanov, p. 169.
196 *But the music business:* Stratemann, p. 132.
196 Variety *reported:* Dodd, "College Rhythm."
196 *"The general preference of white masses"*: Stanley Dance, *The World of Swing*. New York: Charles Scribner's Sons, 1974, p. 10.
197 *"and a few other orchestras"*: "Who Started Swing," *Metronome*, August, 1936, p. 11; quoting an interview with Ellington published in Cleveland on May 20, 1933.
197 *The larger bands required more skilled:* Gunther Schuller, "Arrangement," in *The New Grove Dictionary of Jazz*, ed. Barry Kernfeld, vol. 1, pp. 34–35. London: Macmillan Press; New York: Grove's Dictionaries of Music, 1988.
198 *"swing is not a kind"*: Duke Ellington, interview by Manne Berggren, Swedish Radio, Stockholm, April 29, 1939. Issued on the LP *Duke Ellington in Hollywood/On the Air*, Max MLP 1001, [n.d.].
199 *"In the middle and late thirties"*: Ulanov, p. 166.
199 *The number of jukeboxes:* Samuel S. Brylawski, "Jukebox," in *The New Grove Dictionary of American Music*, ed. H. Wiley Hitchcock and Stanley Sadie, vol. 2, p. 603. London: Macmillan Press; New York: Grove's Dictionaries of Music, 1986. John Stanton, "Swing as a Way of Life," in book accompanying the three-record set *The Swing Era, 1941–1942*, Time-Life Records STL 346, 1971, p. 8.
199 *From a low of 6 million:* Stanton, "Swing as a Way of Life," p. 8.
200 *For I think that:* Martin Williams, "The Men Who Made the Music: Fletcher Henderson, The Musician," in book accompanying the three-record set *The Swing Era, 1936–1937*, Time-Life Records STL 341, 1970, p. 62.

200 *"the most intricate of all"*: John Hammond, Jr., "Ellington on High," *Melody Maker*, December 1932, p. 1055. [Emphasis added.]

202 *"slowly the picture started"*: Stewart, *Boy*, p. 162.

203 *"I'd been with other"*: Ibid., p. 169.

203 *"Jazz is music"*: Burnett James, "Johnny Hodges on Record," *Jazz Journal*, December 1970, p. 25.

203 *"By his refusing to be placed"*: Stewart, *Boy*, p. 163.

205 *For the last two years:* Ralph Matthews, "Are Big Bands Washed Up? Nite Clubs, Hit by Repeal Depression, Want Smaller Orchestras," *Afro-American*, February 29, 1936, p. 11; Franklyn Frank, "Swing Takes Chicago," *Afro-American*, May 9, 1937, p. 11.

205 *"Here is a very bright"*: Giddins, "Notes," p. 41.

205 *He did, and she worked:* Ibid., pp. 41–42.

205 *Mills insisted:* Helen Oakley Dance, booklet notes to the two-disc Ellington recording *The Duke's Men, Small Groups*, Vol. 1, Columbia/Legacy C2K 46995, 1991, pp. 9–10.

206 *Metronome's 1936 poll: Metronome*, May 1936, p. 15.

206 *but Ellington demonstrated:* Ulanov, p. 175.

207 *Rex Stewart recalled one year:* Stewart, *Boy*, p. 193.

207 *Ellington was presented the keys:* "Mayor Shaw Gives Duke Ellington Key to Fair Los Angeles, Sez Levette," *Chicago Defender*, January 19, 1936, p. 21.

207 *Beginning early in 1937:* Ulanov, p. 175.

207 *"being the first orchestra leaders"*: Ibid., p. 184.

207 *Waters and Ellington got top:* program, *Cotton Club Parade, Second Edition*. New York: Cotton Club, 1937. Ulanov, p. 187.

208 *He was heard on twice-weekly:* "Duke Ellington Chronology," p. 4, DEC; Stratemann, p. 143.

209 *The governor, as Duke was called:* Stewart, *Boy*, p. 177.

209 *The companion pieces:* Schuller, *Swing Era*, pp. 90–91.

209 *"Like all of our compositions"*: Duke Ellington, "Duke Ellington Tells the Secrets of His Success," *Chicago Defender*, October 2, 1937, p. 9.

209 Caravan *became something of a hit:* Unidentified notice in the *Peoria Star*, October 24, 1937; in DEPS.

209 *This was a very difficult time:* Ellington/Dance, pp. 70–71.

210 *"Edward's closest friend"*: *Reminiscing in Tempo*, public television documentary produced by Robert Levi, 1991.

210 *Meanwhile, Artie Whetsol's health:* "Ellington Replaces Whetsol in Band," *Down Beat*, April 1938, p. 2; Stratemann, p. 152.

210 *Ellington had now lost:* "2 Musicians Quit Duke Ellington; Health Blamed," *Afro-American*, August 24, 1935, p. 8.

210 *"haunted trumpet players"*: Ellington/Dance, pp. 22–23.

211 *The January 16, 1938, event:* "Basie and Duke Lend Players to Goodman," *Afro-American*, January 29, 1938, p. 10.

211 *Later that night, Ellington:* "Webb 'Cuts' Basie in Swing Battle," *Down Beat,* February 1938, p. 2.

211 *"His was a band that":* Ellington/Dance, p. 71.

212 *When Ellington's forces met Webb's:* "Orchestra Notes," *Billboard,* March 20, 1937, p. 14.

212 *On December 26, 1938:* Red Adams, "Who Has the Greatest Swing Orchestra, Duke or Jimmy?," *Chicago Defender,* January 21, 1939, p. 19.

212 *"Those guys are the Babe Ruths":* Al Monroe, "Swingin' the News," *Chicago Defender,* November 1, 1941, p. 20.

212 *now reports stated he'd play:* David Bratton, Jr., "Outside Listening In," *Brooklyn Times,* February 23, 1933; "Duke to Carnegie," *New York City News,* February 23, 1933; untitled clipping, *Radio Daily,* January 24, 1938; all in DEPS.

213 *"a concert hall without walls":* Albert Murray, *Stomping the Blues.* New York: McGraw-Hill, 1976, pp. 183–84.

213 *On May 29, 1938:* "Duke Ellington Is Winner in 'Swing' Session: Famous Band Adds to Its Many Laurels," *Chicago Defender,* June 4, 1938, p. 19; "Outdoor Swing Carnival Developed Oddities; Addicts Finally Got Tired," *Variety,* June 1, 1938, p. 40.

213 *By mid 1938, swing:* "Cab, Duke and Satch Grossed over 4 Millions," *Afro-American,* July 16, 1938, p. 11; cites and quotes an article in *Down Beat,* "Black Bands Who Made over $1,000,000 Arouse Interest of Big Bookers."

213 *Ellington's tenth show:* Ellington, *Music,* p. 88. "Duke Writes Complete Score," *Afro-American,* March 12, 1938, p. 11. Joel Whitburn, *Pop Memories, 1890–1954: The History of American Popular Music.* Menomonee Falls, Wisconsin: Record Research, 1986, p. 148.

214 *the "band feature":* program, *Cotton Club Parade, Fourth Edition.* New York: Cotton Club, 1938.

214 *recordings of it "have already":* "Duke Ellington's New Song Tops 'Must' List," *Chicago Defender,* August 13, 1938, p. 19.

214 *"about brought the ceiling":* Tommy Berry, "Jitterbugs Riot to Hear the Duke," *Chicago Defender,* November 26, 1938, p. 18.

214 *free improvisation, or "jamming":* "Duke Ellington Tells the Secrets of His Success," *Chicago Defender,* October 2, 1937, p. 9.

215 *"Many a popular song grew":* Dance, "Hodges," p. 19.

215 *were composed almost by unanimous:* "Duke Ellington Tells the Secrets of His Success."

215 *"Hodges addressed to his leader":* Giddins, "Notes," p. 44.

215 *"we all brought bits":* Stewart, *Boy,* p. 209.

216 *biographer James Lincoln Collier:* Collier, *Ellington,* pp. 304–5.

216 *As a composer, Ellington seems:* Ibid., p. 186.

216 *"The memory of things gone":* Boyer, p. 27.

216 *"He always wrote"*: Ellington/Dance, p. 164.

216 *In December 1937*: "Breakdown of Network Plugs," *Variety*, December 22, 1937, p. 40.

216 *In February 1939*: "The Duke Swings: Record Crowd of 12,000 Hear His Band at N.A.A.C.P. Dance," *Chicago Defender*, February 18, 1939, p. 18.

217 *Ellington had always been*: Gordon Parks, *To Smile in Autumn: A Memoir*. New York: W. W. Norton, 1979, pp. 118–19.

217 *"in a large Austin hotel"*: Ulanov, p. 180; "Duke Ellington Plays for Texas U. Prom: Harlem Boys Bound for Fair Los Angeles," *Chicago Defender*, January 5, 1936, p. 21.

217 *"Over 8,000 of the elite"*: "Bill Robinson, Ethel Waters, Duke Ellington Among Stars," *Chicago Defender*, February 13, 1937, p. 21; see also "Duke Ellington Sets Record as Eight Thousand Californians Dance to His Music," *Chicago Defender*, February 13, 1937, p. 21.

217 *"the first time a Race"*: "Duke Ellington's Band Plays at Orpheum in Memphis," *Chicago Defender*, December 4, 1937, p. 18.

217 *"Ellington's melodies are heard"*: "Duke Sets the Pace in Themes," *Afro-American*, July 2, 1938, p. 10.

218 *"I took the energy"*: Simon, p. 187.

218 *"a beautiful woman among"*: Ellington/Dance, p. 76.

218 *As when he left Edna*: Ibid., pp. 76–77; Collier, *Ellington*, p. 207.

219 *When Ellington went off*: Ellington/Dance, p. 78.

219 *by 1938 he had learned*: Ibid., pp. 77–78.

219 *One day*: Ulanov, p. 207; *Reminiscing in Tempo*, television documentary.

219 *Ellington broke with Mills*: "Hear Duke Ellington May Break with Irving Mills," *Chicago Defender*, March 4, 1939, p. 19.

219 *The two swapped their stock*: "Wm. Morris Plans Mature," *Variety*, April 12, 1939, p. 39; "Ellington and Mills in Split," *Down Beat*, May 1939, p. 1.

219 *"No Negro writer"*: Ulanov, p. 206.

220 *Mercer Ellington implied*: Collier, *Ellington*, 195.

220 *While Mills's fairness and honesty*: Ibid., p. 194.

220 *"There is no point now"*: Ellington/Dance, p. 82.

220 *"He had always preserved"*: Ellington, *Music*, p. 89.

220 *In less than a year, Ellington*: "Ellington to Victor," *Variety*, February 21, 1940, p. 34.

220 *Ellington took his dismay*: Duke Ellington, "Situation Between the Critics and Musicians Is Laughable," *Down Beat*, April 1939, pp. 4, 9; "Duke Concludes Criticism of Critics," *Down Beat*, May 1939, p. 14.

221 *"hundreds of jitterbugs"*: Onah L. Spencer, "French J-Bugs in Wild Welcome for Ellington," *Down Beat*, May 1939, p. 9.

221 *"There were a lot of people"*: Stewart, *Boy*, p. 182.

221 *"We were accorded an uproarious"*: "Ellington Gave Concert in Bomb-Proof Hall! Crowd Rioted in Holland; Nazis Tossed Valet into Jail, Reveals Duke's Diary," *Metronome*, June 1939, pp. 10, 35.

221 *The reviews were glowing*: Arthur Wilcox, "Ellington Gets Rave Notice for First Paris Concert," *Melody Maker*, April 8, 1939, p. 11.

221 *"By what orchestral imagination"*: "Concerts et Recitals: Le Langage du Jazz—Style Nègre et Style Blanc les Familiers du Piano et du Chant," *Le Figaro*, April 7, 1939. Translation by Monique Steiner.

221 *"wowed the Parisians"*: Hugo Speck, "Ellington Bd. Whams Paris," *Variety*, April 19, 1939, p. 48.

222 *"related to the rhythm"*: Boyer, p. 22.

222 *"Such music is not only"*: Ibid., pp. 22–23.

222 *"disappointed real fans a bit"*: "Foreign News: Holland," *Metronome*, June 1939, p. 22.

222 *"As we were heading across Holland"*: Bigard, p. 75.

222 *A mix-up on April 9*: Duke Ellington, "Reminiscing with the Duke," *Afro-American*, August 1, 1942, p. 11.

223 *"really accepted throughout"*: Bennie Aasland, interview by Patricia Willard, Jaarfala, Sweden, August 20, 1989, DEOHP.

224 *"This is orchestral art"*: *Aftonbladet*, Stockholm, April 17, 1939. English translation in DEC.

224 *"This presentation was a Jazz-Concert"*: *Ny Dag*, Stockholm, April 17, 1939, DEC.

224 *"The platforms of the railway stations"*: *Nya Dagligt Allehanda*, Stockholm, April 16, 1939, DEC.

224 *"The enthusiasm of Duke's listeners"*: Ibid., April 17, 1939.

224 *"Their refined appearance"*: *Dagens Nyheter*, Stockholm, April 17, 1939, DEC.

224 *"I was awakened"*: Duke Ellington, "Ellington Gave Concert in Bomb-Proof Hall!" *Metronome*, June 1939, p. 10.

224 *"ten little girls"*: Ibid., pp. 10, 35.

225 *their tour was cut short*: Bigard, p. 75; Stewart, *Jazz Masters*, pp. 139–40.

225 *"I was never so glad"*: Bigard, p. 75.

225 *met in New York by 500*: "Duke Ellington in States from Europe," *Chicago Defender*, May 13, 1939, p. 21; "Duke Likes Europe but U.S.A. Better: Noted Pianist-Maestro Had a Successful Tour," *Chicago Defender*, May 20, 1939, p. 20; "Ellington Lands in New York," *Down Beat*, June 1939, p. 7.

226 *"Europe is a very different"*: Ulanov, p. 217.

Essential Ellington, 1935–39
Page
228 *"a little dulcet piece":* Stanley Dance, booklet notes accompanying the three-record set, *The Ellington Era, 1927–1940, Vol. 1,* Columbia C3L39, 1964.
229 *The angular melodies:* Schuller, *Swing Era,* p. 103.

7: MAKING MASTERPIECES, 1939–43
Page
231 *"Why, young man, I'm going to":* Ellington, *Music,* p. 149.
231 *In January, Strayhorn had shown:* Leonard Feather, "Men Behind the Bands: Billy Strayhorn," *Down Beat,* October 1, 1940, p. 11.
231 *While the orchestra was in Europe:* Ellington, *Music,* p. 152; Ellington/Dance, p. 80.
231 *Strayhorn began to crack:* Billy Strayhorn, "The Ellington Effect," *Down Beat,* November 5, 1952, p. 4.
232 *"He had had enough training":* Ellington/Dance, p. 80.
232 *Strayhorn mentioned that he wanted:* Ellington, *Music,* pp. 152, 498–99.
233 *"always the most unselfish":* Ellington, *Music,* p. 156.
233 *"Duke was a father figure":* David Hajdu, "Something to Live For," *Village Voice Jazz Special,* June 23, 1992, p. 15.
233 *According to Mercer Ellington:* Ellington/Dance, p. 67.
233 *Strayhorn's arrival also created:* Andrew Homzy, "Me and You," *Village Voice Jazz Special,* June 23, 1992, p. 5.
234 *Blanton revolutionized jazz bass:* Shuller, *Swing Era,* p. 111.
234 *Blanton loved nothing more:* Bigard, pp. 73–75; Stewart, *Boy,* p. 197.
234 *"His amazing talent":* Stewart, *Boy,* p. 196.
234 *"I'm not going to stand":* Ellington, *Music,* p. 164.
234 *Back in 1935 and 1936:* Leonard Feather, "Duke Hires Ben Webster," *Down Beat,* February 1, 1940, p. 1.
234 *always wanted to play:* Crow, p. 249.
236 *"Ben was inspired":* Dance, *World,* p. 76.
236 *"Ben would watch over the kid:"* Stewart, *Boy,* p. 197.
236 *"Every time there was an addition:"* Dance, *World,* p. 77.
236 *"we write to and for":* "Duke Tells 'Em a Thing or Two," *Down Beat,* September 15, 1942, p. 2.
237 *When a new player came in:* Ellington/Dance, p. 64.
237 *Ellington typically gave his new:* Ibid.
237 *Feuds between band members:* Stewart, *Boy,* pp. 192–93.
237 *"An unbelievable esprit de corps":* Ibid, p. 171.
237 *"After our very successful":* Ibid., p. 189.
237 *Record sales rose 51 percent:* "Cutting Wax," *Down Beat,* January 15, 1940, p. 14. Russell Sanjek, *From Print to Plastic: Publishing and Pro-*

moting America's Popular Music, 1900–1980. Brooklyn: Institute for Studies in American Music, 1983, p. 20.

238 *New swing bands seemed:* Paul Eduard Miller, " 'Money Invested in Swing Music Will Keep It Alive,' Says Miller," *Down Beat*, April 15, 1940, p. 6.

238 Variety *and* Billboard *reported:* "Ellington Got $1530," *Variety*, October 18, 1939, p. 39; "Ellington & Gordon Gravy for Turnpike," *Billboard*, October 21, 1939, p. 9; "Duke a Junior League Hit," *Billboard*, October 28, 1939, p. 9.

238 *The orchestra's usual fee:* "Bands Ask Top Money," *Billboard*, March 9, 1940, p. 9.

238 *It contained an extraordinary provision:* "Ellington to Victor: Back on 75-cent Pancakes Through Transfer," *Variety*, February 21, 1940, p. 34; Leonard Feather, "Duke Hires Ben Webster," *Down Beat*, February 1940, p. 1; "Ellington Switches to Victor Feb. 23," *Billboard*, February 24, 1940, p. 9; "Duke Ellington Now Recording for Victor," *Chicago Defender*, February 3, 1940, p. 20.

238 *That's all bunk!:* " 'Sure I'm Commercial'—Says Duke Ellington," *Melody Maker*, May 13, 1939, p. 9.

239 *By 1939, a dispute:* "ASCAP Monopoly Is Threatened," *Down Beat*, March 1, 1940, p. 2.

239 *The result was a ban:* Sanjek, *From Print to Plastic*, p. 24.

240 *Twenty-year-old Mercer:* Leonard Feather, "Duke's Kid Makes a Wobbly Debut," *Down Beat*, January 1, 1940, p. 6.

240 *"Shorty Baker came into the band":* Ellington/Harman, May 27, 1964.

240 *"Hey, you've got my note!":* Dance, *World*, p. 39.

241 *"a lust for life":* Boyer, p. 50.

241 *"the best of the Ellington band's":* Schuller, *Swing Era*, p. 114.

241 *"It was a great show":* Don McKim, "Duke a 'Gold Mine' in Canada," *Down Beat*, May 15, 1940, p. 20.

241 *"Duke is a great guy":* Dance, "Impressions," p. 18.

242 *As* Down Beat *indicated:* Ted Toll, "Ellington Lauded as All Time Greatest" *Down Beat*, September 1, 1940, p. 3.

242 *"Not only is the music superb":* Barrelhouse Dan, "Record Reviews," *Down Beat*, April 15, 1940, p. 15.

242 *"Duke was very elegant":* Giddins, "Notes," p. 45.

242 *"It changed the face":* Schuller, *Swing Era*, p. 129.

242 *"particularly in its execution":* Ibid., p. 130.

243 *the sad news:* Stratemann, p. 162, citing *Down Beat*, April 15, 1940, p. 2.

243 *"took me for a ride":* Ellington, *Music*, p. 120.

243 *"Well, go ahead on":* Cootie Williams, interview by Helen Dance, May 1976, JOHP, pp. 207–8.

243 *"was almost in tears":* Jimmy Gentry, "Nance Takes Cootie Spot with Duke," *Down Beat*, November 15, 1940, p. 1.

243 *Williams said later:* Williams, interview by Dance, JOHP, pp. 215–16.

243 *The departure of Cootie Williams:* "BG Grabs Cootie for Hot Chair," *Down Beat*, November 1, 1940, pp. 1, 23.

243 *in Williams's stead, Ellington chose:* Gentry, "Nance Takes Cootie Spot."

244 *"Ray Nance was a cocky kid":* Whitney Bailliett, *Jelly Roll, Jabbo, and Fats.* New York: Oxford University Press, 1983, p. 61.

245 *"Don't leave me alone":* Giddins, "Notes," p. 47.

245 *"Money was a game":* Dance, "Hodges," p. 27.

246 *According to Mercer Ellington:* Ellington/Dance, p. 181.

246 *In February 1941:* Patricia Willard, booklet notes accompanying the recording *Jump for Joy*, Smithsonian Collection of Recordings R037, 1988, p. 1.

246 *"Ellington spends his spare moments":* [Hobson], pp. 94–95.

246 *"the dream of Duke Ellington":* Tommy Berry, "Charm and Personality, Not Beauty, Woman's Greatest Asset Says Ellington: Famed Maestro Is Planning an All Race Musical," *Chicago Defender*, November 28, 1936, p. 21.

246 *"evolved into a grand emancipation":* Willard, *Jump for Joy*, p. 4.

246 *Financing of $52,000:* Stratemann, p. 170.

246 *"upbeat, satirical, topical":* Willard, *Jump for Joy*, p. 11.

246 *"the hippest thing":* Ibid., p. 29.

247 *"creating that American phenomenon":* Duke Ellington, "Reminiscing with the Duke," *Afro-American*, August 1, 1942, p. 11.

247 Jump for Joy *offered romance:* Stratemann, p. 169; Willard, *Jump for Joy*, p. 19.

248 *"Everything, every setting":* Ellington, *Music*, p. 176.

248 *"comedians came off stage":* Ibid., p. 180.

248 *"In* Jump for Joy": Ulanov, p. 242; Willard, *Jump for Joy*, p. 19.

248 *The show, however, folded:* Stratemann, p. 170.

248 *That it folded and never:* Stewart, *Jazz Masters*, p. 99; Ellington/Dance, p. 165.

248 *Late in November:* Stratemann, p. 188.

248 *Elsewhere in Hollywood:* Ibid., pp. 193–95.

249 *(Incidentally, Welles reportedly said:* Maurice Zolotow, "The Duke of Hot," *Saturday Evening Post*, August 7, 1943, p. 59.

250 *was in some ways a throwback:* Stratemann, pp. 217–18.

250 *In* Reveille with Beverly: Ibid., p. 229.

250 *Sometimes Ellington composed:* Boyer, p. 23.

250 *Duke was in the bathtub:* Willard, *Jump for Joy*, p. 9.

251 *Occasionally, Ellington would arrive home:* Doron K. Antrim, "Rehearsing with Duke Ellington: This Is How the Duke Rehearses—And It Is One of His Secrets," in *Secrets of Dance Band Success*, ed. Doron K. Antrim, p. 30. [New York]: Famous Stars Publishing Co., 1936.

251 *"Ideas?" he replied:* Ellington interviewed on *Interview with Byng Whittaker*, CBC television program, videotaped September 2, 1964.

251 *"The secret of Duke Ellington"*: Antrim, "Rehearsing with Duke Ellington," pp. 25, 30.

251 *When they worked at the Kentucky:* Ibid., p. 25.

251 *"but the boys know it"*: Lionel Hampton, "Swing," *Afro-American,* March 27, 1938, p. 10.

251 *"If Duke Ellington has an idea"*: Antrim, "Rehearsing," p. 27.

251 *Ellington would go through:* Ibid., p. 27.

252 *"was an open-minded man"*: Bigard, p. 63.

252 *"Changes and improvements"*: Antrim, "Rehearsing," p. 29.

252 *Even at the studio:* Simon, p. 191.

253 *"Ellington is a highly original man"*: Stewart, *Jazz Masters,* pp. 93, 99.

253 *"Ellington," added Stewart:* Stewart, *Boy,* p. 157.

253 *"a composite"*: Stewart, *Jazz Masters,* p. 89.

253 *"the more you know him"*: Ibid., p. 101.

253 *"He lives a good deal"*: Burt Korall, "The Roots of the Duchy," *Down Beat,* July 13, 1967, p. 22.

253 *"Edward did seem somewhat"*: Gordon Parks, "Jazz," *Esquire,* December 1975, p. 144.

254 *Ever image conscious:* Gretchen Weaver, "The Duke of Jazzdom," *Bandleaders,* September 1945, p. 45; Boyer, p. 26; Zolotow, "The Duke of Hot," p. 59.

254 *"He loves flash in dress"*: Tommy Berry, "The 'Duke of Ellington' Tells Tommy Berry Many Life Secrets: Claim Bandster Wants Solitude," *Chicago Defender,* May 29, 1937, p. 20.

254 *"his clothes were avant garde"*: Stewart, *Boy,* p. 164.

254 *In rehearsal, he normally wore:* Ibid., p. 145; Berry, "The 'Duke of Ellington,' " p. 20.

254 *"I've had three educations"*: Boyer, p. 49.

254 *"rarely did he forget"*: Stewart, *Boy,* p. 157.

254 *Uninterested in sports:* Boyer, p. 49.

254 *At one time his favorite:* Frank Marshall Davis, "Duke Ellington, 'Just Plain Folks,' Likes Drinks, Cards and Movies," *Afro-American,* February 9, 1935, p. 9.

255 *"It is no secret"*: Ralph Matthews, "Looking at the Stars," *Afro-American,* October 16, 1937, p. 11.

255 *"Folks can't rush you"*: Boyer, p. 38.

255 *Once, sleepily getting off:* Ibid., p. 30.

256 *His appetite was enormous:* Ibid., pp. 25, 31, 34, 47; Weaver, "Duke of Jazzdom," p. 45.

256 *"Duke drew people"*: Boyer, pp. 52–53.

257 *"Hello—is this the beautiful"*: Weaver, "Duke of Jazzdom," p. 48.

257 *"Whose pretty little girl"*: Marian Logan, interview by Sonia Rosario, February 27, 1928, New York City, Yale, p. 2.

257 *"My mother always told me"*: George, p. 94.

257 *"I never knew an angel"*: Boyer, p. 35.

257 *He regarded women "as flowers"*: Ruth Ellington Boatwright, interview by Marcia M. Greenlee, New York City, August 18, 1989, DEOHP.

257 *"It's all in there"*: George, p. 95.

257 *"He craves peace"*: Boyer, p. 35.

258 *Jimmie Blanton, it was clear:* "Jimmy [*sic*] Blanton 'Cupes at Joe Sullivan's Old 'Resting' Sanitarium," *Down Beat*, March 1, 1942, p. 12; "Jimmy [*sic*] Blanton Takes Last Ride," *Down Beat*, August 15, 1942, p. 12.

258 *Ellington wired the money:* Al Monroe, "Swinging the News," *Chicago Defender*, August 8, 1942, p. 22.

258 *Blanton was replaced:* Stratemann, p. 155.

258 *After Pearl Harbor:* Bigard, p. 77; Mike Levin, "Bus Situation to Eliminate Most Colored Bands," *Down Beat*, August 1, 1942, p. 23.

258 *"in all of my years"*: Bigard, p. 66.

258 *"it seemed that things"*: Ibid., p. 77.

258 *"When I told him"*: Ibid., p. 77.

259 *Ivie Anderson resigned:* "Ivy [*sic*] Anderson to Retire; Duke Seeks Replacement," *Chicago Defender*, July 25, 1942, p. 22.

259 *In mid 1942:* Al Monroe, "Swinging the News," *Chicago Defender*, July 25, 1942, p. 22.

259 *"The backgrounds Duke wrote"*: Sonny Greer, "In Those Days," in booklet accompanying the three-record set *The Ellington Era, 1927–1940*, *Vol. 2*, Columbia C3L 39, 1964.

259 *At the end of 1942:* "Ellington Tinted Music Firm Admitted to ASCAP," *Chicago Defender*, January 12, 1942, p. 10; "Robbins Music and Duke Split," *Down Beat*, January 15, 1942, p. 1.

260 *"I'm going to compose"*: Jack Foster, "Manhattan Melody Men, No. 5: Duke Ellington Plays That Cotton Club Jazz Just as He Feels," *New York Telegram*, February 13, 1942.

260 *An account in 1933:* [Hobson], pp. 94–95.

260 *"He is always telephoning"*: H. Allen Smith, "Duke Ellington as a Composer Is in Class Alone," *New York World-Telegram*, September 13, 1938.

261 *walked on stage without the music:* Duke Ellington, "Duke Tells of 10 Top Thrills in 25 Years," *Down Beat*, November 5, 1952, p. 7.

261 *in "the adjoining cabin"*: Duke Ellington, "Black, Brown and Beige," unpublished narrative sketch, p. 2, Ruth Ellington Boatwright Collection, Series 5: Lyrics/Script notes, Archives Center, National Museum of American History, Smithsonian Institution, Washington, D.C.

261 *"The first thing the Black man"*: Ibid., pp. 6–7.

261 *"he had something to live for"*: Ibid., p. 11.

261 *"Come Sunday, while"*: Ibid., pp. 14–15.

261 *"Good souls praying"*: Ibid., p. 19.
262 *"The desire for freedom"*: Ibid., p. 20.
262 *"recognized the contribution"*: Ellington, *Music*, p. 181.
262 *"When things were darkest"*: Ellington, "Black, Brown and Beige," unpublished sketch, p. 26.
262 *"jumped for joy"*: Ibid., p. 25.
262 *"Boola was the hero"*: Ibid., p. 26.
262 *"I couldn't work without"*: Gleason, p. 167.
263 he *"sort of withdrew"*: Schomburg, p. 451.
263 *"I believe its nonacceptance"*: Schuller, *Swing Era*, p. 142.
264 *Fifty years later, analysts:* Scott DeVeaux, *"Black, Brown and Beige and the Critics,"* unpublished lecture, Sonneck Society for American Music, Baton Rouge, Louisiana, February 1992. To be published in *Black Music Research Journal*.
264 *Selling nearly 20 million records:* Boyer, p. 58.

Essential Ellington, 1939–43
Page
266 *reportedly depicting slaves' frenetic dancing:* Leonard Feather, booklet notes accompanying the two-disc set *The Duke Ellington Carnegie Hall Concerts, January 1943*, Prestige 2PCD-45004-2, 1977, p. [8].
266 *Melodically and harmonically sophisticated:* Schuller, *Swing Era*, p. 118.
266 *"The orchestra could roar":* Mark Tucker, booklet notes accompanying the three-disc Ellington set *The Blanton-Webster Band*, RCA Bluebird 5659-2-RB, 1986, p. [9].
266 *Rich sonorities never before heard:* Schuller, *Swing Era*, p. 123.
268 *Billy Strayhorn's melancholy tone poem:* Ibid., p. 134.

8: COMPOSING FOR CONCERTS, 1943–51
Page
270 *a capacity audience of 3,000:* "Ellington May Extend Concerts into Summer," *Variety*, February 3, 1943, p. 35.
270 *a record-breaking crowd of 7,200:* "Ellington's Concert Big $9,400 in Cleveland," *Variety*, February 24, 1943, p. 31.
270 *On April 1, Ellington:* Stratemann, p. 241.
271 *Alternating with a six-piece:* Ibid.
271 *The Ellington orchestra played:* Ibid., p. 242.
272 *Financial records for the Ellington orchestra:* Series 3: Business Records, DEC, includes detailed payroll records and road manager's receipts for the period beginning in 1942. Also helpful was an unpublished paper by Kip Lornell, "The Economics of Ellington in World War II." See also Boyer, pp. 58–59.

272 *lost $18,000 on the engagement:* Boyer, p. 59.

272 *Then, after leaving The Hurricane:* "Duke's Capitol Dates to Net 8G's Per Week," *Afro-American,* October 16, 1943, p. 8.

272 *By late 1944:* Lornell, "The Economics of Ellington," p. 8.

272 *At long last, Ellington:* Stratemann, p. 253.

273 *Jimmy Hamilton recalled that:* Hamilton, DEOHP.

273 *"writes when he feels like it":* Duke Ellington, "Duke Ellington on Arrangers," *Metronome,* October 1943, p. 35.

274 *In June 1944:* Al Celley, interview by Patricia Willard, Philadelphia, July 12, 1989, DEOHP.

274 *A 1944 year-end financial statement:* DEC, Series 3: Business Records, Duke Ellington, Inc., Balance sheets, 1944–45.

275 *"He spends money lavishly":* Boyer, pp. 58–59.

275 *An occasional payment:* "Report for Week Ending March 18, 1943," Series 3, Business Records, DEC.

275 *But both Al Celley and:* Al Celley, DEOHP; Hamilton, DEOHP.

276 *Ellington was astounded:* Ellington, *Music,* pp. 88–89.

276 *Gunther Schuller has posited:* Schuller, *Swing Era,* pp. 102–3.

277 *By 1944:* Csida and Csida, p. 321.

277 *Ellington had been expecting:* Stratemann, p. 238.

277 *A number of Ellington's men:* Ibid., p. 242.

277 *In January 1944:* "Cab, Duke Nix Great Lakes: Won't Play Naval Base Unless Colored Trainees Get One Date," *Afro-American,* January 15, 1944, p. 8.

277 *"love ballads of separation":* Charles McGovern, "American Popular Music During World War II," unpublished paper, 1982, p. 38.

277 *make transcription discs:* Stratemann, p. 261; Jerry Valburn, interview by Mark Tucker, Plainview, New York, March 19, 1987, Yale, pp. 106, 108.

278 *As a result of his work:* Al Celley, DEOHP.

278 *"American swing records":* Kip Lornell, "Duke Ellington and World War II," unpublished paper, citing a clipping from *Billboard,* November 7, 1942, in DEC.

278 *The changes in personnel:* Stratemann, p. 253.

278 *"a new member of the Ellington organization":* Stewart, *Boy,* p. 215.

278 *Also in April 1946:* Collier, *Ellington,* p. 245.

279 *"One note higher":* Don Walsh, "One Note Higher And Only Dog Could Hear Duke's New Tooter," *Variety,* December 27, 1944, p. 31.

280 *"went on to deepen":* Stanley Crouch, program notes for the Classical Jazz Orchestra. New York: Lincoln Center, 1988.

280 *Schuller has argued:* Schuller, *Swing Era,* p. 154.

282 *In 1944, Ellington, Hodges:* "Spivak Gets Crown from TD, Duke Wins, Bing Is New Voice," *Down Beat,* January 1, 1945, pp. 1, 13.

282 *In 1945, Ellington took first:* "Esquire's All-American Band," in *Esquire's 1945 Jazz Book,* ed. Paul Eduard Miller, p. 30. New York: A. S. Barnes & Co., 1945.

282 *In 1946, Ellington swept:* Ellington, *Music*, p. 485.

282 *In 1943, Ellington was presented:* Stratemann, p. 256.

282 *more and more popular:* Maurice Zolotow, "The Duke of Hot," *Saturday Evening Post*, August 7, 1943, pp. 24–25, 57, 59.

282 *By 1945, there were:* Weaver, "The Duke of Jazzdom," p. 46.

282 *"I'm not old enough":* Dance, "Impressions," p. 20.

282 *Despite the mixed reviews:* Stratemann, p. 239.

283 *On the basis of my experience:* "Concert-Goers Good for Jazz, Says Duke," *Afro-American*, January 11, 1943, p. 10.

283 *Like other nightclubs:* Allen Woll, *Black Musical Theatre: From Coontown to Dreamgirls.* Baton Rouge: Louisiana State University Press, 1989, p. 116.

284 *"To be smart or 'arty' ":* Stanley Dance, booklet notes to the two-disc set *The Duke Ellington Carnegie Hall Concerts, January 1946,* Prestige 2PCD-24074-2, 1977, p. [4].

285 *"Duke and Strayhorn":* Hamilton, Yale, p. 23.

285 *"never liked to close":* Ibid., p. 21.

285 *"wants life and music":* Hentoff, p. 76.

286 *"visualized this new world":* Ellington, *Music*, p. 183.

287 *"was for out-and-out protest":* Ibid., p. 185.

288 *"The annual Carnegie Hall concerts":* Ibid., p. 183.

288 *"By 1950," Ellington wrote:* Ibid., p. 190.

289 *"Expressive jazz requires":* Gunnar Askland, "Interpretations in Jazz: A Conference with Duke Ellington," *Etude*, March 1947, p. 172.

289 *"But it was when Mr. Sargeant":* Duke Ellington, "By Duke Ellington," *Needle*, July 1944, p. 10.

289 *While Ellington has been:* Schuller, *Swing Era*, pp. 149, 153.

291 *The bebop musicians worked:* Scott DeVeaux, letter to the author, January 5, 1993.

292 *In November and December 1946:* Simon, p. 32.

292 *a number of directions:* H. Wiley Hitchcock, *Music in the United States: A Historical Introduction,* 2nd ed. Prentice-Hall History of Music Series. Englewood Cliffs, New Jersey: Prentice-Hall, 1974, pp. 229, 231, 232, 237, 238–42, 249.

293 *"eloquent score, brisk ballets":* Brooks Atkinson, "Beggar's Holiday," *New York Times*, January 27, 1946.

293 *"more opera comica":* Robert Bagar, "Theater: 'Beggar's Holiday' a Brilliant Musical," *New York World-Telegram*, December 27, 1946.

293 *after 14 weeks and 108 performances:* Mix [Mike Levin], "Beggars' Show Opulent Affair But Misses Hit," *Down Beat*, January 15, 1947, p. 2; Bordman, pp. 554–55; Stratemann, pp. 280–82.

294 *"His reputation shredded":* Mike Levin, "Reputation Shredded, Duke Should Disband, Mix Claims," *Down Beat*, June 17, 1949, pp. 1, 12, 13.

294 *"trash-worthy of any studio band":* Ibid., p. 14.

294 *One reader added:* letter from Joe Kaymer, Hamilton, Ontario, "Chords and Discords: All About Duke," *Down Beat*, July 15, 1949, p. 11.
294 *A controversy arose:* Charlie Barnet, "Storm Rages over Duke Story: You Made a Bad Error, Mix—Barnet," *Down Beat*, July 15, 1949, pp. 1, 19.
295 *"When I left Duke":* Stanley Dance, *The World of Swing*. New York: Charles Scribner's Sons, 1974, p. 90.
295 *Ellington the bandleader slipped:* Stratemann, p. 316.
297 *"will be used to help":* Papers of David Niles, Harry S. Truman Library, Independence, Missouri.
297 *They had worked out the details:* Raymond Horricks, *Profiles in Jazz: From Sidney Bechet to John Coltrane*. New Brunswick, New Jersey and London: Transaction Publishers, 1991, pp. 65–66.
297 *Evidently Hodges left:* Robert G. O'Meally, "Johnny Hodges: An Appreciation," *Reconstruction*, Winter 1990, p. 25. Jewell, p. 115.

Essential Ellington, 1943–51
Page
298 *With the song* I'm Beginning: Furia, pp. 261–62.
301 *"probably the slangiest":* Ibid., p. 261.
301 *It was on the best-selling:* Elston Brooks, *I've Heard Those Songs Before: The Weekly Top Ten Tunes for the Past Fifty Years*. New York: Morrow Quill, 1981, p. 424.

9: PLAYING FOR TIME, 1951–56
Page
303 *"going to retire":* "New Musicians Mean a New Sound in My Band: Ellington," *Down Beat*, April 6, 1951, p. 13.
303 *"into more enthusiastic blowing":* Barbara Hodgkins, "New Men Continue to Inspire Ellington Band," *Down Beat*, July 27, 1951, p. 3.
304 *"I'm a young bandleader":* Gleason, p. 175.
305 *"He likes to feel loyalty":* Dance, "Impressions," p. 17.
305 *On the contrary, recalled Al Celley:* Al Celley, interview by Patricia Willard, Philadelphia, July 12, 1989, DEOHP.
307 *"He is famous":* Dance, "Impressions," p. 17.
307 *Al Celley, the road manager:* Celley, DEOHP.
307 *and in 1949, Hamilton said:* Hamilton, DEOHP.
307 *"You know, long stretches":* Ellington/Harman, April 1956.
308 *"Harry and I don't talk":* Hentoff, p. 70.
308 *In advance of a one-nighter:* "Boycott Is Asked of Duke Ellington at Mosque Sunday," *Richmond News Leader*, January 22, 1951; "Duke Ellington Cries 'Shame' at NAACP Action Here," *Richmond News Leader*, January 24, 1951; "Ellington Concert Off," *New York Times*, January 29, 1951.

308 *"Duke Ellington's Views"*: Afro-American, December 1, 1951, p. 5.

308 *"too bad that Southern Negroes"*: "Statement by Duke Ellington," December 1, 1951, DEPS.

308 *the Blue Note in Chicago's Loop*: "Blue Note, Chi," Variety, October 6, 1954, p. 65.

309 *"only the Palace and Radio City"*: "NY Paramount Drops Vaude," *Down Beat*, December 2, 1953, p. 4.

309 *But by 1952*: Gault, p. 109.

309 *"Each member of the band"*: Billy Strayhorn, "The Ellington Effect," *Down Beat*, November 5, 1952, p. 4.

310 *Ellington made seven of these "videos"* Stratemann, pp. 336–41.

310 *By 1950, 95 percent of households*: Csida and Csida, p. 328.

310 *"a 1933 low"*: Ibid., p. 327.

310 *"The future of big band"*: Duke Ellington, "The Duke Speaks Out," unidentified magazine, ca. July 1955, pp. 9–10, clipping in JWJ.

311 *However, with one notable exception*: See Stanley Dance, "Duke Ellington and Television," in *Jazz on Television*, pp. 44–51. New York: The Museum of Broadcasting, 1985.

311 *The 33⅓-rpm long-playing*: Csida and Csida, p. 328.

313 *"I never had too much"*: George Avakian, letter to the author, September 11, 1992.

313 *the reason he gave publicly*: "Duke Switches Record Labels," *Down Beat*, May 6, 1953, p. 1.

313 *" 'I want a hit, Dave' "*: Dave Dexter, Jr., *Playback: A Newsman/Record Producer's Hits and Misses from the Thirties to the Seventies*. New York: Billboard Publications, 1976, p. 138.

313 *the last hit singles*: Joel Whitburn, *Pop Memories, 1890–1954: The History of American Popular Music*. Menomonee Falls, Wisconsin: Record Research, 1986, p. 149.

314 *"It's a matter of whether you want to play music"*: John S. Wilson, "Duke Ellington, a Master of Music, Dies at 75," *New York Times*, May 24, 1974, p. 32.

314 *Ellington's years with Capitol*: Dan Morgenstern, personal communication, September 26, 1992.

314 *On stage, as Dick Katz has noted*: Dick Katz, booklet notes to the Ellington recording *Solos, Duets and Trios*, RCA Bluebird 2178-2-RB, 1990, p. [6].

315 *"You know how it is"*: Wilson, "Duke Ellington, a Master of Music, Dies at 75."

315 *"You would never guess"*: H. Allen Smith, "Duke Ellington as a Composer Is in Class Alone," *New York World-Telegram*, September 13, 1938.

315 *"As a band pianist"*: Bigard, pp. 63–64.

315 *"I have never encountered"*: Schuller, *Swing Era*, p. 49.

316 *Wherever he went:* Irving Townsend, "Ellington in Private," *The Atlantic*, May 1975, pp. 78–79.

316 *major new work:* Night Creature: Gid W. Waldrop, "Carnegie Hall," *Musical Courier*, May 1955, p. 14; Charlie Mingus, "Duke Ellington, Carnegie Hall," *Metronome*, May 1955, pp. 41–52.

316 *For six weeks in the summer:* "Ellington Ork Revamped," *Down Beat*, July 27, 1955, p. 7.

317 *"It just seemed like":* Clark Terry, interview with Marcia Greenlee, Bayside, New York, October 10, 1990, DEOHP.

317 *"The only reason we're still in":* Nat Hentoff, "The Duke," *Down Beat*, December 25, 1956, pp. 12, 25.

317 *Then, just when Ellington needed:* "Strictly Ad Lib," *Down Beat*, June 1, 1955, p. 5.

318 *"the protective womb":* Norman Granz, interview with Patricia Willard, Geneva, Switzerland, August 23, 1989, DEOHP.

318 *"I've heard that band members":* Ruth Ellington Boatwright, DEOHP.

318 *"That was my main reason":* Dance, "Hodges," p. 22.

318 *The return of Hodges:* Clark Terry, DEOHP.

318 *"What I heard last night":* "Inside Stuff—Music," *Variety*, January 18, 1956, p. 58.

319 *an approving article:* "The Duke Rides Again," *Time*, January 23, 1956, p. 53.

319 *In May,* Saturday Review: Whitney Bailliett, "Celebration for the Duke," *Saturday Review*, May 12, 1956, pp. 30–31.

319 *"I think it would be better":* Ellington/Harman, April 1956.

319 *"being at the right place":* Gunnar Askland, "Interpretations in Jazz: A Conference with Duke Ellington," *Etude*, March 1947, p. 134.

319 *But at his opening set:* Leonard Feather, "Newport Festival: Saturday," *Down Beat*, August 8, 1956, p. 17.

319 *"What are we":* Nat Hentoff, "The Duke," *Down Beat*, January 9, 1957, p. 20.

320 *boppish ending written by Clark Terry:* Terry, DEOHP.

320 *"was insistent on just driving":* Ibid.

320 *"that really . . . fired Duke":* Ibid.

320 *"One young woman broke loose":* "Mood Indigo and Beyond," *Time*, August 20, 1956, p. 54.

321 *"over on the end of the stage":* Hamilton, Yale, p. 53.

321 *"Don't be rude":* "Mood Indigo and Beyond," p. 54.

322 *"I was born in 1956":* Jewell, p. 110.

Essential Ellington, 1951–56
Page
323 *This kaleidoscopic:* Raymond Horricks, *Profiles in Jazz: From Sidney Bechet to John Coltrane.* New Brunswick, New Jersey and London: Transaction Publishers, 1991, p. 78.

323 *reportedly, the composer himself:* Stanley Dance, booklet notes to the Ellington recording *Harlem*, Pablo PACD-2308-245-2, 1985, p. [4].

323 *"every bit as much":* Jonathan Yardley, "The Duke, Our Unrecognized Royalty," *Washington Post*, May 1, 1989.

324 *"form a link between":* Mark Tucker, booklet notes to the Ellington recording *Piano Reflections*, Capitol CDP 7 92863 2, 1989, p. [5].

10: RENEWING CAREER AND CREATIVITY, 1956–65

Page

325 *shed thirty-five pounds:* Feather, p. 72.

325 *his best-selling LP:* Collier, *Ellington*, p. 264.

326 *"hates talking about the old bands":* Hentoff, p. 76.

327 *"Record companies don't like me":* Irving Townsend, "Ellington in Private," *The Atlantic*, May 1975, p. 79.

327 *"But my loot comes":* Ibid.

327 *finding a "friendly advisor":* Ellington, *Music*, p. x.

327 *great admiration for Ellington:* Townsend, "Ellington in Private," p. 79.

328 *"The man," said Strayhorn:* Hentoff, p. 76.

328 *"Except for 'commissioning' ":* George Avakian, letter to the author, September 11, 1992.

329 *"the compositions of a man":* Peter Watrous, "New Respect for Ellington's Later Works," *New York Times*, April 27, 1989.

329 *"Did you know that a drum":* Townsend, "Ellington in Private," p. 79.

330 *"most self-revealing works":* Ibid., p. 80.

330 *aired a revised and expanded version:* Stratemann, p. 376.

331 *The program was not viewed:* Dan Morgenstern, "Jazz and Television: A Historical Survey," in *Jazz on Television*, p. 22. New York: The Museum of Broadcasting, 1985.

332 *Ellington's Such Sweet* Thunder: Irving Townsend, "When Duke Records," in *Just Jazz 4*, ed. Sinclair Traill and Gerald Lascelles, p. 18. London: Souvenir Press, 1960.

332 Such Sweet Thunder, *though:* Max Harrison, "Duke Ellington: Reflections on Some of the Larger Works," *Jazz Monthly*, January 1964, p. 12.

332 *which carried more prestige:* Stanley Dance, booklet notes to the Ellington recording *Blues in Orbit*, Columbia CK 44051, 1988, p. 3.

332 *They may have chosen the suite:* Irving Townsend, "Duke's Sweet Thunder," *Horizon*, November 1979, pp. 55–56.

333 *"They continued to write":* Dance, notes to *Blues in Orbit*, p. 3.

333 *He would harbor ideas:* Townsend, "Ellington in Private," p. 80.

334 *"takes records more seriously":* Townsend, "When Duke Records," pp. 17, 19, 20, 21.

334 *"He has nurtured the reputation":* Ibid., pp. 16–17.

335 *At one of the Monterey festivals:* Gleason, p. 167.

335 *The independent Ellington:* Townsend, "Ellington in Private," p. 81.
335 *had written twenty-one new songs:* Stratemann, p. 389.
335 *"I'm so damned fickle":* Feather, p. 72.
335 *first performance in Britain:* Stratemann, p. 391.
336 *"He made polite noises":* Townsend, "Ellington in Private," p. 83; Marian Logan, interview by Sonia Rosario, New York, February 27, 1982, Yale, pp. 18–19.
336 *"he thought," as Logan's wife:* Logan, interview, Yale, p. 19.
336 *"He wanted nothing in his life":* George, p. 235.
338 *"It was," he said, "the closest":* Stratemann, p. 441.
338 *While in Paris:* Ibid., p. 432.
339 *"the highest or noblest":* "Honors for Duke," *Down Beat*, August 6, 1959, p. 10; "High Honor to Ellington," *Billboard*, September 21, 1959, p. 4.
339 *On February 22, 1960:* Stratemann, pp. 420.
340 *he canceled an engagement:* Stratemann, p. 444.
340 *a period of reshuffling:* Stratemann, p. 418.
340 *"University of Ellingtonia":* Clark Terry, DEOHP.
341 *"And a couple of times":* Hamilton, Yale, p. 31.
342 *the* Nutcracker *was more:* Stratemann, p. 432.
342 *"What esthetic pleasure":* John McLellan, "Duke's Suites Swinging, but Why Bother?" *Boston Traveller*, April 6, 1961, p. 48.
342 *"is transformed into jazz":* Eddie Lambert, "Quality Jazz 14," *Jazz Journal*, November 1969, p. 11.
343 *"Duke puts everybody on":* Gleason, p. 166.
343 *"To be a great bull-shitter":* [Duke Ellington], typewritten ruminations dated "March 19," p. 11, Ruth Ellington Boatwright Collection, Series 5: Lyrics/Script notes, Archives Center, National Museum of American History, Smithsonian Institution, Washington, D.C.
343 *The trickster embodies many qualities:* John W. Roberts, *From Trickster to Badman: The Black Folk Hero in Slavery and Freedom*. Philadelphia: University of Pennsylvania Press, 1989, pp. 184–215. Alan Dundes, ed., *Mother Wit from the Laughing Barrel: Readings in the Interpretation of Afro-American Folklore*. Englewood Cliffs, New Jersey: Prentice-Hall, 1973, pp. 524–25. Robert D. Pelton, *The Trickster in West Africa: A Study of Mythic Irony and Sacred Delight*. Hermeneutics: Studies in the History of Religions. Berkeley, Los Angeles, and London: University of California Press, 1980, p. 1. Bill R. Hampton, "On Identification and Negro Tricksters," *Southern Folklore Quarterly*, 31 (1967), p. 60.
343 *"I'm not a bank robber":* Ellington/Harman, April 1956.
343 *"I may be a heel":* Feather, p. 72.
343 *"I just happened along one day":* Crow, p. 249.
344 *"I don't find it too annoying":* [Duke Ellington], typewritten ruminations, March 19, p. 1.
345 *"Duke . . . is a lonely man":* Marc Crawford, "A Visit with Mrs. Duke

Ellington: Musician's Wife Lives Quietly in Washington," *Ebony*, March 1959, p. 138.

345 *"He kids around with us"*: Hentoff, p. 74.

345 *In an insightful analysis*: Townsend, "Ellington in Private," pp. 82–83.

345 *There are reports*: Jewell, p. 177; Collier, *Ellington*, p. 208.

345 *Ellington was furious*: Townsend, "Ellington in Private," p. 81.

345 *sudden public scandal*: Stratemann, p. 442.

346 *"He would call upon"*: Townsend, "Ellington in Private," p. 81.

346 *sometimes, averred Hamilton*: Hamilton, Yale, p. 38.

346 *"The band tried several takes"*: Crow, p. 252.

347 *Ellington . . . said hello*: Jon Hendricks, telephone interview by the author, March 18, 1993.

347 *"Part of the explanation for*: Carter Harman, "About the Duke Ellington Tapes," typescript, [1991], p. 24, Carter Harman Collection, Archives Center, National Museum of American History, Smithsonian Institution, Washington, D.C.

349 *"was one of those mystic moments"*: Ellington, *Music*, p. 243.

349 *That November Frank Sinatra*: "Doubling Up of Act and A&R Man Accented Anew with Ellington, Cooke Deals," *Variety*, December 5, 1962, p. 41; "Duke and the Clan: Free-Loaders Mill as Frank Signs Duke," *Billboard*, December 8, 1962, p. 4.

350 *a few of these numbers*: Stratemann, p. 497.

351 *During the rehearsals*: Logan, Yale, p. 17.

351 *In 1961, for example*: Series 3: Business Records, DEC.

352 *the costs of hiring*: Townsend, "Ellington in Private," p. 79.

352 *Despite a terrible winter*: Stanley Dance, jacket notes to the recording *Symphonic Ellington*, Trend TR-529, 1982.

352 *"Syria's first big band"*: "Ellington Recovering from Illness at Damascus Debut," *Variety*, September 18, 1963, p. 55.

353 *"the representative of an oppressed"*: Ellington, *Music*, pp. 308–9.

353 *When the band got to Amman*: Stratemann, p. 474.

353 *According to Jimmy Hamilton*: Hamilton, DEOHP.

354 *During this tour, Hamilton*: Ibid.

354 *The State Department canceled*: Stratemann, p. 474.

354 *the BBC's* Jazz 625: Ibid., pp. 479–81.

354 *Leonard Feather had said*: Feather, p. 71.

355 *Mercer Ellington quit his job*: "Duke Ellington Chronology," typescript, p. [8], DEC; Jewell, p. 141.

355 *"As a road manager"*: Davis, pp. 8–9.

356 *The three-member music jury*: "Duke and the Pulitzer Prize," *Down Beat*, June 17, 1965, p. 12; "Repercussions On Pulitzer Nix To Duke Ellington," *Variety*, May 19, 1965, p. 71.

356 *"It's very too bad"*: "Ellington and the Prize," *International Musician*, July 1965, p. 18.

356 *Critic Nat Hentoff:* Hentoff.
356 *In rejecting a prize for Ellington:* Scott DeVeaux, letter to the author, January 5, 1993.
356 *"a confession, however unwitting":* Jonathan Yardley, "The Duke, Our Unrecognized Royalty," *Washington Post,* May 1, 1989.
356 *"Fate is being kind":* Hentoff, p. 64.
356 *"It doesn't matter":* "Very Too Bad," *Newsweek,* May 17, 1965, p. 94.
356 *the city's Bronze Medal:* Stratemann, p. 507.
357 *"His transition from Washington":* Stewart, *Jazz Masters,* pp. 88–89.
357 *Artie Shaw revealed:* Artie Shaw, interview by Bruce Talbot, Newbury Park, California, October 8, 1992, Jazz Oral History Program, National Museum of American History, Smithsonian Institution, Washington, D. C.
357 *"The greatest thing one man":* [Duke Ellington], typewritten ruminations, March 19, p. 9.
357 *"Every man prays":* Duke Ellington, program notes to *A Concert of Sacred Music.* San Francisco: Grace Cathedral, 1965, copy in DEC. Reprinted in the jacket notes to the LP *Duke Ellington's Concert of Sacred Music,* RCA LSP-3582, 1966.
358 *musically a progression of climaxes:* Gary Giddins, *Riding on a Blue Note: Jazz and American Pop.* New York and Oxford: Oxford University Press, 1981, p. 161.
358 *This was not a Mass:* Ellington, *Music,* p. 267.
358 *Ellington was addressing the people:* Giddins, *Riding,* p. 160.
358 *"commonplace" and "embarrassing":* Max Harrison, "On Record: *Anatomy of a Murder,*" *Jazz & Blues,* February 1973, p. 12.
358 *"a most remarkable religious synthesis":* Raymond Horricks, *Profiles in Jazz: From Sidney Bechet to John Coltrane.* New Brunswick, New Jersey, and London: Transaction Publishers, 1991, p. 87.
358 *"really directed the whole thing":* Gleason, p. 160.
358 *The resulting two programs:* Stratemann, pp. 515–16.
359 *"successful beyond my wildest dreams":* Ellington, *Music,* p. 263.
360 *"Duke Ellington's concert provoked":* Bryant M. Kirkland, "Commentary on Duke Ellington's Sacred Concert," in the jacket notes to *Duke Ellington's Concert of Sacred Music,* RCA LSP-3582, 1966.

Essential Ellington, 1956–65
Page
363 *"There's no performance":* Stanley Dance, jacket notes to *Happy Reunion,* Doctor Jazz FW40030, 1985.
364 *"a newly arrived jazz soloist":* G. E. Lambert, "The Duke Steps Out," *Jazz Journal,* February 1964, p. 4.
365 *The outer movements have:* Gene Lees, review of Ellington's *Peer Gynt Suites Nos. 1 and 2* and *Suite Thursday, Down Beat,* May 11, 1961, p. 30.

365 *"deserted border town"*: Stanley Dance, jacket notes to *Afro-Bossa*, Reprise R9-6069, [ca. 1963].

11: ACHIEVING FINAL GLORIES, 1966–74

Page
367 *The "ecumenical Ellington"*: Ellington, *Music*, p. 266.
368 *"This is the first time"*: Phil Casey, "The Duke Will Play Despite Rebuff," *Washington Post*, December 3, 1966.
369 *Since 1962*: Stratemann, p. 534.
370 *"She felt very exploited"*: Davis, p. 7.
370 *"a very cultured woman"*: Jewell, p. 135.
371 *For instance, once when Ellington*: Ellington, *Music*, p. 156.
371 *"They were that simpatico"*: Logan, Yale, p. 20.
371 *His food had to be minced*: George, p. 177.
371 *His old friend Lena Horne*: Ibid., p. 178.
372 *"Poor little Swee' Pea"*: Ellington, *Music*, pp. 159–61.
372 *Strayhorn's funeral services*: "A Man Beloved for Himself and His Music Receives a Fond Farewell: Blues Strains Bid Strayhorn Adieu," *New York Times*, June 6, 1967.
372 *In the spring*: Stratemann, p. 584.
373 *In 1965, the Ellington orchestra*: Ellington, *Music*, pp. 428, 476.
373 *"There is no place I would rather"*: Dance, World, p. 287.
373 *"Four kisses?"*: George, p. 184. See also Ellington, *Music*, p. 427.
373 *The medal was the supreme*: Ellington's Presidential Medal of Freedom is preserved at the Smithsonian Institution as part of the Duke Ellington Collection.
375 *"I am reminded of the four"*: George, pp. 184–85.
375 *"freedom from hate, unconditionally"*: Duke Ellington, booklet notes to the recording *And His Mother Called Him Bill*, RCA Bluebird 6287-2-RB, 1987.
375 *honors were rolling in*: Stratemann, p. 636; Ellington, *Music*, pp. 476–89.
377 *In December 1967*: Stratemann, p. 561.
377 *That same year, Ellington*: Ibid., p. 558.
377 *"I am that way about"*: Ellington/Harman, April 1956.
378 *"I regard this concert"*: Ellington, *Music*, p. 269.
378 *"all the stars in God's heaven"*: Joe Klee, review of Ellington's record *Second Sacred Concert*, *Down Beat*, June 10, 1971, p. 19.
378 *"You know, Duke"*: Ellington, *Music*, p. 282.
378 *"He often said"*: Logan, Yale, p. 7.
378 *"I'm a hotel man"*: Ellington/Harman, April 1956.
379 *"telephonitis"*: Logan, Yale, p. 2.
379 *"If a telephone rang"*: Gordon Parks, "Jazz," *Esquire*, December, 1975, p. 144.

379 *"avoiding useless and enervating irritation":* Irving Townsend, "When Duke Records," in *Just Jazz* 4, ed. Sinclair Traill and Gerald Lascelles, p. 21. London: Souvenir Press, 1960.

379 *In the late 1960s:* Stratemann, p. 552.

379 *Meanwhile, other members:* Stratemann, pp. 562, 584.

380 *"Johnny is not replaceable":* Dan Morgenstern, jacket notes to the recording *Ellingtonia!*, Onyx ORI-216, [n.d.].

381 *bitter about Ellington's ego:* Lowell D. Holmes and John W. Thomson, *Jazz Greats: Getting Better with Age.* New York and London: Holmes & Meier, 1986, pp. 108–10.

382 *That year, New York's public television:* Davis, pp. 1, 12.

383 *"Sold," exclaimed Ellington:* Jewell, p. 215.

383 *"You can jive":* Ibid., p. 217.

384 *"It is illuminating":* Gary Giddins, *Riding on a Blue Note: Jazz and American Pop.* New York and Oxford: Oxford University Press, 1981, pp. 159–60.

384 *his widow said:* Logan, Yale, p. 13.

384 *"If ever he lost a friend":* Jewell, p. 224.

384 *"I'll never get over this":* Ibid.

384 *but he kept this knowledge:* Tom Buckley, "Fellow Musicians Among 12,500 at Services for Duke Ellington," *New York Times*, May 28, 1974.

385 *On May 15, Paul Gonsalves:* Stratemann, p. 663.

385 *Expressions of loss and tribute:* John S. Wilson, "Duke Ellington, a Master of Music, Dies at 75," *New York Times*, May 25, 1974.

385 *Paul Gonsalves and Tyree Glenn:* George, pp. 254–55.

385 *Most of the mourners:* "Thousands Mourn Duke," *Melody Maker*, June 8, 1974, p. 22.

386 *Stanley Dance delivered:* Wilson, "Duke Ellington, a Master of Music"; George, p. 258.

386 *There were other musical performances:* Stanley Dance, "The Funeral Address," *Jazz Journal*, July 1974, p. 14.

Essential Ellington, 1965–74

Page

388 *Coltrane makes his tribute:* Andrew Homzy, personal communication, April 13, 1991.

388 *a "call to prayer":* Stanley Dance, quoted in Neil Tesser, booklet notes to the Ellington recording *The Far East Suite*, RCA Bluebird 7640-2-RB, 1988, p. [10].

388 *the movement sound mostly improvised:* Tom Piazza, "Black and Tan Fantasy," *The New Republic*, July 11, 1988, p. 40.

388 *The suite is regarded:* Brian Priestley, "Duke Ellington Orchestra," *Jazz Monthly*, March 1969, p. 18.

388 *the former was titled* Blue Cloud: Andrew Homzy, personal communication, April 13, 1991.

389 *Ellington considered the piece:* Stanley Dance, "Recordings Reports: Jazz LPs," *Saturday Review*, April 24, 1971, p. 56.

12: ELEVATING ELLINGTON, 1974–

Page

392 *"The Duke would have wanted":* Tom Buckley, "Fellow Musicians Among 12,500 at Services for Duke Ellington," *New York Times*, May 28, 1974.

392 *In fact, his father had pledged:* Davis, p. 10.

392 *"I discovered when we got there":* Ibid.

392 *"No matter how closely":* Krin Gabbard, review of ten Ellington recordings, *Cadence*, September 1989, p. 77.

392 *"What I objected to":* Davis, p. 11.

394 *"Every show my father":* Ibid., p. 1.

394 *"with a mature and successful":* Ibid., p. 13.

394 *"Ellington Lite":* Ibid., p. 16.

394 *By 1984, Gary Giddins:* Ibid., p. 17.

394 *"Despite their size":* Neil Tesser, "Ellingtonia: Catching Up with a Giant at 90," *Billboard*, July 1, 1989, p. J10.

396 *In 1989, Ellington's star:* "Paramount's Publishing Arm Purchases Ellington Catalog," *Jet*, May 29, 1989, p. 62; Jean Rosenbluth, "Famous Buys Ellington Catalog," *Daily Variety*, May 12, 1989.

397 *"Until very recently":* Austin B. Caswell, "Canonicity in Academia: A Music Historian's View," *Journal of Aesthetic Education* 25 (Fall 1991), pp. 136–37.

397 *"I'm hardly surprised":* Hentoff, p. 64; Nat Hentoff, "The Duke in Private," *Wall Street Journal*, December 9, 1991.

398 *"As long as something is unfinished":* John Miller, "The Duke Who Never Abdicated," [Toronto] *Globe Magazine*, January 22, 1966, p. 11.

398 *an evolving trail of variants:* Gabbard, review of ten Ellington recordings, p. 75.

400 *"He is the man who first recognised":* Francis Newton [E. A. Hobsbawm], "The Duke," *New Statesman*, October 11, 1958, p. 488.

400 *"Stan Kenton," said the conductor-arranger:* Feather, p. 77.

400 *"Ellington's influence":* Davis, pp. 17, 19, 20.

403 *Leopold Stokowski once reportedly asked Ellington:* Handbill for Duke Ellington's January 23 [1943] Carnegie Hall Concert, JWJ.

404 *"I don't think anybody":* Albert Murray quoted in booklet notes to the three-record set *Duke Ellington: An Explosion of Genius, 1938–1940*, Smithsonian Collection of Recordings R018, 1979, p. 2.

404 *"Duke Ellington is the quintessential":* Murray, "Storiella Americana," p. 219.

$\mathcal{E}$LLINGTON'S KEY
MUSICIANS

In its fifty years of existence, the Duke Ellington orchestra employed more than six hundred instrumentalists and singers. The term "sideman" doesn't begin to do justice to Ellington's best musicians, who were great artists in their own right. Here are fifty-three of his most significant instrumentalists and singers who performed with him over extended periods of time.

Alvis, Hayes (1907–72). Bassist with Ellington, 1935–38.

Anderson, Ivie (1905–49). Singer with Ellington, 1931–42.

Anderson, William "Cat" (1916–81). High-note trumpet specialist with Ellington, 1944–47, 1950–59, 1961–70.

Ashby, Harold (1925–   ). Tenor saxophonist with Ellington, 1968–74.

Babs, Alice (1924–   ). Swedish singer periodically with Ellington, 1963–73.

Baker, Harold "Shorty" (1914–66). Trumpeter with Ellington, 1942–44, 1946–51, 1957–59, 1961–63.

Bellson, Louie (1924–   ). Drummer with Ellington, 1951–53, 1954–55, 1965.

Benjamin, Joe (1919–74). Bassist with Ellington, 1970–74.

Bigard, Barney (1906–80). Clarinetist, tenor saxophonist, and composer with Ellington, 1927–42.

Blanton, Jimmie (1918–42). Bassist with Ellington, 1939–41. Nicknamed "Bear."

Braud, Wellman (1891–1966). Bassist with Ellington, 1927–35.

Brown, Lawrence (1907–88). Trombonist with Ellington, 1932–51, 1960–69. Nicknamed "Deacon" and "Rev."

Carney, Harry (1910–74). Baritone saxophonist with Ellington, 1927–74.

Connors, Chuck (1930–   ). Bass trombonist with Ellington, 1961–74.

Cook, Willie (1923–   ). Trumpeter with Ellington, 1951–58. Nicknamed "Ool-Ya-Koo."

Cooper, Buster (1929–   ). Trombonist with Ellington, 1962–69.

Davis, Kay (1920–   ). Singer with Ellington, 1944–50.

Ellington, Mercer (1919–   ). Arranger with Ellington, 1940–43; trumpeter and road manager, 1965–74.

Glenn, Tyree (1912–74). Trombonist and vibraphonist with Ellington, 1947–50, 1972.

Gonsalves, Paul (1920–74). Tenor saxophonist with Ellington, 1950–74. Nicknamed "Mex."

Greer, William "Sonny" (ca. 1895–1982). Percussionist with Ellington, 1920–51. Nicknames included "Sensational Sonny," "The Great Greer," "The Baron," and "Nasty."

Guy, Fred (1897–1971). Banjoist and guitarist with Ellington, 1925–49.

Hamilton, Jimmy (1917–1994). Clarinetist and tenor saxophonist with Ellington, 1943–68.

Hardwick, Otto "Toby" (1904–70). Saxophonist and clarinetist with Ellington, 1920–28, 1932–43.

Hibbler, Al (1915–   ). Singer with Ellington, 1943–51.

Hodges, Johnny (1907–70). Alto and soprano saxophonist and composer with Ellington, 1928–51, 1955–70. Nicknamed "Rabbit," "Rab," and "Jeep."

Jackson, Quentin "Butter" (1909–76). Trombonist with Ellington, 1948–59.

Jeffries, Herb (1916–   ). Singer with Ellington, 1939–42.

Jenkins, Freddie "Posey" (1906–78). Trumpeter with Ellington, 1928–34, 1937–38.

Jones, Rufus "Speedy" (1936–90). Drummer with Ellington, 1966–73.

Jones, Wallace (1906–83). Trumpeter with Ellington, 1938–44.

Jordan, Taft (1915–81). Trumpeter with Ellington, 1943–47.

Marshall, Wendell (1920–   ). Bassist with Ellington, 1948–54.

Miley, James "Bubber" (1903–32). Trumpeter with Ellington 1923–29.

Nance, Ray (1913–76). Cornetist, violinist, singer, and dancer with Ellington 1940–45, 1946–61, 1962–3, 1965. Nicknamed "Floorshow" and "The Captain."

Nanton, Joe "Tricky Sam" (1904–46). Trombonist with Ellington, 1926–46.

Pettiford, Oscar (1922–60). Bassist with Ellington, 1945–48.

Procope, Russell (1908–81). Alto saxophonist and clarinetist with Ellington, 1946–74.

Roché, Betty (1920–   ). Singer with Ellington, 1942–44, 1951–53.

Sears, Al (1910–   ). Tenor saxophonist with Ellington, 1944–49.

Sherrill, Joya (1927–   ). Singer with Ellington, 1942, 1944–45, 1956, 1963.

Smith, Willie (1910–67). Alto saxophonist with Ellington, 1951–52.

Stewart, Rex (1907–67). Cornetist with Ellington, 1934–45.

Strayhorn, Billy (1915–67). Composer and orchestrator who also wrote some lyrics and occasionally played piano, with Ellington, 1939–67. Nicknamed "Swee' Pea," "Strays," and "Weely."

Taylor, Billy (1906–86). Bassist with Ellington, 1934–39.

Terry, Clark (1920–   ). Trumpeter and flugelhornist with Ellington, 1951–59.

Tizol, Juan (1900–84). Valve trombonist, composer, and copyist with Ellington, 1929–44, 1951–53, 1960.

Turney, Norris (1921–   ). Alto saxophonist and flutist with Ellington, 1969–73.

Webster, Ben (1909–73). Tenor saxophonist with Ellington, 1935, 1936, 1940–43, 1948–49. Nicknamed "Frog."

Whetsol, Artie (1905–40). Trumpeter with Ellington, 1920–23, 1928–38. Nicknamed "Flickering Phil."

Williams, Charles "Cootie" (1911–85). Trumpeter with Ellington, 1929–40, 1962–74.

Woodman, Britt (1920–). Trombonist with Ellington, 1951–60.

Woodyard, Sam (1925–88). Drummer with Ellington, 1955–68.

$\mathcal{M}$OST ESSENTIAL ELLINGTON RECORDINGS

Among the hundreds of compact discs of Duke Ellington, here is a selection of the most essential, listed in chronological order. Because of their historical and musical importance, the seven recordings marked with an asterisk are simply not to be missed. This list specifies record labels but not catalog numbers, since they can vary from country to country, and typically differ for editions on record, tape, and compact disc.

Beyond Category: The Musical Genius of Duke Ellington; His Greatest Victor, Bluebird, and RCA Recordings, 1927–1967, two discs, Smithsonian/BMG.

Early Ellington, 1927–1934, Bluebird.

Reminiscing in Tempo, 1928–60, Columbia Legacy.

Swing, 1930–1938, ABC.

The Essence of Duke Ellington, 1937, Columbia.

The Duke's Men: Small Groups, Vol. 1, 1934–38, two discs, Columbia.

Braggin' in Brass, 1938, two discs, Portrait.

The Great Ellington Units, 1940–41, Bluebird. Septets and octets.

The Blanton-Webster Band, 1940–42, three discs, Bluebird.

Duke Ellington & His World Famous Orchestra, 1946–47, three discs, Hindsight.

The Complete Duke Ellington, 1947–1951, Vols. 2 and 5, CBS.

Ellington Uptown, 1951–52, Columbia.

Piano Reflections, 1953, Capitol. Piano, bass, and drums.

Such Sweet Thunder, 1957, Columbia.

Anatomy of a Murder, 1959, Columbia and Rykodisc.

The Great Paris Concert, 1963, two discs, Atlantic.

The Far East Suite, 1966, Bluebird.

And His Mother Called Him Bill, 1967, Bluebird.

Second Sacred Concert, 1968, Prestige.

Beyond Category: The Musical Genius of Duke Ellington: His Greatest Victor, Bluebird, and RCA Recordings, 1927–1967, two discs, Smithsonian/BMG.

SELECTED FILMS AND VIDEOS

The movie industry first utilized the talents of Duke Ellington in 1929, and from then on, he made dozens of film appearances, typically with his entire orchestra and mostly in short subjects. Hollywood rarely asked Ellington to write soundtrack scores: mostly it wanted Ellington and his orchestra as performers. As on record, though, on film Ellington usually played his own compositions, thus leaving a body of filmed performances that document him as both performer and composer. The filmic record of Duke Ellington provides what phonograph records cannot. The viewer can see the brass players' manipulation of the mutes; observe other playing techniques; notice the interaction between Ellington, musicians, and audience; on occasion watch dancing; and witness that always magnetic Ellington stage persona. Here is a selection of Ellington movies and videos, listed in chronological order. Many of these can be found on home video, watched on television, or, occasionally, seen at film or jazz festivals. The six titles marked with an asterisk are especially recommended for Ellington's performances. Unless otherwise indicated, all videos are issued by U.S. companies.

Black and Tan, 1929, RKO short subject, 19 minutes. Utilizing some of the Cotton Club dancers, this film offers *Black and Tan Fantasy, Black Beauty, Cotton Club Stomp,* and others. Home video: included in *Duke Ellington and His Orchestra: Classics, 1929–1952,* Amvest Video.

Check and Double Check, 1930, RKO feature film, 75 minutes. Notable for a spirited *Old Man Blues,* the movie is an otherwise dreadful blackface Amos 'n' Andy comedy. Home video: Video Yesteryear, other publishers.

Paramount Pictorial No. 837: The World at Large, 1933, newsreel short subject, 8 minutes. Includes 2 minutes of *Creole Rhapsody.*

A Bundle of Blues, 1933, Paramount short subject, 9 minutes. Includes *Stormy Weather* (vocal by Ivie Anderson), *Bugle Call Rag,* and the Ellington composition *Rockin' in Rhythm.* Home video: included in *Jazzball,* a 60-minute jazz anthology, Republic Home Video.

Murder at the Vanities, 1934, Paramount feature film, 98 minutes. Includes *Ebony Rhapsody* and a weird scene in which a gangster machine-guns the entire Ellington orchestra.

Hollywood on Parade, 1934, Paramount short subject, 11 minutes.

Belle of the Nineties, 1934, Paramount feature film, 75 minutes. Feature film starring Mae West includes the Ellingtonians performing four non-Ellington pop songs.

*Symphony in Black, 1934, Paramount short subject, 9 minutes. A remarkable short with no dialogue and a soundtrack composed by Ellington. Included in *Duke Ellington and His Orchestra: Classics, 1929–1952*, Amvest Video.

The Hit Parade, 1937, Republic feature film, 78 minutes. Includes the orchestra and Ivie Anderson doing *It Don't Mean a Thing (If It Ain't Got That Swing)*.

Paramount Pictorial No. 889, 1937, 10 minutes. A newsreel short subject called *Duke Ellington Makes a Record*.

Soundies made for movie jukeboxes: *Hot Chocolate, I Got It Bad and That Ain't Good, Flamingo, Bli-Blip, Jam Session*, all 1941, about 3 minutes each. *Hot Chocolate* is a tour de force consisting of the Ben Webster vehicle *Cotton Tail*, while *I Got It Bad* and *Bli-Blip* duplicate scenes from the musical *Jump for Joy*. Throughout the band and singers are instrument- and lip-"synching" to an already recorded soundtrack.

*Cabin in the Sky, 1942, MGM feature film, 99 minutes. Ellington performs *Goin' Up* and *Things Ain't What They Used to Be* in this handsome production directed by Vincente Minnelli. Home video: MGM.

Reveille with Beverly, 1942, Columbia feature film, 78 minutes. Features a delightful *Take the "A" Train*, with Betty Roché's boppish vocal and Ray Nance's infectious showmanship. Home video: included in the 48-minute video anthology *The Swing Era*, from Green Line/Jazz & Jazz (Italy).

Duke Ellington and His Orchestra (Jamboree), 1943, RKO short subject, 10 minutes.

The March of Time, Vol. 10, No. 5; *Upbeat in Music*, 1943, newsreel short subject, 17 minutes.

Date with Duke, 1947, Paramount cartoon/short subject, 7 minutes. Excerpts from *The Perfume Suite*.

*Symphony in Swing, 1949, and *Salute to Duke Ellington*, 1950, both 15-minute Universal short subjects. Home video: excerpts from each included in *Swing*, MCA video (4 videotapes or 2 videodiscs).

Short subjects made for television: *Caravan, VIP's Boogie, Sophisticated Lady, Mood Indigo, The Hawk Talks, The Mooche, Solitude*, all 1952. Snader Telescriptions, averaging about 4 minutes each.

Person to Person, 1957, CBS television kinescope, 30 minutes. Includes a 13-minute interview of Ellington by journalist Edward R. Murrow.

U.S. Steel Hour, 1957, CBS television kinescope, 55 minutes. TV version of *A Drum Is a Woman*.

Timex All Star Jazz Show No. 1, 1957, NBC television kinescope, 55 minutes.

Timex All Star Jazz Show No. 4: The Golden Age of Jazz, 1959, CBS television kinescope, 59 minutes.

Anatomy of a Murder, 1959, Columbia feature film, 160 minutes. Ellington wrote the brilliant score, performed by his orchestra, and had a brief appearance on screen. Home video: Columbia.

Duke Ellington in Amsterdam and Zurich, excerpts from 1958 and 1959 broadcast concerts, 58 minutes. Home video: Green Line/Jazz & Jazz (Italy).

Paris Blues, 1961, United Artists feature film, 98 minutes. A drama considerably enhanced by Ellington's score. Home video: Fox.

Newport Jazz Festival 1962, Bregmore feature film, 52 minutes.

Goodyear Jazz Concert: Duke Ellington and His Orchestra, 1962, film for television, 27 minutes. Six numbers including *Take the "A" Train*. Home video: Yesteryear Video; Discount Video Tape.

Duke Ellington in Europe, 1963–64, performance video, 56 minutes. Shot in Stockholm and London, includes *Star-Crossed Lovers* from *Such Sweet Thunder*, *Dancers in Love*, *The Blues*, and *Tutti for Cootie*. Home video: Green Line/Jazz & Jazz (Italy).

Jazz 625: Duke Ellington in Concert, 1964, filmed for BBC (U.K.) television, 60 minutes. Excellent production.

The Twentieth Century: Duke Ellington Swings through Japan, 1964, filmed for CBS television, 30 minutes.

Interview, with Byng Whittaker, 1964, CBC (Canada) television production, 60 minutes. Fascinating interview.

Love You Madly, 1965, filmed documentary for National Educational Television (U.S.), 110 minutes. Produced by jazz critic Ralph J. Gleason, it's a highly regarded look at Ellington on stage and off, performing both sacred and secular music.

Concert of Sacred Music, 1965, filmed documentary for National Educational Television (U.S.), 60 minutes. Shot at the work's premiere in San Francisco.

Assault on a Queen, 1966, Paramount feature film, 106 minutes. Ellington composed the soundtrack for this mediocre crime drama. Home video: Paramount.

Duke Ellington at the Côte D'Azur, 1966, filmed documentary for ORTF (France), 58 minutes.

On the Road with Duke Ellington, 1967, filmed documentary made originally for NBC television's *Bell Telephone Hour*, 58 minutes. A valuable record of Ellington performing and discussing his music, Strayhorn, and other topics.

Duke Ellington in Berlin, 1969, performance video, 43 minutes. Home video: Green Line/Jazz & Jazz (Italy).

Monterey Jazz, 1970, filmed documentary for U.S. public television, 81 minutes. Includes the *Afro-Eurasian Eclipse*.

The Lou Rawls Show with Duke Ellington, 1971, CBC (Canada) television production, 60 minutes. Ellington does *Satin Doll* and *Sophisticated Lady*. Home video: V.I.E.W. Video.

The Good Old Days Are Tomorrow: The Duke of American Music, 1972, documentary filmed at the University of Wisconsin at Madison, 21 minutes. In this last documentary made during his life, Ellington performs *Black and Tan Fantasy, Satin Doll*, and other pieces.

Memories of the Duke, 1980, Time-Life Films documentary, 85 minutes. Shot largely in Mexico, this video includes Ellington's *Mexican Suite*, as well as *Black and Tan Fantasy, Mood Indigo, Take the "A" Train*, and others. Home video: A-Vision.

The Sacred Music of Duke Ellington, 1982, concert video, 90 minutes. Shot in London after Ellington's death, this production includes singers Adelaide Hall, Phillis Hyman, Tony Bennett, and McHenry Boatwright (Ruth Ellington's husband). Home video: MGM/UA.

Sophisticated Ladies, 1982, video production, 108 minutes. The Broadway revue based on Ellington's songs. Home video: J2 Communications.

A Duke Named Ellington, 1988, documentary biography for Public Broadcasting Service (U.S.), approximately 120 minutes.

Reminiscing in Tempo, 1991, documentary biography for Public Broadcasting Service, approximately 60 minutes.

The Brute and the Beautiful, 1991, documentary biography of Ben Webster, the first Ellington musician to have his own retrospective video, 60 minutes. Home video: Shanachie Entertainment.

SELECTED READING

The body of writings about Duke Ellington is enormous, numbering in the tens of thousands. Here is a listing of forty-some of the most significant books and shorter writings, with an emphasis on material accessible to the general reader.

SELECTED BOOKS

Bigard, Barney. *With Louis and the Duke: The Autobiography of a Jazz Clarinetist*, ed. Barry Martyn. New York: Oxford University Press; London: Macmillan, 1985. Informal, taped reminiscences turned into a book.

Collier, James Lincoln. *Duke Ellington*. New York and Oxford: Oxford University Press, 1987. Some useful information outweighed by the author's hasty research, numerous factual errors, patronizing attitude, and superficial judgments.

Dance, Stanley. *The World of Duke Ellington*. New York: Charles Scribner's Sons, 1970; London: Macmillan, 1971. Reprint. New York: Da Capo, 1981. Comprised primarily of interviews with key musicians in the Duke Ellington orchestra, along with some observations by Dance and Ellington.

Ellington, Duke. *Music Is My Mistress*. Garden City, New York: Doubleday, 1973; London: Allen, 1974. Reprint. New York: Da Capo, 1976. The maestro's own book of memoirs, guarded and rich in positive reminiscences of key people in his life.

Ellington, Mercer, with Stanley Dance. *Duke Ellington in Person: An Intimate Memoir*. Boston: Houghton Mifflin; London: Hutchinson, 1978. Reprint: New York, Da Capo, 1979. A very candid view of the maestro by his son, strong on insights gleaned close at hand.

Frankl, Ron. *Duke Ellington*. New York: Chelsea House, 1988. A short, illustrated biography for juvenile readers.

Gammond, Peter. *Duke Ellington*. London: Apollo Press Ltd., 1987. A general introduction, including an extensive annotated discography.

————, ed. *Duke Ellington: His Life and Music*. Foreword by Hugues Pan-assié. London: Phoenix House; New York: Roy Publishers, 1958. Reprint. New York: Da Capo, 1977. Fifteen essays examine the man, his music, and key musicians.

George, Don. *Sweet Man: The Real Duke Ellington*. New York: G. P. Put-nam's Sons, 1981. An informal series of anecdotes about Ellington's public and private life by a lyricist and friend.

Jewell, Derek. *Duke: A Portrait of Duke Ellington*. New York: W. W. Norton, 1977. A readable biography with more than a few factual errors.

Lambert, G. E. *Duke Ellington*. London: Cassell, 1959; New York: Barnes, 1961. Slim but helpful introduction to Ellington's life and music.

Rattenbury, Ken. *Duke Ellington: Jazz Composer*. London and New Haven: Yale University Press, 1990. Primarily an analysis of five works from 1939 to 1941; fails to draw on recent research and resources, notably the Smith-sonian's Ellington papers; contains many errors.

Rowell, Jules Edmund. "An Analysis of the Extended Orchestral Works of Duke Ellington, circa 1931 to 1972." Master's thesis, San Francisco State University, 1983. Thin on evaluation; concentrates on musical analysis of twenty-eight longer works.

Ruland, Hans. *Duke Ellington: sein Leben, seine Musik, seine Schallplatten*. Gauting, Germany: Oreos Verlag, 1983. Illustrated guide, in German, pri-marily covering Ellington's LP recordings.

Stewart, Rex. *Boy Meets Horn*, ed. Claire P. Gordon. Ann Arbor: University of Michigan Press, 1991. Insightful memoirs of the cornetist through the mid 1940s, including his years with Ellington.

Tucker, Mark. *Ellington: The Early Years*. Urbana: University of Illinois Press, 1991. A definitive study of Ellington's early years (1899 through 1927), including his youth in Washington and his New York period prior to moving to the Cotton Club.

————, ed., *The Duke Ellington Reader*. New York: Oxford University Press, 1993. A selection of many of the most important writings by and about Ellington, selected by a leading Ellington scholar.

Ulanov, Barry. *Duke Ellington*. New York: Creative Age Press, 1946; Lon-don: Musicians Press, 1947. Reprint: New York, Da Capo, 1975. The first biography of Ellington, covering his life through 1945; includes invented dialogue but is breezy and readable.

SELECTED REFERENCE BOOKS

Massagli, Luciano, Liborio Pusateri, and Giovanni M. Volonte. *Duke Elling-ton's Story on Records*, vols. 1–16. Milan, Italy: Raretone, 1966–83. Excel-lent, detailed discography includes the structural plan and soloists for each piece.

Moulé, François-Xavier, comp. *A Guide to The Duke Ellington Recorded*

Legacy on LPs and CDs, Volume 1: Concerts, Radio Broadcasts, Television Shows, Radio Transcriptions, V-Discs, Film Soundtracks. Le Mans, France: A Madly Production, 1992. Aimed at the collector, this 600-plus-page guide, organized by record label, lists the titles of the pieces issued on hundreds and hundreds of LPs and CDs, and also lists identical releases on other labels.

Nielsen, Ole J., comp. *Jazz Records, 1942–80: Vol. 6: Ellington.* Copenhagen, Denmark: JazzMedia, 1991. Updates Timner's discography for post-1941 Ellington recordings, and includes indexes of compositions, persons, locations, cities, and countries.

Stratemann, Klaus. *Ellington Day by Day and Film by Film.* Copenhagen: JazzMedia, 1992. A massive chronicle of Ellington's films and itinerary from 1929 to 1974, the product of awesome research.

Timner, W. E., comp. *Ellingtonia: The Recorded Music of Duke Ellington and His Sidemen.* Third ed. Metuchen, New Jersey, and London: Institute of Jazz Studies and Scarecrow Press, 1988. The best single-volume discography covering Ellington's entire career.

Valburn, Jerry. *The Directory of Duke Ellington's Recordings.* Hicksville, New York: Marlor Productions, 1986. An exhaustive, worldwide listing of Ellington LP records.

―――. *Duke Ellington on Compact Disc.* Hicksville, New York: Marlor Productions, 1993. A thorough index to more than a thousand CDs of Ellington.

SELECTED ARTICLES AND BOOK CHAPTERS

Ellison, Ralph. "Homage to Ellington on His Birthday," *Washington Sunday Star*, April 27, 1969; reprinted in *Going to the Territory.* New York: Random House, 1986, pp. 217–26.

Feather, Leonard. "Duke," in *The Jazz Years: Earwitness to an Era.* London: Quartet Books, 1986; New York: Da Capo Press, 1987. "Duke," pp. 62–70.

―――. *From Satchmo to Miles.* New York: Stein & Day, 1972; London: Quartet Books, 1974. "Duke Ellington," pp. 45–64. A portrait of Ellington primarily as a human being.

Gleason, Ralph J. *Celebrating the Duke: and Louis, Bessie, Billie, Bird, Carmen, Miles, Dizzy, and Other Heroes.* Boston: Little, Brown, 1975. "The Duke," pp. 153–266.

Hentoff, Nat. *Jazz Is.* New York: Random House, 1976. "The Man Who Was an Orchestra," pp. 21–39.

――― and Nat Shapiro, eds. *Hear Me Talkin' to Ya.* New York and Toronto: Rinehart and Co., 1955. "Ellington Plays the Piano, but His Real Instrument Is His Band," pp. 224–38.

Hodeir, André, and Gunther Schuller. "Duke Ellington," in *The New Grove Dictionary of Jazz*, ed. Barry Kernfeld, vol. 1, pp. 330–36. London: Macmillan Press; New York: Grove's Dictionaries of Music, 1988.

Horricks, Raymond. *Profiles in Jazz: From Sidney Bechet to John Coltrane.*

New York and London: Transaction Publishers, 1991. "Classic Ellington," pp. 55–91.

Lambert, Eddie. "Edward Kennedy 'Duke' Ellington," and "The Ellington Sidemen," pp. 77–92 in Albert McCarthy, Max Harrison, Alun Morgan, and Paul Oliver, *Jazz on Record: A Critical Guide to the First 50 Years: 1917–1967*. New York: Oak Publications, 1968.

Morgenstern, Dan, and Ole Brask. *Jazz People*. Englewood Cliffs, New Jersey: Prentice-Hall; New York: Harry N. Abrams, 1976. "The Duke and His Men," pp. 99–124.

Murray, Albert. "Storiella Americana as She Is Swyung: Duke Ellington, the Culture of Washington D.C. and the Blues as Representative Anecdote," *Conjunctions* 16 (1991), 209–19.

Piazza, Tom. "Black and Tan Fantasy," *The New Republic*, July 11, 1988, pp. 36–40. Review-essay of James Lincoln Collier's *Duke Ellington*.

Schuller, Gunther. *Early Jazz*. New York: Oxford University Press, 1968. Chapter 7, "The Ellington Style: Its Origins and Early Development," pp. 318–58, is an important technical/musical study of Ellington's early music.

———. *The Swing Era*. New York: Oxford University Press, 1989. Chapter 2, "Duke Ellington: Master Composer," pp. 46–157, is a splendid musical study, accessible especially to those who read music.

Stewart, Rex. *Jazz Masters of the Thirties*. New York: Macmillan; London: Collier-Macmillan, 1972. "Ellingtonia," pp. 80–142. Anecdotes and remembrances of Ellington, Nanton, Webster, Bigard, and Carney by fellow Ellingtonian.

West, Hollie I. "The Duke at 70," *Washington Post*, April 26, 1969, Section K, pp. 1, 9–10.

Williams, Martin. *The Jazz Tradition*. 2nd edition, rev. New York: Oxford University Press, 1983. Chapter 10, "Duke Ellington: Form Beyond Form," pp. 100–21, is a veteran critic's summation of Ellington, accessible to the average reader.

SELECTED ARTICLES BY DUKE ELLINGTON

"The Duke Steps Out," *Rhythm*, March 1931, pp. 20–22.

"From Where I Lie," *The Negro Actor*, vol. 1, no. 1 (July 15, 1938), p. 4.

"Jazz as I Have Seen It," *Swing*, part I (February 1940) pp. 10–11, 33; part II (March 1940), pp. 9, 32; part III (May 1940), pp. 10, 23; part IV (June 1940), pp. 11, 22; part V (July 1940), pp. 10, 23; part VI (August 1940), p. 10; part VII (September 1940), pp. 8–9, 24.

"Interpretations in Jazz: A Conference with Duke Ellington," *Etude*, vol. 65 (March 1947), pp. 134, 172.

"The Most Essential Instrument," *Jazz Journal* 18 (December 1965), pp. 14–15.

DUKE ELLINGTON NEWSLETTER

The Duke Ellington Society Newsletter is published monthly, offering news, reviews, and articles about Ellington. A subscription comes with membership in the non-profit Duke Ellington Society, PO Box 31, Church Street Station, New York, New York 10008-0031.

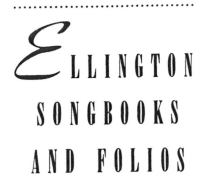

ELLINGTON SONGBOOKS AND FOLIOS

Here is a selected list of Duke Ellington songbooks and music folios for the student, amateur, and professional musician. Ellington wrote nearly all his music for his orchestra, while the versions in these collections are arrangements, mostly for piano and piano and voice. Faithful, note-for-note transcriptions of a number of Ellington's big-band compositions began to be published in 1993 by the Smithsonian's Jazz Masterworks Editions.

PIANO AND PIANO-VOCAL ARRANGEMENTS

Aaron Bridgers Plays Duke Ellington. Piano player No. 1. Paris: Editions Salabert, 1985. 36 pp.

Duke Ellington. Jazz Play-a-Long, Vol. 12. New Albany, Indiana: Jamey Aebersold, 1978. Folio with LP, CD, or cassette tape. 56 pp.

Duke Ellington: In a Mellow Tone. Jazz Play-a-Long, Vol. 48. New Albany, Indiana: Jamey Aebersold, 1990. Folio with CD or cassette tape. 40 pp.

Duke Ellington's Sophisticated Ladies. Melville, New York: Belwin Mills Publishing Corp., 1981. Now published by CPP/Belwin, Miami. 72 pp. Vocal selections from the Broadway show.

The Genius of Duke Ellington: Piano Solos. Miami: CPP/Belwin, 1986. 48 pp.

The Genius of Duke Ellington: Piano Solos, Vol. 2. Miami: CPP/Belwin, 1990. 48 pp.

Georges Arvanitas Plays Duke Ellington. Piano Player No. 3. Paris: Editions Salabert, 1987. 24 pp.

The Great Music of Duke Ellington. Melville, New York: Belwin Mills Publishing Corp., [1973]. Now published by CPP/Belwin, Miami. 143 pp. The most useful collection of his familiar short pieces.

Piano Solo Compilation Album "Hot". Paris: Editions Salabert, 1988. 183 pp. A voluminous collection of piano arrangements of his pre-1940 pieces.

Sacred Concerts Complete. Miami Beach: Hansen House, 1989. 128 pp.

Satin Doll. Stopchorus vol. 3. Paris: Editions Salabert, 1984. 32 pp. Bound with two 7-inch phonodiscs.

Sophisticated Lady. Stopchorus vol. 2. Paris: Editions Salabert, 1984. 32 pp. Bound with two 7-inch phonodiscs.

SIMPLIFIED PIANO ARRANGEMENTS

Duke Ellington Made Easy for Piano, arranged by John Lane. Miami: CPP/ Belwin, 1985. 40 pp.

Duke Ellington's Best: The Wonderful Songs of Duke Ellington in Easy Piano Arrangements by Mark Nevin. Melville, New York: Belwin Mills Publishing Corp., 1970. Now published by CPP/Belwin, Miami. 23 pp.

It's Easy to Play Duke Ellington. London: Wise Publications, 1987. 48 pp.

ARRANGEMENTS FOR GUITAR

Dodge, Spencer. *Fingerpicking Ellington.* London: Amsco Publications, 1985. 63 pp.

ARRANGEMENTS FOR OTHER INSTRUMENTS

The Ellington Collection. Club Date Sessions, Vol. 1. Miami: CPP/Belwin, 1992. Each edition is 40 pages, accompanied by a CD recording, and available for B-flat instruments, C melody instruments, E-flat instruments, and bass clef instruments.

Duke Ellington: Adaptation pour Quintette de cuivres, Vol. 1. Paris: Editions Salabert, 1989. Arrangements for brass quintet.

Duke Ellington: Adaptation pour Quintette de cuivres, Vol. 2. Paris: Editions Salabert, 1989. Arrangements for brass quintet.

INDEX

About the Author

John Edward Hasse is a music historian, musician, and award-winning author and record producer. He serves as Curator of American Music at the Smithsonian Institution, founder and Executive Director of the Smithsonian Jazz Masterworks Orchestra, and Co-Director of America's Jazz Heritage, a partnership of the Lila Wallace-Reader's Digest Fund and the Smithsonian Institution. He is the curator of a Smithsonian exhibition, *Beyond Category: The Musical Genius of Duke Ellington*, that is traveling throughout the U.S. from 1993 to 1996, and producer-annotater of a companion two-disc set of recordings, *Beyond Category*, issued by Smithsonian Recordings and BMG Records. Hasse is also the editor of *Ragtime: Its History, Composers, and Music* and producer-author of the book and three-disc set *The Classic Hoagy Carmichael*, which was nominated for two Grammy awards. He has received two ASCAP Deems Taylor Awards for excellence in writing on music.

Hasse earned a B.A. Cum Laude at Carleton College. an M.A. and Ph.D. degrees from Indiana University. and has performed concerts of ragtime. blues. and jazz at colleges. festivals, and on television.